Regime Change in the Yugoslav Successor States

DEMOCRATIC TRANSITION AND CONSOLIDATION

Jorge I. Domínguez and Anthony Jones, SERIES EDITORS

Regime Change in the Yugoslav Successor States

Divergent Paths toward a New Europe

Mieczysław P. Boduszyński

The Johns Hopkins University Press

Baltimore

© 2010 The Johns Hopkins University Press
All rights reserved. Published 2010
Printed in the United States of America on acid-free paper

9 8 7 6 5 4 3 2 1

The Johns Hopkins University Press
2715 North Charles Street
Baltimore, Maryland 21218-4363
www.press.jhu.edu

Library of Congress Cataloging-in-Publication Data

Boduszyński, Mieczysław P., 1974–
Regime change in the Yugoslav successor states : divergent paths toward a
new Europe / Mieczysław P. Boduszyński.
    p. cm.
Includes bibliographical references and index.
ISBN-13: 978-0-8018-9429-9 (hardcover : alk. paper)
ISBN-10: 0-8018-9429-8 (hardcover : alk. paper)
1. Regime change—Former Yugoslav republics.   2. Self-determination,
National—Former Yugoslav republics.   3. Post-communism—Former
Yugoslav republics.   4. Democracy—Former Yugoslav republics.   5. Former
Yugoslav republics—Politics and government.   6. Former Yugoslav
republics—Foreign relations.   I. Title.
DR1255.B63 2010
949.703—dc22   2009023832

A catalog record for this book is available from the British Library.

*Special discounts are available for bulk purchases of this book. For more informa-
tion, please contact Special Sales at 410-516-6936 or specialsales@press.jhu.edu.*

The Johns Hopkins University Press uses environmentally friendly book
materials, including recycled text paper that is composed of at least 30
percent post-consumer waste, whenever possible. All of our book papers
are acid-free, and our jackets and covers are printed on paper with recycled
content.

For my parents

and

Ms. Betty Borges
who first encouraged me to write

Contents

Figures and Tables

Preface

The states that emerged from the former Yugoslavia followed divergent paths of regime change in their first decade of post-communist transition, only to converge on the road to Europe in the second. As of 2009, all the Yugoslav successor states, save for newly independent Kosovo, are at some stage of the European integration process, at the very minimum having signed Stabilization and Association Agreements (SAA) with the European Union. This means that they are formally committed to implementing the democratic reforms necessary to join the EU. Slovenia has already been a EU member since 2004. Croatia has been engaged in accession negotiations since 2005 and, if all goes well, will join in 2011. Macedonia, Montenegro, and Serbia are also on the European path, as is Bosnia and Herzegovina, despite its problematic internal divisions and slowness on reform. This reflects the victory of pro-Western sentiment in the domestic politics of these countries, but it also reflects the EU's determination to bring the "Western Balkans" into the European and democratic fold.

It was not always this way. Engulfed by war in the 1990s, Bosnia and Herzegovina, Croatia, and Kosovo made headlines on a daily basis. The Federal Republic of Yugoslavia (FRY; also called Serbia and Montenegro) and Croatia were ruled by varying kinds of authoritarian-nationalist regimes; Macedonia owed its existence to Western aid and political support; and Bosnia and Herzegovina emerged from war in 1995 to become an international protectorate. Among the successor states, only Slovenia succeeded in constructing a democratic order in the first decade of transition.

Even in the early 2000s, after electoral revolutions in Serbia and Croatia, the democratic and European prospects of the Yugoslav successor states were not nearly as bright as they are today. In 2004 the Serbian weekly *Vreme* published an illustration by the well-known political cartoonist Predrag Koraksić, better known as "Corax," showing then–Prime Minister Vojislav Koštunica peering into the sky at a ring of stars representing the European Union. Only the prime minister is looking through the wrong end of the telescope, making the stars appear even farther away. Even Albania managed to sign an SAA before Serbia. That same year, in reference to those elusive EU stars, the Slovenian daily *Delo* ran the headline "From red star [the old Yugoslav flag] to gold stars [the EU flag]," signifying Slovenia's formal entry into the EU but also hinting at the paradox of leaving one failed federation only to enter another, still rather insecure multinational grouping thirteen years later. The two images spoke powerfully to the very different places in which these two Yugoslav successor states found themselves in the early years of the new millennium. Slovenia had become a prosperous democracy, one of the first nations in the region to be admitted to the EU. Serbia, by contrast, was damaged by years of nationalism and failed economic policies. Its very borders were uncertain, with Montenegro pushing for independence and Kosovo's largely Albanian population, governed by the international community, demanding sovereignty as well.

This book explains the paths traveled by Slovenia, Croatia, the Federal Republic of Yugoslavia, and Macedonia since 1991, analyzing how and why their paths *diverged* for the first decade of transition and then *converged* as they sought to become members of the EU and NATO in the second (owing to its status as an international protectorate for most of this period, Bosnia and Herzegovina does not play a major role in the study, nor do Kosovo and Montenegro, which only recently gained independence). It argues that the Yugoslav successor states initially followed divergent trajectories of regime change because they embarked on transition from very different starting points. These starting points were rooted in long-term disparities in economic development, reproduced over time and through regimes of varying characters, which in turn shaped the prospects for liberalism after independence and the fall of communism. But post-communist regime change in the Yugoslav successor states has also been powerfully shaped by another factor: the sustained influence of the West and its desire to transfer democratic norms to the Balkans, which helps account for the more recent convergence in democratization and the growth in Euro-Atlantic aspirations.

The kinds of regimes that emerged in the post-communist Yugoslav space were a function of the parameters in which they developed: the structural conditions they inherited from the past and the grand design of the Western liberal project. In this way, the Yugoslav successor states are not unlike other post-communist states in Eastern and Central Europe, but they have rarely been studied as cases of democratization. Yet, their transitions away from a common state, through varying trajectories of regime change and ultimately toward Euro-Atlantic integration, can teach us a lot about post-communist transformation more generally.

This book reflects fifteen years of thinking about political change in Eastern and Central Europe. It owes a great deal to individuals who have thought about such subjects much longer than I have. At the University of California, Berkeley, I am grateful first and foremost to my mentor, Andrew Janos, whose support was unfailing and whose contribution to my intellectual development and, indeed, to my understanding of the world will benefit me long after this book is published. I am equally grateful for the guidance provided by George W. Breslauer, Steven K. Vogel, and John Connelly. I also received encouragement, advice, and financial support from the Berkeley Program in Soviet and Post-Soviet Studies and its executive director, Ned Walker, as well as the Institute for Slavic, East European, and Eurasian Studies, under the leadership of Victoria Bonnell and Barbara Voytek. The support of my graduate school colleagues at Berkeley's Political Science Department was indispensable, especially that of Victor Peskin, my friend and intellectual soul mate. This manuscript is based on my doctoral dissertation, for which I received the Juan Linz Prize for Best Dissertation in the Comparative Study of Democracy. I was honored to meet Professor Linz at the award ceremony, and I, along with all those who study democratization, owe a tremendous intellectual debt to him. I also wish to thank the Johns Hopkins University Press, in particular Henry Tom and Suzanne Flinchbaugh for their faith in this project and Martin Schneider, my copyeditor, for his infinite patience.

Several Foreign Language and Area Studies fellowships, funded by the U.S. Department of Education, facilitated my study of Serbian and Croatian at Berkeley (under the superb guidance of Ronelle Alexander and Charles Greer) and in Zagreb and Novi Sad. The Center for German and European Studies at Berkeley generously funded an early research trip to Croatia, and the Kościuszko Foundation helped defray the costs of my third year of study. My research internship at the Public Policy Institute of California was a wonderful opportunity that broadened my graduate education, and I am grateful to David Lyon and Fred Silva for allowing me to work there.

My fieldwork in the former Yugoslavia was generously funded by the Fulbright program and the International Research and Exchanges Board. There are countless individuals in the four countries that are the subject of this book who gave generously of their time to talk to me about politics in the Yugoslav successor states; there is no way that I could name them all. In Zagreb, I am especially grateful to Radovan Vukadinović, Žarko Puhovski, Goran Ćular, Vlatka Blagus, Ana Đorđević, Boris Kuzmanić, Predrag Bejaković, Alekander Štulhofer, Helmut Fenzl, Loredana Maravić, Eric Verin, Saša Brlek, Kristina Bratičević, Kristina Jurić, Tomislav Stojanov, Dijana Pleština, Tvrtko Jakovina, and Jasmina Beširević. In Ljubljana, I thank Danica Fink-Hafner, Jernej Pikalo, Alenka Krašovec, Jože Mencinger, and Miro Haček. In Skopje, I received valuable assistance from Vasko Naumovski, Svetlana Trbojevik, Maja Gerovska, Gjorgje Ivanov, Ilo Trajkovski, Dane Taleski, Habib Massoud, Armend Reka, and Islam Yusufi. In Belgrade, I was assisted by Marko Romčević, Vučina Vasović, Masaya Furukawa, Živorad Kovačević, and Zoran Slavujević. I also wish to acknowledge the North American scholars who generously shared their knowledge and time with me during the course of my dissertation research. They include Lenard Cohen, Sabrina Ramet, Scott Mainwaring, Ljubiša Adamović, Janusz Bugajski, Ronald Linden, Eric Gordy, Julie Mostov, Ana Dević, and Milada Anna Vachudová. In 2003 and 2004 I presented this research at the University of Notre Dame, the University of Connecticut, and the School of Slavonic and East European Studies at University College London and received valuable feedback.

The writing stage of the manuscript was generously funded by the Berkeley Dean of Graduate Studies Normative Time Fellowship and the American Council of Learned Societies. I spent two years as a lecturer at the University of San Diego, and I am very grateful to Randy Willoughby for the opportunity. At USD, I would also like to thank Christy Soto and Joyce Neu, Dee Aker, and Shelley Lyford of the Joan Kroc Institute for Peace and Justice. During the 2003–2004 academic year, I taught in the Making of the Modern World Program at my alma mater, Eleanor Roosevelt College of the University of California, San Diego. I am grateful to Provost Ann Craig and Reynaldo Guerrero, both mentors to me since my undergraduate years at UCSD, and to Patrick Patterson and Doug McGetchin, my outstanding colleagues in the MMW program. I am equally indebted to my undergraduate mentors: Akos Rona-Tas, who introduced me to both social science and East European studies, and Ellen Comisso, who in supervising my undergraduate thesis always pushed me to do my best work.

The East European Studies Program at the Woodrow Wilson International Center for Scholars has twice contributed to furthering my graduate career:

by inviting me to participate in the Junior Scholars' Training Seminar in the summer of 2002 and by hosting me as research scholar in the summer of 2003. I cannot imagine a more supportive environment in which to have worked on my dissertation; I am grateful to Marty Sletzinger, Nida Gelazis, Meredith Rubin, Sabina Crispen, and Katy Bondy.

I have spent the past six years as a Foreign Service Officer with the U.S. State Department, serving in Albania, Kosovo, and now Japan. During this time, I have had the privilege of meeting some outstanding colleagues who have enriched my understanding of diplomacy and politics: Roxanne Cabral, Charles Morrill, Adolfo Gorriaran, Viki Thomson, Jeff Patmore, Alex Laskaris, Steve Cristina, Steve Zate, Larry Corwin, Elisabeth Corwin, Laura Hochla, Paula Thiede, Wakie Martin, Ed Dong, Stephanie Morimura, Naomi Walcott, Audu Besmer, Kevin O'Connor, Matt Fuller, Ambassador Marcie Ries, and Ambassador Tina Kaidanow. In Tirana, I benefited from the insights and friendship of Eno Trimçev, Bernard Zeneli, Galit Wolfensohn, Erinda Lula, Kujtim Çashku, Aki Ishiwa, Saimir Bajo, Erinda Lula, and Bato Bega. I am also grateful to my Albanian language teachers at the Foreign Service Institute, Ardiana Sinoimieri, Ema Tirana, and Edi Zadrima.

I will also be forever indebted to hitherto unmentioned friends and family who provided support and advice—Grzegorz Gosiewski, Ola Gosiewska, Jan Gosiewski, Stanisław Gosiewski, Maciej Gosiewski, Franciszek Gosiewski, Małgorzata Gnoińska, Stas Currier, Michael Nelson, Michael Carpenter, Rudolf Beran, Randy Ontiveros, Elisha Tilton, Krzysztof Pierścieniak, Deana Slater, Tadashi Anno, Chris Burman, Natalie Burman, Tony Burman, Laura Lamb, Greg Grassi, Steve Reichert, Barrett Heusch, Conor O'Dwyer, Marc Morjé Howard, Bill Hurst, Els De Graauw, Kristina Balalovska, Agnieszka Weinar, Istvan Zsoldos, Jerzy Bąk, Anna Boduszyńska-Bąk, Aleksander Bąk, Wojciech Bąk, Mieczysław Bąk, Janina Boduszyńska, Monica Boduszyński, Thomas Boduszyński, Rick Chalk, Tyler Chalk, Alden Chalk, and Teresa Boduszyński. This book is dedicated to Dr. Mieczysław M. Boduszyński and Basia Chalk, my parents, and my fourth-grade teacher, Ms. Betty Borges, who first encouraged me to write.

Two individuals, latecomers to the project, nevertheless proved essential to its completion. Drew Lehman, among the most amazing people I know, worked tirelessly on the text and graphics. Carrie Bergstrand appeared unannounced at my apartment in Tokyo and has made this book, and my life, much richer ever since.

Abbreviations and Acronyms

JNA • Yugoslav National Army (Jugoslovenska Narodna Armija)
SFRJ • Socialist Federal Republic of Yugoslavia (Socijalistička Federativna
    Republika Jugoslavija)

Croatia
Political Parties and Coalitions

DC • Democratic Centre (Demokratski centar)
HDZ • Croatian Democratic Union (Hrvatska Demokratska Zajednica)
HNS • Croatian People's Party (Hrvatska Narodna Stranka)
HSLS • Croatian Social-Liberal Party (Hrvatska Socialno-Liberalna Stranka)
HSP • Croatian Party of Rights (Hrvatska Stranka Prava)
HSS • Croatian Peasant Party (Hrvatska Seljačka Stranka)
HSU • Croatian Party of Pensioners (Hrvatska Stranka Umirovljenika)
IDS • Istrian Democratic Party (Istarski Demokratski Sabor)
LS • Liberal Party (Liberalna Stranka)
SDF • Serbian Democratic Forum (Srpski Demokratski Forum)
SKH • Croatian League of Communists (Savez Komunista Hrvatske)
SDP • Social Democratic Party (Socijaldemokratska Partija)
SDS • Serbian Democratic Party (Srpska Demokratska Stranka)
SNS • Serbian People's Party (Srpska Narodna Stranka)

Other

RSK • Republic of Serbian Krajina (Republika Srpska Krajina)
NDH • Independent State of Croatia (Nezavisna Država Hrvatska)

Slovenia
Political Parties and Coalitions

DEMOS • *Democratic Opposition of Slovenia* (Demokratična Opozicija Slovenije)

DSUS • Democratic Party of Slovenia's Pensioners (Demokratična Stranka
    Upokojencev Slovenije)
LDS • Liberal Democratic Party (Liberalna Demokratska Stranka)
NSi • New Slovenia-Christian People's Party (Nova Slovenija-Krščanska
    Ljudska Stranka or Nova Slovenija)
SD • Social Democrats (Socialni Demokrati)
SDP • Party of Democratic Renewal (Stranka Demokratične Prenove)
SDSS • Social Democratic Party of Slovenia (Socialdemokratska Stranka
    Slovenije)
SKD • Christian Democrats (Slovenski Krščanski Demokrati)
SLS • Slovenian People's Party (Slovenska Ljudska Stranka)
SNS • Slovenian National Party (Slovenska Narodna Stranka)
ZKS • League of Communists of Slovenia (Zveza Komunistov Slovenije)
ZLSD • United List of Social Democrats (Združena Lista Socialnih
    Demokratov)

Macedonia

Political Parties and Coalitions

DA • Democratic Alternative (Demokratska Alternativa)
DP • Democratic Party (Demokratska Partija)
DPA • Democratic Party of Albanians (Demokratska Partija na Albancit;
    Albanian: Partia Demokratike Shqiptare, PDSh)
DPS • Democratic Party of Serbs in Macedonia (Demokratska Partija na
    Srbite vo Makedonija, Serbian: Demokratska Partija Srba u
    Makedoniji)
DUI • Democratic Union for Integration (Demokratska unija za integracija;
    Albanian: Bashkimi Demokratik për Integrimin, BDI)
LP • Liberal Party of Macedonia (Liberalna Partija na Makedonija)
NDP • People's Democratic Party (Narodna Demokratska Partija)
PDP • Party for Democratic Prosperity (Partija za Demokratski Prosperite;
    Albanian: Partia për Prosperitet Demokratik, PPD)
PDP-A • Party of Democratic Prosperity-Albanians (Partija za Demokratski
    Prosperitet na Albancite; Albanian: Partia për Prosperitet Demokratik-
    Shqiptarët, PPD-Sh)
SDSM • Social Democratic Union of Macedonia (Socijaldemokratski Sojuz
    Makedonije)

SKM • League of Communists of Macedonia (Sojuz na Komunistite na Makedonija)

SPM • Socialist Party of Macedonia (Socialistička Partija na Makedonija)

VMRO-DPMNE • Internal Macedonian Revolutionary Organization Democratic Party for Macedonian National Unity (Vnatrešna Makedonska Revolucionerna Organizacija- Demokratska Partija za Makedonsko Nacionalno Edinstvo)

ZMZ • Together for Macedonia (Zaedno na Makedonija Zveza)

Other

NLA • National Liberation Army (Albanian: Ushtria Çlirimtare Kombëtare, UÇK; Macedonian: Oslobodetelna Narodna Armija, ONA)

Federal Republic of Yugoslavia (Serbia and Montenegro)
Political Parties and Coalitions

DEPOS • Democratic Movement of Serbia (Demokratski Pokret Srbije)

DS • Democratic Party (Demokratska Stranka)

DSS • Democratic Party of Serbia (Demokratska Stranka Srbije)

DZMV • Democratic Community of Vojvodina Hungarians (Demokratska Zajednica Mađara Vojvodine; Hungarian: Vajdasági Magyarok Demokratikus Közössége, VMDK)

G17 Plus • G17 Plus Party

GSS • Civic Alliance of Serbia (Građanski Savez Srbije)

JUL • Yugoslav United Left (Jugoslovenska Udružena Levica)

LS • Liberal Alliance (Liberalni Savez)

NS • Peoples' Party (Narodna Stranka)

SKS • Serbian League of Communists (Srpski Savez Komunista)

SNP • Socialist People's Party (Socijalistička Narodna Partija)

SPO • Serbian Renewal Movement (Srpski Pokret Obnove)

SPS • Serbian Socialist Party (Srpska Partija Socijalistička)

SRS • Serbian Radical Party (Srpska Radikalna Stranka)

SSJ • Party of Serbian Unity (Stranka Srpskog Jedinstva)

SVM • Alliance of Vojvodina Hungarians (Savez Vojvođanskih Mađara/ Hungarian: Vajdasági Magyar Szövetség, VMSZ)

Other

FRY • Federal Republic of Yugoslavia (Savezna Republika Jugoslavija) (1991–2003)

SANU • Serbian Academy of Arts and Sciences (Srpska Akademija Nauka i Umetnosti)

SCG • Serbia and Montenegro (Srbija i Crna Gora) (2003–2006)

UÇK • Kosovo Liberation Army (Ushtria Çlirimtare e Kosovës)

International Organizations

CEFTA • Central European Free Trade Agreement

CFSP • Common Foreign and Security Policy (European Union)

CIVPOL • United Nations Civilian Police Force (Macedonia)

EBRD • European Bank for Reconstruction and Development

EC • European Commission

EFTA • European Free Trade Association

EU • European Union

GATT • General Agreement on Tariffs and Trade

ICTY • International Criminal Tribunal for the former Yugoslavia

IMF • International Monetary Fund

KFOR • NATO-led Kosovo Peacekeeping Force

NATO • North Atlantic Treaty Organization

OHR • Office of the High Representative (Bosnia and Herzegovina)

OPEC • Organization of Petroleum Exporting Countries

OSCE • Organization for Security and Cooperation in Europe

PFP • Partnership for Peace (NATO)

SAA • Stabilization and Association Agreement (European Union)

UNMIK • United Nations Interim Administration Mission in Kosovo

UNPREDEP • United Nations Preventive Deployment Force (Macedonia)

UNPROFOR • United Nations Protection Force (Croatia, Bosnia and Herzegovina)

WTO • World Trade Organization

Map of the Yugoslav Successor States, 2010

Explaining Regime Change
in the Yugoslav Successor States

D espite the potential lessons they hold for comparative politics and area studies, the Yugoslav successor states have rarely been examined as cases of post-communist democratization. This book fills the void by analyzing nearly two decades of regime change in the former Yugoslavia, identifying the internal and external factors that determined whether liberal political orders developed in its successor states. It traces, compares, and explains post-communist transition in four of these states: Slovenia, Croatia, the Federal Republic of Yugoslavia (hereafter FRY), and Macedonia.[1] Bosnia and Herzegovina is not part of the comparison because it is difficult to analyze the extent of democratization where sovereignty has been constrained by an international protectorate, while the remaining successor states, Kosovo and Montenegro, gained independence only very recently.

The divergent trajectories of regime change in the Yugoslav successor states reflect the range of political outcomes in the larger post-communist world. In recent years, scholars have endeavored to explain this diversity. In so doing, they have debated the degree to which post-communist democratization is constrained by history or constructed by the power of human will, politics, and institutions. A primary goal of this book is to address the debate over the determinants of varying paths of post-communist political change.

Another goal is to contribute to the literature on democratic progress where formal democratic rules and practices exist alongside serious problems of legitimacy. The present study addresses this problem of measurement by evaluating democratization along two dimensions: *procedural correctness* (adherence to democratic rules) and *liberal content* (the demonstration of democratic values and the legitimacy of the state). On both dimensions, one finds a whole spectrum of democratic and nondemocratic outcomes among the Yugoslav successor states, providing fertile ground for an inquiry into the forces that shape diverse paths of post-communist regime change. The major part of the book is devoted to the first ten years of transition (1991–2000) in the four successor states, while chapter 8 examines the second decade of regime change.

Two key variables explain post-communist regime diversity in the Yugoslav successor states: (1) varying levels of economic viability among the republics on the eve of their independence (the initial structural conditions of transition);[2] and (2) differing modes of accommodation and resistance to the Western-led effort to transfer liberal norms to the Balkan region. According to this framework, regime change occurred at the intersection of domestic interest and external intention—where the structural legacies of the Yugoslav successor states met Western aims and conditions for Euro-Atlantic integration.

In 2009, save Kosovo, all the Yugoslav successor states are functioning democracies and are formally at some stage of the European Union (EU) integration process. This was not the case in the 1990s. In 1991, on the eve of independence, different degrees of economic viability in each republic set varying parameters for democratization, influencing the strategies of emerging political groups and the expectations of the masses at the time of the first multiparty elections. In FRY and Macedonia, with low levels of economic viability, nationalist and populist political configurations came to the fore and pursued illiberal solutions to socioeconomic decline. In Croatia, where the economy was partially viable, liberal and illiberal groups competed for power on the political scene. Although the illiberal groups prevailed, their undemocratic tendencies were kept in check by a democratic opposition. In Slovenia, with the most viable economy, liberal parties had the political resources to promote a democratic and pro-Western agenda throughout the 1990s.

In the 1990s, the changed international environment, characterized by the Western-led effort to transfer liberal norms to the post-communist world, offered each successor state clear incentives to pursue democratic reform but encountered different levels of willingness to comply with these norms. In Slovenia, democracy was embraced as the means to "reunite" with the West and its institutions, and the path toward Euro-Atlantic integration fortified democratic institutions. In Croatia, democracy was simulated in order to placate Western critics while elites pursued nationalist and authoritarian aims. In FRY, Western conditions were rejected outright and a thinly veiled dictatorship held power, while in Macedonia procedural democracy existed largely thanks to Western political, economic, and security sponsorship, all of which masked a corrupt and illegitimate regime. These differences notwithstanding, all the successor states responded to Western-encouraged liberalism and the powerful incentive of membership in organizations such as the EU and the North Atlantic Treaty Organization (NATO) by instituting some degree of procedural correctness.

External agency became an especially potent force when the illiberal groups that dominated politics in Croatia, FRY, and Macedonia failed to improve living standards by the late 1990s. Coalitions of moderates and reformers in these states came together and embraced Western conditionality in the hopes of defeating ruling anti-systemic elites with the promise of membership in Euro-Atlantic organizations. By neutralizing populist tendencies and helping to strengthen the reformist forces, which ultimately prevailed, the influence of external agency, especially in the form of EU conditionality, helped to surmount obstacles to democratization.

Even after the successor states converged on procedural aspects of democracy after 2000, they continued to diverge in terms of liberal content owing to the sustained influence of initial conditions. Slovenia's post-communist transition suffered from certain democratic deficiencies in the 2000s, but its favorable economic outlook permitted the dominance of democratic, pro-Western political configurations, procedurally correct processes and institutions, and a society united behind the internal and external liberal project. As a consolidated democracy, it was among the first post-communist states to enter the EU, in May 2004. In Croatia, with a more favorably structured economy than its southern neighbors, an ever larger segment of the political elite embraced EU conditionality after 2000, and as the country became a credible EU candidate in 2003, radical populist alternatives were discredited, liberal forces were strengthened, and the country seemed to be on a steady, albeit not painless, path to full democratization and EU membership. In FRY (later Serbia), with much worse economic conditions than Croatia, radical populist forces maintained their influence after 2000 in spite of aggressive Western conditionality. The Serbian public was deeply divided over Western influence, and the country was the last in the region to sign an association agreement with the EU. As such, there was a relatively weaker external impetus for democratization. However, the government that was constituted in the summer of 2008 has moved in a decisively liberal and pro-EU direction, and part of the nationalist camp split off in support of EU integration. In Macedonia, armed conflict broke out in 2001 between Albanian separatists and the Macedonian government, deepening the already existing ethnic divisions. The West stepped in to broker a peace agreement and rescue democratic reform through intense oversight of Macedonia's political institutions, but democratization has continued to be hindered by a lack of legitimacy and deep ethnic divisions exacerbated by poverty; despite achieving candidate status in 2005, membership in the EU is still a distant hope.

The lessons that emerge from the experience of the Yugoslav successor states is that democracy cannot be created out of thin air and that initial conditions are a strong predictor of long-term trajectories of regime change. This is an important corrective to analyses of post-communism that have not adequately acknowledged the limiting influence of structure. Yet actual regime outcomes must be seen in light of Western agency, its ability to transfer liberal norms to the Balkans, and how it confronted domestic structures. Each of these factors—structure and the influence of external agency—is necessary but not sufficient to understand the divergent paths of change that are the subject of this book. Rather than searching for temporally located "legacies" to explain post-communist change, this book emphasizes the influence of two key historical *continuities* in the eastern half of Europe: the political consequences of varying levels of economic development and the dynamics of small states adapting to a shifting external balance of power.

Why the Yugoslav Successor States?

Innumerable accounts have analyzed the breakup of the former Yugoslav federation and the ensuing wars of the 1990s. However, very rarely have researchers examined the Yugoslav successor states in the context of regime transition, whether as individual case studies or within cross-national comparative analyses. Many volumes and articles dealing with comparative post-communist democratization conspicuously left out the Yugoslav successor states. The reasons for this deficiency were multifold, ranging from practical reasons, such as the difficulty of doing primary field research in these countries during times of war, to epistemological reasons, such as the belief that it is not useful to regard polities with fundamental problems of nation and state building through the theoretical lens of democratization studies.[3] Nation-building dilemmas, however, were embedded in the dynamics of post-communist regime change and cannot be separated from this context. There is a need to describe, in a broad comparative perspective, the larger process of regime change that occurred in these countries in order to understand the context in which ethnic conflict and war occurred, as these phenomena are by no means unique to the region.

The existing literature on the former Yugoslavia has been preoccupied with the nature and detrimental effects of nationalism. The methodology of political science often treats nationalism as an independent variable.[4] However, it is necessary to understand the conditions under which ethnic nationalism arises and takes hold and how this shapes the strategies of political elites and the preferences and expectations of the masses. It is thus also critical to see nationalism as a *dependent* variable and, consequently, to understand why illiberal nationalism emerged where and when it did in the first place. When nationalism is treated only as an independent variable, the *timing* of its appearance cannot be explained. Ramet (1984) echoes this idea, noting that nationalism is a variable "whose influence may be critical at some times and under certain circumstances and only marginally significant at other times and [under] other conditions" (quoted in Janos 1997).

The role of the war, assumed by some to be the sole factor precluding what could have been democratic outcomes, must also be reconsidered. Revelations in the published memoirs of leaders in the former Yugoslavia and its successor states[5] and formerly sealed documents and testimony at the International Criminal Tribunal for the former Yugoslavia (ICTY) in The Hague have further confirmed what many already knew: that war was used by nationalist regimes as an instrument of legitimization for undemocratic politics. Although the consequences of war—refugees, occupation, and the need to centralize authority—undoubtedly constrained the democratization process, rulers in war-torn states also demonstrated that their primary goal was to strengthen and expand their power rather than to create genuinely demo-cratic institutions even after armed hostilities subsided.[6] Beyond providing political capital for nationalist elites, armed conflicts also created loyal constituencies of nationalist-authoritarian governments that came to ben-efit directly and materially from the politics and economics of war. Thus, Eric Gordy's (1999) provocative but revealing answer to the counterfactual question on whether an authoritarian regime in Serbia could have been sustained in the absence of war rings true for the rest of the successor states: if authoritarianism could have been maintained without war, there might have not been war in the first place, or at least the intensity and length of the war may have been curtailed. Much less controversially, however, one may note that well after the war was over, the idea of defending national interests in the face of an enemy was used by ruling parties to justify un-democratic practices and hide economic mismanagement. As a prominent political scientist in Zagreb told me, "The transition became embedded in the war, and the war in the transition" (Trazicija se uklopila u rat, a rat u tranziciju).[7]

In terms of historical antecedents and divergence in post-communist out-comes, the Yugoslav successor states represent a microcosm of Eastern and Central Europe and thus contain a reservoir of analogies for the region. With regard to antecedents, the Yugoslav successor states have varying imperial traditions (Ottoman, Habsburg, Venetian) and different religious influences (Eastern Orthodox, Roman Catholic, Islamic) and, at the outset of transition, reflected the entire spectrum of levels of economic development in Eastern Europe (with per capita GDPs ranging from under $1,000 to over $10,000). With regard to outcomes, their post-communist regimes initially also varied along the range of levels of democratization and regime types observed in the region, as illustrated in Table I.1.

Thus, the current void in the literature on the former Yugoslavia as a case of regime change is simultaneously a void in the literature on post-communism. Moreover, the post-communist experience of the Yugoslav successor states may provide important revisions to existing theories of post-communist change. For instance, Yugoslav communism was, at least on the surface, "lib-eral," and yet initially it produced little in the way of post-communist democ-racy, which may lead us to reconsider theories that emphasize the type of communism and its legacies.[8]

Table I.1　Post-communist Regime Types in the Late 1990s

Full substantive democracies[a]	Nearly full substantive democracies[b]	Formal democracies[c]	Between formal democracy and authoritarianism[d]	Semi-authoritarian regimes[d]	Authoritarian regimes[e]
Czech Republic	Bulgaria	Georgia	Albania	Azerbaijan	Belarus
Estonia	Romania	Moldova	Armenia	Kyrgyzstan	Tajikistan
Hungary	Slovakia	Russia	*Croatia*	Kazakhstan	Turkmenistan
Latvia		Ukraine		*Bosnia and*	Uzbekistan
Lithuania		*Macedonia*		*Herzegovina*	*Federal Republic*
Poland					*of Yugoslavia*
Slovenia					

Source: Based on categories developed by Kitschelt (1999).

[a]Regimes that offered a full range of civic and political rights and upheld the rule of law.

[b]Regimes that had generally clean elections and democratic procedures but occasional infringements of civil rights.

[c]Regimes that displayed serious infringements of free speech, civil rights, and political rights to electoral participation. The ruling elite in these countries tended to substantively undermine otherwise fair statutory rules of political competition.

[d]These groups consist of countries where democratic institutions were window dressing designed to legitimize the regime for Western observers.

[e]"Full-blown" dictatorships centered on an individual or ruling clique who exercise unchecked power over the polity.

Notes on Methodology and Case Selection

This book employs the comparative method, focusing on a well-defined set of cases and the unfolding of causal processes and applying systematic comparison to generate explanations of outcomes at the level of national politics.[9] The case selection has empirical, theoretical, and methodological rationales. Methodologically speaking, there is significant and theoretically interesting variance in outcomes across the four cases, and in terms of the two independent variables (economics and external agency), there is also ample variation. Yet, the fact that the four cases emerged from the same multinational state and thus have a common institutional legacy allows for something like a natural experiment, controlling for many factors while isolating others. Moreover, it is possible to control for the effect of certain common starting conditions, such as the imperative of new state formation. Thus, the comparison can be undertaken employing Mill's Method of Difference, which suggests the selection of cases that are structurally similar on important parameters, controlling for as many variables as possible and highlighting the causal variables that explain some key variation between cases. The shared Yugoslav legacy points the observer in two directions with regard to causal factors. On one hand, it points to pre-communist factors or other "deep" structural variables. On the other hand, the shared legacy of a half-century in the same polity may suggest the triumph of contingent factors and human agency. Herein lies another methodological advantage of these cases: they present the researcher with the challenge and opportunity to translate structural factors and other historical conditions into the constraints and opportunities that shape the actions of individuals, who in turn create macro-level political outcomes.

Some words about the "small-N" design of the research are in order. Scholars have noted the problems of causal inference inherent in "small-N" qualitative analysis (King, Keohane, and Verba 1994; Brady and Collier 2004). These problems include conceptual stretching, measurement validity, conditional independence, and the general problem of having too many variables and too few cases. Despite these problems, small-N studies can yield valuable results. As Grzymała-Busse (2002: 15) points out, most analyses of post-communist politics have used either extensions of one-country studies or large-N comparisons of the entire universe of post-communist cases.[10] The strength of the former methodology lies in its empirical richness and its ability to illustrate multiple and complex causes. Its weakness, however, is that it is often unable to draw firm comparative theoretical conclusions. The large-N method, by contrast, can readily eliminate entire groups of potential explanatory variables through statistical regression, but it has more difficulty with causal depth and complexity or the importance of sequence and timing. Thus, a mid-level comparison of cases strikes a compromise between the depth of the single-case study and the generalizability of a large-N study.

In sum, the research design provides a causal account that links distant and recent factors in explaining regime diversity. It takes into account the historical dimension but does not treat leaders and politics as merely passive summarizers of historical and economic conditions. More important for questions of methodology, this strategy avoids the pitfalls of tautology in causally shallow accounts and the lack of plausible causal mechanisms in some structural analyses (Kitschelt 1999).

CHAPTER ONE

Post-communist Diversity

How to Explain the Puzzle of Post-communist Regime Diversity

The combination of divergent political outcomes, a common institutional legacy, and a shared time frame of transformation has made the post-communist region particularly interesting to comparative political scientists.[1] The challenge has been to explain the reality of post-communist regime diversity, which prevailing theories did not predict. When measured in terms of civic and political rights indices developed by Freedom House, there was no region or set of countries with a larger standard deviation on democratization scores in the 1990s. Among the post-communist states, one found instances of liberal democracy, full-blown dictatorship, and everything in between. Today, two decades after the collapse of the Berlin Wall, some post-communist states are members of the EU, while others are autocracies or struggle to maintain stability. As such, questions about the determinants of divergent paths of democratization in the post-communist world have come to dominate the debates of area studies scholars and political scientists.

Post-communist diversity has been a surprise for a number of reasons.

First, it is surprising in light of the common and powerful communist past. Bunce (1999: 757) argues that communism was an "internally consistent," "elaborate," and "unusually invasive" political and economic system, and as such presents one of the best cases social scientists have for the kind of powerful and distinctive past that one would expect to influence post-communist outcomes in a uniform way. Many would not predict democratic or market outcomes at all, given fifty to seventy-five years of regimes that were anything but democratic and market-oriented. Second, communism "remained in place for a long time and was the heir in virtually every instance to a well-established tradition of authoritarian politics and state-dominated economics." Third, diversity is surprising because the East European states emerged from communism into an international environment that was quite consensual in its ideological message: liberalism in politics and economics was hegemonic, with few incentives to pursue alternate paths of development. On the contrary, the incentive to pursue liberalism as a way to enter Euro-Atlantic structures was immense.

The discussion over how best to account for post-communist diversity reflects older debates in the comparative study of democratization. The main divisions in the literature on democratization are between two very different epistemological orientations: structural or configurational theories on one hand, and process and agency–oriented theories on the other (Kitschelt 1992). Put differently, the literature can be categorized into scholars who focus on the structural prerequisites of democracy and those who argue that human agency has the power to "craft" democracy despite the existence of certain unfavorable conditions. In the first group, among the most important works are Lipset (1960), Moore (1966), Luebbert (1991), Rueschemeyer, Stephens, and Stephens (1992), and Huntington (1993). Seminal works of the second group include Rustow (1970), Di Palma (1990), and numerous publications by the "transitologists" Juan Linz, Guillermo O'Donnell, Alfred Stepan, and Philippe Schmitter.[2] As Kitschelt (1992: 1029) notes, central to this debate is the concept of choice in political action itself. For structuralists, "choices represent calculations in light of given preferences and institutional constraints." For those who believe in the power of human agency, "choices are caught up in a continuous redefinition of actors' perceptions of preferences and constraints." The underlying debate, as Hirschman (1970) succinctly stated, is between beliefs in the "probable" (the structuralists) versus the "possible" (the agency-centered scholars).

Bunce (1999: 762) has noted that the position one takes when considering these debates in the context of post-communism is more than just a matter of intellectual taste. Indeed, it reflects different understandings of what has transpired in this part of the world since the collapse of the old system and what is likely to transpire in the future, and it is also likely to lead to different interpretations of communism and pre-communism. One can discern three broad approaches in the literature on post-communist democratization whose differences reflect the kinds of epistemological divisions inherent in the literature on political change mentioned above. Each approach, furthermore, has its own basket of preferred variables and hypotheses.

Pre-communist Legacies

The first of these approaches is preoccupied with the pre-communist history of post-communist states and turns to factors such as historical levels of socioeconomic development, patterns of nation- and state-building in the pre-communist period, the history of ethnic relations, and forms of pre-communist imperial domination and the kinds of institutions, patterns of authority, civil society, and political culture they engendered.[3] Scholars whose work espouses this approach have highlighted differences between Habsburg (with a dense civil society and a relatively high level of development) and Ottoman (with a weak civil society and economic underdevelopment) rule and the consequences of these differences for current developments.

An equally important variable for proponents of this approach is the degree to which liberalism and democracy were part of interwar regimes. Thus, the Czechoslovak interwar experience with democracy is seen as providing democratic capital for post-communist transition, while Bulgaria's prewar autocratic monarchy does not provide such advantages.

Political culture, often defined by religion, is also a key variable in this approach. One hypothesis is that the impersonal-legalist tendencies of Western Christianity provide a more fertile ground for post-communist democracy than the collectivist-paternalistic proclivities of Eastern Orthodoxy and Islam.[4] These differences helped lead the Orthodox-Muslim and Catholic areas of Eastern Europe down differing paths of political development starting in the Middle Ages, and the empires that governed these lands largely reinforced the cultural tendencies of each faith. Thus, this hypothesis maintains that differing religious traditions help to explain the relative democratic success of the predominantly Roman Catholic northwestern tier of Eastern Europe (Poland, Hungary, Czech

Republic) versus the democratic shortcomings of the Orthodox and Islamic southeastern tier (Bulgaria, Bosnia and Herzegovina, Albania, Romania).

Differing levels of economic development, rooted in the pre-communist period, have also been used to explain post-communist diversity. This approach is rooted in the modernization literature of the postwar era, which saw economic development as the precursor to the development of democratic attitudes. Simply stated, the hypothesis is that higher levels of development provide a better setting for democracy than lower levels of development. Post-communist countries with high levels of development are more likely to have a middle class, which constitutes a solid base of support for democratic values, while those with low levels of development will have large populations receptive to populism, nationalism, and other illiberal ideologies.

The degree of ethnic homogeneity versus heterogeneity and the nature of ethnic relations can also be included in this approach as a key variable. A popular hypothesis, formulated well before the demise of communism, holds that societies with ethnic divisions face many difficulties in democratizing their polities (Dahl 1971; Lijphart 1977; Horowitz 2000). When and where they exist, ethnic differences rooted in the pre-communist past create bases of identification that polarize publics and make the kind of compromise and consensus building necessary for democracy much more difficult. Ethnic divisions, furthermore, increase the risk of violence and war, which also complicates the prospects for democracy. Parties will form around ethnic rather than political identities, especially in late-developing countries or in those where ethnic differences coincide with socioeconomic cleavages and strong memories of ethnic strife. Under such conditions, there are incentives for political leaders to exploit any existing or historical distrust and animosity embedded in these ethnic differences. Therefore, ethnically heterogeneous post-communist societies are expected to have a more difficult time democratizing than homogeneous ones.

The pre-communist approach suggests that the communist period was merely a divergence from a preexisting trajectory of development, and the policies and institutions of communism either did little to eliminate pre-communist legacies or only served to reinforce their salience. In this view, the collapse of communism has opened a Pandora's box of pre-communist values, identities, memories, and animosities and led political elites and policymakers to reach into the pre-communist histories of their nations to resurrect everything from state symbols and political parties to laws and institutions.

This approach has been criticized for being overly deterministic and unable to explain those post-communist states that have successfully democratized their polities despite the existence of decidedly negative pre-communist legacies (Romania and Bulgaria). Critics also contend that although it is strong on causal depth, this approach is less effective at making strong causal linkages. How can one demonstrate that interwar democratic cultures (Czechoslovakia) were sustained through half a century of communism and the social, political, and economic upheaval it entailed? The strength of this approach lies in its ability to identify root structural causes that are historical continuities faced by regimes and leaders of various characters in all historical periods as well as temporally rooted legacies. As such, it may actually be quite conducive to cross-regional comparison.

Communist Legacies

The second approach emphasizes the varieties of communist regimes that took shape after the initial Stalinist period.[5] One hypothesis is that communist regimes that allowed more opportunities for civil society to exist outside of state structures created favorable sources of political capital for post-communist democratization. Similarly, those communist regimes that advanced economic and political reforms prior to their fall also created greater chances for post-communist "success" than those that avoided reforms altogether. In the reformist communist regimes, political and economic transition started before the formal end of communist rule, so post-communist reforms were simply a continuation of processes that had started much earlier.[6] Those communist regimes that allowed little room for free speech and autonomous social organizations or avoided reform did not create a base for post-communist democratization. Other proponents of this approach point to the level of institutional pluralism in late communism and argue that where greater pluralism existed, it was more difficult to sustain authoritarianism in the post-communist period.[7]

The advantage of this approach, thus, lies in its ability to highlight continuities and constraints from the powerful communist past. However, like the first approach, this one has been criticized for not assigning enough credit to human agency and post-communist institution building and thus being unable to explain the appearance of democracy "against all odds." In addition, this approach may be faulted for tending to coopt variables that are actually rooted in the pre-communist past as being features of communism, leading one to misunderstand the depth of certain post-communist traits and thus to offer misguided analyses and policy prescriptions. As Ekiert and Kubik (1999) have noted, mistrust and a weak civil society were a part of interwar regimes as much as they characterized communism. Since this approach sees the communist experience as being uniquely powerful, its proponents are skeptical of the comparability of post-communist states.

Post-communist Construction

The third approach argues for the primacy of various features of post-communism to explain political change. In this view, post-communist political outcomes are constructed by human agents, politics, and institutions, not given by history (Fish 1999).[8] The quality, efficacy, and character of post-communist leaders is emphasized[9] as well as the unusual leverage they held in the period of "extraordinary politics" immediately following the collapse of communism. The post-communist construction approach holds that during these periods, social constraints are lowered and the weight of the past becomes less decisive, allowing us to think of transitions in terms of "crafting." The decisions made during these periods are "critical junctures" that "lock in" a subsequent trajectory of political development (Collier and Collier 1991). The mode of transition thus becomes critical in explaining outcomes.[10] This approach also points to the crucial role of institutional design in shaping outcomes, concluding, for instance, that superpresidential systems have had negative consequences for post-communist democratization. Proponents of this approach also hypothesize that proportional electoral systems are more conducive to post-communist democracy than majoritarian ones.

By its very nature, this approach is best suited to the epistemology and analytical tools of "transitology," which focuses on the role and strategic interaction of elites in "crafting" democratic transitions.[11] Because it tends to give little weight to historical factors, it is also more conducive to the kind of cross-regional comparison prominent scholars of democratic transitions have advocated.[12] The significant advantages of this approach lie in the proper credit it gives to human agency, the power of institutions, and the unexpected consequences of post-communist policy decisions. By focusing on proximate factors, this approach is also able to establish plausible causal linkages between explanatory variables and outcomes. Criticisms of this approach include its ahistorical nature, as it overlooks how the past, especially the powerful communist past, shapes the present in post-communist states. Furthermore, critics contend, this approach is causally shallow, inadequately searching for the "why of the why" and thereby overlooking the real root causes of post-communist outcomes.[13] It is possible to show, for instance, that outcomes of the first post-communist elections were crucial in determining subsequent outcomes, but the more important question may be why these elections turned out as they did. The quality of post-communist political competition among parties has also been highlighted by scholars as a determinant of democratization, but it is not clear what makes for robust competition (Ekiert et al. 2007: 16).

The post-communist political construction approach is by its very nature voluntarist, reflecting an epistemology that views almost anything as politically possible given certain "extraordinary" circumstances, a healthy dose of human agency, and the right institutions. Moreover, it is focused on domestic politics. Yet, just as political rumblings in Moscow were able to shift the balance of forces in Warsaw, Budapest, or Sofia during the communist period, so too have the policies, conditions, statements, and progress evaluations of Brussels shaped the constraints, incentives, and strategies of political elites and publics alike in the post-communist period.

Discussion

Each of these approaches can be temporally and epistemologically located. Temporally, the first two reach further back into the past to find determinants of post-communist change, while the third one looks to much more proximate factors. Epistemologically, the first two approaches emphasize constraining factors identifiable a priori and are consequently inheritors of the structural tradition in comparative politics, while the third points to the power of human will, contingency, and institutions in shaping outcomes and thus reflects the voluntarist and institutionalist approaches of the discipline. Moreover, as Kitschelt (1999) has noted, the first two approaches are strong on causal depth but weaker in establishing plausible casual links between antecedents and outcomes, while the third can illustrate causal mechanisms more effectively but is less able to provide causal depth.

Multivariate regression analysis that includes the entire universe of post-communist cases may produce less than satisfactory results because it is difficult to quantify structural variables. For instance, ethnic homogeneity versus heterogeneity has been coded as a dummy variable in large-N studies, yet it is the *content* of ethnic relations that matters much more than the simple

Table 1.1   Approaches to Explaining Post-communist Regime Diversity

Approaches	Variables	Hypotheses	Strengths	Weaknesses
Pre-communist legacies	Ethnic divisions, level of development, religious traditions, political culture, experience with democracy	Favorable precommunist legacies are conducive to post-communist democratization and vice versa	Causal depth, comparability, ability to explain long-term patterns of politics	Lack of causal mechanisms, overdeterminism, lack of attention to agency and contingency
Communist legacies	Type of communist regime (orthodox vs. developmental), extent of reform under communism	Liberal communist regimes were more favorable to post-communist democratization, and vice versa	Acknowledges importance of communist legacy, causal depth	Determinist, unable to account for democratization despite repressive communist legacy
Post-communist construction	Institutional choice, leadership, electoral system	Various. For instance, presidential systems are less amenable to post-communist democratization than parliamentary systems	Strong on causal mechanisms, able to explain surprise cases of democratization	Weak on causal depth

fact of ethnic heterogeneity or homogeneity.[14] Table 1.1 summarizes the three approaches, their associated variables and hypotheses, and their respective strengths and weaknesses.

This is by no means an exhaustive list of the approaches that have been used to explain post-communist political change. Postmodernism and discourse analysis, for instance, have been employed in some accounts of post-communist change.[15] Furthermore, these are ideal types: many studies combine more than one approach or employ variants of one of them by drawing on innovative methodologies. The choice of a given approach is also intricately related to the phenomena that a given research project aims to explain. Single events may be better explained by proximate factors, while long-term patterns of authority are better explained by communist or pre-communist factors. The goal of this "ideal" typology, however, is to identify the main scholarly fault lines so that a set of hypotheses can be generated about the determinants of post-Yugoslav regime diversity.

Explaining Regime Change in the Yugoslav Successor States: Some Hypotheses

Pre-communist Legacies—Culture and Ethnic Divisions

Culture, rooted in deeply ingrained attitudes that developed well before the establishment of the first and second Yugoslavias, has often been used to explain a range of post-Yugoslav phenomena, from nationalism and ethnic conflict to authoritarianism and corruption. A cultural hypothesis would hold that the delegitimization of the communist system combined with political, social, and economic crisis in the 1980s in the former Yugoslavia led to a reemergence of pre-communist forms of political culture and the patterns of authority that they engender. Corrupt and clientilistic forms of communist rule, especially prevalent in the southern Yugoslav republics, only served to reinforce the deeply rooted cultural tendencies of Eastern Orthodoxy. Thus, political vacuums in the north (Slovenia and Croatia) were more likely to be filled by liberal political configurations, while in the south (Serbia, Montenegro, Macedonia, Bosnia and Herzegovina, Kosovo), political forces combining the collectivist and paternalistic tendencies of Eastern Orthodoxy and Islam would most likely come to the fore.

The political culture hypothesis, however, has limits in explaining the political changes that have transpired in the Yugoslav successor states in the post-communist period. At first glance, the contrast between regime types in Slovenia (democratic) and FRY (authoritarian) reflects very different political cultures. Yet, despite a shared Habsburg past, Croatia was much less much democratic than Slovenia in the first decade of post-communist transition. Croatia's Habsburg legacy also suggests that its post-communist regime would be more democratic than Macedonia's, yet in the 1990s on procedural measures the opposite was true. In terms of actual regime substance, the Tuđman regime of Croatia, albeit less repressive on most measures, was arguably more collectivist and patriarchal than its counterpart in FRY, the Milošević regime, despite the latter's Eastern Orthodox cultural context. But even Slovenia and FRY must be placed under greater scrutiny in light of this hypothesis. How can one explain, for instance, that the League of Communists of Slovenia was quite conformist compared to its Serbian counterpart throughout the 1970s? Nor were there any real civil society–based calls for liberalism in Slovenia until the 1980s, while in Serbia of the 1970s, liberal opposition circles flourished. Similarly, in Croatia, even in the first half of the 1980s there was virtually no organized opposition to the hard-line League of Communists that held power until the first free elections.

Another variant of the political culture hypothesis attempts to link post-communist outcomes to the existence of democratic regimes in the interwar period. Given that none of the states in question here were democratic, or even sovereign, in the interwar period, this hypothesis does little to help us understand the outcomes. If anything, Serbia's comparatively longer experience with independent statehood might lead one to predict greater democratization there, and yet this has not been the case.

Similarly, public opinion research carried out in the mid-1980s does not necessarily indicate strong democratic values among people in any of the republics. Though some surveys conducted in the 1980s suggest, in relative terms, greater support for a multiparty system in Slovenia than in Serbia, in absolute terms even the Slovenian figures are not impressive.[16] Public opinion research shows that people throughout the former Yugoslavia seemingly have stronger democratic attitudes than their counterparts in post-communist states that have made greater progress in democratization. Most interestingly, in 1992 only 6 percent of Croatians said that they would support the abolition of parliaments and political parties if given the chance—even though Croatia was well on its way to becoming an authoritarian regime—while 11 percent of Slovenians said they supported this idea, even though Slovenia was on the path to becoming a consolidated democracy![17] There is strong evidence, thus, that it was pluralism itself that engendered democratic attitudes and not the other way around. Put differently, one must understand the victory of pro-liberal forces in Slovenia as a function of certain conditions, incentives, and constraints other than "deeply held democratic values." Conversely, the vocal presence of liberal reformers both within and outside of communist power structures in the 1980s did not assure that liberalism would succeed in post-communist FRY politics. Indeed, as chapter 7 will demonstrate, other forces rendered these liberal forces powerless by the end of the 1980s.

Crude cultural hypotheses are, ironically, quite popular among ordinary people in the countries that are the subject of this analysis.[18] Many a Vojvodanin has told me that the relative post-communist peace and multiethnic harmony of their formerly autonomous region are related to their "non-Balkan traits" (in contrast to their Serb ethnic brethren on the other side of the Danube in Belgrade and further south) and their history as a Habsburg-Hungarian (as opposed to an Ottoman) province. Those from Vojvodina, however, often forget to mention that Slobodan Milošević and his Serbian Socialist Party (SPS) once enjoyed strong support (at least among ethnic Serbs) in Vojvodina, and that many educated citizens of Vojvodina had marched in rallies to demonstrate their support for the Serbian national cause.

It is difficult to separate liberal illiberal cultural predispositions from socioeconomic development and underdevelopment, respectively. It is hard to say, for instance, whether the success of liberal parties in regions like Istria in the 1990s reflects a deeply rooted "civic culture" or simply better economic conditions and, therefore, prospects. It likely reflects the proximity to Italy and all the incentives this creates for greater openness. Much the same could be said for Slovenia. Yet the greatest evidence that economy comes before culture in this chicken-and-egg dilemma is that culture and other values and forms of identity have clearly been mobilized by elites in conditions of economic difficulty. Even where the existence of illiberal political cultures is assumed, the *timing* of the rise of anti-democratic politics cannot be explained by political culture alone. The utilitarian dimension of culture and identity-based mobilization, emphasized throughout this book, strongly indicates that culture must be seen as an *intervening* variable that is necessary but far from sufficient in explaining different paths of regime change in the Yugoslav successor states.

Identity-based mobilization will be important in understanding the role of what is perhaps the most important of pre-communist legacies in the former Yugoslav space, namely, the level of ethnic homogeneity versus heterogeneity in each successor state. There is no doubt that the mobilization of ethnic identity in pursuit of nationalist goals by concrete political actors characterized the fall of Yugoslavia and post-Yugoslav regimes. There is also no doubt that Slovenia's relative homogeneity and the corresponding lack of a geographically based, coherent ethnic minority with a strong identity rendered it lucky in many ways. Most significantly, it meant that illiberal nationalism there could not find a broad following in the absence of groups against which to direct it. Yet, Slovenia has not been without ethnic minority problems owing to the presence of guest workers (*južnjaci,* or "southerners," as they are pejoratively called) from other parts of the former Yugoslavia. Furthermore, the substance of ethnic relations matters more than proportions of majorities to minorities because it relates to the ability of political groups to mobilize identities when circumstances allow. Ethnic homogeneity in Slovenia may better explain why that republic was able to exit Yugoslavia more or less peacefully than why it was able to establish and maintain a liberal democratic regime following independence. Thus, as Ramet (2006: 572) succinctly notes, ethnic plurality as such is not a problem: it becomes a problem when mobilized by elites competing for power.

The ethnic plurality hypothesis is also weakened in the face of comparative scrutiny—both with the other cases that are the subject of this book and with the larger universe of post-communist cases. With regard to the latter, multivariate regression analysis has shown that ethnic heterogeneity and homogeneity fail as predictors of democratization in the twenty-eight post-communist cases (Fish 1998a, 2001). Some post-communist states—most notably the three Baltic republics—have democratized successfully, albeit not always inclusively, despite the existence of large and hostile minority populations. Ethnic Bulgarians in Bulgaria make up the same percentage of the population as Slovenes in Slovenia—but have experienced less success in democratizing their polity than the ethnically heterogeneous Baltic republics. Within the Yugoslav successor states we find equal challenges to the validity of the ethnic plurality hypothesis. In ethnically plural Serbia, where only 66 percent of the population is Serb, ethnic minorities in Vojvodina (Hungarians and others) and Sandžak (Bosniak Muslims) did not always mobilize in a way that was antagonistic to the formation of a post-communist Serbian state. Finally, we should note that authoritarianism in Croatia continued after 1995, when most of the country's Serb minority was no longer present. In sum, the link between ethnic plurality and regime type must be examined in a more sophisticated manner, especially as it relates to other factors such as economic scarcity and shapes the incentives of elites to mobilize ethnicity toward concrete political ends.[19]

Communist Legacies

The former Yugoslavia was understood by many, in Western and Eastern Europe alike, to espouse the most liberal form of politics and economics in the communist world. Pleština (1992) notes that the nation was known for decades as the maverick that defied Stalin, allowed unparalleled freedoms to its citizens, established a new concept of local democracy through worker-managed enterprises, and founded a unique international alliance system as an alternative to the two major power blocs. Those analysts who believe that diverse communist-era patterns of authority are key to understanding divergent paths of post-communist change might predict a high probability for post-communist democracy in all of the Yugoslav successor states. This, of course, has not been the case, which leads one to question the utility of this hypothesis from the outset. However, it may be more helpful to look at differences among the communist power structures of each constituent unit in the Socialist Federal Republic of Yugoslavia (SFRJ), since continual revisions in constitutional arrangements had given each republic an impressive scope of autonomy by the 1970s. Here, we find some plausible answers. The Slovenian party did tolerate more dissent in the political realm in the 1980s compared to Croatia's relatively hard-line regime, a legacy of a crackdown on Croatian communist reformers in the early 1970s. However, Serbia began allowing the same kind of freedoms in the 1970s, and yet Serbia and Slovenia's post-communist regimes by nearly all measures fell on opposite ends of the spectrum in the 1990s. Still, Slovenia's wider-ranging reforms of the 1980s certainly set the republic on a positive course early on. There may be, therefore, some utility in explaining post-communist regime diversity in terms of political differences among the republics during the communist era.

However, challenging some assumptions about the character and consequences of Yugoslav communism raises some serious questions about whether that comparatively open communist system represented the kind of liberalism that could provide a positive foundation for post-communist democratization in any of the republics. Scholars like Ivo Banac are skeptical that anything about the Yugoslav system really provided such a foundation.[20] To the extent that pluralism did exist, it was manifested as competition and conflict among the republics and provinces, a dynamic that took on an increasingly ethnic character in the 1970s and 1980s. It was not the kind of pluralism that provides the building blocks for independent political parties and autonomous social groups, the "civic culture" emphasized by scholars of democracy and democratization. On the contrary, it contributed to building a foundation for nationalist and ethnic-based parties and ideologies. Crises of Yugoslav socialism, unlike those of Hungarian, Polish, or Czech socialism, were never really rooted in broad-based social movements that provided the seeds for a democratic opposition and civil society. Although sizeable dissident groups featured in several of Yugoslavia's constituent republics and provinces, they rarely focused on advocating political and economic reforms. Instead, they increasingly focused on questions of nationality, ethnicity, and independence, which, according to Janusz Bugajski, "diverted popular attention away from the prospect of systemic transformation and . . . strengthened the hand of nationalist and authoritarian politicians in several republics" (2002: xxii). Nor did Yugoslavia's much-touted self-management policies provide an adequate foundation for liberalism or do much to overcome the inherent irrationality of the economic system. In the mid-1970s, whatever genuine workers' self-management existed at the enterprise level began to die out in favor of an authoritarian bureaucratic apparatus (Schierup 1999: 40). As a result, when an economic and ideological crisis came to the fore, nationalist parties gained strength and quickly marginalized any truly liberal political groups. Nationalism became the least common denominator in political competition, while the tasks of building democratic institutions, developing civil society, and establishing the rule of law were largely neglected. As Janos has put it, "Yugoslavia had become the socialist version of a developmental dictatorship rather than the model of popular participation in government" (2000: 276).

Moreover, whatever openness existed in political and economic life did not eliminate the influence of an extensive internal security apparatus that cracked down on stirrings of dissent and dealt harshly with expressions of nationalism in the republics. It was particularly suspicious of the West and interrogated, harassed, and intimidated Yugoslavs who had spent time abroad, such as the *Gastarbeiter*.[21] Yugoslavia's variant of socialism may have promoted modernization, consumerism, and other facets of Western society, but it is harder to make the claim that it shaped democratic attitudes.

Post-communist Political Construction

A healthy dose of voluntarism in the literature on the dissolution of Yugoslavia was a response to overly deterministic accounts, especially those that in some measure underscored "ancient ethnic hatreds."[22] This literature stipulated that power-hungry leaders who manipulated the population through state-controlled media were the real culprits for all that had gone wrong in the region, especially nationalism, authoritarianism, and war. The new emphasis on political leadership and the instrumental aspects of ethnic nationalism was a welcome addition, but it tended to remove the leaders and their ideologies from the context in which they rose to prominence. This context was characterized by eroding central authority and intense political competition within each republic to fill the political vacuum left by the collapse of communist authority and economic crisis. Conditions and prospects varied from republic to republic and shaped different expectations and incentives on the part of both elites and the rest of society. Elites competing for power in this context adapted their strategies and rhetoric according to what best assured their political survival. Without a full understanding of this context, any effort to explain variation among post-Yugoslav leaders misses the crucial variables.

Political construction hypotheses also point to the relationship between post-communist economic reform in the form of liberalization and privatization on one hand and democratization on the other. In the transitology literature, based largely on empirical data from Latin American states, there is much discussion of "sequencing" and a tradeoff between political and economic liberalization.[23] The most basic argument about sequencing is that in order to pursue economic reforms, elites must be insulated from populist demands, so democratic change can only come *after* painful economic liberalization is instituted. The post-communist experience, however, strongly suggests that economic liberalization and democratization reinforce each other rather than being mutually incompatible.[24] The Yugoslav successor states may actually defy this pattern to some degree, but there is little to suggest that the patterns and progress of economic reform can explain the observed divergence in regime type. Slovenia actually pursued limited reform by neoliberal standards in the 1990s, while the type of liberalization and privatization pursued in Croatia only strengthened authoritarian political forces. In Croatia and FRY, post-communist regimes managed to stay in power despite significant economic woes and declines in living standard. Finally, as Hellman (1998) has convincingly demonstrated, partial liberalization may lead to authoritarianism. Hellman argues it was not necessarily the "losers" of transition that constituted the strongest anti-reform coalition, but rather the "winners," the regime insiders who benefited from murky privatizations and other illegal deals. Such trends were evident in Croatia and FRY.

Institutional hypotheses may also be put forward to explain political outcomes in the Yugoslav successor states. Majoritarian and presidential systems, adopted in Croatia, Macedonia, and Serbia in the still-constituted Yugoslavia, could have been the "critical junctures" that ultimately discouraged democratization by concentrating power in single parties and leaders who later used this power to construct authoritarian regimes. Some political analysts, for instance, have attributed the victory and subsequent political monopoly of the Croatian Democratic Union (Hrvatska Demokratska Zajednica, HDZ) in post-communist Croatia to that country's choice of a majoritarian electoral system in 1990.[25] The institutional argument, however, does not hold up very well when subjected to comparative scrutiny, given that in Macedonia, FRY, and Croatia, similar electoral systems produced three different kinds of regimes. Nevertheless, all three of these regimes were less democratic than the regime found in Slovenia, which, to the credit of theoretical and prescriptive proponents of institutional choice, did adopt a more proportional electoral system. At the same time, both Macedonia and Slovenia instituted parliamentary systems, and yet democracy fared differently in each place. Perhaps the most powerful argument against the institutional view is that the political forces that dominated the initial transition in FRY and Croatia had so much popular support that it is somewhat trivial to speculate on what might have changed had the constitutional distribution of power or electoral rules been different.

Discussion

None of the above hypotheses, taken alone, succeeds in accounting for regime diversity in the Yugoslav successor states. Most useful for understanding illiberal outcomes seems to be the ethnic plurality versus homogeneity hypothesis, which can be subsumed under the larger set of factors with origins in the pre-communist period. The politics of ethnic mobilization and ethnic nationalism appear to have precluded the emergence of liberal democracy in FRY, Macedonia, and Croatia, albeit to different degrees. Slovenia's relative homogeneity, by contrast, seems to underlie its democratic success. Yet, the case of post-communist Macedonia, characterized in the 1990s by relative peace, inter-ethnic cooperation in government, and higher scores on procedural correctness, appears to challenge this hypothesis to some extent. And, as noted above, comparative analysis with other post-communist cases also poses a challenge to the ethnic plurality hypothesis. Moreover, the extent of democratization varies widely in ethnically heterogeneous states and does not neatly correlate with the degree of plurality.

What is needed is an understanding of the conditions under which ethnic mobilization and nationalism, expressed as concrete political strategies, appear and ultimately succeed in overcoming liberal responses to economic and political collapse. Conversely, we need to specify the conditions that prevent nationalism from becoming the dominant ideology despite the existence of ethnic cleavages. This does not mean we have to reject such hypotheses outright, but ethnicity, culture, and institutions need to be seen in light of economic conditions to fully account for the kinds of regimes that appeared in the successor states.

Economic Viability and the Promise of Western Integration: A Map of the Argument

This book seeks to specify the conditions that underpinned the emergence of particular regimes in each successor state. The limitations of the hypotheses discussed in the preceding section bring us to the two variables at the center of the argument. The "master" explanatory variable is economics, and more specifically, the level of economic viability of each republic on the eve of independence. The second independent variable is the way in which the successor states adapted to the new international conditions of Western agency and its desire to spread liberal democratic norms to post-communist Europe. The argument can be summarized as follows:

1. Varying structural configurations created varying parameters for liberalism in the 1990s:
   a. Economic viability (Slovenia) represented the most favorable conditions for the rise of liberal political configurations.
   b. Partial economic viability (Croatia) represented conditions in which liberal and illiberal groups competed for power.
   c. Low levels of economic viability (FRY and Macedonia) indicated poor prospects for liberal groups.
2. The way in which Western agency interacted with the initial structural conditions of transition helps us to understand actual regime outcomes:
   a. Where the external agenda of liberalism was compatible with local structures (Slovenia), a process of "contagion" and "convergence" occurred. A credible promise of membership in Western organizations reinforced liberal proclivities and helped to keep democratization on track. *Substantive democracy* emerged.
   b. Where the external agenda of liberalism was partially compatible with local structures (Croatia), a struggle ensued among domestic actors over the appropriateness of Western norms. Conditionality was used by Western states and organizations to promote democratization and met with limited success. *Simulated democracy* emerged.
   c. Where the external agenda of liberalism was incompatible with

local structures (FRY and Macedonia), Western norms had limited impact or were outright rejected. The West, in turn, mixed conditionality and control to promote democracy. It did so through the enforcement of liberal norms, such as human rights, through sanctions and military intervention (FRY), or through direct mandate and financial sponsorship (Macedonia). In the former, *populist authoritarianism* emerged, in the latter, *illegitimate democracy*.

3. After the first ten years of transition, when economic conditions deteriorated and the ruling radical populist parties became delegitimized, part of the elite signed on to the Western project in a bid for international support and domestic political capital (Croatia and FRY, later Serbia, after 2000). As long as the public and elite remained divided over the Western agenda, however, the legitimacy of liberal norms was threatened. Nevertheless, both the public and elites became socialized to Western conditions, albeit to different degrees (Montenegro after 2000, Croatia after 2003, Macedonia after 2004, Serbia after 2008).

Economics: Material Scarcity and the Structure of Authority

Eighteenth- and nineteenth-century materialism provided the foundation for an extensive socioeconomic modernization literature that linked levels of economic development to the existence or nonexistence of democracy. In the classical modernization literature, a high level of economic development is associated with relatively low levels of social conflict and the presence of an educated middle class, which constitutes a critical source of support for democratic rule (Lipset 1960). The desire of the middle class for more representative institutions can also be stated in terms of rational self-interest, along the lines of Barrington Moore's influential dictum "no bourgeoisie, no democracy" (1966). Newer studies have used regression of large statistical samples to show that prosperity is associated with democratic endurance (Przeworski and Limongi 1997). Despite a number of research findings that attempt to challenge the view that wealth is associated with democracy,[26] there is a consistent and fairly strong statistical connection, on a cross-sectional basis, between levels of national income and the extent of democracy in national political arrangements. Furthermore, there is evidence that this same relationship holds over time and that a causal arrow runs from wealth to democracy and not the other way around. This connection is especially strong when one looks at large samples of countries over a longer period of time (Moore

1996: 38–39). Moreover, there is evidence that individual countries tend to become more democratic in proportion to increases in income (Moore 1996: 38). Economics, then, cannot explain short-run processes and temporary shifts in the vertical structure of authority. It cannot explain, for example, the various ways in which some Latin American countries have shifted between various degrees of democracy and military rule in recent decades. It is much more effective at explaining longer-term patterns of political authority.

For post-communist states, this body of theory predicts that countries that embark on regime change at higher levels of wealth enjoy distinct advantages in democratization because "their populations are more sophisticated and better able to accommodate the dislocations of transformation without falling below some minimal material threshold, which could breed desperation and a preference for antidemocratic solutions" (Fish 1998a). A conventional model of transition stipulates that those whose fortunes would be directly hurt by the changes—such as state-sector workers—would come to constitute the biggest source of opposition to democratic and market reform. In countries with a higher level of socioeconomic development, this part of the population is smaller, so one should find fewer impediments to democracy. Moreover, material scarcity makes the kind of political compromise that is crucial to democracy more difficult.

The relationship between development and democracy is central to comparative politics and the study of democratization, and it is no less relevant to policy-making. In the contemporary political science literature, there is an abundance of theory that purports to explain how material prosperity generates democracy: the problem becomes one of sorting out which theories are more plausible. In fact, Lipset's famous study (1960) on the subject generated the largest body of research on any topic in comparative politics. Although empirical observation and statistical regression showed a strong association between development and democracy, there was disagreement on what kinds of causal processes and mechanisms link the two. Yet the causal connection between development and democracy was difficult to ascertain with statistical methods alone. Consequently, a number of theories attempted to explain the causal mechanisms that lead from economic development to democracy. One such approach was the aforementioned body of "modernization theory," which enjoyed a long period of popularity. Modernization consists of a gradual differentiation and specialization of social structures culminating in a separation of the political from other structures, thereby making democracy possible. The specific causal chains consist of sequences of industrialization, urbanization, education, communication, mobilization, political incorporation, and innumerable other social changes that make a society ready to proceed to democratization. As a result the system can no longer be run by command: society becomes too complex, technological change endows new groups with autonomy and private information, civil society emerges, and dictatorial forms of control lose their effectiveness.

Another approach, associated with Moore (1966), posits that the "national bourgeoisie" spearhead the drive for economic development and use parliamentary democracy to establish its political authority and protect its interests. Other Marxian writers have focused on the role of the working classes, whose role becomes more important with economic development and industrialization, in pushing for democracy.[27] Still other approaches argue that the cultural change produced by economic development is key to democracy, but this change will occur differently in Western and non-Western societies.[28] Friedman and Friedman (1980) argue that a free market (associated with high levels of development) helps prevent the power that is inevitably accumulated in the state or political arena from being extended into the economic arena, thereby maintaining political pluralism and enabling economic agents to resist attempts by the state to interfere in the market. More recently, Inglehart and Welzel (2005) have used data from the World Values Survey to show that socioeconomic modernization leads to the kind of cultural change (for example, the strengthening of values such as tolerance) that in turn becomes conducive to democratization.

Classical theories that link overall wealth and socioeconomic modernization with the prospects for liberal democracy provide a general framework in which to examine post-communist democratization, but they need to be adapted in three key respects in order to fit the post-communist reality. First, the notion that a capitalist "bourgeois" class is needed to support democracy must be reconsidered, since traditional class structures were decisively altered under state socialism. The absence of property-owning classes in communist states is particularly important in this respect. Second, the relative dimensions of economic deprivation and the expectations they generate must be considered over absolute notions of wealth and income. The collapse of economic output and declining living standards in the late communist and early post-communist period must be considered alongside post-communist expectations of material standards to discover what segments of society constituted a political challenge to reform. Third, the structure of the post-communist economy and its implications for domestic transformation and international integration appear to be of equal importance to various macro-indicators of wealth, industrialization, urbanization, and education. Communism did succeed at modernization and educational advancement, but it did not necessarily lead to the kind of social change predicted by Lipset. With economies designed to meet the needs of the Soviet bloc rather than competitive global markets, countries that exhibited the highest degree of industrialization under communism have experienced great difficulty adapting to the world economy after the collapse of communism. This has tended to hinder democratic outcomes despite high levels of "modernization." High levels of communist industrialization, in turn, are closely correlated with pre-communist backwardness. Where a socialist industrial structure prevailed, there was usually an entrenched economic elite connected to former ruling parties who were interested in stripping state-owned enterprises of their assets rather than promoting liberalization and privatization. Such groups constituted a serious hindrance to attempts at both economic and political reform.

Levels of economic development in Eastern Europe can be traced first and foremost to historical degrees of backwardness that follow a continental geographic gradient—with development and living standards decreasing as one goes east and south. Communism promoted industrialization and material advancement, but most often in a Stalinist mode such that the historically less-developed states and regions were left, on the eve of communist collapse, with few competitive industries and thus less hope for integration into the global economy. Moreover, despite communist efforts at modernization and industrialization, the historical disparity in development between the developed northwestern and southeastern tiers of Eastern Europe still exists. Yugoslavia was very much a microcosm of this gradient. As chapter 3 will show, in spite of a concrete effort to eliminate the disparities through a policy of income transfer from the richer north to the poorer south, regional economic disparities still defined the former Yugoslavia on the eve of collapse and were strikingly apparent to anyone who traveled throughout the country.

Janos (1984, 1989, 2000) has written extensively about the causes and consequences of disparities in economic development, both between Western and Eastern Europe and within Eastern Europe itself. He argues that the key to understanding both the reproduction of backwardness and how it leads to various forms of bureaucratic authoritarianism is the paradox of poverty necessitating state power and state power creating more poverty. In the East European context, this dynamic is further complicated by a strong international demonstration effect of consumption standards that arises from the geographic proximity of East European states to the centers of development and innovation in the world economy. The desire of both elites and masses in the East to raise their material standards to those of their counterparts in the West without a corresponding increase in production and investment and without the same availability of capital has historically shaped authoritarian rentier states in the region.

The explanatory power of initial economic conditions in the case of the Yugoslav successor states lies in their ability to predict patterns of authority and to provide a means of understanding the underlying constraints to liberalism over extended periods of time. In this manner, one can evaluate the future prospects for democratization. The leverage of economics as an explanatory variable of regime diversity in the Yugoslav successor states lies not in looking at *absolute* but rather *relative* levels of material scarcity, especially when we look at levels of public support for particular political solutions. Relative differences refer not only to disparities among the republics on the eve of dissolution, but also to the extent of economic hardship in the 1980s and 1990s *relative to people's expectations.* Herein lies one key difference between the economic crisis in the Yugoslav successor states and similar crises in other communist states in the 1980s. Citizens of all former Yugoslav republics, but particularly those in the more developed republics and regions, had come to *expect* a high material standard of living. That many educated Yugoslavs were aware that these standards were artificially propped up and unsustainable in the long term ultimately did not matter when prices rose dramatically, unemployment skyrocketed, and weekend shopping trips to Italy were suddenly rendered impossible. Unfulfilled expectations for higher living standards have abruptly terminated the rule of countless post-communist governments that earlier seemed invincible. We must not forget that before 1990, when the notion of incipient war was still unfathomable to most, ordinary Yugoslavs had the same, if not rosier, expectations for post-communist transition as their counterparts in other East European countries beginning their transitions.

Countless polls and anecdotes capture the social frustration of the 1980s crisis years in Yugoslavia. This hopelessness, however, was not only prevalent among the working classes or peasants. In more developed areas and urban centers, it was also widespread among the younger members of the middle class who suddenly could not attain what their parents had taken for granted in the 1960s and 1970s: a stable job with good wages, an apartment, and quite often a vacation home (*vikendica*) on the Croatian or Montenegrin coast. Part of the problem lay in a trend present to different degrees in all of Yugoslavia's regions: an increase in education levels without a parallel increase in jobs (Lampe 2000). Those who did have jobs saw their wages decline precipitously in the 1980s. These people could be found standing shoulder to shoulder with their compatriots from rural areas at rallies for Milošević and Franjo Tudman in the early 1990s. The rise to power of various radical populist groups, thus, reflected a revolution of the middle classes as much as it did that of sectors of the population traditionally considered most vulnerable to economic crisis and thus wary of liberal democracy, such as workers and peasants. The alienation of the educated middle class may explain that among the first and strongest advocates of extreme nationalism were many prominent intellectuals.[29] Radical populist regimes in Belgrade and Zagreb would not have come to power were it not for a temporary alliance uniting nationalist intellectuals, disaffected middle classes, and communist opportunists who later brought semirural workers into this improbable coalition and adopted various extreme ideologies to replace the now-defunct Titoism. In Slovenia, the middle classes were much better off and less receptive to such appeals. To the extent that the middle classes were among the core of the disenfranchised parts of the population that turned to anti-liberal political solutions in the late 1980s, the economic argument advanced here differs in an important way from the kinds of arguments seen in the classical socioeconomic modernization literature.

The global economic changes of the 1970s and 1980s and the winding down of the Cold War were much more painful for Yugoslavia, despite its higher living standards and expectations than, for example, Poland, where the economic crisis was even deeper and things arguably could not get much worse.[30] Many crucial factors that propped up the Yugoslav economy began to disappear in the 1980s: easy access to foreign credit, a safety valve for unemployment through guest worker programs, and stable markets for its goods in the East and West. The ultimate blow came when the global distribution of power began to change with the rise of Mikhail Gorbachev in Soviet politics, for it was Yugoslavia's special place in this distribution of power and its ability to balance the rival superpowers that helped legitimize the entire system.

The extent to which these changes affected each republic varied, ensuring that the consequences for politics in each republic following independence would be unique.

When speaking of relative deprivation, one cannot ignore the growing gap in living standards between the Yugoslav republics and the states of Western Europe, which millions of Yugoslavs had visited as guest workers and tourists. Expectations were high because many Yugoslavs had fully anticipated that they were inevitably moving toward the material standards of the West. Social frustration rose quickly when it became clear that, far from those expectations being realized, living standards were actually declining. Rather than being directed at the inherent irrationalities of the Titoist economic system, this frustration became focused on ethnic and national issues and radical populist solutions by the late 1980s. The extent to which this occurred, however, varied by republic, more than aggregate indicators suggest. Different levels of development and varying structures, reproduced over many decades, created different patterns of elite competition in each republic and had lasting political consequences when political pluralism was introduced in 1990.

The intent of this book is to explain economic conditions as a determinant of regime type rather than as a determinant of state dissolution. Though it is true that explanations for breakup and regime diversity overlap to some extent, economics is actually a variable that may go further in explaining the latter than the former. There are many good arguments that point to noneconomic factors, such as agency and ideology, as causes of the dissolution. And there is the issue of explaining the inherent economic irrationality of cutting off important markets and trade links. In doing this, even Slovenia initially suffered, for many of its manufactured goods depended on markets in the southern republics of Yugoslavia.[31] Moreover, the dissolution of Yugoslavia came just as the economic reform plan of the Ante Marković government was showing some results, which tends to weaken somewhat an economic explanation for the breakup (Jović 2001: 239). However, despite the rhetoric, ideology, and the "fog of war" surrounding the breakup, what elites in each republic ultimately confronted when given free elections and independence were particular economic structural inheritances that directly shaped republican-level politics. In fact, the structural strengths and weaknesses of each economy were magnified when the republics for the first time stood alone, facing the challenge of integrating into the global market without the benefit of access to the subsidies, credits, and markets that had sustained them during the Yugoslav period. Thus, economic considerations may not have played a primary role in some republics when decisions were made about secession, but they played a much more central role in republican-level politics when independence loomed on the horizon. Some republics, such as Macedonia, may have simply been too poor to pursue a viable state-building project, much less a liberal one.[32] As one Macedonian told James Pettifer a short while after the referendum for independence, "What are we going to build a new state with? Tobacco plants?" (2001: 19).

The International Factor: External Agency and Domestic Politics

While the initial economic conditions of transition can account for the general liberal or illiberal substance of the regimes that took shape in each successor state in the 1990s and beyond, they cannot explain every shift in adherence to procedural correctness, nor can they explain the outcome of every election or the strategies of given leaders at particular moments. Here the role of external agency does a much better job. Theorizing on how external structures of power affect domestic politics represented a critical paradigm shift in the discipline. States henceforth were no longer viewed in isolation but rather as part of a larger system (Janos 1986). From this paradigm shift there emerged a number of literatures on the international sources of domestic politics, among them a prominent literature in the 1970s on the political and economic consequences of externally dependent development. Nevertheless, much of the democratic transitions literature that appeared in the 1980s conspicuously left out the external factor. Some scholars of democratic transitions even explicitly spoke of the primacy of domestic over international factors. It was only later that some of these same scholars, regretting their earlier omission, brought the international dimension back into their analyses of democratization.[33]

Many of the early works on post-communist Europe also did not give adequate attention to the external factor, except that now this omission seemed all the more conspicuous since it was clear from the outset of transition that its course would be fundamentally shaped by the hegemony of the West and, indeed, that to some extent democracy on the Eastern half of the continent would owe its very existence to Western engagement and conditionality.[34] In later works, the role of the external factor in structuring post-communist elite behavior is too frequently ignored, sometimes described but rarely theorized. More recently, a proliferation of articles and books have appeared that bring the external factor, and especially EU conditionality, into their theories and analyses of post-communist transition, explaining how the West successfully transmitted liberal norms to the post-communist world.[35]

That post-communist elites and parties across geographic space and the political spectrum were equating the systemic change with a "return to Europe" reinforced the new structures of external influence into which the former communist states entered. Western states and organizations, for their part, embarked on their own scramble for influence over the eastern half of Europe. They had geopolitical and economic interests but also a more inchoate desire to welcome long-lost relatives back into the family. The interests of states and organizations such as the EU, NATO, and the United States were underpinned by a desire for self-validation, which they could accomplish by remaking the post-communist states in their likeness. The project of EU enlargement has as much to do with validating the legitimacy and universal applicability of liberalism in politics and economics as with the objectives of global and regional political and economic integration. After all, if liberalism failed in the West's very "backyard," where could it succeed?

These two dynamics—an Eastern push for the West and a Western push for the East—combined in such a way that from the very beginning of the transition political elites in post-communist countries were maneuvering in a space that existed between domestic realities and the conditions of Western liberalism, especially the conditions associated with membership in Euro-Atlantic organizations. The incentives and constraints, and ultimately the political and policy choices, pursued by these elites reflected a balance that was struck between these two often competing imperatives. Western integration and support held out powerful material benefits for elites in particular. However, though many post-communist elites professed to want to join NATO and the EU, they differed in their ability and willingness to meet the conditions for doing so.

It was easier in countries that were structurally predisposed to joining the West—whether by geography, culture, or economics. In these states, an acceptance of Western conditionality created a self-reinforcing mechanism, a path dependent process in which a post-communist state became "coopted" into the integration project in a number of legal, political, economic, and psychological ways that raised the costs of turning back. Though material and other incentives may have triggered the process, it ultimately resulted in a substantive alteration of beliefs among both elites and masses. Such processes, as the concluding chapter of this book will argue, are illuminated by the literature on norm transfer and international socialization. Schimmelfennig (2002: 1) called the process of EU integration the "most massive international socialization process currently underway in the international system."

In those post-communist states where elites saw little interest in adapting to Western conditionality or where the prospects for membership in the EU or NATO were poor to begin with, nationalism and other forms of radical populism prevailed over both liberalism and any desire to join Euro-Atlantic organizations. However, the same factors that helped bring illiberal regimes to the fore also meant that liberalism could not succeed in the absence of Western engagement and the incentive of membership in NATO and the EU. This process was self-reinforcing in that the costs for ruling parties who depended on nationalism as a legitimizing factor to change course were quite high, while their pursuit of illiberal policies meant that their states were left out of the process of Western integration, making them fall further behind their counterparts who already were busy implementing the democratic reforms needed to join NATO and the EU. In other words, a powerful external impetus for reform was not present, making democratization much more difficult. However, where authoritarianism faltered for economic reasons and because of popular resistance, a window opened for Western conditionality to exert its leverage toward democratizating previously illiberal regimes.

Since no post-communist regime—even those that blatantly disregarded democratic norms—perceived that it could afford to disregard Western conditionality completely, the daily domestic political dynamics of regimes that deviated from liberalism often entailed ad-hoc adjustments of rhetoric and policies: speaking to the importance of minority rights, passing laws on civil society, tinkering with budgets to reduce social spending. This was an attempt to receive a better "report card" from a Western monitoring organization or to ensure continued financial support. These policies, however, were not underpinned by substantive liberalism. Shifts in policies or laws often reflected "simulated" democratization to win Western favor rather than suggesting a sincere commitment to liberalism.

Janos (2001) has provided a framework to help us understand the relationship between a new external structure of power and domestic political outcomes. To supplement existing paradigms of post-communist change, Janos offers a framework that sees communist to post-communist systemic change as a transition from one international regime (Soviet-dominated) to another (Western-dominated). Though he admits that by itself, this paradigm has limits in fully explaining outcomes, he demonstrates that a universalist external project of liberalism produces different results when it encounters varying local structural realities.

Politics in the most classic sense of the word, in this view, occurs where the external and the internal meet, and hence political outcomes are a product of external intent (Western liberal universalism) and domestic interest (rooted in structure). Part of the success of the Western agenda in a given country depends on the public's threshold of tolerance: in other words, how long society is willing to tolerate external conditionality and its consequences without seeing rewards. The rewards, in turn, are related to what legitimizes the quest for Western integration in the first place among East Europeans, that is, the promise of higher living standards. But, as Janos writes, "Legitimacy by expectation, as opposed to direct trade-offs, has its perils" (2001: 248). It is thus in the "teetering" cases, where there are substantial parts of the population and powerful political groups skeptical of or hostile to the Western liberalism, that the greatest threat to liberalism is posed.

As the above discussion suggests, it is not enough to import existing understandings of hegemon-client relations to the post-communist context. As with the economics variable, the particularities of the international dimension of post-communist transitions need to be acknowledged. First, external hegemony in the post-communist world is about the subtleties of "soft power" à la Joseph Nye (2004) rather than power in its absolute or relative manifestations. Thus, every statement by the EU Commissioner for Enlargement in Brussels hinting at the status of a potential candidate nation could be the flap of the butterfly's wings that generated storms in Warsaw, Bratislava, Budapest, or Zagreb. Elites in the East held their collective breath for the next "grade" they would receive on democratic performance, as this would determine their access to foreign aid, favorable terms of trade, loans, and general respectability in the international arena (Pop-Eleches 2007a: 145).

Unlike Western hegemony during the Cold War, which was at times more interested in cultivating "friendly" regimes rather than liberal ones, the current Western liberal agenda, codified in the EU's Copenhagen criteria, has mandated real democracy in the post-communist states. The extent and invasiveness of the conditions have been truly unprecedented. Yet, so are the potential benefits to be derived from membership. While existing theories of hierarchical relationships in the international system often focus on the negative inducements for compliance, Western hegemony in post-communist Europe is often based on the power of positive inducements that can be used as a source of domestic political capital. As this book will show, by explicitly linking certain policies with the prospects for aid and integration, supporting nongovernmental prodemocracy groups, or implying that a certain election outcome will bode well or poorly for membership, Western conditionality can also change the domestic power balance between liberal and illiberal forces (Pop-Eleches 2007a: 147).

Some of the explanatory leverage of the external factor in the Yugoslav successor states is related to the unique geopolitical position of the former SFRJ and how its position changed as the Cold War wound down. At the outset of transition, the former Yugoslavia simply was no longer on the foreign policy radar screens of Western governments. In sharp contrast to countless conspiracy theories about the intentions of external actors that seem to be especially popular in Serbia, in reality many Western governments, most significantly the United States, simply did not show much concern for Yugoslavia at all from the mid-1980s until the outbreak of war in 1991. There were other, more important trouble spots to attract Western attention, such as the Soviet Union and Iraq. Some have even suggested that intelligence reports indicating that Western countries would not intervene in a Yugoslav armed conflict emboldened Slobodan Milošević to pursue military action in Croatia.[36]

The neglect of a country which was dependent in so many ways on its special relationship with the West had direct and determining domestic consequences. Although it adversely affected the entire country, the degree to which Yugoslavia's demise as an object of geopolitical interest affected each republic also varied. The less-developed republics and regions depended more on the financial resources afforded by access to Western aid, while the more developed republics were angry that most of this aid was being diverted to irrational development projects in the south and were eager to have more control over state revenues from export earnings. Serbia depended more than other republics on the political prestige derived from Yugoslavia's special geopolitical status, such as its leadership of the non-aligned movement. The developed republics and regions benefited more from access to Western markets. The external factor, then, is critical in understanding the post-communist transitions of the Yugoslav successor states in a broader comparative perspective, since it was their particular difficulties in adapting to the new international order that put them in a more difficult position than Poland, Hungary, or the Czech Republic despite ostensibly more favorable starting conditions on some parameters.

Though neglect in the international arena characterized the initial stages of the post-communist transition, the Yugoslav successor states soon became subject to the same pressures and incentives to pursue liberalism as other states in the region. External agency acted as a magnetic field, attracting certain segments of the elites and public while repelling others. The promise of membership in the EU or NATO could be used as a source of political capital by liberal elites wherever there was a receptive audience. By contrast, the external factor can also be painted as a threat by nationalist elites seeking to stake their legitimacy on popular perceptions of an outside enemy threatening state sovereignty.

The promise of Euro-Atlantic integration meant that the incentives to pursue some threshold of procedural democracy were enormous, both because of the perceived rewards of doing so and the feared costs of not complying. Even rulers and ruling parties with clearly authoritarian inclinations adhered to basic tenets of electoral democracy. As such, the external factor clearly helps us to understand the existence of procedural democracy in the absence of strong structural underpinnings. For example, Macedonian elites, acutely aware of the very real threats to their state's, and by extension their own, survival, adhered to formal democracy in the 1990s under the close supervision of Western governments. However, the quality and viability of Macedonian democracy was always in question, given that ethnic Albanians, representing twenty-five percent of the population, not only challenged the legitimacy of the regime but also the legitimacy of the state itself. In Croatia, the continuing need for Western support, combined with a semi-viable pro-Western opposition and a significant pro-Western impetus in society, compelled the Tuđman regime to ensure that certain facets of formal democracy were functioning. By conditioning aid or other rewards on democratic reform, the West has "encouraged" actors to simulate democratic behavior. Thus, external agency can explain the existence of a procedural democracy where economics would predict none, but it alone cannot account for a democratic regime with a high level of liberal content.

CHAPTER TWO

Characterizing Regime Type

In the end, the "quality of democracy," to use the currently fashionable phrase, does matter for its very survival.

POLITICAL SCIENTIST ADAM PRZEWORSKI

Measuring Post-communist Democratization

Although it would be highly optimistic to think that post-communist countries should exhibit anything but "Schumpeterian" democratic orders (in which, at the very least, elites compete for power) during the initial period of transition, it is nevertheless important to recognize variation in the liberal content of post-communist regimes in order to understand their prospects for further democratization, ability to withstand domestic crises, and capacity to respond to changes in the international balance of power and global economy.[1] Thus, this study measures democratic progress on two dimensions: in terms of a given regime's adherence to the procedural norms of democracy on one dimension (procedural correctness) and in terms of its liberal content on the other.[2] For the purposes of this study, liberal content will be measured according to three main components: legitimacy (both democratic legitimacy and legitimizing principles), liberal presence on the political scene, and the nature of political cleavages.

Scholars note that many post-communist regimes have been neither democracies nor dictatorships; rather, most have been hybrid cases, exhibiting features of both incipient democratization and residual authoritarianism and combining "the uncertain results of democracy with the uncertain procedures of authoritarianism" (Bunce 2000: 715).[3] The challenge for political scientists, then, is to provide some order and meaning to a set of what are largely semi-democratic cases.[4] There have been important distinctions even among the hybrid cases that tell us a lot about the quality, viability, and durability of a post-communist democracy and thus allow us to understand the conditions necessary for liberalism to succeed in the longer term.

Conceptualizing and Measuring Democracy: "Minimalist" versus "Maximalist" Understandings

Many authors have noted the various problems inherent in the enterprise of measuring and conceptualizing democracy.[5] This is not to mention diverse popular understandings of democracy, which are contingent on culture, class, education, and a host of other factors.[6] There appears to be more agreement about what features of a polity indicate that it is *not* a democracy than exactly what indicates that it *is* a democracy. For example, a one-party state such as China is universally recognized as undemocratic, but there is debate over whether regular elections and the existence of democratic institutions alone make a democracy: the case of India is paradigmatic. Such disagreements can be boiled down to a difference between "minimalist" and "maximalist" understandings of democracy.[7]

The minimalist understanding is best articulated by Dahl's (1956) notion of "polyarchy": a polity is democratic to the extent that there exist institutionalized mechanisms through which the mass of the population exercises control over the political elite in an organized fashion.[8] Juan Linz expands this definition to the rights of democratic participation: he summarizes the "criteria for democracy" as the "legal freedom to formulate and advocate political alternatives with the concomitant rights to free association, free speech, and other basic freedoms of person; free and nonviolent competition among leaders with periodic validation of their claim to rule; inclusion of all political offices in the democratic process; and provision for the participation of all members of the political community, whatever their political preferences" (1978: 5).

The maximalist notion of democracy is based on the idea that real democracy exists not only when political actors comply with the democratic rules of the game but also when these rules are seen as legitimate by both the actors themselves and a large section of the public. To this, "maximalists" might add the following criteria: a free and vibrant civil society, effective institutions, widely held democratic values, and public consensus over issues concerning the state, its borders, and who belongs within these borders.

Positive scores on quantitative measures of democratic procedure, often based on the minimalist understanding of democratization, indicate that democratic rules have been accepted to some degree but also have a number of limitations. First, the political elite and other powerful groups can manipulate the rules such that any measurement of democracy that relies only on procedures has the potential to be seriously misleading (Moore 1996: 40). Second, although advanced industrialized countries such as Italy and Japan are placed at the high end of quantitative measures of democratic procedure, there are serious questions as to whether publics in those states have the same degree of control over their elites as citizens of Sweden or Australia (Moore 1996: 40). Third, procedural correctness is easy to institute and equally easy to abolish in emerging democracies and thus may indicate a temporary effort to meet external expectations or to appease internal opposition rather than a pointing to a real commitment to democratic rules. Fourth, democratic procedures, even where they persist over time, do not necessarily tell us anything about the legitimacy of a particular regime type: that is, whether the majority of society, even when it disagrees with particular policies or leaders, agrees on the basic rules of the democratic game and perceives the state and its institutions to be legitimate. Measures of procedural correctness, therefore, help one to gauge just that—the existence of formal procedures and institutions—but taken alone are insufficient measures of liberal democracy.

This is especially true when we consider that many regimes in the world fall into the category of "electoral democracies," with regular elections but weak levels of democratic substance. Diamond (1999: 34) notes that the gap between electoral and liberal democracy has grown markedly during the latter part of the "third wave," forming one of its most significant but little-noticed features, while Schmitter and Karl observe that "however central to democracy, elections occur intermittently and only allow citizens to choose between the highly aggregated alternatives offered by political parties, which can, especially in the early stages of a democratic transition, proliferate in a bewildering variety" (1991: 78). This is a fact that some Western policymakers, eager to point to the success of democracy by citing successful elections, have at times failed to grasp.

Maximalist conceptions of democracy and their accompanying measures have their own set of pitfalls. To some extent, this reflects the fact that the question of how extensive liberty must be before a political system can be termed a liberal democracy is a subjective, normative, and philosophical one (Diamond 1999: 31). Maximalist conceptions can set too high a standard, thus leading to pessimistic conclusions for new and fragile democratic polities. Methodologically speaking, they may not properly delimit the concept under consideration (Munck 2009: 16). Moreover, maximalist notions of democracy may be rooted in Western cultural biases about what the "proper" ingredients of democracy should be.

The normative and methodological limitations of maximalism notwithstanding, the very nature of post-communism renders procedural measures alone insufficient in capturing the character of a regime. Democratic progress and "backsliding" of the kind that move a state up or down on a quantitative scale of democracy often represent a temporary shift in a regime's adherence to democratic procedures and not necessarily a substantive change in its commitment to liberalism. "Backsliding," then, is not the *cause* of democratic regression; rather, it is a *symptom* of deeper deficiencies in the liberal *content* of a regime.

Measuring Regime Type in the Yugoslav Successor States: Two Dimensions

The division of the dependent variable into two components in this study serves several important purposes. First, by juxtaposing procedural correctness with liberal content, we will see that procedural correctness alone, while representing a significant and normatively desirable step above unbridled authoritarianism, does not necessarily indicate progress in terms of the internalization of liberal norms. Second, separating these two dimensions of regime type will show that the existence of procedural correctness with a parallel lack of liberal content is particular to post-communist regimes that have an interest in espousing some procedural democracy in order to placate international critics and, by so doing, to gain political or material rewards even when they have few real democratic inclinations. In such cases, there may also be domestic political rewards in winning concessions from the West or appearing "European." Third, the addition of the second dimension allows greater leverage and precision in describing the character and democratic prospects of hybrid regimes. Fourth, and most important, separating the two dimensions will allow us to show how each independent variable shaped regime type: procedural correctness with low levels of liberal content are characteristic of a regime adapting to external conditions, while procedural correctness buttressed by democratic substance reflects economic health.

The First Dimension: Measuring Procedural Correctness

With regard to its minimalist definition, democracy is always a matter of degree: the extent to which the elite is controlled and influenced by citizens. Yet, as Moore (1996: 40) notes, this definition is not so helpful if one wishes to determine degrees of democracy since it refers to a power relationship, which is very hard to measure. Thus, we must rely on an indirect measure, that is, democratic *procedures*, which relate to the existence of mechanisms, institutions, and laws that enable citizens to exercise control over their leaders:[9]

- The proportion of the population eligible to vote;
- The existence of various categories of elections and the extent to which they are free and fair;
- The contribution of elections to the choice of the chief executive and the membership of the legislature;
- The extent to which control of the state and its key decisions lies with elected officials (and not democratically unaccountable actors or foreign powers);
- The extent to which the power of the executive is checked by other branches of government;
- The extent to which the military is under civilian control;
- The degree of freedom enjoyed by the media and the extent to which citizens have unfettered access to alternative sources of information;
- The degree to which the regime allows for individual and collective political activity (freedoms of speech, movement, association, petition, and assembly);
- Beyond elections, the extent to which citizens have multiple, ongoing channels for expression and representation of their interests and values, including independent associations and movements, which they have the freedom to form and join;
- the strength of the rule of law (often measured by the degree to which corruption pervades public life);
- Whether individual and group liberties are effectively protected by

an independent, non-discriminatory judiciary whose decisions are enforced and respected;

- The extension of civil, political, and cultural rights afforded to ethnic and national minorities;
- The extent to which state repression and coercion exist (the degree to which the rule of law protects citizens from unjustified detention, exile, terror, and torture, not only by the state but also by organized non-state or anti-state forces).

Freedom House measures how governments around the world adhere to the above principles and how their adherence changes over relatively brief intervals of time, so its evaluations of the procedural dimension of post-communist regimes provide a good starting point to examine the differences between our four cases.[10] Table 2.1 shows the Freedom House scores given to the Yugoslav successor states in the 1990s on political rights, primarily measuring the quality of elections, and civil liberties, focusing on the freedom of expression. When seen over time, the numbers are fairly consistent, indicating that each regime exhibited fairly stable patterns of adherence or non-adherence to democratic procedures. The numbers also illustrate a continuum among the four cases, such that Slovenia's post-communist regime consistently adhered to democratic procedures, Macedonia's adhered to some procedures some of the time, Croatia's did so to a lesser degree, while FRY's regime consistently ignored democratic rules.

The Second Dimension: Liberal Content

As noted above, three main indicators will be used to evaluate the level of liberal content in the Yugoslav successor states: legitimacy, the nature of political cleavages, and liberal presence in the party system. Legitimacy, perhaps the most important indicator of liberal content, will be split into two related components: democratic legitimacy and legitimizing principles. Democratic legitimacy refers to the extent and nature of public support for a particular regime: is it based on strong democratic feelings, is it based on populist and illiberal attitudes, or is there no strong support for democracy at all, even where ostensibly democratic forces are in power? Legitimizing principles refer to the appeals a regime uses in seeking support: are these appeals based on liberal themes or nationalist and populist ones? The extent and nature of political divisions will be measured by looking at cleavages in the party system and the content of public discourse. Do these cleavages reflect those

Table 2.1   Freedom House Scores of Procedural Correctness, 1991–1999
(political rights, civil liberties)

Country	1991–1992	1993–1994	1995–1996	1996–1997	1998–1999
Slovenia	2, 3	1, 2	1, 2	1, 2	1, 2
Macedonia	3, 4	4, 3	4, 3	4, 3	3, 3
Croatia	3, 4	4, 4	4, 4	4, 4	4, 4
FRY	6, 5	6, 6	6, 6	6, 6	6, 6

Source: Freedom House, Nations in Transit, various issues.
Note: Based on a scale from 1 to 7, with 1 representing the highest level of freedom and 7 the lowest.

that exist in stable Western democracies (urban-rural, secular-religious), or are they based on divisions that are bound to become deeply divisive? Liberal presence in the party system will be measured by the influence and electoral success of liberal versus illiberal political configurations on the political scene. The focus will be not only on parties holding power but also on opposition parties since they constitute the "regime in waiting." Do they constitute a viable liberal alternative?

The concept of political legitimacy has a long history in the discipline of political science. An early approach was offered by Weber (1968), who defined and analyzed legitimacy as the subjective belief of individuals and groups in the normative validity of a particular political order—more simply stated, legitimacy refers to a public belief in a particular regime's right to rule. Since coercion in itself is insufficient to maintain order, every state must rely on some other legitimizing principle to uphold its existence. Weber identifies three general types of legitimate domination: rational-legal, traditional, and charismatic. Subsequent works on legitimacy (Friedrich 1972, Barker 1990, Offe 1984, Habermas 1976, and so on) have to varying degrees criticized and modified Weber's ideas, but the important idea for our purposes is that the ways in which regimes legitimize themselves vary, and the strength of a particular legitimizing principle or ideology will depend on the degree to which it is embraced by the public, which in turn is rooted in various historical factors. However, all legitimizing principles are *not* equal when measured with the yardstick of liberalism.

Legitimizing Principles

Barker (1990) writes, "The desire to justify one's domination is as great as the desire to dominate" (Barker 1990, quoted in Malešević 2002: 84). Since the ways in which regimes justify their rule are not equal in terms of their liberal content, the nature of legitimizing principles in post-Yugoslav regimes should tell us a lot about their democratic quality. A regime whose legitimacy rests on appealing to ethno-nationalist sentiment has much lower liberal qualities than one whose legitimacy is derived from promoting democratic and economic reform. This can be measured by examining the political platforms, rhetoric, and policies of ruling parties. Thus, on this dimension the post-communist Slovenian regime receives the highest liberal content rating since its legitimizing principles were entrance into European structures, democratization, and economic growth. Macedonia receives a "medium" ranking because its post-communist governments, though mostly avoiding radical populism, relied mainly on international support as a legitimizing principle; only occasionally does one see in their rhetoric and policies a commitment to liberal ideals. Moreover, the extensive corruption, clientelism, and nepotism that have characterized Macedonia's transition indicate that, using Weber's terminology, "traditional" (that is, illiberal) rather than "legal-rational" sources of legitimacy (or for those left out of clientelist networks, illegitimacy) were prevalent. FRY and Croatia, autocracies from 1991 to 1999, are ranked low since the legitimacy of regimes in both states rested largely on variants of radical populism, especially ethno-nationalism. A combination of nominal acceptance of certain democratic procedures with illiberal legitimizing principles (Croatia and Macedonia and to some extent FRY) defines "simulated democracy," a regime type in which elites don't really like democracy but "fake" it at certain times to meet concrete political ends and pacify external critics. Table 2.2 summarizes the legitimizing principles of each regime and their corresponding level of liberal content.

Democratic Legitimacy

Another important dynamic to consider when using the concept of legitimacy to evaluate the degree of liberal content is the extent to which a society "buys" a regime's legitimizing strategies. Legitimacy, as Lipset has written, also depends on "the capacity of a political system to engender and maintain the belief that existing political institutions are the most appropriate or proper ones for the society" (1960: 86). Yet, as in the case of legitimizing principles, the extent to which society sees a certain ideology as legitimate or, alternatively, the *reasons* it perceives a regime to be legitimate or illegitimate is important when determining the liberal quality of a regime. A full-fledged nationalist and authoritarian regime that has strong support in society can be

Table 2.2   Liberal Quality of Legitimizing Strategies, 1990s

Country	Regime-legitimizing strategies	Level of liberal content
Slovenia	European integration, democracy, economic growth	High
Macedonia	Stability, international recognition, limited use of democracy and European integration	Medium
Croatia	Nationalism, protection against external enemies, creation of independent state. Nominal use of democracy and European integration	Low
Federal Republic of Yugoslavia	Nationalism, protection against external enemies, economic populism	Very low

legitimate but measure very low on liberal content, for instance. All regimes also ultimately depend on meeting the material expectations of society, and can only rely on nationalism and other forms of populism for so long before severe material scarcity damages the "effectiveness" component of their legitimacy. However, illegitimacy based only on economic dissatisfaction does not measure high on liberal content. Thus, that a regime is removed mainly because of popular discontent with material standards and is replaced by one that is critical of its predecessor does not necessarily testify to the liberal content of the new regime, since the nationalist component of the previous regime's legitimacy was never really condemned. It is only after a longer process of attitudinal and cultural change and a rise in living standards that the more liberal sources of legitimacy espoused by the new regime take root, though their success is also contingent on meeting society's economic expectations. Put another way, a nationalist and authoritarian regime may become illegitimate because of economic decline, but if this illegitimacy results in a change of government without a parallel increase in the legitimacy of democracy and its institutions, we are not necessarily witness to regime change in the direction of higher liberal content.

The Second Dimension: The Extent and Nature of Public Divisions

Lipset writes that the "extent to which contemporary democratic political systems are legitimate depends in large measure upon the ways in which the key issues which have historically divided the society have been resolved" (1960: 86). The extent and degree of public divisions, thus, directly affect

Table 2.3 Nature of Public Divisions as Exhibited in Party Orientations, 1990s

Country	Types of divisions	Level of liberal content
Slovenia	Redistribution, church-state relations, re-privatization, communist past	High
Macedonia	Existence of state, deep ethnic divisions	Very low
Croatia	Borders of state (Herzegovina, Krajina, Slavonia), acceptance of Western agenda, deep ethnic divisions	Low
Federal Republic of Yugoslavia	Nature and borders of state (Federal Republic of Yugoslavia federal relationship, Kosovo), Serbia's place vis-à-vis the West, deep ethnic divisions, democracy as an appropriate framework	Very low

legitimacy. These divisions refer to the horizontal integration of a political community. Put differently, we are interested in the proportion of the population that identifies with the state as it exists, that is, the state as it is defined on a map within internationally recognized borders. The position of ethnic minorities is critical in this respect.

One method of illustrating such divisions is to use direct indicators: for instance, simply asking people about their views on relevant issues. This study will occasionally refer to surveys that show the extent of public division over key matters. However, such surveys are notoriously flawed, especially since out of context, people may not betray their true attitudes. Potentially much more effective indicators of the kinds of public divisions that affect liberal content are cleavages displayed in the party system. Table 2.3 reveals that the nature of cleavages as exhibited in the party system varied significantly among the four cases and suggested varying levels of liberal content.

The Second Dimension: Liberal Presence on the Political Scene

In discussing legitimizing principles above, we have already spoken to the character of ruling parties to some extent. However, it is equally important to consider parties and groups that are not necessarily in power but influential in society, especially since undemocratic practices may keep them out of power even when they have strong public support. Furthermore, parties out of power constitute the alternative to ruling parties, and the extent to which they represent a *liberal* alternative is vital. Although one may argue that the undemocratic character of the regime itself does not allow room for opposition parties to espouse liberalism, in none of the four cases was the regime so repressive that opposition parties were not allowed to articulate their positions. By assessing the character and strength of parties, we have a powerful means of evaluating the liberal content of a given regime.

CHAPTER THREE

The Development of Disparity

Što južnije, to tužnije. (The further south you go, the sadder it is.)
POPULAR SAYING IN THE FORMER YUGOSLAVIA

Historical Roots of Regional Economic Inequality

This chapter traces the development of economic disparity in the former Yugoslavia through time and space.[1] The history and features of each republican economy can tell us a lot about its economic viability—not only with regard to its ability to construct a viable market economy but also in terms of its capacity to adapt to a global market *given independence.* Anyone who has traveled in the former Yugoslavia or who has visited its successor states cannot help but be struck by vast disparities in regional economic development. That which is immediately apparent to the casual observer is easily confirmed by a range of quantitative measures suggesting the continuation, reproduction, and intensification of a regressive north-south economic gradient over time and through regimes of differing characters. Although one of the most obvious contrasts in development exists between the lands of the former Habsburg Empire (Croatia, Slovenia, and Vojvodina) and those of the former Ottoman Empire (Bosnia and Herzegovina, Macedonia, much of Serbia proper, Kosovo, and Montenegro),[2] the actual spatial distribution of development is more complicated and transcends imperial, republican, ethnic, cultural, and other kinds of boundaries.

Physical geography has been one cause of regional economic disparity. There are distinct regions in the former Yugoslav lands, endowed to varying degrees with natural resources, access to water navigation, good soil for agriculture, and proximity to the prosperous economies of Western Europe. The mountainous areas of present-day Bosnia and Herzegovina, Montenegro, southwest Serbia, the Dalmatian hinterlands of Croatia, and northern Kosovo had been the most isolated, unfertile, and least developed. These areas were historically the greatest sources of out-migration. The Adriatic coastlands (especially Dalmatia) belong geographically to the Mediterranean world and benefited from trade and technological transfer, and much later, tourism, but also suffered from poor soil, lack of rainfall, and lack of access to navigable rivers to facilitate trade with the inland areas. Central Serbia, parts of Kosovo, and Macedonia are endowed with natural resources and good agricultural land, and yet remained undeveloped due to poor economic planning as much as geographical isolation. Some mining and heavy industry were developed there under Yugoslav communism. Vojvodina, to the north of Central Serbia, as well as the lands of present-day eastern Croatia (Slavonia), are fertile agricultural lands and served as the "breadbaskets" of both the first and second Yugoslavia, though their economic well-being was historically subject to fluctuations in the market demand and price of agricultural products. The Croatian and Slovenian hill lands were the most developed region of the Yugoslav lands, with skilled labor and a tradition of production in areas such as ironworks, machinery, textiles, furniture, electrical appliances, building materials, and food processing.[3] This region benefited historically from proximity to West European capitals and an extensive transportation infrastructure, constructed under the Habsburg Empire, that further facilitated trade with the West.[4]

Habsburg and Ottoman rule magnified the existing economic disparities. The Austro-Hungarian Empire was far wealthier and more technologically advanced than its Ottoman counterpart. Differences in patterns of rural organization were also critical, as the overwhelming majority of the Yugoslav peoples were peasants. In all of the former Habsburg territories (Croatia, Slovenia, Vojvodina) agricultural landholdings were larger and more efficient compared to those in the former Ottoman territories, and there were well-organized cooperatives to coordinate production and distribution and provide credits to farmers at single-digit interest rates (Singleton 1986: 155). By contrast, farmers in the Ottoman Empire had no such organizations, and when economic crisis and impoverishment struck the agricultural sector in the first Yugoslavia, indebted farmers in places such as Bosnia and Herzegovina were forced to borrow at rates of interest approaching 200 percent (Singleton 1986: 155).

The experience of World War I further reinforced the disparities in development, as its effects were far less devastating for Slovenia and Croatia than for Serbia, Montenegro, and especially Bosnia and Herzegovina, where there were enormous casualties and destruction of infrastructure. After World War I, the first Yugoslavia (1918–1941) largely failed as a developmental state. Its economic policies consisted of rapid but limited and highly protected industrialization, largely financed by foreign capital, which hurt the average consumer and made the Yugoslav economy highly dependent on external capital and yet not integrated with Western markets (Pleština 1992: 11). This foreign-owned or dominated industrialization relied on cheap local labor and emphasized the extraction of raw materials in the southern regions and processing and manufacturing in the northern regions, thus continuing the legacy of differentiated development (Pleština 1992: 13). As a result, between 1918 and 1938 Slovenia developed two times faster than Serbia, six times faster than Bosnia and Herzegovina, and twenty-five times faster than Montenegro.[5] Infrastructure, especially transportation, was largely neglected, leaving the poorer regions with primitive Ottoman-era roads and few rail links. The agricultural sector was also ignored, such that a full-scale "scissors" crisis developed in the late 1920s in which widening prices between agricultural and manufactured goods left many peasants with enormous debts. This crisis was exacerbated by the dramatic fall in world demand for agricultural exports in the 1920s (Woodward 1995b: 23). Given that the economies of the southern regions were almost entirely dependent on agriculture, the crisis was particularly acute there, further impoverishing an area that was already backwards relative to the northern regions.[6] These stark disparities among the first Yugoslavia's regions can also be illustrated through a comparison of illiteracy rates. Less than 20 percent of the population of Bosnia and Herzegovina and Macedonia was literate, while in Serbia only around 30 percent could read and write. The difference between Slovenia, where the literacy rate was above 90 percent, and Croatia-Slavonia, where it was under 70 percent, was also significant.

The economic failures of the first Yugoslav government, writes Pleština, were "aggravated by the bureaucratic mentality of civil servants who viewed the state as a means for private accumulation and by the existence of a quasi-capitalist class relying on state contracts, rather than on the dynamic, self-propelled capitalist entrepreneur whose drive for industrialization might have alleviated peasant poverty through industrial (urban) employment" (1992: 12).[7]

The increasing economic stagnation and dependency of interwar Yugoslavia led to political chauvinism, division, and ultimately, chaos. In the end the royalist leadership in Belgrade undermined federalism, independent political parties, and other democratic institutions and instituted a centralized absolutist regime in their place. Conflicts between Serbs and Croats increased, and with these conflicts came heightened political repression facilitated by the apparatus of a police state. The first Yugoslav experiment had resulted in an illegitimate state with large inter-regional disparities and hostilities. Such hostilities and continuing economic immiseration led to the rise of political radicalism, most notably the Četnici in Serbia and the Ustaše in Croatia, who were subsequently coopted in World War II by external powers with their own imperial agendas for the Balkan region.

For a state that was already underdeveloped, the effects of World War II were catastrophic, leaving Yugoslavia even less industrialized and more rural than when it entered the war (Woodward 1995b: 63). Foreign occupation and civil war led to disease, a refugee crisis, homelessness, and the death of 11 percent of the prewar population. The economic effects were devastating, particularly in the southern regions, where fighting had been heavier.[8]

Thus, all the Yugoslav lands were very undeveloped compared to the lands of Western Europe. Their backwardness was deepened by the experience of imperial tutelage, war, and economic mismanagement, and they remained essentially poor peasant societies until the victorious communists began an intensive industrialization drive after World War II and formation of the second Yugoslavia (1945–1991).[9] The overall poverty of Yugoslavia notwithstanding, disparities in development among the regions were quite evident when Tito's communists consolidated their power in the mid- to late 1940s. Figure 3.1 provides a telling picture of early communist regional developmental differences through indices of per capita regional products.[10] In 1947, Kosovo's per capita regional product was less than half the average of the newly formed socialist federation, while Slovenia's was 62 percent higher than this average.

The stated goal of the communist leaders was to rectify these disparities and promote a more equal mode of development.[11] However, as the next sec-

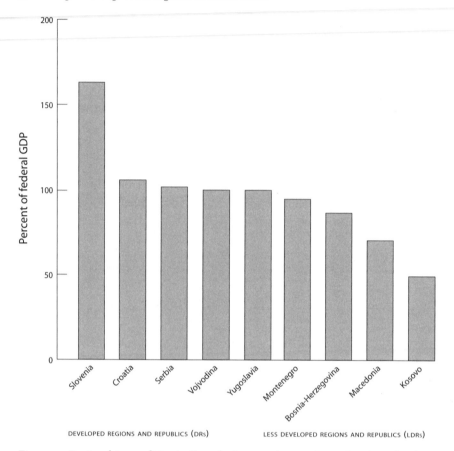

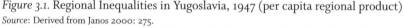

DEVELOPED REGIONS AND REPUBLICS (DRs)   LESS DEVELOPED REGIONS AND REPUBLICS (LDRs)

Figure 3.1. Regional Inequalities in Yugoslavia, 1947 (per capita regional product)
Source: Derived from Janos 2000: 275.
   Note: Index, Yugoslavia = 100. "Serbia" refers to Serbia proper, without Vojvodina and Kosovo.

tion will show, their efforts largely failed. Indeed, the disparities increased between 1945 and 1989, leaving each republic and region with very different economic prospects on the eve of their independence.

Efforts and Consequences of the Yugoslav Communists to Combat Regional Inequality

Prewar levels of production were attained fairly quickly through a combination of social mobilization by the newly formed communist government and massive income transfer from abroad in the form of reparations from

Hungary, Italy, and Germany and aid from the United States and the United Nations (UN) (Pleština 1992: 15).[12] Although the federation-wide economy rebounded in terms of total production, the problem of uneven regional economic development remained as stark as ever, and as a whole Yugoslavia was still a very poor country.

The problem of regional disparity, notes Bombelles (1991: 440), was recognized and specifically addressed as early as 1946 by Boris Kidrič, the Politburo member and president of the Economic Council and Chairman of the Federal Planning Commission, who said that "uneven economic development [is] one of the great difficulties in the current process of development . . . [and that] the principle of brotherhood and unity, which is the basis of our federation, categorically demands elimination of this unevenness." In official Yugoslav policy, the "undeveloped states" came to be known as less-developed republics and regions (LDRs), including Macedonia, Bosnia and Herzegovina, Montenegro, and Kosovo. Serbia proper, despite its relative poverty, was not included among the LDRs for various political reasons. The developed regions (DRs) thus included Serbia proper and its northern province, Vojvodina, as well as Slovenia and Croatia.

The nature of the policy strategies adopted by the communist authorities to even the balance of regional development is key to understanding not only why the overall program of regional development failed but also why the less developed republics and regions were left with unfavorable economic legacies despite absolute gains in modernization and industrialization. A Stalinist approach to large-scale industrialization in sectors such as metallurgy, steel processing, and power was adopted from the outset. The construction of such heavy industries and other large-scale public projects was enabled by mass mobilization and the suppression of prices for raw materials and agricultural products, which had a decidedly negative impact on the regions and republics that provided most of these goods: namely, the LDRs and Vojvodina. At the same time, Slovenia, the most developed republic, received a highly disproportionate amount of investment, as it was thought that this would maximize output. Such overtly discriminatory policies were explained to Pleština as necessary for national security at a time when the Soviet threat loomed large because of Yugoslavia's abrupt split with the USSR in 1948. Thus, the only special provision made for the LDRs during the first Five-Year Plan (1947–1952) was the granting of special tax relief and some grants-in-aid (Pleština 1992: 21–28).

The DRs had a great structural advantage. Slovenia, Croatia, and to a much lesser extent parts of Serbia proper were already industrial areas of Yugoslavia before the war. The workers in these areas were more educated and efficient, steeped in the industrial tradition, and in general more receptive to the demands of modernization (Pleština 1992: 44). Due to the spatial distribution of the fighting, these prewar industries were much less likely to have been damaged if they were located in Croatia and Slovenia, and it was also these same industries that were initially targeted by the communist regime to be expanded or converted. The investments they obtained early on to expand production came at the expense of development funds for the LDRs, so the regional inequity was widening just as the country reached a critical juncture with opportunities to pursue regional development, as table 3.1 shows.

The initial Five-Year Plan was followed by the announcement of what was to become the internationally heralded Yugoslav "National Road to Socialism," whose cornerstones included social rather than state ownership of the means of production; worker management; decentralization of political and economic decisions from the federal government to republics, communes, and enterprises; and a greater reliance on market signals as guides to resource allocation. These were codified in constitutional changes in 1953 and, along with non-alignment in foreign policy, became the basic principles of Yugoslav communism (Pleština 1992: 27).

Yet, even under decentralization the primacy of geopolitics continued to compel policymakers to emphasize overall, rather than regional, development, which in practice meant continued economic discrimination against the LDRs and a flow of resources into heavy industrial projects rather than infrastructure and other foundations of long-term development. The decentralization also signaled the beginning of what was to become a continuing pattern of political jockeying for the economic interests of one's republic or region, a pattern in which the DRs often emerged victorious since they could legitimately argue that investments in their areas would yield maximum returns. Montenegro was an exception among the LDRs, effectively using its political leverage to win economic concessions in inter-republican battles even though investment there continued to produce poor results (Pleština 1992: 33).

By the mid- to late 1950s, the geopolitical threat had disappeared with Soviet-Yugoslav *rapprochement*, the inflow of aid from the United States, and the formation of the non-aligned bloc, and yet no important shift in policy toward

Table 3.1   Indicators of Development in Republics and Regions, 1953

Republic or region	Industrial workers (per 100)	Agricultural population (index)	Completed high school (%)	Less than 3 grades of schooling (%)
Yugoslavia	33	100	6.6	42.1
Slovenia	77	68	11.2	15.2
Croatia	40	93	7.3	30.5
Vojvodina	29	103	7.5	28.4
Serbia[a]	27	110	7.0	44.5
Bosnia and Herzegovina	31	102	4.1	67.2
Macedonia	16	103	3.8	50.7
Montenegro	0.2	100	5.3	40.9
Kosovo	16	119	2.3	71.2

Source: Pleština (1992: 45–46).
[a]Serbia proper, without Vojvodina and Kosovo.

the LDRs occurred. Indeed, the policy of under-pricing raw materials continued into the late 1960s (Pleština 1992: 32–33). This did not mean that there were no industrial investments in the poorer republics—in politically powerful ones, such as Montenegro, money flowed into all kinds of projects, from highways to steel mills. The problem with these investments was that they were often an irrational use of scarce material resources, such as the "political factories" that began to appear in the 1950s. Other kinds of projects—such as the massive investment in military industries in Bosnia and Herzegovina—may have raised the aggregate growth figures but also did little in terms of establishing a viable long-term base for economic development. The legacy that these political projects bequeathed to the LDRs is one of inefficient, loss-making enterprises that could hardly be used to support the economy of a newly independent state, much less compete in the global marketplace.

The second Five-Year Plan yielded impressive results in the federal economy and at last some advantages for the LDRs, especially Macedonia and Kosovo, which were provided with a guaranteed volume of investment for development projects chosen by the center.[13] Still, a satisfactory plan for their development did not emerge. The lack of a comprehensive plan meant that the investment projects that were approved were often political in nature, and due to a soft budget constraint the state propped up many failing enterprises in LDRs for years. Alternatively, investment in the LDRs was channeled to defense industries, which had neither a productive use nor a consumption benefit. Added to this was the continuing lack of equitable valuation of the LDR's products, and the failure of the state to promote development in areas where the LDRs would have the greatest comparative advantage—such as the labor-intensive processing and manufacturing industries. Finally, agricultural investment during this period benefited the DRs much more than the LDRs because it encompassed only the social sector, much more prevalent in the former than the latter (Pleština 1992: 49–50). Meanwhile, regional inequality continued to increase.[14]

Improvements in the infrastructure of the LDRs did occur, but only after the Federal Fund for the Accelerated Development of the LDRs was put into place in 1965–66 as part of the third Five-Year Plan (Pleština 1992: 40–41). The source of funds for this new development agency was a special tax on fixed assets of all firms in Yugoslavia (Pleština 1992: 73), and part of the strategy entailed sending economic advisors from the developed north to the undeveloped south. Still, this constituted limited help for the LDRs.

The Development Fund never got off the ground, mainly for political reasons, among them the mutual suspicion between officials in the LDRs and economic experts from DRs sent as advisors to consult in the south. From the perspective of the LDRs, the DR experts had ulterior motives (such as making sure that factories that might compete with DR enterprises were not built and enriching themselves on state expense budgets) and were not genuinely interested in promoting development in poorer regions, while the DR advisors saw their colleagues in the LDRs as corrupt and uneducated. The Development Fund could not step in to help quell this mutual suspicion since it had limited powers to monitor the management of funds once they were distributed (Pleština 1992: 80–85). An analysis of the infrastructure investment in each of the republics and autonomous provinces during this period of reform shows a glaring movement away from equalization. During this period, the LDR definition shifted to include less-developed parts of Croatia, Bosnia and Herzegovina, and Serbia, and more measures to promote decentralization were enacted. Ironically, it was precisely decentralization that prevented more development because it led to continual political deadlock. As the republics and regions gained more autonomy, their representatives in federal organs acted increasingly as interest groups, fighting for the narrow economic interests of their respective "constituencies." In these battles, the interests of DRs and LDRs naturally diverged, with the LDRs generally favoring centralization and statist policies and the DRs pushing for liberalization and greater decentralization. With the failure of *jugoslovenstvo* (the effort to encourage a supra-national Yugoslav identity)[15] and given that republican and regional boundaries overlapped with ethnic boundaries, these intra-federal political battles over economic issues took on an increasingly ethno-national tone in the late 1960s.

However, in the 1960s political and economic interests did not always co-incide with ethnic boundaries or identities, and coalitions between DRs and LDRs were formed at certain political junctures. Confronted with the fear of Serbian domination, Croatia and Slovenia were able to convince Bosnia and Herzegovina and Macedonia to join them in a fight against centralization (Pleština 1992: 66–67), allowing them to prevail. Investment was increasing in the LDRs, but there was a negative correlation between the size of inflow and efficiency of capital use (Ocić 1998: 5).

All the talk of economic reform and development did much to raise expec-tations among ordinary people. When these expectations were not realized, social unrest appeared. In 1968, strikes by students in Belgrade against condi-tions at the university and high unemployment spread to encompass other quality of life issues. At the end of the 1960s there were also strikes and riots organized by Albanians in northwest Macedonia, no doubt a product of feel-ings of economic deprivation. The unrest culminated in the Croatian rebel-lion (*Hrvatsko Proljeće*, "Croatian Spring") of 1971, which initially was based on grievances arising from perceived economic discrimination and resulted in a crackdown by Tito on reformist elements in the League of Communists of Croatia.[16]

The 1971–1975 period was witness to yet another Five-Year Plan (the fifth), which also promised to deal with the problem of regional inequality. As in previous plans, the Development Fund was to be the principle means of in-tervention. However, the less developed areas of developed republics and re-gions were no longer under the Development Fund's jurisdiction; they were now to be under the supervision of their respective republics and regions. Kosovo was now given special consideration and generous terms of repay-ment given its very low level of development. The reforms did have a positive impact on the growth of the LDRs—in fact, the growth was not only higher than it had been under the previous Five-Year Plan, it was also marginally higher than growth rates in the DRs (Pleština 1992: 96–97). Yet, relative to population, the DRs continued to receive more investment than the LDRs. Moreover, investment did not reflect past performance, so that Montenegro continued to receive the highest levels of investment despite poor returns, which Pleština (1992: 100) attributes to the over-representation of Montenegrins in key party organs. This was true for other forms of aid, such as development credits from the World Bank. Thus, politics, and not economic rationality in terms of optimum use and allocation of resources to promote regional development, governed development policy in the LDRs, and the consequences for remedying disparities between developed and undeveloped republics and regions were decidedly negative. Even when enterprises were built and other forms of investment took place, the LDRs continued to suffer from structural problems such as a low level of education and a neglected agricultural sector. The return of many guest workers from Western Europe in the mid-1970s in response to a continent-wide recession hurt the LDRs (as well as Croatia), as many of these workers came from the poorer regions and republics and their jobs abroad provided a critical safety valve for unemployment, while their remittances of hard currency were critical for republican budgets and family income. In general, external economic shocks, such as Yugoslavia's sharply increasing balance of trade deficit, were much more acutely felt in the LDRs than the DRs.

The sixth Five-Year Plan, implemented in the late 1970s, relied on the Development Fund as the main means of intervention but included new measures, among them a plan to integrate and coordinate enterprises among republics and regions that ultimately failed. Efforts at regional development were increasingly rendered futile by a growing economic crisis. Yugoslavia's foreign debt skyrocketed, reaching $18 billion in early 1980. The Gastarbeiter continued to return in record numbers, swelling the ranks of the unemployed. Personal incomes began to decline, for the first time in nearly three decades (Pleština 1992: 106). Again, this overall economic crisis was felt most strongly in the LDRs. Growth did indeed occur in the LDRs under the sixth Five-Year Plan, though instead of the expected 20 to 25 percent above the Yugoslav average, growth only exceeded this average by around 7 percent (Pleština 1992: 114). The disparity between the DRs and LDRs, however, failed to narrow. Subsequent efforts in the last ten years of the SFRJ to promote regional development also failed, for all of the reasons cited above, as did the last-ditch attempts to introduce market mechanisms into the economy. Thus, writes Pleština (1992: 124),

> The result for regional development was that 35 years after the [Communist Party of Yugoslavia] had come to power, its goal of bridging economic inequal-

ities between the developed and the less developed republics and regions had not been achieved. The effect on the political stability of the country was becoming palpable. Ten years after the Croatian crisis shook the Yugoslav regime, economic grievances once again took on a violent ethno-nationalist manifestation. In the decentralized, post-Tito Yugoslavia of the early 1980s, where pursuit of economic interests had acquired de-facto legitimacy these proved much more difficult to contain and, ultimately, impossible to subdue.

It is important to emphasize that despite irrational or even discriminatory patterns of regional development policy, large amounts of money *were* transferred from the richer north to the poor south, as demonstrated by Bombelles (1991). These transfers came at an expense, not only to the net donor republics but also to the economy as a whole. However, the reason why these investments were not yielding returns in the LDRs was quite evident by the 1980s. Namely, the Development Fund was financing a large number of *promašene investicije*—"bad investments." This term, however, is really a euphemism for the corrupt political projects of local party machines that lined the pockets of a select group of apparatchiks but did little to promote overall development of the regional or republican economy. "Bad investments" increased as economic decline deepened and competition for resources and jobs became fierce. At the end of the 1980s, the media, such as the Belgrade weekly *NIN*, were unabashedly reporting on the scope and substance of some of these irrational projects (Bombelles 1991: 459). Among them were factories that were constructed but never started production, factories that were only partially completed and then abandoned, and factories that were operating at a fraction of their capacity. The Development Fund tolerated, or had to tolerate, the misdirection of its resources since it had no control of these funds once they were allocated to the regional or republican level. Although the healthier economies of the DRs had "bad investments" of their own, these projects did not have nearly as negative an impact as they did in the LDRs, where the legacy of clientelism and corruption carried on into the postcommunist period, now reproduced in ethno-national, rather than simply political, ties.[17]

Thus, during the communist period, the economic disparities between the DRs and LDRs had increased, as shown in table 3.2. The DRs became richer, while the LDRs became poorer. Croatia's per capita gross regional product (GRP) increased by 12 percent relative to the Yugoslav average, while Kosovo's GRP fell from half the Yugoslav average to almost one third of that aver-

Table 3.2   Regional Disparities during Communism
(per capita regional product)

Republic or region	1947	1965	1975	1986
Slovenia	162	177	201	179
Croatia	105	120	124	117
Vojvodina	100	122	121	133
Serbia[a]	101	95	92	94
Montenegro	94	71	70	80
Bosnia and Herzegovina	86	69	69	80
Macedonia	70	70	69	75
Kosovo	49	39	33	36

Source: Janos (1997: 33).
  Note: Index, Yugoslavia=100.
  [a]Serbia proper, without Vojvodina and Kosovo.

age. Although the Yugoslav economy had experienced a major transformation, by the 1980s inter-regional differences were as great as they had been historically, and in some cases even greater.

Pleština concludes her study of regional development in communist Yugoslavia by noting that increasing decentralization simply could not be reconciled with the desire to bring the LDRs up to par with the DRs. The vast disparities in development among the republics and regions created equally divergent interests, and the highly decentralized institutional structure enshrined in the 1974 constitution meant that politics began to revolve exclusively around republican interests. The particularization of interests, in turn, was given ideological legitimacy by Edvard Kardelj, architect of Yugoslavia's economic system, in the late 1970s. Federal institutions had become forums in which to pursue and preserve the narrowly defined economic interests of one's republic or region.

In this pursuit, the developed regions were automatically favored in the increasingly market-oriented Yugoslav economy. The institutions themselves were designed such that federal representatives directly depended on the regional organizations that elected them, and this resulted in their acting almost exclusively on behalf of their respective regions, rather than as representatives of the federation as a whole. This, in turn, led to the "parcelization" of the federation, with negative effects for overall development, especially for the development of the LDRs. The result for the LDRs was to further relegate them to a permanently disadvantaged position. On the one hand, decentralization and the introduction of market mechanisms had created a situation in which the economically weaker and less competitive LDRs were unable to draw the capital necessary for investment or to find markets for their products. At the same time, the ideological justification of the pursuit of particular interests condoned this situation in which they were less competitive (Pleština 1992: 113).

The regional pursuit of scarce economic resources was, in the final analysis, the key element in the coalition building and the most important determinant of political action. Although the coalitions varied over time and often transcended ethno-nationalist interests, economic grievances began to be increasingly articulated in the language of ethno-nationalism, especially during the period of severe crisis. By the end of the 1980s competition for scarce resources *among* republics and regions became competition among political elites *within* these republics and regions for even scarcer resources.

The Economic Crisis of the 1980s and Its Consequences for the Republics

The Roots of the Crisis

Despite its failure to make the regional distribution of development more equitable, communist Yugoslavia was an effective developmental state through the 1960s and, to some extent, the 1970s.[18] Development was felt everywhere, including the poorer regions and republics, where standards of living increased dramatically with the modernization of extremely backward economies. However, even in its best days, the Yugoslav economy suffered from a range of imbalances, irrationalities, and deficiencies, which coexisted with, and in many ways were related to, the problem of regional economic inequality. Agricultural growth was sluggish despite the reversal of collectivization efforts. Unemployment was a lingering problem—it did not reach crisis levels in the 1970s only thanks to the critical safety valve provided by sending one million guest workers to advanced industrialized countries, which at its peak constituted a substantial portion of the total Yugoslav workforce. The system of workers' self-management was largely inefficient and stimulated the inflationary economy that was needed to support it. Many large state-owned enterprises operated as monopolies with unrestricted access to capital, which was doled out according to political criteria. Punitive taxation and restrictions on inheritance discouraged private enterprise in almost all sectors other than tourism, artisan manufacture, and construction, such that remittances from abroad continued to provide as much income as legally registered, private enterprise (Lampe 2000: 319). There was a chronic problem with investment in industries in which Yugoslavia had a comparative disadvantage as well as duplication of industries in two or more republics and regions. This last problem was intimately related to the federal structure, which had given the republics broad powers over everything from educational policy to international trade. Continuing foreign trade and balance of payments deficits drained hard currency reserves and led to giant debts. Central intervention was needed but difficult to achieve precisely because of the decentralization described in the previous section. Furthermore, divergent interests in the absence of strong central institutions meant that regions and republics had the power to block needed reforms.[19] Members of central party organs were responsible to constituents in their home republics or regions—and were inclined to portray themselves as defenders of their respective unit's interests against exploitation by the others.

The Effects of the Crisis

These economic deficiencies were magnified during the oil shocks of the 1970s, triggering what Lydall (1989) has called "the great reversal." A steadily rising standard of living in previous decades had partially muted grievances even in the poorest regions and republics, but by the end of this reversal, standards had fallen so quickly and dramatically that the second Yugoslavia, its leaders, and its basic principles were rendered illegitimate. The initial response of the technocratic federal government to the looming crisis was to combat the slowdown with extensive foreign borrowing, which was made possible by the large amounts of capital flowing into Western banks from the newly formed Organization of Petroleum Exporting Countries (OPEC). The borrowing policy did manage to sustain a reasonable rate of growth for several years. But this kind of growth was unsustainable, indeed in many ways artificial. While the GNP grew at a rate of 5.1 percent, the rate of foreign borrowing was increasing at an annual rate of 20 percent (Janos 2000: 278). Yugoslavia's economy was rapidly falling deeper into a hole of debt that helped to seal its doom. The "bubble" burst in 1979, and the following figures from Janos (2000: 278) illustrate the consequences, painfully felt in the 1980s:

- Between 1979 and 1985, Yugoslavia accumulated $25 billion in foreign debt;

- During this same period, the Yugoslav dinar plunged from 15 to 1,370 to the U.S. dollar;
- Half of the income from exports went to service the debt, rendering earnings gleaned from foreign trade and tourism inconsequential;
- Real net personal income declined by 19.5 percent;
- Unemployment rose to 1.3 million job-seekers;
- Internal debt was estimated to be $40 billion.[20]

Thus, in the 1980s the Yugoslav economy entered a period of sustained crisis from which it never recovered. All of these downward trends were closely correlated with the regional differentiation of the economy, meaning that they were more acutely felt in the south than the north, spelling certain political trouble.

The Belgrade political scientist Vladimir Goati called the economic crisis of the 1980s the "epicenter of a society in crisis" (1989: 19; "epicentar društva u krizi"). In 1988, national income declined by 1 percent, agricultural output declined by 5 percent, unemployment stood at 16.8 percent, the inflation rate was some 340 percent, and the foreign debt had reached an all-time high of nearly $30 billion. The purchasing power of the average Yugoslav fell to the 1960 level as monthly salaries plummeted to less than 50 dollars for a factory worker and to 155 dollars for professionals (Pleština 1992: 133), leading to a sharp increase in personal debt. Pleština writes that by 1989 "chaos was the only word to describe a situation in which inflation had reached 1.5 percent a day, or more than 2,500 percent for 1989" (1992: 137). Shortages for many goods became the norm everywhere. By 1990, the economic infrastructure itself was becoming unraveled. This was most evident in the Development Fund itself, which simply ceased to function when Slovenia and Croatia refused to pay their dues. The final nail in the fund's coffin was the emergence, at the end of the decade, of statistics showing that the development gap had increased even further in the 1980s.

Consequences for the Republics

This crisis, then, had very different consequences for each republic. Aggregate indicators actually masked the true decline in poorer regions. The economic structures of the LDRs had always been more vulnerable to recessions and were thus very badly hurt by the 1980s crisis. The effects of this crisis, combined with the structural deficiencies or advantages of each republic, shaped very different economic circumstances in each entity of the SFRJ in the late 1980s. Even in Croatia, the second most developed of the DRs, structural problems and regional poverty were exposed as a result of the crisis.

Slovenia had the most developed economy and was best able to weather the 1980s crisis. Its workers were by far the most productive and the best compensated of any other republic. Compared to the other republics, unemployment was very low and savings were high. Quite significantly for its looming independence, Slovenia had the most favorable debt situation, the highest foreign currency reserves, and the greatest potential to service its debt and maintain foreign currency reserves given its active and highly developed export sector. Croatia's economy, albeit much more developed than the LDRs to the south, had been adversely affected by the 1980s crisis, which had exposed some serious deficiencies in its economic structure. These deficiencies included overdependence on guest workers (both as a safety valve for unemployment and as a source of hard currency remissions), poor and unproductive regions (such as the Krajina), and an uncompetitive industrial sector. The republic's income fell such that it only marginally exceeded the national average by the end of the 1980s. The economy of Serbia was deeply hurt by the crisis, and any benefit from Vojvodina, a DR, was countered by negative effects from southern Serbia and Kosovo, both extremely poor regions whose misery only deepened in the 1980s. Bosnia and Herzegovina, Macedonia, and Montenegro were all in dire economic straits by the end of the 1980s and experienced sharp declines in living standard and high unemployment. Moreover, their weak industrial base was dominated by loss-making heavy industries and mining, which were uncompetitive in the global market.

The Problem of Unemployment and Its Regional Distribution

The deteriorating conditions of life that characterized 1980s Yugoslavia were reflected in soaring unemployment rates. In the late 1980s, the unemployment rate in Yugoslavia was over 17 percent, with another 20 percent underemployed. Unemployment, in fact, was a chronic problem in Yugoslavia.[21] Suffice it to say, however, that unemployment, along with inflation, had reached socially and politically dangerous levels in the 1980s. Some 60 percent of the unemployed were now under twenty-five years of age and almost that same percentage had at least a secondary education. The demographic phenomenon of a growing number of relatively educated and young segments of the population confronting a labor market with diminishing prospects was politically explosive. The lack of *perceived* opportunities was especially critical in shaping hopelessness and a search for new political solutions. Public opinion research conducted in 1987 found that 79 percent of the respondents doubted that there was any avenue open to escape the accumulated economic problems. Of the Yugoslav population, 84 percent felt that their economic fortunes and sense of personal security were in decline (Lampe 2000: 333–34). So the sharp rise in unemployment reflected not only a tight labor market but also a broader social crisis and the erosion of Yugoslavia's substantial middle class, a potential core of support for liberal reform. In part owing to the growing unemployment rate, by 1984 one-quarter of Yugoslav families were living below the poverty line, and this figure was substantially higher in the LDRs (Lampe 2000: 323).

As might be expected, the regional distribution of unemployment was uneven. Even in the 1970s socially dangerous levels of unemployment prevailed in Macedonia, Kosovo, and other intra-entity regions. Riots and strikes in Kosovo in the 1980s were a direct consequence of an extremely high unemployment rate. Unemployment became a serious problem in urban centers such as Belgrade as well, where the jobless rate was as high as 25 percent in the 1980s. This was due in part to large migrations of ethnic Serbs from rural areas (Lampe 2000: 334–35). The general trend, in any case, was increasing unemployment as one moved from north to south. Thus, Slovenia had virtually full employment and was not threatened by the social instability that comes with high unemployment rates. Croatia's unemployment rate, though at first glance relatively low, masked high levels of unemployment in poorer regions, a generally high level of underemployment, and excess labor in many public enterprises. Moreover, it did not take into account the large numbers of Croats temporarily working abroad in Western Europe. If they were added to the registered job seekers, the unemployment figures would have been even worse. In the other republics and regions, the very high levels of unemployment led to increasing calls for new political solutions.

The unemployment problem (figure 3.2) and the fall in real income that accompanied it emerged in the context of a population that was used to a relatively high standard of living, augmenting the general feeling of frustration. Many Yugoslavs, through travel or work in the West, had been exposed to high consumption standards. Unemployment was an especially sensitive

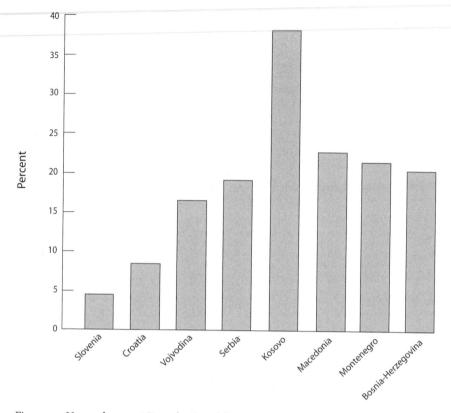

Figure 3.2. Unemployment Rates by Republic or Region, 1990 (end of year)
Source: Derived from Appendix table 6-9, Woodward 1995b: 383–84.
  Note: Yugoslavia = 15.9%. "Serbia" refers to Serbia proper, without Vojvodina and Kosovo.

issue in terms of unfulfilled expectations since the workplace, particularly in the social sector, was an important basis of one's identity in the Yugoslav system. Due to such heightened expectations, the relative psychological deprivation experienced by many Yugoslavs during the 1980s crisis was deeper than that felt by their counterparts in other Central and East European countries.

Youth unemployment was at even higher levels. In Kosovo, Macedonia, Montenegro, and Bosnia and Herzegovina, the situation had reached catastrophic proportions. In these republics, high unemployment rates were the most poignant indicator of conflicting trends in 1980s Yugoslavia, as noted by Lampe: "rising levels of higher education and diminishing chances for graduates to find employment." In fact, the rise in literacy and educational opportunities was one of the unambiguous achievements of Titoist Yugoslavia. However, these advances were only meaningful if they led to good employment opportunities and social advancement. Such opportunities were available in the 1960s and 1970s to the parents of unemployed young people and allowed them to sustain a relatively high standard of living. This state of affairs was no longer available in the 1980s in most LDRs: the government could now promise jobs to only half of university graduates (Lampe 2000: 339–41). Again, a potential constituency for liberalism instead became a group receptive to populist themes.

Unemployment had another negative effect throughout Yugoslavia. Namely, the fierce competition for jobs and income in conditions of great scarcity was leading to an expansion of the secondary economy and corruption. Moreover, networks of corruption were increasingly based on ethnicity—as was access to state resources. The rapid modernization of the LDRs with its focus on quantity over quality created high expectations—especially given demonstration effects of living standards from the DRs and frequent promises of quick and even development—and thus, as Ocić writes, the "revolution of rising expectations" in the LDRs gave way to the "revolution of rising disappointment and frustration" (1998: 9).

A Note on Intra-republican Disparities

So far we have considered economic disparities among republics and regions, mainly because the federal Yugoslav state dissolved along republican boundaries, the bare outlines of the successor states that are the subject of this study. The exceptions, of course, were Montenegro and Serbia, two republics that stayed together in a single successor state until 2006, and Serbia's two autonomous regions, Vojvodina and Kosovo, which lost their autonomy in the late 1980s and also remained in the common state with Serbia and Montenegro. Just as one must acknowledge the role of Kosovo's relative poverty in shaping political developments in Serbia in the 1980s, it is equally important to consider the role of economic disparities *within* other republics. In fact, that official Yugoslav development policy stubbornly divided republics and regions into "developed" and "less developed" without taking into greater account intra-entity disparities also undermined the goal of equitable regional development (Ocić 1998: 1). The political significance of less developed regions within certain republics, furthermore, went beyond their relative underdevelopment, since the poorer areas often coincided geograph-

ically with large concentrations of ethnic minorities, leading to political vola-
tility, creating a base for nationalism, and making it difficult to distinguish
ethno-national grievances from economic ones. Thus, Kosovo, by far the poorest region of Serbia, was overwhelmingly populated by ethnic Albanians; the
Krajina, a poor area of Croatia, had a majority of ethnic Serbs; Herzegovina,
an undeveloped area of Bosnia and Herzegovina, had many Croats; and western Macedonia, also impoverished, was largely populated by ethnic Albanians. This nexus of regional poverty and ethnic unrest became salient not
only in the impending conflicts but also in shaping the kinds of political attitudes that emerged in each republic in the period immediately prior to dissolution. There were also intra-republican disparities that did not correspond
to the spatial distribution of ethnic groups, and yet their relative poverty led
them to be both a target and source of support for radical populism, as in
southern Serbia, parts of Croatia, and much of rural Macedonia.

The Dependence of the Yugoslav Economy on the Cold War Order

Patterns of regional development in communist Yugoslavia must be seen
in the context of the international order.[22] It is important to understand Yugoslavia's special position within this order, the benefits it derived from this
position, and the effects that a change in the external balance of power had
on Yugoslavia's economic and political fortunes. In addition, each republic
had a different stake in Yugoslavia's favored geopolitical position. Yugoslavia's
viability, both political and economic, was based in large part on the benefits
it derived from its favorable position between "West" and "East." This position, argues Susan Woodward (1995a: 21–46), was one of three critical "bases
of stability" of the Yugoslav system. Concrete and vital economic benefits were
derived from Yugoslavia's strategic importance, and these, in turn, shaped Yugoslavia's internal and external politics. According to Dyker, "The history of
the Yugoslav economy could be written in terms of capital import." Indeed,
"in the immediate post-war period in particular, capital import provided the
nexus, not only of economic evolution, but indeed of political developments
too" (1990: 155). It was the promise of economic aid that initially brought
Tito into an alliance with Stalin, and it was by cutting off that assistance that
Stalin later sought to discipline Tito. It was the need for massive aid and "soft
loans" from the United States that compelled Tito to adopt a less repressive
internal order and allowed the West to maintain Yugoslav neutrality and independence in the Cold War world order (Dyker 1990: 155).[23] After the U.S.

handouts ended, Yugoslavia repeatedly received credits from the World Bank, other international financial institutions, and consortia of private Western banks (often encouraged by Western governments), all of which provided a critical infusion of capital for infrastructure and the consumer sector.[24] In exchange, "socialist Yugoslavia played a critical role for U.S. global leadership during the Cold War: as a propaganda tool in its anti-communist and anti-Soviet campaign and as an integral element of NATO's policy in the eastern Mediterranean" (Woodward 1995a: 25). Furthermore, in a global economy that was governed by political, rather than economic, criteria, Yugoslavia's "neutral" position gave it access to markets in both the advanced industrial countries of the West and the developing countries of the third and communist worlds.

The economic benefits of Yugoslavia's strategic position had begun to decline well before the end of the Cold War, mainly due to changes in global markets. A deep recession in Western Europe sent many Gastarbeiter home, demand for Yugoslav goods in Eastern markets fell, and the supply of foreign capital dried up. All of these factors helped to precipitate the 1980s crisis, while the nature of the crisis itself exposed the extent of Yugoslavia's economic dependence on external factors. These changes in the unforgiving global market notwithstanding, Cold War political logic prevailed and Yugoslavia still managed to receive help from the International Monetary Fund (IMF) in the form of aid and also from increased exports to the USSR and China. The continuing interest of both in maintaining Yugoslav economic viability "demonstrated the economic value to Yugoslavia of maintaining its policy of non-alignment" (Singleton 1986: 277).

However, these benefits were only sustainable so long as the Cold War, and thus the basic interests of its participants, remained intact. Everything changed with the developments in Moscow and other capitals of the Warsaw Pact in the late 1980s, and suddenly Yugoslavia lost its strategic importance to the outside world. The effect was devastating for Yugoslavia's internal order. Two images capture the change in Yugoslavia's relative importance: the first, while Yugoslavia was still of strategic value, of the thirty-three heads of state and sixteen heads of government in attendance at Tito's funeral in 1980; the second, after the fall of the Iron Curtain, of federal Prime Minister Ante Marković desperately and, ultimately, futilely attempting to seek financial aid and support in the West to keep the Yugoslav federation intact in 1990, as told by Zimmermann (1996).

The Cold War was truly Yugoslavia's lifeblood, both in terms of economic sustenance and political legitimacy, so its demise hurt the country severely, in a much more direct and negative way than other East European states emerging from communist rule. However, the international changes had a more adverse effect on some republics than others. All the republics except Slovenia and Montenegro, for instance, benefited significantly from the export of labor and the remissions it provided. The unfinished goods and raw materials produced in the LDRs depended heavily on demand in and access to markets in the East; these sectors of the economy were inexplicably less protected than secondary industries (Pleština 1992: 70). The LDRs were much more dependent than the DRs on Western financing of domestic consumption. All the LDRs—in particular Macedonia and Kosovo—depended heavily on international aid, much of which was channeled specifically to them. The aid and conditions included priority of access to foreign exchange credits extended by the World Bank, federal assumption of repayment of foreign loans, lowering of customs duties on imports of certain products to the underdeveloped areas, provision of extra foreign exchange to industry in the LDRs, and a number of similar measures (Bombelles 1991: 465). Serbia, though formally considered a DR, derived not only economic benefits but also political prestige from Yugoslavia's international position, especially since the capital of Yugoslavia was Belgrade. Its interest in greater centralization in part reflected this reality. In Belgrade, there was a belief that the West for its own reasons would guarantee Yugoslav independence and economic and political stability.

Slovenia and Croatia, on the other hand, benefited from decentralization when it came to independently making foreign trade deals and retaining hard currency. In other words, as the international environment and internal reforms began to push Yugoslavia to participate more fully in an expanding world economy, Serbia and other LDRs had even greater reason to push for re-centralization. This, however, was related not only to the changing international environment but also to the character of the internal Yugoslav market.

Initial economic conditions are indispensable to understanding the postcommunist transitions of the four states that are the subject of this study. Very different levels of development tell us a lot about the economic viability of each republic given independence—such differences in levels of development, in turn, are a good predictor of the chances for liberalism. In brief, the further an area was from northern markets, the existence of developed transportation networks, and the benefits of early industrialization (light manufacturing, industrial habits, and literacy) and the larger the proportion of the population employed in agriculture, in noncreative occupations (army, security forces, and civil service), in low wage and non-accumulative industries, the greater was it hurt by the crisis in the 1980s and the less economically viable it was, thereby constraining the emergence of a liberal regime. Thus, the starting point of transition in each Yugoslav successor state was a unique structural context that established the parameters for the subsequent regime transition.

Economic viability, then, can be defined as the ability to sustain economic growth and acceptable living standards at the pre-independence level after secession.[25] Independence meant sharp declines in living standard for parts of the population who had come to expect better, especially compared to their counterparts in other post-communist states. For them, the economic decline of the 1980s and the subsequent economic shocks of independence were an instance of "decremental deprivation," the effects of which are described by Ted Robert Gurr. Gurr (1970) points out that discontented people are most susceptible to new doctrines when they do not understand the origins of their discontent and feel insecure in their social environment. The real test of economic viability, in other words, came once the successor states were exposed to the pressures of the post–Cold War global economy.

CHAPTER FOUR

Simulated Democracy

Croatia's Transition in the 1990s

The war became embedded in the transition, and the transition in the war.
CROATIAN POLITICAL ANALYST MIRJANA KASAPOVIĆ

The Road to Nationalist Authoritarianism

The regime that ruled Croatia in the 1990s exhibited both authoritarianism and a particular brand of simulated democracy designed to assure a baseline level of Western support. The first ten years of post-communist transition were dominated by the entrenched power of one nationalist political party, the Croatian Democratic Union (Hrvatska Demokratska Zajednica, HDZ) and its founder and leader, President Franjo Tuđman.[1] The Tuđman regime used ethnic nationalism, authoritarian populism, and economic clientelism to consolidate and legitimize its hold on power. Early in Croatia's post-communist transition, liberal reform and integration into Western structures were deemphasized in favor of national issues. The initial conditions of Croatia's transition are the first step to understanding the character of the HDZ regime. Croatia's economy was partially viable at the outset of transition and independence: although there were well-established sectors and industries, there was also a substantial part of the economy, developed under communist industrialization, that was negatively affected by the years of economic crisis and the loss of unified markets after independence. The Croatian economy depended heavily on a few semi-viable sectors and some volatile ones like tourism as well as sending workers abroad as a source of hard currency remittances and as a safety valve to relieve domestic unemployment pressures. In this regard, Croatia's economic structure was quite different from that of Slovenia, more than aggregate indicators might suggest.[2] Economic downturn was most heavily felt in Croatia's poor interior (the former Habsburg military frontier or Krajina), which also happened to be ethnically mixed.[3] It was the populations of such underdeveloped and ethnically mixed regions that came to constitute the strongest base of support for radical populist parties that advocated ethno-nationalist positions: the ethnic Serbian Serbian Democratic Party (Srpska Demokratska Stranka, SDS) and the Croatian nationalist HDZ.[4]

The nationalists blamed Croatia's economic woes on Belgrade and Croatia's Serbs, and used them to justify the displacement of ethnic Serbs from positions of economic and political influence. The positions were doled out to HDZ insiders such that the new regime's anti-Serb policies at times resembled a grab for dwindling resources more than a real effort to rectify ostensible inequalities.[5] Along with the ethnic Croat residents of the impoverished economic hinterland, the HDZ insider beneficiaries of misappropriated state resources became among the firmest supporters of the regime.

In the 1990s, Croatia's mixed economic structure was reflected in the presence of liberal and pro-Western parties on the political scene. Though often fragmented and weak compared to the HDZ, these political groups nonetheless kept the regime in check and were available as a democratic alternative when the HDZ's rule collapsed at the end of the 1990s.

It was the political exploitation of the so-called Homeland War (*Domovinski rat*) by the regime that helped to entrench President Tuđman and the HDZ in power. The HDZ's record in winning this war and defending Croatian sovereignty was used to justify anti-democratic politics and clientelistic practices by the ruling party. Critics of the regime could be labeled anti-patriotic, Yugo-nostalgic, or enemies of the state. Initially, Belgrade and Serbs in general were cast as the new state's primary enemies, but after 1996, with the Serbs mostly gone and the war over, the HDZ turned its attention to a new enemy of Croatian sovereignty, the West and its organizations, which were increasingly chastising the Tuđman regime for its undemocratic politics.

Nationalist rhetoric became the baseline of political competition in the

1990s. Criticizing the ethno-nationalist agenda effectively meant political sui-cide. It was the divisive politics of nationalism that kept the liberal opposition divided and marginalized. By using the war as its legitimizing principle, the HDZ regime managed temporarily to attract a large cross-section of society inclined toward liberalism. The creation of a sense of vulnerability and a state-sponsored nationalist mentality, fostered by the extensive use of historical mythology and symbols, helped keep the HDZ in power. War politics also added new beneficiaries to the HDZ's growing clientelistic network: war veterans and their families, ethnic Croats in Herzegovina, arms dealers and other war profiteers, and residents of war-ravaged areas, all of whom became firm HDZ supporters and were duly rewarded in a number of ways. As the economic situation deteriorated, the HDZ invoked the war to divert attention from reform and solidify its hold on power.

Yet, one cannot fully understand the character of the Tuđman regime without acknowledging the way external forces shaped its nature and demise. Though many foreign officials intuitively distrusted President Tuđman, the West's initial policy toward the post-communist Croatian regime ranged from begrudging tolerance to open support. Some Western countries pursued a policy of tacit support for the Tuđman regime because it was seen as a counter-weight to a greater evil, the Milošević regime in Belgrade. The financial and military support provided by Western countries was much needed by Zagreb, and hence Tuđman and the HDZ maintained a facade of democracy to avoid alienating their Western "friends." However, such support was contingent on continuing hostilities in neighboring Bosnia, and after the Dayton Agreement the West's threshold of tolerance for Tuđman's undemocratic behavior declined significantly. In the second half of the 1990s both the United States and the EU actively began pushing for democratization, supporting the opposition and sponsoring the expansion of civil society while chastising the Tuđman regime for its infractions against democracy. Consequently, Tuđman and the HDZ were under increased pressure to reform, and their response was twofold and somewhat contradictory. On one hand, the regime began to vilify the West as an enemy of Croatian sovereignty, while on the other it went out of its way to show a democratic face to the West.[6] Certain domestic constituencies may have believed for a time that the West and its liberal agenda were a threat to Croatian sovereignty, while those who derived benefits from the HDZ regime did not raise their voices in protest. However, the West actively courted other constituencies, those that were pro-Western in their orientation and those that were beginning to see through the HDZ's instrumental appeals to nationalism, especially as the economic situation worsened. Certain political groups, most notably the communist successor Social Democratic Party (Socijaldemokratska Partija, SDP), saw incentives in allying themselves with the West and promising EU and NATO integration in their public appeals.

The relative strength of the pro-Western part of society in Croatia compared to FRY explains why the pro-EU and pro-NATO rhetoric was much stronger in the Tuđman regime than the Milošević regime. As time passed and it became clear that Croatia was being left behind other post-communist states in the race to join NATO and the EU, support for Tuđman and the HDZ fell dramatically. Support for the Western-allied opposition parties rose, especially as the West began to employ the carrot of membership in Euro-Atlantic organizations and the stick of isolation when Tuđman balked at implementing liberal reforms. The final nail in the HDZ's coffin was the disastrous economic situation that prevailed by the end of the 1990s, in which nearly one-quarter of the country's workforce was unemployed.

Formal Democracy: The Record

It is no small irony that while the HDZ fiercely opposed communism, once in power it treated all institutions as an extension of the party, installing a politically loyal *nomenklatura* in all positions of influence, just as the communists had done (Ottaway 2003: 113). In this manner, Tuđman and the HDZ controlled the judiciary, the security apparatus, parts of the private sector, and the media.

Although the Tuđman regime allowed regular and free elections, electoral manipulation did take place—though not necessarily through the ballot box. First, the HDZ tended to call elections on a whim, and especially at times when it was guaranteed victory. These included the height of the summer holidays, or after military campaigns, or when patriotism was at its peak (Ottaway 2003: 113). Elections were called with the shortest possible notice, which was deliberately designed to hamper the efforts of the opposition and maximize the number of parliamentary seats. Gerrymandering of districts to give weight to friendly rural constituencies was common. Croats in the diaspora, mostly of right-wing political persuasions, were not only enfranchised but also given special seats, which magnified their influence (Ottaway 2003:

113). Parliamentary elections were nonetheless regarded as generally free and fair by international observers.[7] The three cycles of parliamentary elections held in the 1990s were not marred by the irregularities that were commonplace in Macedonia and FRY. Such irregularities would have sullied the democratic face that the Tuđman regime was so eager to show to the West. Presidential elections were deemed unfair, however, with the Organization for Security and Cooperation in Europe (OSCE) concluding that the 1997 election "did not meet minimum standards for democracies" (quoted in Karatnycky et al. 1999:178).

Many democratic transgressions were recorded in the media sphere, and it takes only a cursory glance at papers like *Večernji List* or HINA (Croatian Press Agency/Hrvatska Izvještajna Novinska Agencija) reports in the 1990s to see that the big media outlets were simply tools of the regime. Croatian Radio-Television (Hrvatska radiotelevizija, HRT) was also a mouthpiece of the government.[8] Yet, in the area of media, too, there was a conscious effort to simulate democracy. The press, for instance, was privatized early on to give an impression of independence, but most press outlets were owned and run by HDZ insiders.[9] Later in the 1990s, some notable exceptions appeared: *Novi List* of Rijeka and the famous *Feral Tribune*. However, the latter in particular came under consistent and fierce attack from the regime and was left with massive debts from legal fees.[10] Security services were also used to harass opposition journalists. Some independent publications, such as *Nacional, Globus,* and *Jutarnji List* got stronger and more critical toward the end of the 1990s. Yet, the problem with press freedom, even for such independent publications, was related to the government's full control of the distribution of papers through its monopoly company, Tisak.[11]

Even though the legal system was nominally established on the model of a Western liberal democracy, Tuđman and the HDZ's influence in all spheres was undeniable. For instance, an extra-constitutional body created by Tuđman, the Council of Defense and National Security, resembled something like a *politburo* that often took over functions of the parliament. The judiciary was used to prosecute journalists for insulting the president, offending public morality, and exposing the state's top-secret documents (Malešević 2002: 229). Judges who challenged the HDZ's policy of interfering in the legislative system were quickly replaced. The minister of justice had broad discretionary powers over the appointment and removal of judicial personnel.[12]

The constitution initially was mostly democratic, although over time it was tailored to give Tuđman sweeping powers. Highly majoritarian electoral rules translated into great advantages for the ruling party. Although minority rights were guaranteed in the 1990 constitution under pressure from the West, they were seen as insufficient by most ethnic Serbs, even after a more comprehensive guarantee of rights was passed in the May 1992 Constitutional Law of Human Rights and Freedoms and the Rights of National and Ethnic Communities or Minorities (Bugajski 2002: 588). Moreover, the constitution proclaimed the newly independent state to be a state of ethnic Croats, which alienated the Serbian community. In practice, minority rights, especially those of ethnic Serbs, were trampled upon in every possible way.[13] The regime tolerated abuse of ethnic Serbs, and Serb refugees who wished to return faced serious bureaucratic and other obstacles (Karatnycky et al. 1999: 194).

A key instrument of Tuđman's rule was the use of the state security services. After being purged of ethnic Serbs, the state security apparatus was turned into an HDZ organ. It was used extensively to spy on and harass regime opponents, and it was rewarded with privileged access to state assets. Many of the HDZ's first members, in fact, were ethnic Croatian members of the former Yugoslav security services. The military, too, was subject to political control. Professional officers who dissented from the regime's position were fired and replaced with political loyalists (Ottaway 2003: 114).

Parliament (known as the Sabor) legislated as a democratic institution, at least when viewed from a distance. However, close examination reveals that HDZ supermajorities acted as a rubber stamp for policies dictated by Tuđman and other top HDZ officials. It was widely reported that Tuđman had a habit of intimidating any HDZ deputies thought to be straying from the government line (Kearns 1998: 252). Tuđman always personally chose the prime minister. In any case, Tuđman could in theory bypass the Sabor and legislate by decree, since the new constitution gave him such powers (Ottaway 2003: 114).

Civil society, virtually nonexistent under communism, was most evident in post-communist Croatia in the form of hundreds of externally financed nongovernmental organizations (NGOs). Some served the thousands of people affected by the war, while others were concerned with human rights and democracy. The government waged campaigns against those that criticized the regime, labeling them foreign lackeys and enemies of the state. They were also subject to unfair taxation and other bureaucratic obstacles. Yet, in the end NGOs were tolerated, as part of the broader strategy of simulating pluralism.[14]

The entrenched power of the HDZ and Franjo Tuđman did not rest on flawed democratic rules but rather on a host of other ways in which Croatia's rulers guaranteed their political power.

The First Elections

After the suppression of the 1971 Croatian Spring rebellion, there was a long period of political quiescence in Croatia, which became known within Yugoslavia as the "silent republic" (Bartlett 2003: 33).[15] The Croatian League of Communists (Savez Komunista Hrvatske, SKH) was among the most conservative in the Yugoslav federation, and dissent was dealt with harshly. Signs that change was imminent appeared in the late 1980s when Ivica Račan, a reformer, was elected leader of the SKH and added "Party of Democratic Change" to the SKH name. However, by this time the SKH was largely discredited for failing to bring Croatia out of economic crisis and to deal with the rising inter-republican conflict. The SKH had no choice but to call for free elections in 1990. This call, however, was hardly the result of popular pressure; rather, besides being a response to the advent of pluralism in neighboring Slovenia, it was also a last-ditch effort on the part of the SKH to seek a popular mandate for its rule.

Pluralism begat intense competition among emerging parties and personalities. Initially, there were liberal voices among the countless new political parties and groups, but over time they were edged out by those adopting nationalist positions. The first new party to be established in Croatia was the Croatian Social-Liberal Party (Hrvatska Socialno-Liberalna Stranka, HSLS). It was set up by Dražen Budiša and other anti-communist intellectuals from the Zagreb political scene (Bartlett 2003: 33). Soon afterwards, in June 1989, the HDZ was established by Franjo Tuđman, a former communist Partisan general-turned-dissident. His appeal was for national reconciliation in Croatian society, especially between former Partisans and supporters of the Ustaša regime. The other part of his platform called for the privileged position of Serbs in the state administration to be reversed. Besides finding a solid base in rural Croatia, the HDZ enjoyed strong support outside Croatia's borders, in places such as Canada, the United States, and Herzegovina (Bartlett 2003:

32). Over time, the HDZ's rhetoric became openly chauvinistic with regard to the ethnic question. Tuđman implied that republican borders would need to be revised in order to assure that all ethnic Croats were living in a Croatian state, claimed that Bosnian Muslims were actually ethnic Croats, and launched verbal attacks on Croatia's Serb minority (Bugajski 2002: 584). As Belgrade became increasingly confrontational and ethnic tensions inside Croatia increased, the HDZ broadened its constituency substantially using populist nationalism, so that by the time of the first elections it resembled a broad movement.[16]

As the HDZ and other parties came onto the political scene, a section of the Serb Krajina elite began to organize its own party, the SDS. Whipped up by reporting in the Serbian press that equated the HDZ with the wartime Ustaša (Bartlett 2003: 35) as well as by the HDZ's own divisive rhetoric, the SDS became openly hostile to the Croatian state. At first the SDS argued for full autonomy within Croatia, but over time it became a client of Milošević and nationalist politicians in Belgrade, and adopted a much more hard-line stance.

The first elections were held in April 1990 in an atmosphere of fervent nationalism buoyed by strong anti-Serb and anti-communist sentiment. More than 1,700 candidates vied for 356 seats in what was then a tricameral legislature (Bugajski 2002: 583). Three entities dominated the electoral competition: the HDZ, the SKH-SDP, and the centrist Coalition for National Understanding, made up of five major liberal parties. Several other parties ran independent of any coalition, notable among them the SDS. The HDZ won comfortably on its platform of national sovereignty, while liberal parties were marginalized. The HSLS-led Coalition for National Understanding did not succeed in winning any seats at all.

The ruling communists had clearly been unprepared for the renewed wave of nationalism mobilized by the HDZ and Belgrade. Ironically, the SKH had designed a majoritarian electoral system that was supposed to work in its favor. Actually, it worked in favor of opposition: the HDZ gained 55 of 80 seats in the Sabor, 206 out of 351 seats in all three chambers. The SDP, many of whose members had migrated to the HDZ, accepted the results and Croatia's new rulers could lay claim to democratic legitimacy.[17]

The HDZ at first argued for a confederal solution to Yugoslavia's problems, but independence was already on the mind of many, and soon the government's policy moved decisively in this direction. In May 1990, the new Sabor elected Franjo Tuđman as president, while Stjepan Mesić, the last head of the collective presidency of the former Yugoslavia, became prime minister. In December 1990, a new constitution was introduced declaring Croatia to be the homeland of the Croatian nation, a strong negative message to ethnic Serbs. The constitution also proclaimed the republic's sovereignty and right to secede from Yugoslavia and established a new bicameral parliament.

Along with the constitution, a new citizenship law was passed that allowed ethnic Croats living abroad to apply for citizenship (Bartlett 2003: 36). As a result, large numbers of ethnic Croats in neighboring Bosnia and Herzegovina became Croatian citizens, as did many others in the Americas and Australia. A much stricter law, by contrast, governed the citizenship rights of non-ethnic Croats. Moreover, the adoption of state symbols associated with the World War II–era fascist Ustaša regime further alienated ethnic Serbs. The new parliament also immediately set to work changing the names of streets and squares to make them more "Croatian" and proceeded to remove signs using the Cyrillic script from Serb-populated areas.

The preoccupation with sensitive state symbols, writes Bartlett (2003: 21), showed the political immaturity of the HDZ, while the lack of attention given to pressing matters of political and economic transition showed that the HDZ was driven by a populism that led people to believe that the Serbs were the cause of all of their woes, economic and otherwise. The new government dismissed many ethnic Serbs from the police, the judiciary, the media, and the educational system. Ethnic Serb managers were also dismissed, and small businesses were appropriated. Many Serbs were subject to officially sanctioned harassment that led them to leave their jobs and apartments, which were quickly taken over by Croats. Such policies pointed to the economic dimension of Croatian nationalism.

The response of the ethnic Serbs was the breakaway republic known as the Srpska Republika Krajina.[18] In August 1990, roadblocks were set up in Serb-populated areas of the Krajina (known in Croatian as the *revolucija balvana*, "revolution of the tree logs"), making travel and shipping between Zagreb and the Dalmatian coast very difficult. The Serbian secret police from Belgrade were instrumental in instigating and organizing the Krajina rebellion (Judah 1997: 170). Both sides began to arm themselves, and sporadic fighting erupted. Soon afterwards ultranationalist paramilitaries from Serbia entered the fray.

A referendum on independence was held in May 1991. Eighty-three percent of registered voters turned out for the plebiscite, and 93 percent voted in favor of independence. However, the Krajina Serbs refused to participate. Intervention by the EU and U.S. Secretary of State James Baker convinced Slovenia and Croatia to delay their calls for independence temporarily.

As the fighting escalated, Tuđman created a government of national unity that included the HDZ's communist adversaries. Yet, political options were also greatly constrained. The opposition was basically silenced despite its presence in parliament. Voices of peace and reason were sidelined. One example was the infamous killing by HDZ functionaries of Slavonian police commander Josip Reichl-Kir, who had put substantial effort into reassuring local Serbs that they would not be harmed.[19] Meanwhile, the Serbian-controlled Yugoslav National Army (Jugoslovenska Narodna Armija, JNA), acting in support of the Krajina Serbs, overran eastern Croatian lands and expelled the ethnic Croatian population. It also attacked coastal towns like Šibenik and Dubrovnik. Bugajski writes: "Serbia's intervention on behalf of the Knin insurgents caused the authorities in Zagreb to view the Krajina Serbs as puppets of Milošević rather than as citizens with legitimate concerns about their status. As a result, the Tuđman government was at first reluctant to negotiate seriously with the Serbs and unwilling to discuss the question of territorial autonomy—a discussion that Zagreb calculated would fuel 'Greater Serbian' irredentist pressures" (2002: 586).

The first major battle was fought for the eastern Slavonian city of Vukovar. It became a powerful symbol of Croatian resistance and the fight for independence. Ultimately, the fighting stopped under pressure from the international community, and the UN declared demilitarized zones in Krajina and Slavonia, but by this time Croatia had lost control of a third of its territory. The Serb militias were not disarmed, and continued to operate with impunity (Bartlett 2003: 34). Few ethnic Croat refugees returned, and the de facto division of the country became the status quo for the next three years. By December 1991, five thousand were reported dead, countless thousands were injured, and over a quarter million refugees had fled or were expelled from the conflict zones (Bugajski 2002: 588).

The outbreak of war had profound consequences for domestic politics. Political competition was curtailed, and the extremist wing of the HDZ was greatly strengthened and began to promote itself as the defender of Croatian sovereignty and interests. Later, this would be used to cover up economic mismanagement and quell political dissent. In becoming a justification for undemocratic politics, the war placed necessary political and economic reforms on the back burner. It was clear that certain elements within Croatia's new political establishment had a vested interest in war and, ultimately, were able to benefit from it materially. The best evidence for this is that there was negligible effort on the part of the HDZ to acquire the support of the country's Serb population (Bugajski 2002: 584). Bartlett observes:

> Critically for the future development of Croatia, the political parties had been unable to secure an accord between Serbs and Croats in the process of gaining independence. There was no Serb-Croat coalition in the pre–First World War tradition of Pribićević and Supilo, or in the wartime tradition of Hebrang. Rather, the forces of Croatian separatism gained ascendancy. Later on, Stipe Mesić was to say that one of the greatest mistakes of the new government was its failure to immediately make an alliance with the Serbian Democratic Party, which instead boycotted meetings of the *Sabor*. (2003: 37)

Despite the loss of territory and some controversy over his willingness to defend Vukovar, Franjo Tuđman emerged from the year of conflict as a powerful and popular leader (Bartlett 2003: 41). He moved quickly to marginalize the opposition and to curtail the power of the independent media, justifying these actions by saying that it was unrealistic to pursue economic reforms and allow criticism of the government in conditions of war (Pusić 1994: 386). In early 1992, he won a major victory when most of the international community decided to recognize a sovereign Croatian state. At the same time, however, over the objections of the HDZ, a United Nations Protection Force (UNPROFOR) of 14,000 troops was dispatched to the conflict areas.

The early transition took place in conditions of uncertainty and resurgent nationalism. Although liberal options competed on the political scene, they were ultimately crowded out by the politics and rhetoric of nationalism. That which had been competition over material resources turned into divisive ethnic competition. In such conditions, political and economic reform was hardly discussed, and nationalist populism became the legitimizing principle of the post-communist regime.

Subsequent Elections and Party Politics

The 1992 and 1995 Elections

In 1992, the HDZ announced the suspension of the national unity coalition and called for new elections in order to capitalize on postwar popularity.

New electoral rules were instituted that included a mixed majoritarian system. This reversion turned out to be a shrewd tactic—the HDZ was riding a wave of popularity, and the opposition entered parliament fragmented into a number of small parties. The elections were held against the backdrop of lost territory, the outbreak of war in neighboring Bosnia and Herzegovina, and a sense of vulnerability and uncertainty. Not surprisingly, voters rallied around the government. The HDZ was returned to power with 44 percent of the vote, much more than the second-largest party, the HSLS. This was sufficient under the mixed electoral system to ensure an absolute majority of seats. A new government was formed and led by Prime Minister Hrvoje Šarinić.

The opposition was fragmented, with the largest opposition party, the HSLS, gaining only 17 percent of the vote and just over 10 percent of the seats. The reformed communist SDP gained only 11 seats, having lost support of the moderate Serbs in the Krajina, who now had their own administration. The center-left Croatian People's Party (Hrvatska Narodna Stranka, HNS) got six seats, while the far-right Croatian Party of Rights (Hrvatska Stranka Prava, HSP) and the agrarian Croatian Peasant Party (Hrvatska Seljačka Stranka, HSS) gained three seats each. The Serbian People's Party (Srpska Narodna Stranka, SNS), representing urban Serbs, got three seats. Thus, parties with clearly authoritarian inclinations captured over 50 percent of the vote. Parties with nominally democratic programs (if untested liberal credentials) won the remaining vote.

Presidential elections were also held in 1992. Unlike before, the president was elected by popular vote. Tuđman claimed a clear victory with 57 percent of the vote. In a subsequent election for the Upper House (Dom Županija, "House of Counties") and for local governments in 1993, the HDZ maintained preeminence, though with lower numbers than before (Bartlett 2003: 35). The main beneficiaries of the local elections were Dražen Budiša's HSLS and the HSS. In Istria, the Istrian Democratic Party (Istarski Demokratski Sabor, IDS) emerged as the most powerful force and began to argue for a greater degree of regional autonomy, making it a principal enemy of the HDZ, who feared that Italy was coveting its former territories. Thus, despite the HDZ's dominance in domestic politics, the local elections showed that there was an impetus in the public for more liberal politics. Many still trusted the HDZ to provide security and promote nationalist issues and thus voted for it at the national level, even as they voted for the opposition in local elections.[20]

Nevertheless, after 1992 the HDZ was firmly entrenched in power. As a party, it still represented a broad but tenuous coalition of various elements within the nationalist movement. The key to future policy lay in the elements that could consolidate their domination over the party, and by 1993 it was clear that the extremist wing had done so.[21]

The elections of 1992 and 1993 did show, on one hand, that pluralism in the form of multiparty competition had taken root in Croatia. On the other hand, it was also clear that the HDZ was willing to use unfair tactics to make sure that it would retain power. The HDZ did achieve some domestic policy successes, among them an economic stabilization program that brought inflation under control and the acquisition of aid from international financial institutions. Marko Škreb was declared to be the best central banker in Eastern Europe. Things looked quite good for the ruling party, while the opposition was in disarray (Bartlett 2003: 46). Yet, one-third of the country's territory was in open rebellion without representatives in central government organs, while hundreds of thousands of Croatian citizens were displaced from their homes, creating serious legitimacy problems for the regime.

The regime's subsequent policy of open confrontation and half-concealed territorial ambitions in Herzegovina[22] propelled the right wing elements within the HDZ to the top and simultaneously moved the regime in the direction of authoritarianism.[23] Dozens of moderate HDZ members left the party in protest of its decision to pursue armed conflict with the Bosnian Muslims in the hopes of creating a Greater Croatia. The policy also created dilemmas for Croatia's international relations: whereas before Tuđman could portray Croatia as the victim of Serbian aggression, now it was clear that Croatia itself had become an aggressor.[24]

The regime had a choice on how to deal with the Krajina para-state. It could have sought to negotiate with the Serbs to peacefully reintegrate them into the country with guarantees of rights and autonomy. This option became increasingly feasible as Milošević withdrew Belgrade's support for the rebels. However, Tuđman and the HDZ were deeply resentful of UNPROFOR's presence in the country and what they saw as the international community's effort to maintain the status quo, effectively legitimizing an illegal breakaway entity (Bartlett 2003: 47). Moreover, any recognition of Serbian autonomy would have seriously hurt the HDZ in the eyes of its supporters, many of whom clearly wanted the Serb problem to be solved in a less accommodating way.

The ultimate choice to launch an all-out offensive against the Krajina rebels reflected not only these interests but also deepening anti-Serb sentiment in international public opinion following the notorious massacre in Srebrenica, Bosnia and Herzegovina in the summer of 1995.[25] This led to two major military operations dubbed Storm (Oluja) and Flash (Blijesak) in late summer 1995 in which the Croatian Army (Hrvatsko Vojsko, HV) recaptured all of the lost territories in a matter of days. The Krajina Serbs had been alerted to the impending action and organized columns of refugees that became one of the largest movements of people in recent European history. The JNA did nothing to help them.[26] As for the Tuđman regime, it claimed that it had urged the Serbs to remain—that they would not be harmed or arrested as long as they were not war criminals. This fact notwithstanding, many war crimes were committed by the Croatian Army and documented by human rights organizations.[27] The "liberation" of the Krajina, then, was to become a major liability for Croatia down the road, both in terms of accounting for war crimes against Serb civilians and implementing very unpopular refugee return policies.[28] It also had profound demographic consequences: Croatia was now a much more homogenous nation with a population over 90 percent Catholic and Croat.

The domestic political consequences of Storm and Flash were a boon to Tuđman and the HDZ. Bartlett writes: "Croatia was swept by a tide of euphoria and celebration. Tuđman traveled to Knin and in a masterly stroke of propaganda kissed the Croatian flag flying from the battlements of the medieval Knin castle, which had been the seat of the medieval Croatian King Tomislav, and had an enormous symbolic importance for the new Croatian state. Tuđman was at the pinnacle of his power and popularity. Had he left office at that point, he may well have been remembered as a national hero" (2003: 47). Tuđman's position was further strengthened with the Dayton Agreement and the end of the war in Bosnia.[29] Confident of international support and buoyed by talk of NATO accession, Tuđman moved to strengthen the position of the HDZ further, and an effort to construct a cult of personality around him as the "father of the nation" was also under way. The right wing had triumphed within the party, and the democratic opposition was marginalized. Questioning the motives of the regime was tantamount to questioning the supremacy of national issues and the achievement of Croatian sovereignty, and no political group was willing to do so.

New elections were called a year early, at the end of 1995, once again to capitalize on the HDZ's popularity. In what was now a pattern of behavior by the ruling party, the electoral rules were adjusted to favor the HDZ. Now, out of a total of 127 seats, 80 were allocated by proportional representation, 28 according to majoritarian constituencies in the counties, and seven seats were reserved for national minorities.[30] The number of seats reserved for ethnic Serbs was reduced from 13 to 3, a final symbolic removal of Krajina Serbs from political life. In addition, 12 seats were reserved for non-resident diaspora Croats, a guaranteed HDZ constituency. Enfranchising the Herzegovina Croats magnified their political influence.

The HDZ returned to power with an overall 45 percent of the vote and a majority of 75 seats in the 127-seat parliament, which was also enough votes to amend the constitution (Karatnycky et al. 1999: 177). The HDZ won 21 of the 28 single-member constituencies and, as expected, all 12 of the diaspora seats. Research showed that the HDZ did particularly well in poorer rural areas and in areas affected by the war. It also attracted large numbers of votes from older and less educated people (Kasapović 2001: 83).

However, taking into account the timing of the election, the wild popularity of the HDZ, and its profound advantages in terms of organizational and media resources, the liberal and pro-Western opposition parties actually fared quite well, winning a total of 45 seats. Some opposition parties felt emboldened to criticize the HDZ and its top leaders for their accumulation of wealth at the expense of the masses of people. The opposition did best in larger cities such as Zagreb, Rijeka, and Split, and the liberal IDS won the majority of votes in Istria (Kasapović 2001: 123).

These results and other developments following the end of the war indicated that at least part of the public was unwilling to tolerate authoritarianism and international isolation. When the HDZ lost control of the Zagreb city council during the same elections, Tuđman reacted with a heavy hand, refusing to recognize the results. He vetoed the opposition choice of mayor four times, saying that the capital city could not be turned over to "enemies of the state," and a political crisis erupted. The crisis lasted over a year, until finally Tuđman prevailed and appointed his own nominee for the post. In the end, however, the Constitutional Court ruled in the opposition's favor.

The regime's abuse of power was again demonstrated in November 1996 when the government attempted to shut down the popular independent Zagreb radio station Radio 101 (Bartlett 2003: 62). This move outraged the citizens of Zagreb, who turned out for a 100,000 strong protest against the curtailment of media freedom. Tuđman was able to overcome the protest, which he labeled the work of foreigners, but in many ways it signaled the beginning of the end for the HDZ, especially among the urban classes.[31] The middle and educated classes were to become increasingly frustrated with the country's obvious distance from Europe compared to the other transition countries and more and more hostile to the Herzegovinians and other rural refugees and migrants who were not only changing the character of Croatia's cities but also exercising disproportionate influence in public life and the economy.[32] Many were also outraged at the regime's use of various security services for political purposes.[33]

With the war over, all Croatian citizens began to turn their attention to issues like economic improvement. Things did get better for a while but then in 1998 began to take a decisive turn for the worse. The lack of progress in reform was now quite evident, and the HDZ regime found it harder to play the national security card to justify these deficiencies. Instead, it began to point the finger at Western embassies and the NGOs they funded as the latest enemies of Croatian sovereignty. Although authoritarianism began to look increasingly anachronistic (Bartlett 2003: 72), a growing number of people in the HDZ had a vested interest in ensuring the survival of a single-party authoritarian state because of their material interest in the prevailing order. The opposition, however, continued to suffer from disunity, which was mainly the consequence of disputes among various personalities and egos.

As HDZ-style authoritarianism continued into the late 1990s and the economy went downhill, it was evident that Croatia was being left out of the process of Euro-Atlantic integration. Tuđman nonetheless continued to toe a pro-Western line at home as the press reported his meetings with various Western dignitaries. However, the state-controlled press did not report that at these meetings Croatia was being chided for its democratic deficiencies. When news of outside criticism did make it into the Croatian media, the regime responded by branding critics enemies of Croatian statehood or accused the EU of wanting to recreate Yugoslavia with its "regional" approach to integration. The latter line of attack worked quite well in raising Euroskepticism among some Croatians, at least for a time.

However, there were limits to this strategy, and opposition parties could increasingly point to the international isolation brought upon Croatia by the HDZ and affirm their own pro-Western credentials, especially when Western governments and organizations began to support regime change in Zagreb openly. Thus, in the process, parties like the communist successor SDP became enthusiastic pro-Europeans not so much by virtue of a long history of internationalism but because it had become an expedient source of political capital and outside support at the time. Over time, of course, this tool became a responsibility (and even a liability) as power came within their grasp and expectations of EU and NATO membership rose.

Tuđman as an individual remained popular and won the 1997 presidential elections with 61 percent of the vote. However, his deteriorating health and the preeminence of the Herzegovina wing and tycoon capitalists in the party apparatus meant that daily policy was often outside of his direct grasp.[34] Strong links continued to be maintained between ministries in Zagreb and political leaders in Herzegovina, and the owners and managers of many prominent Zagreb firms were HDZ insiders from Herzegovina. This was well known and widely reviled: indeed, by the end of the 1990s, Herzegovina had become a political liability for Zagreb. One opinion poll conducted by the Croatian weekly *Globus* in 1998 showed that more than 80 percent of respondents said that Herzegovinians ruled the country and should be held responsible for all of its social, economic, and political problems (quoted in Oh 2003: 15).

Thus, while the HDZ may have enjoyed broad support at the beginning of transition, by the second half of the 1990s the urban educated classes had largely abandoned ship. However, it would take more than this part of society to remove the HDZ from power. To win the other part, the economic situation would have to deteriorate drastically, which, with the onset of a deep recession in 1998 and the collapse of a number of important regional banks, then happened. Unemployment and poverty rates rose steadily, real incomes declined, and income inequality increased. A general strike held in early 1998 spoke volumes about the public mood: eighty thousand took to the streets to protest the government's social and economic policies (Oh 2003: 17). Graffiti scrawled during this period on the pension administration near my apartment in Zagreb read, "Tito! Give Us Back Our Pensions!" invoking memories of better economic times under his rule.

The pursuit of partial economic reform and the deficiencies of Croatia's initial conditions had come back to haunt the regime. For years, despite gains in macroeconomic stabilization, little structural reform had taken place. Privatization was a cover for protectionist policies that ensured the interests of HDZ-affiliated tycoon capitalists who were more interested in increasing their personal wealth, stripping assets, and engaging in conspicuous consumption than in pursuing productive accumulation.[35]

It was in the context of economic downturn, international pressure, and a unifying opposition that the HDZ lost support in the last two years of the 1990s. The death of ailing President Tuđman in November 1999 was also the symbolic death of the HDZ, at least as an anti-systemic nationalist party. Elections held in January 2000 dealt a resounding victory to a coalition of pro-Western liberal opposition parties.

The Role of Franjo Tuđman

In order to understand the first post-communist Croatian regime, one must understand the biography, personality, and role of its main protagonist, the late president Franjo Tuđman.[36] In World War II, Tuđman had fought with the Partisans and subsequently became a major general in the JNA. He later earned a controversial doctorate in history and in the 1960s became the director of Croatia's Institute for the History of the Workers' Movement.[37] Tuđman was also on the Executive Committee of Matica Hrvatska, a dissident organization that reexamined recent Croatia history based on new data and challenged sensitive doctrines about World War II, moving into direct conflict with the basic tenets of Titoist Yugoslavism. Consequently, Tuđman was imprisoned and stripped of his military rank, giving him instant fame as a Croatian patriot.

After leaving prison, Tuđman continued to write revisionist accounts of modern Croatian history and also began cultivating relationships with the anti-communist Croatian diaspora. As the Croatian sociologist Žarko Puhovski explained to me, it was not necessarily easy for him to enlist the right wing émigré community since they were inherently distrustful of a man who had been one of Tito's generals.[38] Thus, Tuđman was forced to prove his nationalist credentials, and did so by making extremist statements such as his since-infamous assertion that he was glad his wife was neither a Serb nor a Jew. In the late 1980s he was actively raising funds for a new political party and propagating the doctrine of unity among Croats of different political convictions and familial political histories.

In 1989 the HDZ was founded; from the beginning it had many émigré anti-communist dissidents among its core members. Croatian diaspora communities happily showered Tuđman and the new party with millions of dollars, unaware that some of these funds were being used by their compatriots in the homeland to build villas and buy yachts.[39]

Tuđman surrounded himself with all the wrong kinds of advisers, mainly ultranationalist members of the diaspora and corrupt local opportunists. He struck shady deals with international arms dealers and the ostensible enemy—Slobodan Milošević's Serbia—itself. It is by now a well-documented fact that Milošević and Tuđman made secret plans to divide Bosnia and Herzegovina between them, and some accounts even claim that Tuđman was ready to sacrifice Vukovar and other frontline towns in exchange for other territories.

Tuđman was described by many who knew him as a man with clear authoritarian and megalomaniacal tendencies.[40] He surrounded himself with blind loyalists and quickly punished dissent. In the public sphere, he gradually established a personality cult that portrayed him as the father of the nation. Tuđman's pictures and posters were to be found in every corner of Croatia, and songs were written depicting him as a prince or king. Some textbooks compared him (in a positive light) to the wartime Ustaša leader Ante Pavelić (Malešević 2002: 199), and official propaganda emphasized the need for a strongman in Croatia (Bugajski 2002: 597).

The Croatian president also indulged in nepotism. Tuđman appointed his son, Miroslav, to several important positions, including chief of the Croatian secret service. His daughter, Nevenka, and his grandson, Dejan, overnight became owners of several banks, supermarket chains, and other businesses. Similarly, the relatives of the highly influential minister of defense, Gojko Šušak, were given many influential posts in various ministries and the state administration (Malešević 2002: 230).

The HDZ regime, then, was characterized in large part by the charismatic authority of President Tuđman, who enjoyed popular support even as his party faltered. Yet, the pervasive sense of relief felt by many after his death[41] and the fact that only one foreign head of state attended his funeral spoke volumes about his legacy.

The Main Parties and Their Orientations:
The HDZ and the Right Wing

The HDZ's policies reflected to a large degree the preferences of its "extremist wing," as this was the faction of the party that gained prominence in the early 1990s and comprised the party's administrative apparatus. Many within Croatia saw it as a "movement" much more than a party in the classic sense (Čular 2000: 35). This is justified to the extent that the HDZ was from the beginning a collection of many disparate elements that united for electoral purposes. In this sense, Oh (2003) notes that Tuđman's goal to unite the domestic left wing and nationalist diaspora succeeded, but this did not mean that the HDZ's policies reflected a compromise among its various ideological persuasions. Instead, as noted above, the right wing of the party took control for most of the 1990s. Yet a careful examination of its program and policies also reveals many ideological inconsistencies and contradictions, perhaps a result of its internal diversity. The HDZ party program, for instance, incorporated references to democracy, Catholicism, historicism, national reconciliation, economic reform, a statist economy, unification with Herzegovina, Europe, and independence.

The founders of the HDZ were motivated by both nationalism and anticommunism. Some were veterans of the Croatian Spring rebellion who had fallen out with the SKH. Others were SKH members who opposed the official pro-Belgrade stance. Still others were members of the nationalist diaspora, political émigrés or their descendants from the fallen Independent State of Croatia (Nezavisna Država Hrvatska, NDH). Thus, there were, at least initially, very different understandings within the HDZ of modern Croatian history, which Oh (2003) argues actually helped deepen divisions in Croatian society rather than overcome them. In terms of intra-party affairs, Oh observes that it was very difficult to coordinate these different viewpoints, so the party became increasingly centralized.

The right wing of the party was disproportionately made up of the "Herzegovinian lobby" that came to hold major sway over policy in the mid-1990s. Among its best-known members were Vladimir Šeks and the hard-line defense minister Gojko Šušak. Šušak was an émigré Croat from Canada but had roots in Herzegovina, parts of which are overwhelmingly Croat and poor and have close historical ties to Croatia proper. It is no surprise, then, that the party program called for the "territorial integrity of the Croat nation within its historical and natural borders" (quoted in Oh 2003: 9). Herzegovinians were all but promised reunification with Croatia. At the other extreme of the party were the left-oriented elements that had abandoned the defunct SKH. Prominent members of this wing, such as Stjepan Mesić, left the party early in opposition to Tuđman's Bosnia policy. The third wing of the party was made up of managers, technocrats, and government officials who did not make major decisions on policy but simply carried out orders and knew how to deal with Westerners. Ideologically, they were moderates who tempered some of the regime's anti-Western leanings. Yet they did not leave the party even when they disagreed with its policies because they often had vested material interests in remaining a part of it. Former foreign minister Mate Granić belonged to this wing. In general, the moderate and left wings prevailed in executive positions (except for Defense and Interior), while the right wing dominated the party apparatus (Oh 2003: 14).

The HDZ initially attracted a broad following, but many from the urban and educated classes stopped supporting it in 1996. This left the HDZ with a strong base of unskilled workers, pensioners, the unemployed, and others who were promised a better life in a sovereign Croatia and in European structures. However, these people abandoned the party once they realized that living standards were declining rather than increasing and that Europe had closed the door to the Tuđman regime.

The policies of the right wing of the HDZ, moreover, were not far removed from those of other ultranationalist groups on the political scene, such as the HSP, whose share of the vote in parliamentary elections increased throughout the 1990s and beyond.[42] Irvine (1997: 3) has identified the following seven characteristics of the Croatian Right:

1. An insistence on the historical continuity of the Croatian state and the state-building accomplishments of the interwar Ustaša fascist movement and the independent NDH.[43]
2. An emphasis on achieving Croatian independence through military means.
3. The establishment of a strong authoritarian or semi-authoritarian state.
4. Territorial expansion into Croatia's "historical, natural, and ethnic borders."
5. A struggle for survival against "natural enemies."
6. A conservative social policy based on close ties with the Roman Catholic Church.[44]
7. An isolationist foreign policy based on anti-liberal and anti-Western views.

What differentiated the HSP and other right wing groups from the ruling HDZ? To some degree, the political ambitions of individual leaders set the parties apart. Later in the 1990s, the HSP began to criticize the HDZ for its

alleged corruption and willingness to concede to Western demands. Moreover, the HSP was able to push the debate further to the right with editorials
in the state-controlled press.

One key characteristic of the HDZ was its anti-Western orientation. This
was not an outright rejection: HDZ officials never rejected the prospect of EU
membership, for instance, and in fact continued to insist that they would
bring Croatia into European structures. Further, the posts of foreign minister
and various ambassadorships were given to individuals who put a democratic
face on the regime. However, in its domestic rhetoric and in its policies, the
HDZ displayed a deep ambivalence toward Western norms, as Irvine has argued: "The liberalism spawned by the West, [the Croatian nationalists] argue,
has failed to speak to the spiritual nature of man and his need to understand
himself in the context of a particular community or nation; only the particu-
larity of the nation gives meaning to the life of the individual. The specificity
of the Croat nation and its unique mission provide individual Croats with a
sense of their true and satisfying mission in the world" (1997: 7). At times this
ambivalence was expressed by the HDZ as a profound suspicion of the West,
despite the HDZ's emphasis on Croatia as a bulwark of Western Christianity
and European civilization against the East. UNPROFOR was portrayed as an
occupying force, and Western demands were said to be incompatible with
Croatian national values. The HDZ's anti-Western stance came to constitute
a main factor distinguishing it from the opposition parties, who by the end of
the 1990s were expressing a clear desire to cooperate with the West and work
toward meeting the conditions necessary to enter the EU and other Western
organizations.

The HDZ's economic policy, on the other hand, was unclear. In its official
program, the HDZ declared support for market mechanisms and institutions,
yet it also advocated strong state involvement in the economy and other populist measures. In practice, although a certain degree of economic reform was
carried out, serious structural reform was avoided and privatization was carried out in such a way as to benefit and reward HDZ loyalists, a practice that
propelled the Croatian economy to crisis at the end of the 1990s.

Although the HDZ had a rhetorical and at times procedural commitment
to liberal democracy, there were elements within the party who questioned
the benefits of democratic institutions.[45] One such individual was Mladen
Schwartz, a member of Tuđman's inner circle: "Democracy has its positive
characteristics. I would be mad to deny that. However, there are limitations

to democracy and that is why we must look for alternatives. I think that in this day and age, democracy will not benefit the Croatian nation and I am prepared to present arguments in support of that" (quoted in Malešević 2002: 43; see also Schwartz 2000). Tuđman, as might be expected, occasionally reigned in such rhetoric in fear of alienating Western diplomats and observers.[46]

The Main Parties and Their Orientations: The Opposition

On the left of the political spectrum lay the SDP, the successor to the defunct SKH. Although by the end of the 1990s it had become the most popular opposition party, it did not really have democratic credentials. However, its decision to adopt a pro-Western tone and accept Western support put it firmly in the democratic camp. The SDP was led by Ivica Račan, a reformer within the former SKH. Though not known for his charisma or interpersonal skills, he was nonetheless a skilled politician. The SDP's program reflected social democratic values, though once in power after January 2000 its actual economic program was quite neoliberal in scope.[47] In the early 1990s, the SDP was totally discredited and operated on the margins of political life, gaining a modest number of seats in local and national elections. It focused on narrow concerns, such as labor union activity, and quietly regrouped. The SDP's political opening came at the end of the 1990s, when the economy was in crisis and support for the HDZ fell precipitously. It was then that the SDP seized on the opportunity to promote a pro-European agenda. However, an ongoing problem for the SDP was coalition building: several other parties in the democratic camp were wary or outright hostile to participating in a coalition with the former communists. It was only when public opinion shifted in favor of the SDP and Western organizations began to engineer an opposition coalition that this could be overcome.

The HSLS, as noted above, was formed by former participants in the 1971 Croatian Spring. It was a centrist party made up of both conservative and more leftist elements. It initially attracted the votes of educated people interested in developing civil society and free enterprise and bringing Croatia into Europe. The conservative wing was led by Dražen Budiša, the ex-dissident and well-known politician. Budiša was more interested in dealing with national issues than pragmatic issues of economic and political reform. As a result, the HSLS split into two factions in January 1998 following a bitter dispute between Vlado Gotovac, leader of a more left-leaning group, and the more conservative Budiša. The dispute was over the decision of some HSLS deputies to cooperate with HDZ, a move opposed by Gotovac. Gotovac and his followers left HSLS to form the Liberal Party (Liberalna Stranka, LS) and announced that they were willing to cooperate with other groups to oust the HDZ (Kearns 1998: 252). From that point on, the LS consistently attracted a loyal base of urban, educated voters. The party's program was centered on ending HDZ rule (Bugajski 2002: 605).

To the left of the LS in economic terms was the HNS. It was organized after the 1990 elections by Savka Dabčević-Kučar, who had been Croatia's premier in the 1960s but was later removed from office for her involvement in the Croatian Spring (Bugajski 2002: 601). The HNS demanded a free press and the rule of law and advocated equal rights for all citizens and the protection of ethnic and cultural minorities and social groups with special needs. It was also pro-Western in its orientation. The HNS experienced some notable defections in 1992 and 1995, when some prominent members left to join the HDZ. However, it continued to play an important role as part of the democratic opposition.

The HSS, led by Zlatko Tomčić, was another democratic opposition party that garnered a respectable number of seats in parliamentary elections. The HSS could claim to be the oldest political party in Croatia, having been originally established in 1904 by two brothers, Ante Radić and Stjepan Radić.[48] It was an extremely influential force in Croatian and Yugoslav politics during the 1930s and was outlawed by the Ustaša fascists in World War II. The party's platform was democratic and pro-market but also advocated social welfare for the disadvantaged, especially for small farmers, which gave it a populist edge (Agh 1998: 195). It had a clear sense of Croatian national identity without engaging in the exclusivist rhetoric and policies of the HDZ.

Several regional groupings also were part of the democratic opposition. The most important in terms of membership figures and electoral influence was the IDS. Established in 1990 in the city of Pula and led by Ivan Jakovčić, it adopted a strongly regional position, stating that the central government should deal with issues such as the army, the police, finances, and foreign policy, and leave the rest to regional governments. This platform was based on the belief that the highly centralized HDZ regime did not recognize uniquely Istrian regional interests, and especially the rights of its sizeable Italian minority (Bugajski 2002: 620). In particular, it backed economic self-determination and close economic ties with Slovenia and Italy, which undoubtedly reflected its advanced economic status and close historical ties to

Italy and Slovenian Istria. For this reason, it also adopted a decisive pro-EU position.

The IDS remained troubled by the HDZ's national chauvinism and xenophobia, arguing that the regime's emphasis on nationality would undermine Istria's multiethnic character. Instead, it advocated a state that respected the rights of all of its citizens regardless of nationality, religion, race, or language. Not surprisingly, the IDS came into direct and fierce conflict with the HDZ, which included it on its ever-growing list of "enemies of the state." Later, when the IDS received support from the Italian right, the HDZ claimed that the IDS's activities constituted irredentist agitation (Bugajski 2002: 621). The IDS had strong showings in local elections, tending to win over 70 percent of the vote in Istria.

The Main Parties and Their Orientations: Ethnic Minority Parties

A number of ethnic minority parties also were part of the democratic opposition, among them small groupings representing Croatia's Hungarian, Roma, and Slavic Muslims. Given the size of the ethnic Serb minority, however, the parties representing it were the most important. Three Serb parties emerged in the 1990s. The first was the SDS, which was formed in the town of Knin in 1989. Led by Jovan Rašković, the SDS aimed to acquire extensive rights for Croatia's ethnic Serbs. After the HDZ came to power in the 1990 elections, the SDS concluded that Croatian Serbs must seek some kind of institutionalized autonomy in order to assure their rights (Bugajski 2002: 616). However, the SDS did not give much time or energy to its promise to negotiate with Zagreb and work within the parliamentary system. Shortly after the April-May 1990 elections, it pulled its five deputies out of the Sabor and embarked on the road of confrontation. The party became increasingly radicalized such that Rašković, who had shown some willingness to compromise with Zagreb, was replaced by the radical nationalist Milan Babić, who forged close ties with Slobodan Milošević and the JNA. In December 1991, Babić and his associates unilaterally declared the Republic of Serbian Krajina (Republika Srpska Krajina, RSK), and ruled the region in the style of a civilian-military dictatorship from then on.

Babić and his followers wanted to push for quick unification with Serbia, but Milošević, fearful of an extended war and international sanctions, exerted intense pressure on the Krajina Serbs to delay such a move. Belgrade later succeeded in replacing Babić with Goran Hadžić, who negotiated with

Zagreb and the UN to establish a UN protectorate in the occupied areas of Croatia. This status quo prevailed until 1995, with the SDS firmly entrenched in power and its leaders enriching themselves through various forms of war profiteering. After the 1995 military operations against the RSK, the SDS ceased to play a part in the Croatian political scene.

In sharp contrast to the SDS, the Serbian Democratic Forum (Srpski Demokratski Forum, SDF) and SNS were interested in the politics of accommodation. They represented mainly urban, educated Serbs, since the SDS really had managed to rally only Serbs in Krajina. The SNS acted as a forum for Serbs who regarded Croatia as their homeland and concerned itself mainly with cultural and representational issues (Bugajski 2002: 615). Its extremely conciliatory tone toward the blatantly anti-Serb HDZ led many to charge that it was merely a creation of the Tuđman regime, designed to counter the radical demands of the Krajina separatists and show a democratic face to the West. While it is true that the SNS leadership shirked from asserting Serb rights for fear of retribution, it did at times criticize the HDZ government for encouraging discrimination against Croatian Serbs.[49] The SDF, by contrast, criticized both the SNS for acting as a HDZ front organization and the regime for its blatant disregard for the rights of Serbs and tried to build ties with Serbian intellectuals in the Krajina.

In sum, the first ten years of Croatia's post-communist transition were dominated by illiberal political configurations with a radical populist and anti-systemic agenda. Though the HDZ comprised more moderate elements as well, it was for the most part run by the extremist wing. However, liberal, pro-systemic parties were very much part of the political scene, particularly in the second half of the 1990s. They managed to win around 40 percent of the vote in the 1992 and 1995 elections, kept a check on the regime's more extreme tendencies, and were waiting as a liberal alternative when the HDZ faltered.

Loci of Political Conflict

Offe (1984) and Linz and Stepan (1996) concur that liberal democracy presupposes the existence of stable borders and a consensus on who should live in them. Throughout the 1990s, the main loci of political conflict reflected deep divisions over basic questions about the nature of the Croatian state. The existence of these divisions lowered liberal content and signaled significant impediments to the development of a substantive democracy. Divisions were reflected in an extremely polarized political scene, one in which labels like "communist," "fascist," "Ustaša," and "Bleiberg murderer" were tossed about freely.[50] One conflict was over the very definition of the Croatian state, whether it should be constituted as one of ethnic Croats or as one of all its citizens. It was the HDZ's decision to opt for the former that ultimately helped lead to the Krajina Serbs' refusal to recognize an independent Croatian state and attempt to secede.

Croatian elites and the public were also deeply divided over Croatia's place in Europe, with the internationalist democratic opposition advocating full Western integration based on meeting liberal norms and the HDZ and its nationalist allies arguing that meeting such norms would compromise Croatia's sovereignty and Croatian "national values." The Roman Catholic Church was often used to justify the latter.

The HDZ found its strongest support in the countryside, while the constituency of the democratic opposition, meanwhile, resided primarily in urban areas. The urban-rural divide, in turn, corresponded to the kinds of sharp regional economic differences within Croatia, and to some degree it also corresponded to a split in society over democracy itself, with just 50 percent of respondents to a survey saying that democracy is always the best system and over one quarter responding that a strong leader is necessary (Čular 2000: 42).

Despite Tuđman's mission to unite the supporters and opponents of the NDH, divisions over Croatia's recent history continued to matter a great deal. Just as Tito had temporarily frozen such differences through political authoritarianism and a commitment to Yugoslav unity, so did the Tuđman regime gloss over such painful divisions in deference to the larger state-building task. The divisions were to reemerge after 2000, when the HDZ lost power. As Tomac (1992: 61) has written, Croatia was a country where World War II was not over, at least in terms of fighting between the right-wing émigrés and home-based leftist Partisans.[51]

The HDZ and the Politics of War

Nearly a decade after the end of armed hostilities on Croatian soil, a large body of evidence points to the many ways in which the HDZ regime used war to its political and material advantage.[52] From the very beginning of the war, HDZ insiders in Croatia and Herzegovina profited handsomely from war-related activities such as the smuggling of arms and other contraband. Bićanić

(2001: 169) writes that the decision to purchase arms with no transparency opened the door to widespread corruption and war profiteering and forged a close link among politicians, arms dealers, smugglers, and other underworld figures. Politicians, in turn, remained hostages to these interests. After the war, veterans were given a number of exclusive benefits, such as the right to import cars duty-free, which turned them into a loyal HDZ constituency. Veterans' groups were used as virtual front organizations for the HDZ, which mobilized ex-soldiers and their allies to protest any internal and external regime critics, saying that they were undermining the sanctity of the Homeland War. The Homeland War is said to have lasted from 1991–1995, though the actual fighting, fierce as it was, occurred only at the beginning and the end of the conflict, when the Croatian Army crushed the Krajina rebels in late summer 1995.[53] This does not mean that the impact of the war was not felt in daily life, even in regions where there was no fighting. Economic production fell to half of prewar levels and refugees flooded into Croatia from Bosnia every day, filling every hotel and sports complex.[54]

The negative political, economic, and social repercussions of the Homeland War notwithstanding, it ultimately was used by the HDZ as the key component of a larger myth about the founding of the post-Yugoslav Croatian state, a myth in which Tuđman and his party defended Croatian nationhood against various enemies, thereby facilitating the creation of an independent Croatia and fulfilling the Croats' "thousand-year old dream." The HDZ's portrayal of the Homeland War was one of a cleanly fought battle of national liberation, which strayed greatly from the reality of the war and the way in which it was conducted. This view of the war nonetheless became a key source of its legitimacy. In the late 1990s, as the economy failed and Croatia was left out of the process of Western integration, the doctrine of the Homeland War arguably became the HDZ's *only* source of political capital. Yet sources of legitimacy are not equal in terms of their ability to elicit public sympathy, and issues of the nation and state creation are always powerful in mobilizing support, especially when memories of war are fresh. As such the democratic opposition for a long time found it quite hard to match the strength of this appeal. Once, after the HDZ performed poorly in local elections, Tuđman declared that the election showed that "all enemies of the HDZ are also enemies of the sovereign Croatian state," one of countless such pronouncements (quoted in Malešević 2002: 233). The use of such rhetoric allowed the HDZ regime to turn each election into a plebiscite on Croatian independence, creating an atmosphere of nationalist fervor that put the opposition in an impossible position (Ottaway 2003: 117). Questioning the conduct of the war, after all, meant questioning the way in which the independent Croatian state had been created.

The war was also used in electoral politics. The point was made in an earlier section that elections were called to coincide with successful military maneuvers: the reverse may also be true, that military offensives were planned to coincide with upcoming elections (Ottaway 2003: 117). Most prominently, the war was used as Tudman's justification for illiberal practices, reflected in his 1993 comments in response to domestic and international calls for greater democracy. "We have democracy," he said, "and in our war conditions we even have too much of it. We are even allowing some anarchy but of course we will have full freedom and total democracy when we liberate every inch of land" (quoted in Kearns 1998: 247). When every inch of land *was* liberated, Tudman did not keep his promise, and the authoritarian practices of the HDZ continued.

The International Dimension of the Croatian Transition

Croatia had historically been pulled in different directions with regard to its international relations: on one hand, it had long been part of two South Slav unions, and yet also had a coast with a strong Mediterranean orientation. Large parts of Croatia also belong firmly to the central European geographic, cultural, and trade sphere, in large part due to their long period of development in the Habsburg Empire. However, the presence of ethnic Croats in neighboring Bosnia and Herzegovina meant that foreign policy was made in reference to these regions as well. Economic networks reflected this varied orientation, with links to the west, south, and east.

There was, nevertheless, a strong impetus to direct the gaze of post-communist Croatia toward the West. The HDZ, in fact, came to power promising to bring Croatia "back" to Europe. There was a concerted effort on the part of the HDZ regime to market Croatia abroad as a Central European, and not Balkan, state. Joining European structures was positively viewed by an overwhelming majority of the Croatian public, though many of these people did not connect the dots between economic and political conditionality and membership in Europe. At the same time, there were domestic political incentives to bringing the Herzegovinian Croats into the transition project.

Since the Herzegovinian Croats were resident in a neighboring state and in a backward region with very different political traditions, however, this effectively meant orienting Zagreb's foreign policy away from Europe and toward the Balkans. Thus, the decision to support the Herzegovinian Croats and pursue irredentist policies in Bosnia helped in part to shape Zagreb's ambivalent attitude toward Europe and the West.

Tuđman justified the lack of progress on democratization to Western diplomats by continually emphasizing Croatia's victimhood at the hands of the Serbs. These Western officials, for their part, were under no illusions about Tuđman's true intentions, but there was a clear strategic interest in supporting Serbia's main adversary in the Balkans. Western diplomats refused to talk of ethnic cleansing even after the expulsion of 150,000 Serbs from the Krajina in August 1995 (Kearns 1998: 248). Yet, the West had an equally compelling interest in not allowing Tuđman to overstep his bounds and to construct a full-blown dictatorship on the doorstep of Europe. Thus, simulated democracy served the purposes of both the Tuđman regime and Western governments, at least while the war raged in neighboring Bosnia and the issue of the Krajina remained unresolved. Since domestic democratic movements were temporarily silenced, the practice of simulating democracy became institutionalized. Hence, until 1995, the pro-Western impetus was sidelined and the West itself pursued an improvised foreign policy in Croatia based on the imperatives of containing a war. The situation changed radically after 1996, when there was no longer the perceived need to prop up the Tuđman regime to counter the Milošević threat.

Human rights organizations had long been pressing Western governments to take a more proactive approach in condemning the anti-democratic tendencies of the Tuđman regime.[55] In 1996, Western countries began to respond. The West understood that Tuđman would now have to begin to fulfill domestic aspirations for European integration, and it would be more difficult to use the war as an excuse for delaying their fulfillment. The problem was that even if Tuđman's pro-Western rhetoric was sincere, by the late 1990s he had, with his rhetoric and policies, placed Croatia firmly on the path of nationalism and authoritarianism.

Starting in 1996, Western politicians, officials, and diplomats began to block Croatia's links with Western institutions to compel the Tuđman regime to improve its democratic record. In the first half of 1997, official statements criticizing Croatia's lack of democracy began to emanate from the U.S. Embassy.[56] When Madeleine Albright assumed the post of U.S. secretary of state in 1997, U.S. pressure ratcheted up significantly. One low point was reached in October 1997 when Tuđman "was forced into the humiliating position at a Council of Europe meeting in Strasbourg of defending Croatia's human rights record against the backdrop of open U.S. attempts to secure his country's suspension from the organization" (Kearns 1998: 248).

Germany, a strong supporter of Croatian independence and its struggle against Serbian aggression, began to criticize the Tuđman regime openly. During the 1997 presidential elections, Hans-Dietrich Genscher, the German foreign minister at the time of Croatia's independence in 1991 and a very popular personality in Croatia, was openly calling for Croatians to support the opposition candidate, Vlado Gotovac.

The HDZ response was to launch an attack on Western criticism, saying that it was seeking to undermine Croatian sovereignty, that it was supporting Milošević in Belgrade, and that it was part of a larger strategy to recreate Yugoslavia. But Croatia had already become part of a broader strategy, one in which it was seen by the West as a potential model for reform in the region and a way to demonstrate the rewards that democratization can bring (Field 2000: 135).

The EU had been closely involved in Croatian affairs from the outset of transition. However, its failure to "seize the hour of Europe" and stop the war discredited it among many former Yugoslavs, Croats included. In the decade after Croatia's independence in 1991, the EU provided over 367 million euros in emergency and recovery aid to Zagreb (Tull 2003: 137). Other kinds of aid, however, were frozen due to concerns over Croatia's democratic record.

Following the end of the war, the EU began to reorient its policy away from solely humanitarian assistance toward conditional support based on concrete reforms. A regional approach and a policy of encouraging regional cooperation became cornerstones of the Stabilization and Association (SAA) process of EU accession, formulated in 1999. However, it was this very approach that gave Tuđman the ammunition to suggest that the EU was indeed trying to recreate Yugoslavia, in fact a new "Euroslavia" (Cohen 1997: 111). The EU's regional approach did create greater ambivalence toward Europe among Croats, since after years of war there was genuine revulsion toward the notion of cooperation with the likes of Milošević's Serbia.

Tuđman was not ideologically anti-Western, and in fact he probably would have gained politically in the long term had Croatia made progress on its accession to Euro-Atlantic structures. But he was also a shrewd politician, and calculated that the short-term costs were too high. He knew that strong support for the EU in Croatian society was divorced from the actual process needed to join the organization and that granting more rights to Serbs or allowing for the mass return of refugees would be too high a political price to pay since any potential benefits that Croatia would derive from it in terms of EU membership were far away. The legitimacy of the HDZ regime, in the end, rested on a nationalist project and on noncooperation with its southern neighbors. In the 1990s, little progress was made on EU accession, and relations between Zagreb and Brussels remained difficult until January 2000.

By the late 1990s, then, Croatia was left out not only of the EU accession process but also of NATO and the Partnership for Peace (PFP) program and other important international organizations like the World Trade Organization (WTO). However, by this time the West's policy of isolation also began to pay off. Economic isolation in particular helped turn the tide of public opinion against the HDZ regime.

There was a significant part of the Croatian public, larger than that in Macedonia or FRY, that was favorably disposed toward the West. They were represented by the democratic opposition parties and targeted by the Western governments and organizations that actively worked toward regime change in Zagreb. By 1997 both the EU and United States were launching a full assault on the Tuđman regime, which they accused of committing transgressions against democracy as well as blocking cooperation with the International Criminal Tribunal for the former Yugoslavia (ICTY) and preventing the return of Serbian refugees. Western willingness not only to withdraw support from but also to shun the Tuđman regime emboldened the domestic opposition.

Western funding poured into NGOs that sponsored seminars on democracy and media, trained and financed opposition parties, and educated and mobilized voters.[57] Significantly, some of these organizations conducted polls that predicted an opposition victory in the next elections. These polls were enthusiastically received, as they were seen to be more objective than those conducted by Croatian media organizations (Krickovic 2001: 9). Other, more focused Western-sponsored polls were made available to opposition parties to help them sharpen their message to voters. Help was also provided in forming coalitions, thereby allowing the democratic camp to overcome years of disunity.

The opposition parties, in turn, saw this as a critical opportunity to adopt a firm pro-Western platform. Some smaller liberal parties had always run on such a platform, but the communist successor SDP had not been explicit in its desire to meet Western conditionality. In 1999 the SDP declared its willingness to carry out the tough reforms necessary to begin to negotiate Croatia's accession into Euro-Atlantic organizations. The incentive of membership was not necessary for those groups and parts of the public that had been firm in their pro-Western orientation from the beginning. Rather, it was parties like the SDP and other parts of the Croatian public that may earlier have been ambivalent but now saw clear incentives in jumping on the pro-EU bandwagon, especially as the economic situation deteriorated. The story is not simply that of a repressed opposition and demobilized public "saved" by the West from a dictator: rather, it is about a sufficiently large number of political groups and people making a "rational choice" about where their interests lay.

Thus, the demise of the HDZ and its ultimate fall in January 2000 coincided with a concerted effort on the part of the West to criticize Croatia's human rights and democracy record and take proactive measures to help precipitate regime change in Zagreb (Kearns 1998: 247). Regime change, consequently, was due not only to domestic factors but also to the pull of the West and its concrete strategies in Croatia. The West and its organizations had won the hearts and minds of at least part of the public. The other part may have been reluctant to cede Croatia's sovereignty by giving in to the many Western demands but was also deeply dissatisfied with Croatia's economic situation and either saw no other choice or hoped for a potentially bright material future in Europe.

Economic Performance

Despite a relatively successful program of stabilization, the 1990s Croatian economy was characterized by steep falls in production, real wages, and income and rising unemployment. GDP fell by one third in the first five years of transition (see figure 4.1). Real wages were reduced to the level of the 1960s, while household income was at half the level achieved in 1990 (Bellamy 2001: 34). In contrast to other post-communist states, and more than other Yugoslav successor states except Slovenia, Croatian firms had been exposed to market forces. Croatia was an established producer in some sectors, such as ships and pharmaceuticals (Bićanić 2001: 159). Thus, economists point

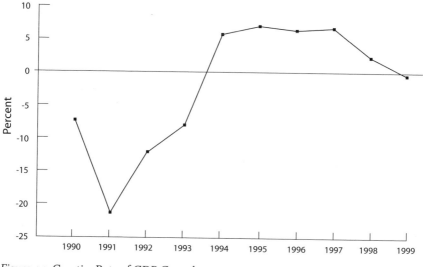

Figure 4.1. Croatia, Rate of GDP Growth, 1990–1999
Source: Jeffries 2002: 227.

to major reform failures on the part of the Tuđman regime, including the failure to implement such basic measures as liberalization, privatization, restructuring of large enterprises, bank rehabilitation, and small business promotion as well as a failure to reach a growth consensus (Franičević and Kraft 1997: 1). The precise economic effects of the war were debated, with the Tuđman regime apparently inflating them for political purposes.[58] Yet, as chapter 3 showed, the Croatian economy suffered from many structural weaknesses, including an overdependence on remittances from Gastarbeiter and tourism. Dependence on remittances made the economy less open than statistics implied and less likely to withstand the shocks of independence, not to mention war. Tourism itself was declining prior to independence, and serious improvements in infrastructure were needed. Certain parts of the country suffered from industrial decline, and unemployment was a growing problem. The service sector was undeveloped, small businesses were underrepresented, energy use was wasteful, and small-scale agriculture was inefficient and undercapitalized.

There is no doubt, however, that the negative economic repercussions of the war were significant. Some cities such as Vukovar were completely destroyed. Industrial capacity and infrastructure were destroyed. Ten percent of the housing stock was destroyed or damaged, as were nine large regional hospitals. Economic networks within and outside the country were severed. Landmines rendered large swathes of land unusable. Bartlett observes:

> A large part of the decline occurred before the war began. Measured in terms of GDP, total output fell from the equivalent of HRK 74 million in the third quarter of 1990 to HRK 59 million in the second quarter of 1991, or by 20 percent. After the war began in the middle of 1991, output fell further HRK 49 million, or by 17 percent. Clearly more than half of the cumulative decline in output was due to the breakup of Yugoslavia and the loss of traditional markets in the southern republics. The war only made a bad situation worse. Between 1990 and 1992 the number of people in full-time employment fell by over 300,000. Registered unemployment increased from 160,000 to 267,000, an increase of 66 percent. (2003: 89)

In short, there was an economic base for populism in Croatia before the war began. However, radical populists entrenched themselves not only through the politics of nationalism and war, as argued above, but also through economic clientelism. Besides HDZ clientelist networks, there was also a related informal economy, based on traditional networks, that operated within ethnic groups and regions. The networks among Herzegovinians in Bosnia, Zagreb, and abroad, in fact, provided the cornerstone for Croatia's version of crony capitalism.

Not all economic policies were unsuccessful. A very successful stabilization program launched in 1993 brought down inflation and introduced exchange rate stability (Franičević and Kraft 1997: 1).[59] Some liberalization measures, such as lower import taxes, were also introduced. The most visible sign of the success of the stabilization program was the restoration of confidence in the domestic currency, which allowed people to sell their hoarded foreign currency holdings for Croatian dinars (Bartlett 2003: 95). Most important, the policy brought inflation down from a high of nearly 40 percent in late 1993 to less than 5 percent in 1994 (Bartlett 2003: 96). Croatia had been admitted to the IMF and World Bank in early 1993, and once these stabilization measures were implemented, it was offered a line of credit.

The cost of this stabilization policy was high short-term interest rates, which discouraged investment and growth. Although the National Bank had lowered its own interest rate, this had little impact on the actual rates charged to individuals and businesses, since in the process of monetary tightening the central bank ceased issuing credits to the commercial banks (Bartlett 2003:

97). The banking sector was able to maintain high rates due to lack of competition in that sector, but large amounts of bad loans ultimately led to its collapse. Nevertheless, the success of the stabilization program compelled the National Bank to introduce the new Croatian currency (the kuna) in 1994.[60]

An economic recovery ensued after Dayton and the liberation of occupied territories in 1995. GDP grew by over 6 percent between 1995 and 1997 before slowing to just 3 percent in 1998 (Bartlett 2003: 100). Part of this recovery was due to bringing excess capacity back into use, repairing damaged factories, and restoring communications and transportation networks. Investment also grew at a healthy rate[61] and inflation remained low, but this may have been because registered unemployment remained quite high at 14 percent (Bartlett 2003: 100). The economic recovery was also greatly facilitated by inflows of foreign aid and loans. The World Bank in particular invested in major infrastructure projects in the post-Dayton period.[62] The several years of success after Dayton led to an increase in Croatia's credit rating and praise from the international financial community.

However, problems left over from the pre-independence period and bad policies pursued by the Tuđman regime were accumulating to the detriment of longer-term economic growth and health: a deteriorating balance of payments position due to poor export performance (in part due to being left out of European free trade agreements such as Central European Free Trade Agreement (CEFTA) and SAA agreement with the EU); a lack of recovery in the tourism sector; low levels of foreign direct investment (FDI); a large, nominally privatized loss-making state sector in need of restructuring; a banking sector on the verge of collapse with enormous amounts of bad assets; underdevelopment of the small business sector; a looming pension fund crisis, with the average age of pensioners only 61; and large state expenditures to support a large army and police force and generous benefits for veterans.[63]

Privatization in Croatia: The Road to Crony Capitalism

These problems were compounded by an increasingly corrupt privatization process that put already failing industries in the hands of regime insiders, who used their position to strip the firms of any valuable assets. Privatization legislation was introduced early, in part to fulfill conditions for help from international financial institutions. A privatization agency was established with the power to install managers, who were then to initiate privatization. However, under strict political control, it often chose HDZ party insiders, who did little to restructure the firms and make them viable. Kearns describes how privatization became a sham:

> Legislation on privatization was passed as early as spring 1991 and stressed a number of options... all proposals for privatization, however, had to be approved by the same Agency for Restructuring and Development which had been involved indirectly in press censorship. This ploy served two distinct political purposes. On the one hand it was designed to ensure the destruction of any remnants, legal as well as practical, of the old Yugoslav self-managed economy in which enterprises were socially rather than state owned. It was also, however, designed to give the government the opportunity to abuse the subsequent privatization of enterprises by selling the best companies to its political friends. (1998: 253)

The net result was that a new class of regime-friendly entrepreneurs was created—many of whom happened to be members of the former communist elite—and they, the *winners* of partial reform, had a vested interest in upholding the system of semi-authoritarianism.[64]

Privatization, writes Bićanić, "was an all-out failure" (2001: 170). It did not generate revenue, foreign investment, or foreign management experience. The corporate governance issue was not solved. Workers were coerced into relinquishing assets, and instead a nationalist capitalist class emerged through Tuđman's policy of putting the Croatian economy in the hands of loyalists. Therefore, ownership transformation was used to develop cronyism and a system of clientelism. But it also left the state as the pseudo-owner of countless ailing firms, many of which were already in trouble at the end of the communist era.

The Onset of Crisis

Besides leading to public outcry, the regime's economic policies led to an economic recession, and then crisis, in 1998.[65] Bićanić writes that "apart from price and exchange rate stability, economic policy has not lead to financial sector and monetary stability, nor has it managed to generate growth and favorable changes in the real sector" (2001: 171). Financial instability began in 1998 as the foreign and domestic debt skyrocketed. International indebtedness increased from $2.4 billion in 1993 to $6.1 billion in 1997, reaching 33 percent of GDP (Bartlett 2003: 109). This experience "gave a practical demonstration of how the growth of the economy was being held back by a structural balance of payments constraint as any upturn in the economy tended to suck in imports unmatched by growth in export revenues" (Bartlett 2003: 109).

The net effects of a politicized, partially reformed economy that had been weak in several key respects from the outset culminated in the collapse of the banking sector in 1998 and 1999, a devastating blow to the Croatian economy. In September 1999 Lehman Brothers advised foreign firms not to invest in the Croatian economy until regime change occurred (Bartlett 2003: 117). Many firms were on the verge of collapse, kept alive by subsidies from the government. Unemployment continued to grow, surpassing 20 percent in 1999 (see figure 4.2). In Eastern Slavonia and other war-torn areas, unemployment was as high as 80 percent, but foreign aid was only a fraction of what was flowing into Bosnia.[66]

Actual wages remained at 1980s levels while prices doubled. Surveys showed that the public was most concerned with the economy, corruption, unemployment, and social welfare and not with issues such as sovereignty and national survival (Bellamy 2001: 22). Most Croatians felt that they were poorer than before independence. Poverty increased dramatically, as did income inequality, since whatever growth had taken place in the 1990s benefited the small HDZ-affiliated elite. Much of this growth, furthermore, had been based on borrowing, leading to a $15 billion domestic and foreign debt (Judah 1997: 20). Despite the post-1995 gains, the Croatian economy was still 21 percent behind its 1989 GDP.

An analysis of post-communist Croatia in the 1990s suggests at least two counterfactuals. Would things have turned out differently had the Croatian Spring not been repressed in 1971 and the development of pluralism been essentially frozen until 1989? Had there not been a war, would liberal democracy have had a brighter future in post-communist Croatia? With regard to the first question, the Croatian Spring did not display the qualities of a true movement for liberal democracy[67]—whether it would have been if the national question had not been present is yet another counterfactual beyond the scope of this analysis.

With regard to the second question about the detrimental effect of war on liberalism, we have shown that war helped to tip what was a precarious balance between liberals and radical populists toward the latter. Yet, I also recall Eric Gordy's (1999) observation about Serbia: namely, if an authoritarian re-

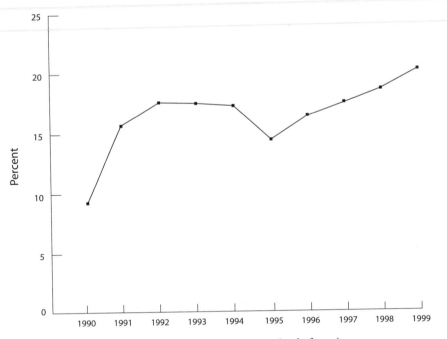

Figure 4.2. Croatia, Unemployment Rate, 1990–1999 (end of year)
Source: Jeffries 2002: 227.

gime could have been sustained in the absence of war, perhaps there would
have been no war in the first place. This is a direct way to summarize a more
nuanced argument made in this chapter about the way in which the politics
of war became embedded in the transition, and how certain elements within
the ruling party derived great political and material benefit from the war. As
this chapter has argued, war allowed leaders to rally people around issues of
collective survival, sovereignty, and the national cause, thereby avoiding any
real debate over the war itself or any major state policies. It also allowed the
regime to neglect real political and economic reforms and instead pursue a
kind of crony capitalism that enriched a few but brought the economy to its
knees by the end of the decade.

But the larger point is that Croatia's transition did begin with a precarious
balance between liberals and populists, and of all the analysts I interviewed,
not a one argued that liberalism would have been assured in the absence of
war, Milošević, Tuđman, Bosnia, and so on. The precarious balance reflected
differences in Croatian society that had been brought to the fore by the 1980s
economic crisis. These differences were manifest in Croatia's mixed economic

structure: in the economically viable urban areas compared to the depressed hinterland and all the cultural and ethnic divisions that corresponded to this disparity. "Development without modernization" was an apt characterization for how parts of Croatia had developed under communism. There were clear illiberal proclivities in Croatian society, and the electorate was hardly a politically mature one in terms of its understanding of democracy (Glavaš 1994). The war contributed greatly to turning otherwise liberal and internationalist parts of the public toward the HDZ's radical populism and strengthened the Balkan orientation of Croatia's foreign policy.

The vacillation of the Tuđman regime between simulated democracy and outright authoritarian practice reflected both domestic and international factors, as did the presence, influence, and program of the opposition parties. On the domestic front, levels of support for liberal opposition parties suggested a real impetus for more liberal politics, much more than in FRY. Liberal opposition parties consistently won over 40 percent of the vote in parliamentary elections, and they were able to moderate the more extreme tendencies of the Tuđman regime.

This chapter has also argued that the international dimension of transition is key to understanding the nature of regime change in post-communist Croatia. The promise of membership in the EU and other Western organizations turned out to be a powerful impetus for change, especially when the Tuđman regime was delegitimized as a result of corruption and economic failure. The acceptance of the Western agenda by the opposition parties and then by an ever-growing part of the public depended on socio-cultural factors, but also on Western strategy in the late 1990s. The opposition ultimately found political capital and material assistance in Western support. But an elite acceptance of the Western liberal agenda did not mean that it had been accepted by the masses. This required a longer socialization process, but the elite acceptance was crucial in jump-starting this process.

The international factor also helps to explain the simulated character of Croatian democracy. Because there was a sizeable domestic pro-Western constituency, and because Tuđman depended on Western support for security purposes and his own political survival, he did not find it in his interest to reject Western liberalism altogether. It is clear that Tuđman made concessions only when absolutely forced to do so by the international community. Moreover, Tuđman's message that he would turn to democratization once the war was over was clearly intended for Western consumption. By the late 1990s, the HDZ regime was constantly vacillating between permitting and repressing democratic institutions in reaction to Western pressure. Thus, the important conclusion is that to the extent that procedural democracy existed in Croatia in the 1990s, it did not reflect a substantive commitment to liberalism on the part of the elites.

Despite the existence of procedural correctness, there were a number of indicators of low liberal content in the Tuđman regime. First, there were deep divisions among parties over basic issues about the state, and the regime had decidedly illiberal legitimizing principles. Tuđman attempted to overcome public divisions by rewriting history and constructing myths, much like Tito had done before him. Given the rejection of Croatian sovereignty by the Krajina Serbs, the regime also suffered from a serious democratic legitimacy problem. Analysts have noted that clear state borders are a prerequisite of democratization, but in the case of Croatia the disputed borders were themselves very much a consequence of the mode of post-communist transition. If the success of Croatian democracy depended on its territorial integrity and security, then the sad conclusion is that democracy in Croatia depended on solving the Serbian problem.[68]

By the end of the 1990s, nationalist, paternalistic authoritarianism and the development of a rentier state led Croatia down the road to international isolation and economic crisis. This dire situation helped to propel parties with a pro-Western agenda to the forefront in 1999. The real test of commitment to democratic rules, as Croatian politician Ivo Škrabalo noted, was whether the HDZ would surrender power.[69] Many contend that had Tuđman lived, he would have never allowed the opposition to come to power, but by 1999 the momentum was clearly against the HDZ.

When the HDZ was ultimately defeated in January 2000, it was due to dissatisfaction with the economy, corruption, and international isolation. It did not reflect a universal condemnation of the nationalist project, nor did it indicate unconditional acceptance of Western liberalism. The public divisions that had existed under the HDZ regime, moreover, were still there. However, Croatia's economy had potential, and there was genuine and widespread pro-European sentiment in society, which meant that divisions over the appropriateness of Western liberalism could be overcome by a decisive entry onto the road to European integration, the road on which Croatia's new leaders embarked in 2000.

CHAPTER FIVE

Substantive Democracy

Slovenia's Transition in the 1990s

> No concern at all. Most of our savings and reserves are in Austrian schillings.
>
> SLOVENIAN OFFICIAL IN 1991, UPON BEING ASKED IF THERE
> WAS ANY CONCERN ABOUT THE BELGRADE BANKS HOLDING
> THE RESERVES OF THE YUGOSLAV FEDERATION.

The Road to Liberalism: Favorable Initial Conditions

Economic viability underpinned the procedurally and substantively liberal regime that guided Slovenia's post-communist transition in the 1990s. Favorable initial conditions enabled the repeated success of liberal political configurations in elections and contributed to a broad consensus among varying social groups on a liberal project of reform and European integration. A strong economic base allowed democratic transition to proceed without becoming bogged down in issues of the nation. Slovenia had not only the most favorable structural starting conditions among the Yugoslav successor states but indeed some of the most favorable initial conditions of all transition economies as well. These conditions included its geographical location, skilled human capital, and significant trade links with the West that had been established and strengthened during the 1970s and 1980s. With an economic structure in which industry contributed 43 percent and services 51 percent to total output, Slovenia's level of development resembled many West European economies. As a result of these advantages, Slovenia quickly was able to redirect its vanishing inter-republican trade to the West, thereby generating a fast economic turnaround. Throughout the transition, economic success lent credibility to liberalism and prevented voids in legitimacy that could be filled by radical populism.

The story of Slovenia's transition is not about "critical junctures" but rather a strong structural foundation for liberalism. However, there is little support for the notion that deeply internalized liberal political values—or demonstration of a strong democratic political culture—can explain both the procedural and substantive liberal qualities of Slovenia's post-communist regime.[1] Transition did not instantly produce democratic attitudes. Favorable economic prospects and the positive inducements of joining Europe helped to shape a pluralist orientation on the part of elites and masses and, ultimately, to create and reinforce democratic attitudes in the long run.

However, Slovenia's liberal political order was not guaranteed, nor has its transition from communism been without its bumps and diversions. Besides initial conditions that favored liberalism, the external inducement of EU membership was a powerful force constraining the influence of radical populist groups in the Slovenian polity. Thus, what began as an instrumental recognition on the part of elites that Slovenia's economy and state survival depended on positive relations with the West led to a process in which the substantive beliefs of both elites and masses were shaped in such a way that liberalism became the "only game in town."

The regime that consolidated power in 1990s Slovenia, however, was not without illiberal blemishes in areas such as elite continuity, transparency, and minority rights. These shortcomings notwithstanding, the prominence of liberal political forces and programs since the outset of transition and an elite and mass consensus on democracy as the appropriate political order for the country set Slovenia apart from the other three cases examined in this study. From the earliest days of transition, both elites and the public built a consensus on the appropriateness of seceding from Yugoslavia, pluralism as the organizing principle of political life, the European integration policies of all governments, and a pragmatic concern for the economy. Slovenia's economic success reduced the level of potential conflicts that were translatable into nationalist issues. It precluded divisions over basic questions about the state, its borders, and the people within those borders.[2]

Nationalism, Liberalism, and Legitimacy in Post-communist Slovenia

Nationalism

Slovenia's post-communist regime was substantively, and not just procedurally, liberal, in large part because it was not pervaded by illiberal nationalism and because liberalism itself and the project of democratization and European integration were seen as legitimate by the vast majority of Slovenians.

Independence in Slovenia started not only in the name of the nation, but also in the name of democracy (Harris 2002: 66). Secession was pursued as the means to rejoin Europe and establish a democratic system. In Croatia, FRY, Lithuania, Slovakia, and other post-communist states, the political and economic dimensions of transition were subordinated to the national question, which had negative repercussions for the process of democratization. By contrast, in Slovenia democratization and independent statehood formed a mutually compatible dynamic. Nationalism did emerge as a defense, especially during the tumultuous period following Slovenia's secession from the Yugoslav federation, but it never translated into a legitimizing principle for the regime.[3] Nor was the Slovenian transition cast as a struggle against internal or external enemies. From the beginning, it was characterized in terms of themes such as "democracy," "human rights," "Europe," and "freedom." Certainly Slovenia's higher degree of ethnic homogeneity mattered, but relative homogeneity does not necessarily preclude the appearance of illiberal nationalism. There were potential targets inside and outside Slovenia for ethnic nationalist entrepreneurs to exploit, and to some degree and at certain times there were attempts to exploit them—but never to the extent that this occurred in neighboring Croatia.

Ethnic nationalism was also tempered by the early pursuit of Western markets and political support from the EU. The strong pro-European orientation among leaders of varying political stripes and the conscious recognition that displays of nationalism would seriously hurt Slovenia's standing in the eyes of the EU also constrained nationalism. Even the overtly nationalist Slovenian National Party (Slovenska Narodna Stranka, SNS) in its program mentioned Slovenia, albeit independent, in European structures as its first point (Harris 2002: 198–99). Slovenia's aspirations toward Europe, of course, were not merely economic but political and cultural as well. They were fortified by events in other parts of the failed SFRJ: to be pro-European was to be anti-Yugoslav and anti-Balkans. In the end, Europe itself embraced Slovenia's brand of pro-European separatism, "not least because it was anti-Yugoslav—that is, anti-Milošević" (Jović 2001). The momentum toward Europe, in turn, was sustained by economic viability and growth.

Minority Rights

The topic of minority rights can be quite sensitive in Slovenia. There was never any discrimination in terms of deficiencies in the legal framework. In contrast to the other successor states, the Slovenian constitution starts with the premise that Slovenia is the state of Slovenian citizens and not the "state of the Slovenian nation" (Kuzmanić 1999: 121). This fact notwithstanding, one of the central problems with the Slovenian constitution was the introduction of the concept of "autochthonous national minorities." This reference applied primarily to Austrians, Italians, and Hungarians and dated back to the situation immediately following World War II, specifically the border disputes with Italy. Tito's regime had later used these minorities to try to create channels of communication with the West and to protect Slovenian minorities in Italy, Austria, and Hungary. Thus, special recognition of the three minorities was a legacy of Yugoslav-era policy and remained in force after Slovenian independence. However, it created problems when it did not apply to the estimated 200,000 people from other Yugoslav republics who had migrated to Slovenia, mainly to seek better employment opportunities. Officially, these groups did not exist (Kuzmanić 1999: 122). This led to considerable protest by domestic and international human rights groups but surprisingly little complaint by the EU.

On the Legitimacy of Slovenia's Democratic Order

Democratic transition in Slovenia rested on a broad consensus about vital issues of national interest and a commitment to democracy (Harris 2002: 154). Thus, Slovenia's post-communist regime in the 1990s was characterized by high degrees of the kind of legitimacy outlined in chapter 2. The overwhelming majority of the Slovenian population recognized the state within its existing borders and consented to the authority of the government. Radical elements were neutralized by the momentum toward liberalism and Europe before they had a chance to succeed. Democracy in Slovenia, then, was legitimate, making it likely to succeed in the long term.

However, a lack of adequate debate in Slovenian society on certain issues and a passive acceptance of elite continuity and lack of transparency on the part of the electorate signals "thin democracy" to some.[4] On the lack of debate—I disagree in light of the intense debates that have taken place in both the Slovenian Parliament and in public discourse about issues such as the role of the Roman Catholic Church. The kind of consensus that did exist, such as an unequivocal commitment to EU accession and democracy, is the kind that stabilizes and guarantees, rather than threatens, liberalism. The alternative, deep political divisions over fundamental issues about the state, has precluded substantive democracy in the other three cases being examined here.

Formal Democracy: The Record

On 23 December 1991, Slovenia adopted a new constitution that proclaimed the country to be a democratic republic governed by the rule of law.[5] Just two issues aroused serious controversy: abortion rights and the structure of the Parliament. In the end, the right to an abortion was guaranteed, and the constitution also enacted a parliamentary system with a bicameral legislature, the National Assembly (Državni Zbor).[6] In addition, the constitution mandated a National Council (Državni Svet). It was to serve as an advisory body with members representing key social, economic, local, and professional interests—a clear legacy of communist-era corporatist arrangements. In all areas, democratic rules were codified in the Slovenian constitution, and the institutions that are mandated by the document functioned as prescribed in the 1990s. For example, elections were held regularly, no violations of electoral rules were noted (Lukšič 2001: 44), and there were no difficulties relating to the separation of powers.

The new constitution mandated a parliamentary system, similar to that of Macedonia but in sharp contrast to the semi-presidential systems adopted in Croatia and FRY to serve the ambitions of Presidents Tuđman and Milošević, respectively. Unlike the other successor states, the electoral system was highly proportional. This system, however, also produced intense battles among parties in the Parliament. Just two years into independence, Slovenia had a new constitution, a politically pluralist landscape with ten parties in the Parliament, a free press, and an independent judiciary (Ramet 1993: 869).[7]

However, progress was slower in some notable areas. The media was often subject to political influence. Ambiguity emerged over the status of civil-military relations, with allegations of misuse of the military by defense minister and former leader of the Slovenian youth movement, Janez Janša (Vankovska and Wiberg 2003: 160–82). Police and security services, however, were fully reformed and enjoyed a high level of trust among the public (Kuzmanić 1999: 127).

Civil society thrived in the 1990s, though ironically not with the same vibrancy as it did in the 1980s: as Gantar notes, after 1990 civil society retreated back into the "semi-public, semi-private sphere" (1994: 359). Trade unions were increasingly independent, but business associations were just appearing and lacked such independence (Kuzmanić 1999: 128). A number of NGOs working in the area of human rights made important accomplishments. Yet, in general, political parties took the place of what was previously "political society" and dominated public discourse.

In sharp contrast to all of the other successor states, the rule of law seemed to take root in Slovenia. Legal business practice restrained the grey economy, which was estimated to account for only 10 percent of Slovenian GDP (Lampe 2000: 403). Levels of corruption were much lower than in the other three cases, and indeed much lower than in most post-communist states. Thus, on the criteria of procedural democracy identified by Kaldor and Vejvoda (1998: 6) as inclusive citizenship, the rule of law, separation of powers, free and fair elections, freedom of expression and alternative information, associational autonomy, and civilian control of armed forces, Slovenia placed quite high.

The First Elections

Slovenia's advanced economic status was unquestionable when it was still part of the SFRJ, but nothing suggested that free elections would appear. On the contrary, the leadership in Slovenia maintained relatively tight rule by Yugoslav standards into the 1970s (Bukowski 1999: 76). Apart from the increasing activity of "new social movements" (NSMs) and independent publications in the late 1980s, concentrated chiefly in urban areas and dominated by young people, there was little evidence of burgeoning democracy in Slovenia.

Free elections, instead, were largely a by-product of local elites seeking to legitimize their struggle against an ever more oppressive Belgrade.[8] This made the start of transition in Slovenia different from other communist countries: indeed, the transition to pluralism in Slovenia was begun for reasons having little to do with the broader processes occurring in the region (Ramet 1993: 869). No pacts or "round tables" stimulated the democratic transition. In fact, the Slovenian government conducted no formal talks with opposition groups (Bukowski 1999: 85). Yet by 1990 a broad consensus existed among the regime and opposition groups on the direction in which Slovenia should go, that is, away from Yugoslavia and toward democracy and Europe. This was a result of the need for a united front in identifying an alternative approach to that of Milošević's policies in Belgrade, and it was shaped by the favorable structural conditions discussed earlier.

In between Slovenia's economic viability and its liberal regime outcome lay an important intervening variable—the democratic transformation of the League of Communists of Slovenia (Zveza Komunistov Slovenije, ZKS) at the end of the 1980s. At its eleventh congress, the group declared itself to be a modern political party of the left and a supporter of democracy, basic human rights, and the market economy and changed its name to the Party of Democratic Renewal (Stranka Demokratične Prenove, SDP) (Bukowski 1999: 82). The activist League of Socialist Youth also became a political party: the Liberal Democratic Party (Liberalna Demokratska Stranka, LDS).

Thus, a decisive step toward liberalism was taken when the liberal faction of the ZKS took control in 1986 and ousted conservatives from the party leadership. The ascent of the liberal wing was a key development in the Slovenian "proto-transition" that shaped later reforms, and its subsequent decision to pursue multiparty elections was the contingent choice that shaped the path to liberalism. It was the ability of liberals to consolidate power within the party that created the possibility for change.

However, it was structural conditions that ultimately shaped the strategies of the reformist wing of the Slovenian communists. Their counterparts in the Serbian League of Communists (Srpski Savez Komunista, SKS), after all, were also undergoing an internal struggle in which a younger, reformist wing prevailed, except that "reform" in the Serbian case came in the form of Milošević's decidedly illiberal "anti-bureaucratic revolution," a response to the conditions prevailing in Serbia and in particular Kosovo. Thus, it would be a wrong to see the ZKS strategy in entirely voluntarist terms, but it would also be wrong to give too much credit to broad popular mobilization. To the extent that such mobilization existed, it was largely limited to a progressive social agenda, urban areas, and younger strata of the population. Structural conditions, particularly those economic factors that dictated a pro-European orientation, mattered most in determining ZKS strategies.

During this internal party turnover, Milan Kučan, the liberal communist, became president of the Slovenian League of Communists and "the *de facto* arbiter of Slovenian political life" (Ramet 1993: 869). It was Kučan's wing of the party that led the drive for the introduction of a multiparty system in their republic, and it was also Kučan's wing of the party that began to use the slogan "*Evropa Zdaj!*" (Europe Now!) to argue that Slovenia's political interests could only be advanced in Europe, and thus that Yugoslavia, and in particular Serbia, represented everything that was anti- or un-European (Jović 2001). In December 1989 the Slovenian Parliament adopted a package of new laws on elections and political association, effectively legalizing political pluralism (Ramet 1993: 870).

Events in Belgrade arguably had saved the Slovenian communist leadership from complete delegitimization and helped stimulate their pro-Western strategies. On the former point, the ability of the communist leaders to portray themselves as defenders of Slovenian interests against threats from Belgrade was an important source of political capital. On the latter point, the logical response to Milošević's onslaught was to seek support in the West, which could only be accomplished by pursuing political pluralism. The ZKS's ultimate decision to support multiparty democracy, then, could be interpreted as a way to preserve both Slovenian autonomy and its own political fortunes in the midst of a legitimacy crisis.

The first elections were held in April 1990; as the first multiparty elections in the still-existing SFRJ, they were a "showcase" for the entire country (Cohen 1993: 89). About twenty political parties participated in the parliamentary elections, and presidential elections were held at the same time. Kučan, who had recently stepped down as the head of the communist party, easily won election as president of Slovenia. To the surprise of many observers, the reformed communists were unable to prevail in the legislative elections. The SDP was the major vote getter, but could not overcome the combined strength of a broad anti-communist coalition calling itself DEMOS (an abbreviation of Demokratična Opozicija Slovenije).

The DEMOS coalition was headed by Jože Pučnik, a former philosophy professor who had spent the previous twenty years living in exile in West Germany. Lojže Peterle, the leader of the Christian Democrats (one of the largest DEMOS members) assumed the post of prime minister after the victory. In reality, DEMOS was not all that united but was rather a "hodgepodge of social democratic, Christian democratic, agrarian, and ecological ideas along with a commitment to parliamentary democracy and a free market economy" (Cohen 1993: 90). The unifying theme, of course, was to defeat the ruling Communist Party, and all DEMOS members agreed on the fundamental principles of democracy and market reform. Cohen writes: "For Slovenian voters, the election contest essentially boiled down to a choice between reform socialism and post-socialism. On several other important matters, however, the positions of the competing parties were not that far apart. For example, all the major parties favored Slovenia's closer association with the European Economic Community as well as a loose confederation of Yugoslavia's republics that would allow Slovenia full sovereignty over its internal affairs and require only a limited commitment to other areas of the existing federation" (1993: 90). However, calls for confederal arrangements were clearly failing, and the DEMOS coalition began hinting at full Slovenian independence, saying "Yugoslavia as a concept is exhausted. Slovenia simply wants to join Europe and is not willing to wait for the rest of Yugoslavia to catch up with it" (quoted in Cohen 1993: 90). On this point, the former communists were more cautious.

However, like many coalitions initially united by opposition to a common adversary, this one found that staying together once in power was much harder than staying together in opposition. The loose DEMOS coalition endured a stormy eighteen months in power, with intense criticism over its privatization policies. Ultimately the Peterle government fell in the face of battles over privatization and a deteriorating economic situation. Their shortcomings aside, Slovenia's first leaders were clearly committed to democratization and European integration, and set newly independent Slovenia firmly on the path of both.

Subsequent Elections and Party Politics

Peterle's coalition began to come apart by early 1992 when three parties left the government over disputes about privatization and abortion (Lampe 2000: 392). Peterle's calls for Slovenian society to return to traditional Catholic values did not resonate with much of the population, and general public dissatisfaction opened a window of political opportunity for the LDS to form a new coalition. The LDS was led by Janez Drnovšek, at one time a member of the SFRJ's collective presidency; he made Peterle the foreign minister in return for the support of the Christian Democrats (Slovenski Krščanski Demokrati, SKD). In April 1992, after withstanding two votes of no confidence, the Peterle government fell, and Drnovšek became prime minister and put together a left-oriented interim government. New legislative elections, as well as presidential elections, were held in December 1992 with high voter turnout. Kučan easily won reelection as president. In the legislative elections, the LDS prevailed with 23.3 percent of the vote. The right-of-center SKD came in second, with 14.5 percent and the SDP third, with 13.6 percent. The radical right SNS, headed by the fascist-leaning Zmago Jelinčič, received 9.9 percent of the vote, which has been attributed by many analysts to the economic difficulties surrounding the initial transition.[9] The SNS vote came heavily from disaffected rural areas and included protest votes from unemployed persons and national chauvinists. It was the strongest showing that any radical populist, anti-systemic party would ever have in post-communist Slovenia. The SNS was ultimately discredited and marginalized and was even forced to accept a pro-European orientation.

This government survived until the 1996 elections, after which Drnovšek barely managed to eke out a center-right coalition when a member of the SKD switched his affiliation to Drnovšek's renamed Liberal Democracy of Slovenia. Drnovšek managed to forge an agreement with the center-right Slovenian People's Party. Thus, what had been a center-left coalition from 1992 to 1996 became a center-right coalition after the 1996 elections. The nationalist SNS's share of the vote was just a third of what they had received four years earlier, due no doubt in part to accusations that its leader, Jelinčić, had worked with the Yugoslav-era Interior Ministry. But, it was also in no small part due to advancements in the EU accession process prior to the election. Drnovšek and his program of liberal reform were fortified by an economic picture that was mixed to some extent but on balance quite reassuring (Ramet 1997a: 214). Drnovšek's personal approval rating stood at around 60 percent in late 1996 (Gow and Carmichael 2000: 165), and he managed to survive until 2000 through sheer political acumen—but at a cost to reform. Meanwhile, Kučan was easily reelected as president in 1997.

Thus, in terms of the principal leadership posts, there was much continuity in the 1990s, with Kučan and Drnovšek enjoying strong support and prevailing in multiple elections. In the context of a parliamentary system, however, Kučan had limited powers, and Drnovšek's maintenance of power was subject to fierce debates and realignments in the party system.[10] "While the system encouraged cooperation and coalition government," write Gow and Carmichael, "it also required sufficient harmony and consensus between a number of parties for there to be an effective government: thus the character and platform of each of the main parties were important" (2000: 146).

The Main Political Parties and Their Orientations

Compared to the other three cases in this study, research indicated a general stabilization of the Slovenian party system in the 1990s (Lajh and Fink-Hafner 2001: 129). By the end of the decade the political scene was dominated by a few key parties with relatively clear and stable positions, half occupying the center-left of the political spectrum (mostly with roots in the communist party) and half the center-right (with roots in the non-communist opposition). All were strong supporters of Slovenia's integration into the EU and collectively captured well over 80 percent of the vote. The most important of these parties on the center-left was the LDS, led by Drnovšek. The roots of the LDS were in the reform wing of the ZKS, and it inherited certain advantages such as the organizational know-how and resources of its predecessor as well as perceptions of the positive role of the ZKS in its final years. In terms of policy orientation, the key elements of the LDS program were "its outward-looking program of integration with international, and particularly, European organizations, such as the European Union and NATO—as well as a domestic program focusing on measures such as privatization and economic stability to facilitate European integration" (Gow and Carmichael 2000: 147). In this sense, it laid claim to the "traditional inheritance of the Liberals in Slovenian politics: serving the national cause through integration in a wider framework which *inter alia* allows the development of business" (Gow and Carmichael 2000: 147). The other center-left parties included the United List of Social Democrats (Združena Lista Socialnih Demokratov, ZLSD), the Democratic Party of Slovenia's Pensioners (Demokratična Stranka Upokojencev Slovenije, DSUS), and SNS. The ZLSD (formerly the SDP), like the LDS, had its roots in the former communist party, but in the party's less radical, though certainly not conservative, elements (Gow and Carmichael 2000: 147). Its platform was to the left of the LDS and included calls for social justice and social provision, as well as social ownership and protection of jobs, rather than privatization and full economic reform. The DSUS emerged from the LDS, maintained close links with it, and effectively became something of an interest group for a rapidly growing group of retirees (Gow and Carmichael 2000: 148). The SNS, while also a product of the former communist party, adopted a program that was staunchly nationalist and anti-communist and yet on some points quite leftist in its economic orientation—much like Zhirinovsky's party in Russia.[11]

The parties to the right of center focused more on Slovenian identity and the protection of Slovenian national interest, but all were pro-European and pro-market by the end of the 1990s. The Slovenian People's Party (Slovenska Ljudska Stranka, SLS), led by Marjan Podobnik, claimed to derive its legitimacy and inspiration from the interwar party of the same name, but its ideological orientation was much more European in nature. The SKD, led by Lojže Peterle, was very similar except that it reflected a more clerical orientation. Both parties were more cautious on the point of European integration than the LDS, though as integration moved forward they tempered much of their Euroskepticism.[12] The final prominent center-right party was the Social Democratic Party of Slovenia (Socialdemokratska Stranka Slovenije, SDSS), led by former *Mladina* correspondent and political prisoner Janez Janša. Its ideological orientation was often unclear except for Janša's increasing use of the party as a platform to criticize other leaders and advance his personal ambitions, thus marginalizing the party. It is notable that aside from Jelinčič's SNS (completely marginalized after 1996), no parties put forth a serious challenge to Western liberal norms. Put differently, in post-communist Slovenia, no anti-democratic alternatives seriously challenged the prevailing liberal order and Western liberal agenda.

Loci of Conflict in Slovenian Politics

The level of consensus among Slovenian parties on issues of national and international integration was almost paradoxical given the intense competition in domestic affairs. That foreign policy never became a prisoner to domestic affairs showed the strength of the EU impetus. Tonči Kuzmanić observes that "however important the differences between and conflicts among the Slovenian political parties, they are always framed by a strong view of the 'national interest,' meaning those relating to Slovenia's democracy and future in Europe" (1999: 124). The remarkably cohesive response to Italian opposition to Slovenia's bid to join the EU is a case in point. Surprisingly, the greatest debate over foreign affairs has revolved around a number of contentious issues in Slovenia's relationship with Croatia.[13] Moreover, Slovenian anti-communism certainly contained anger, but not in the same way as in Poland, and in general less divisive disagreements over evaluations of the Yugoslav period allowed for political compromises and coalitions of various stripes, such as the liberal-right coalition that governed after the 1996 elections.

Moreover, some domestic issues generated intense and even divisive debate among parties, at times destabilizing the government, leading to frequent shifts in the composition of ruling coalitions and impeding the passage of legislation. Yet none reflected the kinds of divisions that preclude the building of a liberal order.

One locus of conflict was over the appropriate role of the Roman Catholic Church in society, with the SKD in particular lobbying for a clerical social agenda. Interestingly, the Slovenian Catholic hierarchy itself has not been united, though as elsewhere in the post-communist world it certainly saw the end of communism and Yugoslavia as an opportunity to reassert its "traditional" role. The re-privatization and restitution issue was closely connected to the clerical one, as the Roman Catholic Church was a major landowner in the interwar period. On balance, the anticlerical forces prevailed in the 1990s, but with some major concessions to the Church. Some of the other most politically contentious issues were over privatization, in particular the rights of foreigners to buy land. Widespread resistance to foreign ownership was tempered only by the realization that a complete ban would not be in accordance with the EU's acquis communautaire, and both political elites and the public ultimately gave in.

Such debates were played out in the party system and not in daily life. In fact, they were often exclusively in the domain of what Kuzmanić has called Slovenia's "partitocracy" (1999: 123). In the 1990s, political debate in Slovenia moved almost entirely from the public sphere to the political system, both a cause and a consequence of public disillusionment with parties and politicians. But this cynicism with political institutions was no different than that recorded in other post-communist states. Make no mistake: endless decision-making and chaotic parliamentary disputes among various political parties impeded reforms and the functioning of state institutions, but they never threatened an elite commitment to democratic rules, cohesion on fundamental issues concerning the state, or a continuing belief in democratic institutions on the part of the public. Nor did they generate anything resembling political violence. Slovenians were critical of those in power (Toš et al. 1995:

11) but not of liberalism itself, and the nature of the cleavages themselves resembled those in many developed Western democracies.[14]

The External Impetus for Liberalism

Liberalism in Slovenia would not have succeeded without Europe, meaning a consistent and credible promise of membership from Brussels, as well as the numerous ways in which a pro-Western, pro-European orientation defined the rhetoric and policies of the transition. As in many other postcommunist countries, Europe created euphoria among Slovenians before most really understood what integration into Europe would entail, and, for that matter, before most really grasped the implications of parliamentary democracy and a free market. Europe, for its part, was not ready to welcome the Slovenians with open arms, and when Slovenians realized this, the euphoria turned into disappointment. In fact, the first cadre of post-communist leaders found that they had to engage in intense lobbying abroad to prove Slovenia's democratic and pro-European intentions (Rupel 1994).

Yet, despite Europe's initially cool reception of Slovenia, Slovenia's leaders relentlessly pursued the goal of EU integration so that, after a while, a seemingly unshakable social consensus existed on the imperative of EU membership to assure stability, democracy, and prosperity in Slovenia. By the mid-1990s the public, for its part, was under no illusions about the drawbacks of membership. However, as Harris (2002: 199) notes, these kinds of attitudes were prevalent in EU member states as well, and 94 percent of Slovenians continued to believe that Slovenia would benefit from membership.

Regular EU Commission reports on progress were well publicized in Slovenia and, as noted below, often succeeded in realigning political forces and public opinion on certain issues. The EU, in other words, relied on a credible offer of membership to provide a strong enough impetus for reform. Since most major political parties and a majority of their constituents supported EU membership, the EU found that passive leverage was a sufficient strategy to motivate most elites to abide by EU demands (Lindstrom 2004). Moreover, though it is difficult to cite systematic evidence for this, the EU was willing to "tolerate" Slovenian transgressions at times because they paled in comparison to the authoritarian politics of the other Yugoslav successor states. The Slovenian leadership, for its part, used the threat of delay in admission to the EU to achieve compliance when difficult and unpopular issues were at stake.[15]

In terms of elite strategy, much of the early push for the EU was dictated by the simple fact of Slovenia's small statehood and the need to establish markets for Slovenian exports with some haste to compensate for those lost with the dissolution of the SFRJ. Small states, as Katzenstein (1985: 25) has written, depend on big foreign markets, and Slovenia's two million inhabitants could only provide a satisfactory market if the national economy exported more than 50 percent of its output (Brinar 1999: 245).

On 6 March 1995, after a long dispute with Italy over property restitution, Italy lifted the veto on Slovenia's association agreement with the EU. This led to the Europe Agreement of 1996, which gave persons who had lived in Slovenia for more than three years preferential access to Slovenia's real estate market (Sabič 2002: 106). However, this necessitated amending the Slovenian constitution in the face of strong public opposition. Amazingly, through a sustained pro-EU public information campaign and intra-party arm-twisting, the Parliament adopted Article 68 in 1997, which abolished the constitutional prohibition of the purchase of land by foreigners and was a prerequisite of the association agreement. The vote was 81 to 1 in favor. Soon Slovenian property rights laws were harmonized with those in force in EU member states, and on 10 June 1996, Slovenia signed an association agreement with the EU, the first Yugoslav successor state to do so. On 4 February 1998, Italy accepted $62 million from Slovenia in compensation for property seized from ethnic Italians who fled after World War II. As soon as the problem with Italy was solved, Slovenia was placed on EU's "coveted list for accession" (Lampe 2000: 394). On 16 July 1997, the European Commission recommended that Slovenia open negotiations in early 1998 for entry to the EU. The invitation was formally approved at an EU summit in December 1997, and formal negotiations began in March 1998 (Jeffries 2002: 362).

The dispute with Italy and its solution shows the high degree of consensus with which an otherwise fragmented party system rallied around important decisions relating to EU accession. Second, it shows how the political party elite was able to rally support for unpopular measures when EU accession was threatened. Third, and most important for the discussion here, it demonstrates the "passive leverage" with which the EU succeeded in forcing the Slovenian leadership to fall in line. Finally, in a more general sense, it shows how the promise of EU admission was the key force that pushed certain reforms through at critical moments where disunity would have otherwise prevailed.

There is a great deal of other evidence that shows not just that the EU mattered in realigning domestic political forces and public opinion but also that it mattered specifically in keeping the liberal project on track when it faltered. Requirements imposed by the acquis also acted as a powerful impetus to force governing elites to initiate reforms with little public appeal, such as minority protection laws for non-indigenous groups, which Slovenia finally adopted at the end of the 1990s. They marginalized the influence of radical populists like the SNS, whose influence began to decline with the imminence of the association agreement. Other parties of the more moderate right who were initially Euroskeptics tempered their rhetoric over time. Evidence exists that in the long run this was not just an instrumental acceptance of EU norms but rather a process in which attitudes changed. For instance, xenophobic and ethnocentric attitudes persisted despite early democratization, but data also show that they were tempered as the EU accession process continued (Bernik 1997: 67). The political elite was also transformed. One Slovenian legislator spoke to me candidly about the influence of the EU in intra-party affairs: "The EU, the acquis, always loomed in the background. At party conferences we were lectured on the next item on the EU agenda. We were encouraged to educate our constituents about the EU. Important decisions on party positions were never taken without first consulting with appropriate persons, and the EU reaction was always considered. In many cases this made further debate in parliament unnecessary. I didn't always agree with this, but we were on a determined course."[16]

Any sign that Slovenia was straying from the EU's path—such as during the fierce party battles of the second half of the 1990s—would elicit warnings not from the EU itself but from President Kučan, who reminded warring parties that the EU accession process was at stake.[17] Other domestic organizations issued similar warnings. For instance, Helsinki Watch, criticizing Defense Minister Janša's misuse of the military and security services, wrote: "With that kind of behavior . . . Slovenia is setting up for itself a very poor recommendation for admission to the European Union and to Europe in general" (Ramet 1997a: 207). Needless to say, such statements were widely publicized and turned public opinion against Janša. The government also embarked on an ambitious public relations campaign to promote the EU and the benefits of membership and tried to appease those fearful that Slovenia would lose its sovereignty with the slogan "*Slovenija Doma v Evropi*" (Slovenia, House in Europe) (Government of the Republic of Slovenia 2001: 50). The EU, for its part, issued mostly positive statements regarding Slovenia's status, all of which were immediately cited by elites as evidence of the appropriateness of their policies.[18]

However, at the end of the 1990s, the EU also began to be more critical of slowness in certain areas of reform. A 1998 report in particular came as a shock to the leadership. There were no major complaints about corruption, as there were in other candidate states (Jeffries 2002: 370–71), but the report also cited slow progress in adopting certain parts of the acquis communautaire, mainly owing to the fractious coalition. According to the report, Slovenia lagged behind other candidate countries in administrative and economic reforms, especially in the area of competition in certain sectors and in the free movement of capital. Slovenia was no longer to be forgiven for its challenge to the neoliberal consensus in the economic sphere, a challenge that had kept living standards high but also, in the eyes of the EU and international financial institutions, eroded Slovenia's international competitiveness. These reports had the effect of mobilizing the government to begin to pursue reforms so that subsequent reports were more positive in tone. By the beginning of the new millennium, Slovenia was among the applicant states that had made the most progress in negotiations.

Here we have focused on the EU as the primary external actor shaping regime change in post-communist Slovenia, but others should be mentioned as well. NATO membership was also a priority for Ljubljana, and 66 percent of the population supported the government's endeavors to join (Bugajski 2002: 650). However, at NATO's Madrid summit in May 1997, alliance leaders excluded Slovenia from the first round of enlargement, a devastating blow to the Slovenian leadership. Among the concerns raised by NATO leaders were Slovenia's relations with other states in southeastern Europe. Nevertheless, at the same time Slovenia was singled out as a prime candidate for the second wave of expansion if it continued to pursue political and military reforms (Bugajski 2002: 651). The immediate effect of Slovenia's exclusion was a decrease in NATO support among the public, but it also increased public support for, and thus the momentum toward, the EU.

Economic Performance

Favorable initial conditions notwithstanding, Benderly and Kraft recall that Slovenia's size initially raised questions about economic viability given independence. They also note, however, that "far smaller states operate without difficulty in a European context" and that "the presumption that economic prosperity requires a large state makes less and less sense in a world in which the economies of scale of traditional manufacturing no longer matter, natural resources matter less, and economic integration makes borders less relevant anyway" (Benderly and Kraft 1994: x). In fact, despite a number of setbacks and problems, Slovenia's economy marched steadily forward in the 1990s, justifying the strategies of those who designed the country's independence and democratic transition. The first two years were, admittedly, difficult. During 1991 and 1992 Slovenia experienced a period of declines in income and production and a sharp rise in unemployment, which stood at 14.2 percent in 1992 (Zapp 1996: 61).[19] New private firms were creating jobs rapidly, but not as rapidly as layoffs in the former state-owned sector were eliminating them (Zapp 1996: 62). This was due to a number of factors, most notably the economic shocks that resulted from the loss of former Yugoslav markets. Lost markets and, in many cases, lost assets in other Yugoslav republics created liquidity problems for a number of firms, since they had long subsidized their exports to the West with the generous profits they received from domestic sales. To find new Western business to replace the lost Yugoslav markets, producers had to sell at or below variable costs (Zapp 1996: 61). Losing the Yugoslav market, in fact, had worse consequences than the Slovenian government had anticipated (Zapp 1996: 61). Economic problems resulted also from unexpected pressures, such as the sudden influx of 60,000 refugees from the war in Bosnia and Herzegovina (Ramet 1997a: 208) and sanctions imposed against the entirety of the former Yugoslavia (Bojnec 2000: 1332). Slovenia's tourism sector was also adversely affected.

Following this period of economic decline, a period of recovery ensued. The decline in industrial production slowed from -13.2 percent to -2.8 percent, the rate of inflation was reduced thanks to the establishment of monetary independence, and an increase of 1.3 percent in GNP was recorded (Ramet 1997a: 207). This turnaround, however modest, was critical in keeping the reformers in power and the reforms on track and simultaneously keeping populist forces on the margins of the political scene.[20] It was facilitated above all by a successful stabilization program that included a restrictive monetary and fiscal policy (Bojnec 2000: 1333). Moreover, the currency was stabilized, thanks in part to the efficacy of a fully independent Bank of Slovenia (Rupel 1994: 321) and the successful introduction of the Slovenian tolar, which marked the decisive break with the Yugoslav economy (Zapp 1996: 62). Throughout the 1990s, the tolar was remarkably stable (Zapp 1996: 62). A real testament to the currency's strength, however, were Slovenia's strong foreign currency reserves, about $2 billion in the mid-1990s, and the high share of exports in the GNP (more than 60 percent). In other words, the foreign demand for Slovenian goods and services kept the tolar strong. In a relatively short time the fledgling Slovenian government was able to achieve the kind of macroeconomic stability that federal authorities in Belgrade had attempted with no success prior to the SFRJ's collapse.

By 1994 the economic recovery gained real momentum. That year, the growth rate was 5.3 percent, and industrial production increased by 6.4 percent (Ramet 1997a: 207). This growth contributed to stabilizing the unemployment rate and stimulating a rise in real income so that several years later Slovenia was one of the few post-communist states to register higher total aggregate income than in 1989. The country was able to solidify its standing in the global economic arena by acceding to the General Agreement on Tariffs and Trade (GATT) in the fall of 1994 and by coming to an agreement for cooperation with the European Free Trade Association (EFTA) in 1995. In September 1995, Slovenia was admitted to CEFTA.

Several trends in the early 1990s, however, indicated some long-term problems in the Slovenian economy. Supply-side and structural adjustment policies in particular encountered difficulties. Domestic investment declined steadily during the early 1990s, reaching its lowest point in 1993 (Bojnec 2000: 1333). The greatest criticism of Slovenian economic policy has centered on its inability to attract FDI, deemed crucial for firm restructuring and international competitiveness.[21] The main reason for persistently low levels of FDI in Slovenia was the legal framework that governs privatization policy, which offered few opportunities for external participation in Slovenia's privatization process (Bojnec 2000: 1334).[22] The priority, instead, was given to internal management and labor buyout privatization schemes—in other words, "insider privatization."[23] These privatization policies, besides generating their share of controversy and scandals, were quite ironic, given Slovenia's openness to external trade. They were, however, a result of a concrete legacy of the communist period: the self-management system that only really worked well in Slovenia as well as a general wariness among the Slovenian public of foreign ownership.[24] Enterprise managers in particular assumed a politically powerful role during a period of ambiguity between federal and republican authority, creating new internal mechanisms to maintain the cooperation and support of their workers and working alongside political parties to defeat privatization proposals that threatened their interests (Zapp 1996: 63). Yet there were two sides to this coin: even as the workers' councils and managers constrained the adoption of a privatization policy that would give a greater role to outsiders, they (especially the workers) consistently supported liberal political options, in stark contrast to their counterparts in FRY, for instance. This may be seen as a concerted effort to "pay off" a potentially anti-European constituency rather than the result of certain policy constraints, but either way it is certain that the support liberal parties received from workers and managers in the social sector was crucial in building a liberal regime. Stano-jević has argued that a "side effect" of Slovenian privatization was that it con-tinued Slovenia's tradition of corporatism, in which the political elite sought the support of labor, making labor an important partner in the privatization process (1994: 164).[25] The macroeconomic fallout, however, was clear: due to delayed and contentious privatization, the share of FDI in Slovenia's GDP remained substantially lower than the corresponding level of FDI in front-runner transition economies such as Hungary, Estonia, and the Czech Re-public, leading some analysts to question whether the Slovenian economy would remain competitive in the long term.[26] These problems with the trans-parency and effects of Slovenia's policy of ownership transfer notwithstand-ing, privatization in Slovenia never became what it did in the other three successor states examined in this study: a non-transparent privatization pro-cess whose only beneficiaries were cronies of the ruling regimes. Nor did it prevent the restructuring of firms from taking place—unlike Croatia, FRY, and Macedonia, many bankrupt or loss-making industries were closed down (Bartlett 2000: 148). Ultimately, a compromise approach to privatization was approved, though it took several years to implement, so that by 1995, 868 Slovenian firms had their privatization plans approved by the Privatization Agency (Zapp 1996: 64). Despite evidence that significant assets were still held by managers and other insiders by the end of the 1990s, in general the government's privatization plan was "met with both market and political acceptance" (Zapp 1996: 71).

Privatization, then, proceeded amidst intense parliamentary battles. Large-scale privatization was slow. By July 1998, 90 percent of privatization programs reached their final stage (Jeffries 2002: 380). The small commercial and service sectors were fully privatized at the end of the 1990s, but the state still held shares in around two hundred large companies, which were heavily criticized for their style of management (Jeffries 2002: 381). Minority shareholders were treated with contempt, further scaring away foreign investment. The involvement of workers meant that management could not resist demands for higher wages. In the area of restitution, most cases remained to be settled.

External trade, however, compensated for many of Slovenia's economic deficiencies and consistently fueled growth. Slovenia's primary exporters in the 1990s were a diversified group of internationally recognized firms, as shown in table 5.1.

Slovenia was able to establish most favored nation trading status with the EU in 1993. The aim of full membership in the EU, in fact, became the most important goal of Slovenian trade policy. The proof of this was how quickly its trade was reoriented toward West European markets: in 1987, 35.7 percent of Slovenia's exports went to the rest of Yugoslavia. By 1993, this figure had dropped to 15.9 percent and by 1994 the EU was Slovenia's largest trading partner, with around 66 percent of its exports going to the EU and 69 percent of its imports coming from the EU. Slovenian exchange rate policy was designed not only to reinforce macroeconomic stabilization but also to promote economic integration with the West (Rupel 1994: 316).

Bojnec (2000) finds that both older and newer enterprises were steadily increasing the share of their products and services they sold on international markets in the 1990s. The dependence of the Slovenian economy on exports was calculated to be 57.4 percent, while the measure of total dependence on international trade (exports plus imports as percentage of GDP) stood at 116.3 percent (Ferfila and Phillips 2000: 10). The economic imperative of EU membership thus aligned perfectly with the political one discussed in the previous section.

Driven by exports, economic growth thus marched forward in the 1990s, registering impressive growth rates (figure 5.1).

Despite, or perhaps because of, the lack of reform in key areas, Slovenia's

Table 5.1   Primary Slovenian Exporters, 2001

Firm	Activity
Revoz	Manufacture and marketing of cars
Gorenje	Manufacture of household appliances
Krka, Tovarna Zdravil	Pharmaceutical products
Prevent	Car seat covers, work clothes, and gloves
Lek	Pharmaceutical and chemical products
Sava Tires	Manufacture of tires
Impol	Aluminum production
Mura	Clothing manufacture
Talum	Aluminum production
SZ Acroni	Production of iron, steel, and ferro-alloys

Source: Slovenian Chamber of Commerce and Industry, www.gzs.si/.

economy was growing. Lack of reform in areas such as capital liberalization and a worker buyout–dominated privatization model shielded many Slovenians from the kind of transition pains experienced by their counterparts in other post-communist states. Slovenia was not immune from demonstrations resulting from economic dislocations, but they were not disruptive, confrontational, or anti-systemic (Bukowski 1999: 90). Whether Slovenia's rejection of many tenets of neoliberalism would hurt its international competitiveness in the long run remained to be seen. For the moment, negative economic legacies of political management and unaccountable social ownership could be overcome with a high level of development and a diversified economic structure as well as a relatively successful industrial policy (Petrin 1995).

By the end of the decade, some of Slovenia's economic problems had been remedied with reform, in part forced by the EU. Privatization, albeit imperfect, was nearly complete. Capital flows were liberalized, and Ljubljanska Banka, Slovenia's largest bank, was restructured to the satisfaction of domestic customers and international financial institutions, though the problem of uncompensated depositors from the rest of the former Yugoslavia remained (Lampe 2000: 334).

Hence, in 2000 the IMF submitted the following assessment of the Slovenian economy: "Slovenia is among the most successful transition economies of central and Eastern Europe. It has a functioning market economy, a stable macroeconomic environment with sustainable growth, the highest standard of living and investment ratings among transition countries, and has made

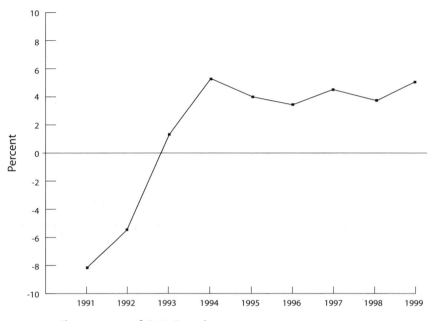

Figure 5.1. Slovenia, Rate of GDP Growth, 1991–1999
Source: www.nationmaster.com.

significant progress towards convergence with the EU" (quoted in Phillips and Ferfila 2000: 179). However, structural problems were also noted by the World Bank (1999) and in an EU progress report:

> Slovenia is a functioning market economy. Provided that it implements the remaining reforms to increase competition in domestic markets, it should be able to cope with competitive pressure and market forces within the Union in the near term … remaining restrictions to capital movements are progressively being removed, in the context of managed exchange rates. However, the persistent inflation, linked to widespread indexation … remains a concern. Labor markets are not sufficiently flexible. The authorities should now progress with the implementation of the announced structural reforms and privatization in a number of essential sectors such as banking and insurance.[27]

Inotai and Stanovnik (2004: 355) observed that slow privatization, low levels of FDI, and a weak banking sector made the Slovenian economy of the late 1990s substantially less competitive than the economies of Hungary, the Czech Republic, and Poland.

These deficiencies notwithstanding, the greatest testament to Slovenian economic success was the growth in real per capita income. In this respect, Slovenia was outperforming not only the other post-communist economies but also EU members Greece and Portugal, whose per capita incomes it overtook as the new millennium dawned. At $15,000, this figure represented 73 percent of the EU average.

Moreover, Slovenia's budget deficit and public debt compared favorably with EU members. Among transition countries, it had the lowest inflation rate, the highest GDP per capita, and the lowest unemployment rate (except for the Czech Republic). It had settled all of its debts from the Yugoslav period and, according to investment risk analysts such as Dun and Bradstreet, Slovenia had the lowest level of risk among all transition economies (Government of Slovenia 2001: 54).

However, Slovenia's level of development was evident in more than just aggregates such as income. Human development rates also testified to a high standard of living: for instance, at 4.9 per 1000 live births, the infant mortality rate was among lowest in the world (Government of Slovenia 2001: 76). On the Human Development Index global scale, it ranked 28th in 1997. The growth of income inequality was low in Slovenia: while the Gini coefficient rose 65 percent in Bulgaria in the initial years of transition, in Slovenia it rose by only 17 percent, the lowest of all the transitional economies. It registered a poverty rate of 13.5 percent, also lowest among Central and East European countries, where it was one quarter to one fifth of the population (Toš and Miheljak 2002: 21).

Slovenia embarked on its transition much better structurally prepared than the other three cases in this study. This chapter has demonstrated that favorable starting conditions characterized by high levels of economic viability shaped a liberal orientation on the part of Slovenia's post-communist elites and public, and continued economic success reinforced the liberal project of reform. However, economic viability was merely a necessary—and not a sufficient—determinant of a post-communist regime that was both procedurally and substantively liberal. This chapter has also illustrated how the promise of EU membership reinforced the liberal project. For economic reasons, Slovenia was forced to nourish links with the EU, and in the long term the EU and the EU accession process became the guarantors of Slovenian liberalism by "coopting" most of Slovenian society into the acquis agenda. Cooptation was made possible, in turn, by economic conditions that underpinned pro-EU attitudes. In this sense, economic viability and EU incentives formed a mutually reinforcing dynamic that in turn legitimated democratic institutions.

If, as Pridham (1990) argues, the first decade is a crucial test of whether democracy will hold, then the prospects for Slovenian liberalism looked good at the end of the 1990s. There was little to suggest that the achievements of the 1990s could erode. No serious alternatives to democracy were on the political scene, and democratic institutions functioned smoothly. Yet, as Slovenia marched forward into the new millennium, several questions remained. Given its determination to reject many tenets of neoliberal market ideology, would it be able to maintain competitiveness internationally as globalization proceeded apace? Given its reliance on exports to the EU as an engine of economic growth, what kind of political fallout would there be if a sudden downturn took place in Western Europe? In many ways, economic success had made Slovenians more sensitive to gains and losses. Finally, could populism appear once EU membership was realized, that is, once elites no longer felt constrained?

CHAPTER SIX

Illegitimate Democracy

Macedonia's Transition in the 1990s

Elated by their good business cooperation, [ethnic Albanian leader] Xhaferi and [Prime Minister] Georgievski thought that finally Albanians and Macedonians also became brothers. They forgot that cooperation between politicians doesn't necessarily mean cooperation among ordinary citizens who have [gained] nothing from luxury, privileges, and corruption of power.... That is why today Albanians don't even believe their own political parties.

KIM MEHMETI, MACEDONIAN ALBANIAN WRITER, POET,
JOURNALIST, AND TRANSLATOR, ON THE 1998–2001
VMRO-PDA COALITION GOVERNMENT.

Difficult Initial Conditions

Macedonia's transition in the 1990s was deeply troubled, characterized by political instability and deep divisions among its people. The main hindrance to establishing a liberal post-communist regime in Macedonia was its lack of economic viability as an independent state and the reproduction of poverty in the 1990s and beyond. Poor economic conditions characterized the starting point of Macedonia's post-communist transition: few competitive modern industries with little to no export potential, a high degree of dependence on Yugoslav markets and federal aid disbursements, a large agricultural sector, and no service sector to speak of. Pettifer notes that Macedonia was "at the bottom of the federal heap in every way, in terms of wage or output levels, literacy, social and educational provision, or any other measure" (2001: 20). Economic malaise was deepened by a number of negative externalities in the 1990s—an economic embargo against Macedonia imposed by neighboring Greece, international sanctions against the FRY and a large influx of refugees as a result of the war in Kosovo. Poor economic conditions translated into intense competition over very scarce resources, which intensified conflict between Macedonia's ethnic Slav and Albanian populations. A deteriorating economic situation in the 1990s had the net effect of further reducing employment and diminishing other economic advancement opportunities, which raised the general level of resentment in the ethnic Albanian community. Ethnic divisions were reflected in the open hostility of many ethnic Albanians toward Macedonian sovereignty, rendering the state itself illegitimate in the eyes of a large portion of its population. Moreover, ethnic divisions were especially acute in light of a comparatively young, and thus insecure, Macedonian national identity.[1] The economics of extreme scarcity were also at the root of rampant corruption on the part of all governments in the 1990s, which led to a deep public mistrust of state institutions. Ethnic divisions and corruption, in turn, severely weakened the Macedonian state and its institutions.

Macedonia's lack of economic viability was partially and temporarily overcome by extensive Western involvement, which acted as a guarantor of economic survival and macro-political stability in the short term. The West prevented ethnic divisions from turning into divisive politics and violence and also forced the political elite, acutely conscious of the need for international support in order to ensure their state's—and, by extension, their own—political survival, to fall in line with the basic tenets of procedural democracy. However, the elites saw little incentive to pursue anything but a thin facade of democracy. Instead, nominal cooperation with the Western project in the form of multiethnic coalitions became a convenient cover for complicity in organized crime and corruption, which some have blamed for the 2001 outbreak of a "mini war" between ethnic Albanian rebels and the Macedonian army.[2] The convenience of this arrangement went beyond such motives, though: Macedonian elites could point to the presence of ethnic Albanians in government structures to show that adequate rights were being afforded the country's Albanian community and remain in the West's good favor, while Albanian elites could claim to be fighting for the rights of their constituency. Elites, then, largely benefited from this arrangement, while the public grew cynical and detached. The West, for its part, consistently praised Macedonia's relative stability and peace, and yet at the same time it did little in the way of offering a credible promise of membership in Western organizations. In fact,

Western involvement may have provided a false sense of security. According to Macedonian scholar Mirjana Maleska, one troubling and unexpected result of Western sponsorship in the 1990s was that Macedonian elites, in denial about the looming conflict, actually began to believe that Macedonia was comfortably stable.[3]

The Macedonian case is one of procedural democracy "simulated" by elites to gain and maintain some threshold of Western support but mostly lacking in substantive liberalism, much more so than Croatia. The low liberal content in post-communist Macedonia was reflected in low levels of democratic legitimacy, deep ethnic cleavages, division over basic issues about the state, and the large presence of illiberal groups and parties on the political scene. The Macedonian case is also a powerful, and tragic, illustration of the limits of illegitimate democracy in the long term, especially when the commitment, reach, and public acceptance of liberalism is shallow.

Formal Democracy: The Record

Many accounts were quite optimistic about Macedonia's democratic institutions and procedures in the 1990s, singling out the seemingly successful efforts at interethnic cooperation in government for praise.[4] To the extent that democratic institutions functioned, albeit imperfectly, the positive view of these accounts was not unwarranted. In spite of seemingly insurmountable odds, Macedonia did have for most of the 1990s a somewhat procedurally correct democratic order that included regular elections, a parliamentary system, and progress in a number of key areas such as media freedom and minority rights.[5] Part of the optimism on the part of observers reflected Macedonia's *relative* success: compared to the authoritarian politics of FRY and Croatia and the bloodshed in Bosnia and Herzegovina, Macedonia appeared to be an oasis of relative peace and stability.

Although formal democratic institutions were in place, their day-to-day functioning was highly flawed. Democratic rules were often not enforced. While there was little evidence of outright rigging of elections, there was ample evidence of irregularities that produced illegitimate results. For instance, the Organization for Security and Cooperation in Europe (OSCE) concluded that the 1994 elections, the second round of which was boycotted by an important party and its supporters, were marred by irregularities (Karatnycky et al. 1999:

389). In general, all elections in the 1990s were characterized by chaos and the threat of instability.

The judiciary was barely reformed in the 1990s. It was slow and inefficient, and in 1997 research found that eighteen of thirty courts were not performing their duties. Moreover, surveys revealed that 50 percent of the population had no trust at all in the judicial system (Karatnycky et al. 1999: 397), a number that would only grow. According to the 1997 report of the Helsinki Committee for Human Rights, "The quality of trials and verdicts is also very low, a fact being confirmed by the great number of annulments." The report also stated that "judges, instead of seeing their role in the protection of civil rights and freedoms and of legality and fairness of the proceeding, see themselves as active partners of the prosecution" (Karatnycky et al. 1999: 397). It also cited political interference in the work and selection of judges and criticized the limited rights of defendants, who were often not afforded public defenders.

There were a number of media outlets, although until the end of the 1990s most were under government ownership and thus subject to political control. For instance, during the University of Tetovo crisis in 1995, Macedonian-language papers were uniformly critical of ethnic Albanian demands. It was quite ironic that Albanian-language papers, also under government subsidy, were often so inflammatory in their ethno-nationalist rhetoric. Perhaps the small percentage of Slavic Macedonians who understand Albanian explained this. Independent print media outlets did begin to appear in the second half of the 1990s with well-known titles such as *Nova Makedonija, Utrinski Vesnik,* and *Dnevnik.* There were few television outlets, mostly under government control, but they nonetheless proved to be generally reliable sources of information (Karatnycky et al. 1999: 377).

The Macedonian constitution was somewhat contradictory on the point of minority rights. On one hand, it guaranteed equal rights to all groups, and yet at the same time it defined Macedonia as the "national state of the Macedonian nation." In practice, despite the presence of Albanian politicians in all of the governments constituted in the 1990s, little progress was made in the 1990s on language and educational rights for ethnic Albanians, which caused repeated incidents of instability, rioting, and violence. Ethnic Macedonian elites continually promised change. Ethnic Albanian politicians at times genuinely fought for these rights, while at other times, they "pretended" to fight for them but in reality engaged in political maneuvers to protect their positions and influence. Discrimination against Albanians was commonplace, especially in employment and in abuses by the police.

Pluralism was weakened between 1994 and 1998, when several major parties were left out of the Sobranie (Macedonia's legislature) and the political process, allowing the ruling parties, mostly former communists, to entrench themselves in state institutions and benefit from insider financial deals (Cabada 2001: 100). Aside from admonitions by the highly interventionist international community and harsh extra-parliamentary criticism by opposition parties, the ruling Social Democratic Union of Macedonia (Socijaldemokratski Sojuz Makedonije, SDSM) had few checks on their power.

The rule of law was extremely weak, with corruption and graft pervasive at all levels of government and business, leading to widespread distrust of state institutions. In 1999, the Berlin-based Transparency International ranked Macedonia 66th out of 99 possible positions. It shared this ranking with Egypt and Ghana. Political parties were a main site of corruption and used patronage and quasi-privatization to enrich their members (Hislope 2002: 35). A weak indigenous civil society did not have the resources to counter such trends, and as such action was only taken when high-ranking officials were exposed and shamed by the media, their political opponents, or foreign NGOs.

In sum, in the 1990s Macedonia's post-communist regime only superficially adhered to the democratic procedures stipulated in its constitution. Much of the procedural correctness that existed was thanks to extensive foreign involvement.

The First Elections

Macedonia was the last of the Yugoslav republics to hold free elections. There was little to no impetus for such elections among the republican political elite and public, and they were held largely because everyone else in the region was holding free elections at the time. Nor was there a strong impetus for independence in a republic whose livelihood depended on political and financial support from the rest of the SFRJ. When the republic did finally opt for independence, it was less by design than by default (Janos 2000: 391). Macedonia prepared for its first elections as central Yugoslav controls weakened and the communist stranglehold gave way to nationalist and autonomist forces on the political scene. One group in particular—the Internal Macedonian Revolutionary Organization–Democratic Party for Macedonian National Unity (Vnatrešna Makedonska Revolucionerna Organizacija–Demokratska Partija za Makedonsko Nacionalno Edinstvo, VMRO-DPMNE) gained popularity quite quickly with its appeals to Macedonian nationalism, historical symbols, and lost territories. VMRO's leader was the young and fiery nationalist writer Ljupčo Georgievski. Although it renounced the terrorist tradition of its prewar predecessor of the same name, VMRO pledged to continue its nationalist political traditions. The other major contenders in the elections were the reformed League of Communists of Macedonia (Sojuz na Komunistite na Makedonija, SKM), now pledging support for democracy and market reform and led by the young Branko Crvenkovski; the ethnic Albanian Party for Democratic Prosperity (Partija za Demokratski Prosperitet, PDP; Albanian: Partia për Prosperitet Demokratik, PPD); and the Marković-led Alliance of Yugoslav Reform Forces. The high-turnout elections held in late 1990 produced a fractured parliament in which no party or coalition secured a clear majority, though VMRO won the most seats. It was unable to form a governing coalition because of lack of adequate support, in part because it did not have enough qualified individuals within its ranks. The elections were held against a backdrop of ethnic tension, resurgent nationalism, growing ruptures among the Yugoslav republics, and serious economic decline.

Exit polls suggested that voting was entirely along ethnic lines (Perry 1997: 233). This was true not only of the two largest ethnic groups (Macedonians and Albanians): Serbs voted as a bloc for ethnic Serb parties, Roma for Roma parties, Turks for Turkish parties, and so on. In circumstances of uncertainty and economic scarcity, ethnic groupings offered the most security for Macedonia's diverse peoples. Reform programs, if proposed at all, were vague. Besides ethnicity, parties were split over the communist past and the Yugoslav period as well as Macedonia's future sovereignty, with the SKM still promoting a confederation of Yugoslav states and the VMRO pushing for outright independence (Bugajski 2002: 725).

After three rounds of balloting, there was still no clear majority, and a precarious balance was achieved among reform communists and Macedonian and Albanian nationalists. Although VMRO had performed poorly in the initial rounds, it successfully used nationalist issues to surge in the runoffs. The assembly later elected former communist and Tito ally Kiro Gligorov as president. It was Gligorov who had been the impetus behind the formation of a "government of experts" as a solution to the parliamentary deadlock. This was important, as it sidelined the nationalists at a critical moment and established a precedent in which Gligorov overshadowed the Sobranie in key decisions. Gligorov's legitimacy derived from his patriarch-like status and support among all of Macedonia's ethnic groups.

With VMRO unable to form a government, an expert government took shape with Skopje University professor Nikola Kljusev at its head. Only two of fifteen ministers had any party affiliation. As the new administration seemed determined to avoid any escalation of ethnic tensions, one deputy premier and two government ministers were ethnic Albanians (Bugajski 2002: 726). The Albanian PDP also obtained chairmanships in key parliamentary committees as well as representation in judicial bodies, including the Supreme Court. Although the government was officially nonpartisan, the former communists, closely allied with Gligorov, took the lead in parliamentary affairs.

Conscious of its perils, President Gligorov was hardly a supporter of Macedonian independence. But as Slovenia and Croatia departed the federation and it became clear that Milošević was bent on war, independence became imminent. Fortunately, in part due to a personal relationship between Serbian and Macedonian JNA commanders as well as JNA troop requirements in Croatia and Bosnia, Gligorov was able to negotiate a peaceful withdrawal of federal troops and equipment from Macedonian territory.[6]

A referendum was held on 8 September 1991, and nearly 70 percent of eligible voters opted for independence. However, most ethnic Albanians, organized by their parties, refused to participate in the referendum, citing non-acceptance of the constitution. Symbolically, this mass boycott by over 20 percent of the population also meant non-acceptance of the state, a fact that injected a large dose of illegitimacy into the post-communist Macedonian nation-building project. Nonetheless, independence was declared in December, and a slow and difficult process of international recognition ensued.

The government of experts under Nikola Kljusev oversaw the initial phases of transition. It established a stable government, introduced a sound anti-inflation program that included the introduction of a new currency, the denar, and presided over the creation of a new military. It resigned in July 1992 after a no-confidence vote promoted by the SDSM (this was the new name of the SKM), Liberals (Liberalna Partija na Makedonija, LP), and Socialists (Socialistička Partija na Makedonija, SPM), who sought a political government. VMRO, with the most deputies in the Sobranie, tried to form a new government but again failed to garner the necessary support, overshadowed by Gligorov and the extensive organizational apparatus of the former communists. Instead, a new government headed by thirty-year-old Branko Crvenkovski and made up of a four-party coalition including the PDP and its more radical ethnic Albanian ally, the People's Democratic Party (Narodna Demokratska Partija, NDP), the SDSM, and the Liberals was brought in and made stability and prosperity its chief goals. Although a number volatile issues arose, the government worked closely with the United States, the EU, President Gligorov, and ethnic Albanian leaders to resolve differences peacefully. Yet the constitutional status of ethnic Albanians remained unresolved, and the economic situation kept getting worse. The dilemma for the government was to give serious consideration to Albanian expectations without antagonizing influential nationalists (Szajkowski 2000: 256). VMRO, meanwhile, continued to play a disruptive role in interethnic relations with its radical populist rhetoric and actions, like the creation of ethnic Macedonian self-defense committees in Albanian-populated areas. Moreover, being just as fiercely anti-communist and anti-Western as it was nationalist, it criticized the government for its communist roots and tendency to give in to Western demands.[7]

Subsequent Elections and Party Politics

The 1994 and 1998 Elections

The next elections were held in the fall of 1994. With its power firmly entrenched and backed by the popular President Gligorov, the grand coalition led by the SDSM did very well. The 1994 election was crucial in terms of its importance for the future direction of the fledgling state. Despite the ruling coalition's advantages, VMRO had significant support among ethnic Macedonians most hurt by the harsh economic transition and those living in areas heavily populated by ethnic Albanians.[8] Round one led to a victory for the Alliance for Macedonia, a three-party coalition led by President Gligorov and made up of the SDSM, the LP, and the SPM. The two main opposition parties, the Democratic Party (Demokratska Partija, DP) of Petar Gošev and VMRO, blasted the outcome as fraudulent and demanded new elections (Perry 1997: 235). They called for a boycott of the second round of voting. As a result, only 57.5 percent of the eligible constituency cast votes in the second round. The opposition parties began a massive campaign to discredit the elections, organizing protests and marches throughout the country and claiming that the elections had been rigged. International election monitoring organizations found irregularities in the elections but declared them to be valid. Nevertheless, allegations of ballot rigging, fraud, and destruction of ballots lingered, and two election commissioners resigned their posts (Perry 1997: 235).

As a result of the boycott, 95 percent of the seats were captured by members of the Alliance for Macedonia—the SDSM got 58 seats, the LP took 29, and the Socialists took 8 seats. Of the remaining mandates, 10 went to the PDP, 4 to the NDP; the remainder went to an assortment of small parties and 7 independents (Perry 1997: 236).

In 1994 the PDP, the main Albanian party, underwent an internal split when a radical faction led by Arben Xhaferi left the party, criticizing its gradualist program for the integration of ethnic Albanians and its willingness to cooperate unconditionally with ethnic Macedonian parties. In time, local PDP offices throughout western Macedonia began to fall to Xhaferi's splinter group, the Party of Democratic Prosperity-Albanians (Partija za Demokratski Prosperitet na Albancite, PDP-A; Albanian: Partia për Prosperitet Demokratik–Shqiptarët, PPD-Sh), later renamed the Democratic Party of Albanians, (Demokratska Partija na Albancite, DPA, or, in Albanian, Partia Demokratike Shqiptare, PDSh). The more moderate faction of the PDP joined the governing coalition.

Buoyed by the lack of an intra-parliamentary opposition and the support of the West, the government enjoyed an easy ride until February 1996, when the coalition broke down after the Liberals, led by Stojan Andov, withdrew from the government, objecting, among other things, to the disproportionate representation of Albanians in the Crvenskovski cabinet at the expense of other coalition partners. Pressured by the West, whose support it desperately needed, the SDSM had indeed made efforts to include ethnic Albanians in governing structures and in important state organs like the judiciary and diplomatic missions. The newly formed Xhaferi-led Albanian opposition claimed that these were just superficial moves aimed to quell Albanian opposition and criticized the ethnic Albanian cabinet members for doing little to support the plight of Macedonian Albanians. Gligorov tried to keep the coalition together, but to no avail. Crvenkovski ultimately was forced to reconstitute the government, which now excluded LP members, while the overall representation of ethnic Albanians rose from four to six. Meanwhile, public opinion polls reflected deep cynicism and distrust among the public toward the government: only 10 percent said the government was functioning well, while 69 percent believed change was necessary (Perry 1997: 235).

The VMRO was a highly vocal extra-parliamentary opposition, and a radical nationalist one at that. It criticized the government constantly for its accommodation of ethnic Albanians and its cozy relationship with the West. In 1996, it organized a nationwide petition drive for early elections and organized parallel, illegal elections when this strategy failed. However, with the firm support of the West behind it, the extensive organizational advantages and resources it had inherited from its communist predecessor, and the aversion of many Macedonians to potential conflict, the ruling coalition prevailed. At times the SDSM used the threat of instability to garner support for its agenda.[9] In general, the SDSM seldom showed a commitment to real pluralism, but, as former foreign minister Denko Maleski explained to me, "A low level of democracy at that time may have saved us from war."[10]

Over the next two years the SDSM became increasingly arrogant in the eyes of the public. For average Macedonians the economic situation had deteriorated even further so that most of the population was dependent on the informal economy and remittances from relatives in the West to survive. Unemployment had risen to socially dangerous levels and was especially prevalent among new entrants to the labor force. Corruption scandals began to engulf the Crvenkovski government, and by the time of the 1998 elections, it was seen as deeply illegitimate. Even its Western supporters could not rescue it now, but to the extent that they did try to save a political configuration that was perceived as corrupt and ineffective in the eyes of the public, it delegitimized the West and the external project of liberalism itself. So it was no surprise when in the 1998 elections, over 45 percent of the vote went to a coalition of VMRO and a newly formed party, the Democratic Alternative (Demokratska Alternativa, DA).

Surprising, however, was the announcement that Xhaferi's DPA would participate in the coalition, which effectively meant an alliance of Albanian and Macedonian extreme nationalists. However, both Xhaferi and Ljubčo Georgievski campaigned with greatly moderated rhetoric, in no small part because they understood the risks of alienating the West.[11] The improbable coalition was also a result of political forces within the Albanian bloc: sharp disagreements between the PDP (associated with the ousted SDSM coalition) and DPA leadership gave Xhaferi a golden opportunity to secure cabinet positions for himself and his DPA colleagues. Xhaferi nonetheless issued a warning to his VMRO partners: "The DPA has acquired its reputation among Albanians with the fight for realization of the basic social, educational, and cultural rights and de-blocking of some relations which cause irregularities in the election process. If it turns out that our hopes for resolving these key problems were in vain, we will step out of the government" (quoted in Szajkowski 2000: 260). The VMRO's rhetoric and policy proposals were also moderated because of its alliance with the DA, a nominally liberal party led by Vasil Tupurkovski, a highly popular politician who understood the imperatives of working with the Western presence in Macedonia. Despite concerns about VMRO, Tupurkovski and the multiethnic coalition that claimed to support Macedonia's membership in the EU and NATO briefly appeased the West. The newly formed government also promised to work toward interethnic harmony and economic recovery. Nonetheless, it was not nearly as solid a partner of the West as its predecessor. Efforts to fix the economy and lessen ethnic divisions largely failed, in part owing to the escalation of the war in neighboring Kosovo. In the end corruption and organized crime became virtually synonymous with the VMRO coalition.

The Role of Kiro Gligorov

It would be impossible to discuss the post-communist Macedonian political scene without mentioning the key role of President Kiro Gligorov, who was returned to office in 1994, but by an extremely slim margin, barely edging out Ljubčo Georgievski of VMRO. Gligorov, who remained in the post of president until 1999, was a member of the last Titoist generation of post-Yugoslav leaders. During World War II, he had been a Partisan sympathizer, and in the SFRJ, he held top economics posts in Belgrade as well as posts in the presidency of the SFRJ and the Central Committee of the League of Communists of Yugoslavia. He was among the creators of a 1965 marketization program that never worked. When he ascended to the presidency of Macedonia, he soon assumed the role of a "father of the nation." Though he was clearly not a great democrat, Gligorov was also not a "father" in the authoritarian mold of Croatia's Franjo Tuđman. Rather, he played the role of a benevolent leader who could rise above many political conflicts and broker inter-ethnic cooperation by balancing the exclusionary demands of the nationalists with the inclusionary demands of the ethnic Albanian parties; he also pacified the nationalists at several key junctures. Furthermore, he declared repeatedly that Macedonia had no territorial aspirations against its neighbors and negotiated the peaceful withdrawal of the JNA from Macedonian soil, assuring its sovereignty. In so doing, he worked closely with and was strongly supported by the West, which exposed him to criticism by nationalists. He worked with the West because he had an acute understanding of Macedonia's internal and external vulnerability, and he knew that Western support would not be forthcoming if Macedonia became an authoritarian state. In light of nationalist pressure, cooperation with the West often meant privately giving in to Western demands while publicly rejecting them. He remained highly popular (a kind of successor to Tito in a country in which Tito's portrait still hangs from many walls); indeed, a 1995 poll gave him a 95 percent approval rating (Perry 1997: 246–47). More important, both ethnic Macedonians and Albanians viewed him in a positive light. In the mid 1990s, 76 percent of Albanians and 93 percent of ethnic Macedonians considered President Gligorov to have "considerable beneficial influence in inter-ethnic relations" (Najčevska et al. 1996: 93). He was the only politician, in fact, to transcend the divisive ethnic boundary. He understood that material conditions had a lot to do with the progress of ethnic relations and Macedonian state legitimacy among Albanians, saying: "The most important thing for us would be for Macedonia to be developed economically. And if we live better in Macedonia than in Serbia, Kosovo, Bulgaria, and Albania, then Albanians will remain here" (quoted in Liotta 2001: 249).

It was President Gligorov who requested that a UN peacekeeping force monitor Macedonia's post-communist transition. His role was so critical in the 1990s that when on 3 October 1995 twenty kilograms of explosives detonated in a car next to Gligorov's and nearly killed him, the government was seriously destabilized. LP leader and President of the Sobranie Stojan Andov became interim president. Gligorov survived but lost an eye and was left with shrapnel fragments in his head. Those responsible for the assassination attempt were never identified.

The Main Parties and Their Orientations

At one point in the 1990s there were as many as sixty parties registered in Macedonia, which was quite extraordinary for a country of two million people.[12] However, only a few really mattered. It was difficult to speak of a truly liberal democratic party in post-communist Macedonian politics, especially since nearly all parties were mono-ethnic. It was possible to identify parties who spoke to democracy and the free market more than others, and it was also possible to categorize parties by the degree to which they expressed willingness to work with the West and toward integration into its institutions. The three most liberal parties were the DP and LP and Tupurkovski's DA. All supported a free market, an inclusive democracy, and Macedonia's integration into NATO and the EU. They maintained extensive contacts with Western organizations and states. Yet, at times, they exhibited nationalist tendencies and opposed extending full rights to ethnic Albanians (Perry 1997: 243), as evidenced by Andov's abrupt departure from the ruling coalition for what he perceived to be overrepresentation of Albanians in government. The LP's roots were in Marković's reformist forces, and its membership was made up of enterprise managers and others in the business community, many of whom benefited from the shady privatization deals of the 1990s. The DP sought to be a much more nationally oriented alternative to the LP and SDSM. It was led by Petar Gošev, the only politician really known in Macedonia at the outset of transition because he had built his career in the SKM rather than in Belgrade. The DP portrayed itself as pro-EU and pro-NATO. It was not nearly as nationalistic as the VMRO or PDP, but its membership nevertheless was mostly made up of ethnic Macedonians. Along with VMRO, it withdrew from the 1994 elections and called for a boycott of the second round. Despite espousing an economic program that fell on the far left of the political spectrum, the Socialist Party was ethnically inclusive and tolerant, at least nominally, and could be included among the liberal and pro-Western parties. In some ways, due to strong Yugo-nostalgia among the Macedonian population, it exerted influence disproportionate to its size.

While composed of some members with genuine democratic inclinations, for the most part the SDSM spoke the language of liberalism in order to please Macedonia's Western sponsors and therefore ensure their continued support. Beyond this facade, however, it often acted undemocratically and jealously guarded its power and influence. It was a highly undemocratic organization internally. While it spoke to greater inclusion for ethnic Albanians and included them in governing coalitions, they were given insignificant portfolios and relegated to second-class status. And the SDSM took a decidedly hard-line stance toward calls for expanded Albanian language and educational rights, as demonstrated in the University of Tetovo conflict described later in this chapter. Its young leadership, and Prime Minister Branko Crvenkovski in particular, learned to speak in the language of democracy, human rights, and the free market, thus showing a consistently democratic face to the West. Many Macedonians, aware of the SDSM's flaws, nevertheless supported the party because it was perceived as the better of two evils and was, after all, the party of the popular president Gligorov.[13]

VMRO started the decade as a virulently nationalist party and ended it as a corrupt political machine that simulated a commitment to democracy.[14] It showed itself to be interested in power above all else, and since power could not be achieved without the West's blessing, like the SDSM it fell in line with the basic tenets of formal democracy. VMRO's leader, Ljupčo Georgievski, was an avowed anti-communist nationalist and an advocate of Macedonian independence since the 1980s and maintained close contact with the Macedonian diaspora, among whom there was no shortage of radicals. Throughout the 1990s, VMRO claimed a membership of 150,000, by most estimates greatly inflated.

By choosing the VMRO name, it sought to connect with most important icon of Macedonia's history but openly denounced violence. Until 1998, its program had decidedly illiberal connotations that antagonized not only Macedonian Albanians but also Macedonia's neighbors. It sought to unite Macedonians and Macedonia in a single state and advocated the return of property confiscated by neighboring sates. In so doing, it implicitly challenged state borders, which inflamed passions in Greece. VMRO was openly anti-Albanian, explicitly opposing more rights for the Albanian minority, claiming fear of a Greater Albania. During the 1990 and 1994 campaigns, VMRO argued that multiculturalism was a threat to Macedonian unity and would lead to federalization and ultimately to war. According to Georgievski, there was no future for a multiethnic state in the Balkans. With the campaign slogan "Macedonia is for Macedonians," VMRO made it clear that ethnic Albanians would be kept in their place should the nationalists take power (Williams 2000: 113). It was no surprise, then, that among its most ardent supporters were ethnic Macedonians living in regions populated by ethnic Albanians, where ethnic tensions were highest, though it also enjoyed strong support among unemployed industrial workers, farmers, rural residents, and uneducated people, in other words, those most adversely affected by the shocks of the 1980s crisis and post-communist economic transition.[15] As economic conditions got worse and competition for resources increased, VMRO's simple and radical populist message resonated with the disaffected segments of society. Besides promoting inter-ethnic divisions, the VMRO also played to divisive fears among ethnic Macedonians.[16]

Although decidedly focused on narrow ethno-national concerns, among the ethnic Albanian parties the PDP was the most liberal, interested in compromise, and committed to working within the framework of an independent Macedonian state. It consistently focused on pragmatic concerns, such as promoting employment and educational opportunities for Albanians. But it gradually lost influence and its leader, Nevzat Halili, lost credibility as a declining economy and the efforts of certain political entrepreneurs radicalized rural Albanians.[17] One such entrepreneur was Arben Xhaferi, who, like his VMRO counterpart Georgievski, espoused openly nationalist views. As described earlier, he broke off from the PDP, forming the PDP-A (later the DPA) and called for radical, rather than incremental, change in extending rights to Albanians. This caused a rift within the "rump" PDP: Halili was ousted as leader, and Abdurahman Aliti emerged as the head of the officially recognized faction. Aliti continued to cooperate with the Crvenskovski administration, though at a cost to government stability.

Xhaferi took a decidedly hard line and attracted poorer and less educated segments of the ethnic Albanian electorate. Some of his statements in the early 1990s suggested that ethnic Albanians were ready to secede from Macedonia if not afforded adequate rights, which greatly increased tensions in the mixed ethnic areas of western Macedonia. He also cautioned that violence between nationalities would be a likely outcome if the government did not enact major reforms. The PDP-A's vice president, Menduh Thaçi, a former dental student, was even more radical, arguing that if "Macedonians go on refusing Albanians' demands, there will be bloodshed here . . . only Albanians hold the key to stability in this country." Such talk, however, frightened and alienated not only ethnic Macedonians but many Albanians as well (Perry 1997: 240).

In the end, however, very much like Georgievski, Xhaferi showed himself to be more of a pragmatist than a fundamentalist when he decided to sign on to the VMRO-DPA coalition. His reward was a tangible eight ministerial posts and tacit Western support, which he very well knew he would need in order to achieve any kind of real influence in post-communist Macedonia. In other words, his interests in political power and its spoils ultimately superseded any ideological commitment. Yet, the radical program that the PDP-A had been promoting in Albanian-populated areas could not be abandoned overnight, and certain elements in the party continued to espouse extremist positions in their localities even as the top leadership showed a conciliatory face to the West.

Parties representing Macedonia's other ethnic groups (Slavic Muslims, called *Torbeši*; Turks; Roma) were also present on the political scene but exercised limited influence and generally had very moderate programs.[18] There was one notable exception: the Democratic Party of Serbs in Macedonia (Demokratska Partija na Srbite vo Makedonija, DPS, Serbian: Demokratska Partija Srba u Makedoniji). Though it clearly did not represent the views of all of Macedonia's forty thousand ethnic Serbs, the DPS was involved in a number of anti-Macedonian activities and maintained ties with ultranationalist leaders Željko "Arkan" Ražnajtović and Vojislav Šešelj in Serbia proper as well as with the Serbian Orthodox Church. For good measure, the DPS was anti-American, anti-NATO, and anti-EU.

The Nature of Political Cleavages

The post-communist Macedonian political scene, then, reflected deep divisions in Macedonian society that painted a bleak picture in terms of the liberal content of the polity. The most significant division was ethnic, between the country's Slav Macedonian and ethnic Albanian populations. Macedonia's people voted entirely along ethnic lines throughout the 1990s and lived in parallel societies. This ethnic division was simultaneously a rift between ethnic Albanians and the independent Macedonian state, which many ethnic Albanians did not see as legitimate.

Yet, deep divisions were present among ethnic Macedonians as well, especially in terms of their acceptance of Western liberalism. Though nationalism in Macedonia did not have the wide support it did in Croatia and Serbia due to various insecurities and uncertainties about Macedonian national identity itself, anti-Western sentiment was mobilized at numerous points in the 1990s. Macedonian elites felt that they had no choice but to submit to Western influence—but this did not mean that it had wide acceptance on the ground. Indeed, to some degree it had the opposite effect, delegitimizing both the government and the Western project, especially when the public perceived that the West was supporting corrupt and inept politicians.

The widespread perception of corruption and ineffectiveness, in fact, characterized the deepest division of all in Macedonia by the end of the 1990s: that between the people and their government and its institutions. Public opinion polls conducted throughout the 1990s revealed a profound distrust of the state and all of its institutions (Perry 1997). Reports of corruption and abuse of by persons at the highest levels of power abounded. Macedonians were deeply distrustful of political parties, the Sobranie, the police, the judiciary, and virtually every other key state institution. In their place, they relied on traditional and informal networks to acquire goods and services, to mediate disputes, and to conduct everyday life, all of which deepened intra-ethnic solidarity. There was the collapse of a pyramid scheme in 1997 promoted by a Bitola-based savings institution, which bilked 30,000 customers of $90 million (Karatnycky et al. 1999: 399). There were stories of corruption in the Interior Ministry, with companies owned by friends or relatives of ministry officials given lucrative contracts. Macedonians, furthermore, were exposed to corruption in everyday life and transactions. Routine state services, such as power or trash removal, functioned irregularly.[19] It is no wonder that Macedonians came to see their government as deeply illegitimate and the state itself as a rent-seeking, unaccountable, indifferent entity. If this is how Slav Macedonians felt, asked Hislope, "How can Albanians be asked to sign on to the regime" (2002: 36)?

Indeed, ethnic Albanians, besides being disconnected from the idea of a Macedonian state, also did not perceive that their own leaders were working in their interests, leading to a rift between ordinary Albanians and their political elite, which left a void in legitimacy that was easily filled by radicalism. So interethnic cooperation at the top was not an indication of a positive move toward a multiethnic society but rather a vestige of facade democracy, window dressing that kept elites in the good favor of the West and their pockets lined with money earned through illegal transactions involving Western financial aid.[20] Slav Macedonian parties pretended to cooperate with ethnic Albanian ones, and ethnic Albanian parties often pretended to represent their ostensible constituency's interests. This certainly guaranteed a certain degree of stability and a preservation of parliamentary government, but it did little to ensure stability and legitimacy in the long run.

The Ethnic Albanian Minority, the Politics of Inequality, and State Legitimacy

The "Albanian factor" has dominated post-communist Macedonian politics.[21] There was rarely any relief from the pressure of politicized ethnicity. As

Pettifer observes, ethnic Albanians were seen as "having a practical veto over the future of the state" (2001: 138).

The very question of just how many Albanians there are in Macedonia is a deeply politicized one, with ethnic Albanians accusing the Macedonian government of deliberately undercounting them and ethnic Macedonians accusing ethnic Albanians of inflating population figures to make more demands on the state. It is clear that both sides have engaged in manipulation to suit political ends. The most credible census conducted in the 1990s under the auspices of the EU counted 443,914 Albanians, or 22.9 percent of the total population, and 1,288,330 Macedonians, or 66.6 percent of the total population. Even these figures, however, have been disputed by Albanian groups. Not in dispute was the fact that Macedonia's Albanians were the fastest growing population group in Europe in the 1990s (Hislope 2003: 131).

Albanians claim to be descendants of extinct Illyrians, who lived in the Balkans well before the days of Alexander the Great. In Macedonia, they live in a crescent-shaped region that begins in Kumanovo to the northeast, stretches through Skopje to Tetovo in the northwest, and then reaches south along the Albanian border to Debar, Gostivar, and Struga. As Muslims, during the duration of the Ottoman Empire, they were treated better than their Orthodox counterparts. They did not fare so well under Titoist communism compared to other groups for a number of historical reasons. A combination of political repression and economic exclusion pushed them to the sidelines of society, making them the primary participants in an informal economy. Traditional, clan-based, conservative patterns of rural life reinforced this role (Hislope 2003).

They are separated from Slav Macedonians by both religion and ethnicity. The two groups live side by side and yet function in complete segregation in virtually all spheres of life. Social networks are intra-ethnic, as are places of employment. Unlike Bosnia, intermarriage is virtually nonexistent, and a large majority of both groups said that they would never consider marrying someone from the other (Najčevska et al. 1995: 78). Mutual stereotypes reinforce suspicions. Casual racism against ethnic Albanians pervades Macedonian life. Ethnic Albanians are commonly referred to with the pejorative "*Šiptari*," and even educated Macedonians advance a view that sees Albanians as inferior. Such stereotypes are reinforced by the fact that large numbers of ethnic Albanians, who never benefited from SFRJ-era urbanization and modernization, live in poorer rural conditions in extended families in which women are afforded inferior status. Albanians, in turn, scoff at the construed nature of ethnic Macedonian identity and are irritated by Macedonians' obsession with history.[22]

The fear of a greater Albania has fueled ethnic Macedonian nationalism and attitudes toward Albanians to a large degree. This fear arises first and foremost from the fact the fact that Albanian populations in the region are geographically contiguous. Given the international community's clear opposition to such a project, Albania's rejection of such a possibility, and the very weak desire of most Macedonian Albanians to join Albania proper due to even worse economic prospects there, such fears were largely unfounded, yet they were driven by both nationalist ethnic Macedonian politicians and ethnic Albanian extremists. Slav Macedonian insecurity was also based on demographic trends in the Albanian community.[23]

Interethnic relations and the position of the Albanian minority were shaped first and foremost by the politics of inequality. Inequality between Slav Macedonians and Albanians was largely a holdover from communist-era socioeconomic structures and was intensified by poor economic prospects following independence. By every possible measure, ethnic Albanians were worse off than their Macedonian counterparts. In the area of education, schools where Albanians is taught were generally inferior, and there was no officially recognized university teaching in Albanian in the 1990s. As a result, Albanian children regularly dropped out after eight years of compulsory education (Perry 1997: 259). Of the 27,000 students enrolled in higher education in the mid-1990s, only 1.5 percent were ethnically Albanian. Eighty percent of prisoners were ethnic Albanians. A high percentage of Albanian youth were unemployed, faced poor economic prospects, and regarded violence as an acceptable form of political expression. They were seriously underrepresented in state institutions, a major source of employment in the absence of viable private sector. Among Albanians, unemployment stood at 60 percent, while it was only 30 percent for Slav Macedonians (Hislope 2003: 2008).

Not all Albanians were poor. Many were beneficiaries of the flourishing secondary economy, with major advantages in the market environment.[24] This also fueled the perception among Slav Macedonians that most ethnic Albanians are thieves and criminals. Ethnic Albanians were also overrepresented among guest workers in Western Europe, which translated into remittances for many ethnic Albanian families. In the 1990s, Macedonian Albanians may have been doing better than their ethnic kin in Kosovo or Albania proper, but as Hislope (2003) notes, they did not see these places as a benchmark. This fact notwithstanding, they were in an inferior material position as a whole and in times of economic scarcity, when many Slav Macedonians were struggling, demands for greater equality were likely to lead to conflict. In post-communist Macedonia, there were few resources to go around, and Slav Macedonians claimed them because they perceived themselves to be the "owners" of the new state. It was no wonder that when the ethnic Albanian National Liberation Army framed its struggle in 2001 as a fight for greater equality, it struck a resonant chord. This overlap of ethnic, religious, and economic differences meant that there were few cross-cutting cleavages of the type emphasized by scholars as critical to political compromise and stability. An editorial in the Albanian-language daily *Flaka a Vëllazërimit* captured the issue of inequality when it asked rhetorically, "How can a state succeed when one part of its population is educated, while the other is semi-literate? Does Macedonia have a greater interest in having [ethnic] Albanian children selling cigarettes on the streets than in working with computers?" (quoted in Hislope 2003: 59).

This inequality, and the discrimination perceived to cause it, lay behind low levels of ethnic Albanian support for a Macedonian state and its institutions. While among Slav Macedonians there was a very low level of trust in state institutions, ethnic Albanians simply did not recognize these institutions and relied on alternative ones in daily life.[25] In the 1990s, this was seen in everything from such non-state-affirming activities as a refusal to recognize the constitution and a boycott of the referendum for independence to the flying of Albanian national flags in localities where ethnic Albanians predominate and a practice that especially irritated Slav Macedonians, cheering for the Albanian soccer team in international matches and singing the Albanian national anthem. Furthermore, taxes were rarely collected in some Albanian-populated areas, where even the police did not dare to enter.[26]

It was in this context that several destabilizing interethnic conflicts occurred in the 1990s in which large-scale violence was averted largely by the intervention of the international community:

- Throughout the 1990s, there was conflict over the wording of the constitution and its exclusion of ethnic Albanians.
- In 1992, police and ethnic Albanians clashed in the Skopje neighborhood of Bit Pazar. Four persons were killed and thirty-six injured. Extremists were ready to fight, but PDP leaders called for calm.

- In 1993 authorities announced the discovery of a plot by an unknown group, the All-Albanian Army, to overthrow the government. High-ranking ethnic Albanian officials, including two cabinet ministers, were named in the plot. The Albanian community labeled the news as a hoax that could subsequently be used as an excuse to repress Albanians. Nevertheless, the news struck fears of extremism in most Macedonians and made ethnic relations deteriorate. This incident led to the PDP shakeup described earlier.
- In 1995, there were skirmishes and violent protests over the Albanian-language University of Tetovo. The Macedonian government initially closed the institution in 1995, leading to a riot and one death. Ethnic Macedonians interpreted the university as a challenge to state authority; Albanians saw it as a challenge to the status quo and a chance to increase their educational opportunities and their chances to participate in state administration. Attempts to close down the university were halted under Western pressure, but the regime refused to recognize the institution. President Gligorov came under severe pressure from the nationalists not to recognize it and claimed that it was the work of Albanian separatists. The incident greatly strengthened the PDP-A and Albanian radicals.
- In 1997, mayors of Albanian-populated localities raised the Albanian flag over city halls, which led to violent exchanges with the Macedonian police and army.

Due to Western ambivalence, government inaction, and the failures of Albanian politicians themselves, many of these issues remained unresolved at the end of the 1990s. Resentment among ethnic Albanians grew, as did the interethnic divide. The average Slav Macedonian, meanwhile, was convinced that ethnic Albanians were already being given too many rights. The influx of massive amounts of Albanian refugees from Kosovo in 1999 only exacerbated tensions. When I first visited Macedonia in 2000, the situation was clearly at the breaking point.

The Role of External Forces in Macedonia's Transition

In post-communist Macedonia, Yugoslav paternalism was replaced with Western paternalism, which kept the state viable and the transition peaceful and asked only for a functioning democracy in return. Throughout the 1990s, "the success of [Macedonia's] democratic transition was tied to the influence of external actors as much as the internal development of the political system" (Cabada 2001: 101). An array of actors were involved in Macedonia's early post-communist transition: international organizations like the UN and the EU, individual states, and international financial institutions like the IMF and World Bank, which were all but creating the state budget throughout the 1990s. The OSCE mission was especially involved in the political sphere, helping to broker agreements among political parties (Stoilovski 1999: 85–95). Various international NGOs were active in monitoring Macedonia's transition: their reports were enough to cause political firestorms, change policies, and even determine elections, which caused great resentment among Macedonian politicians of all stripes.[27] They became, in many ways, Macedonia's de facto civil society and were often staffed by young, educated Macedonians who saw their presence as a beneficial employment opportunity. In day-to-day political life, foreign influence over the government remained very strong, "with a small committee of EU and American ambassadors acting in a highly interventionist way over many policy and practical issues" (Pettifer 2001: 128).

In general, the Western project in Macedonia went through two phases. In the first, external actors were interested in maintaining stability at any cost, while in the second, they began to shape the content of state policy under the general theme of liberalism. Macedonian elites, for their part, became adept at simulating democracy, which often meant saying one thing to international officials while doing another. The public was deeply ambivalent and at times distrustful of Western motives; when, as one Macedonian politician described to me, "Americans began imposing their ideas of ethnic quotas on us," the Western project lost support among many ordinary Slav Macedonians.[28] Throughout the 1990s, while supporting Macedonian sovereignty, the West sent very ambiguous and, at times, contradictory messages about the prospect of Macedonian membership in Western organizations. By the end of the 1990s, Macedonians had no clear idea of when and if they would be admitted to NATO or the EU. Part of the problem was that pro-Western attitudes existed in Macedonia out of a profound sense of weakness rather than a genuine desire to pursue liberal reform.

The West, however, did not address itself to the serious interethnic problem until it was too late, perhaps mistakenly believing that the interethnic coalitions it had encouraged reflected actual relations. The elites in these coalitions, for their part, were happy to play the part and derive the benefits that come with political power. In the Sobranie, ethnic Albanian elites consistently denied support for a greater Albania but at the same time did not sign on to state institutions and used inflammatory rhetoric in their home constituencies, giving more radical members of the Albanian community room to pursue separatistism. In the same manner, Slav Macedonian elites spoke the language of multiculturalism and human rights in front of international officials but did little to implement the kind of policies that would increase the rights of ethnic Albanians.

Relations with Greece

The most difficult relationship turned out to be with Greece, which refused to recognize Macedonian independence because of objections to the use of the name "Macedonia," the flag, and accusations of irredentist claims on Greek territory in the Macedonian constitution. Greece blocked Macedonian cooperation with the EU and its membership in a number of international organizations. When other countries went ahead and recognized Macedonian sovereignty, Greece imposed a crippling trade embargo on the country, which by some estimates cost the Macedonian economy $40 to $50 million (Williams 2000: 26). Eventually the United States helped broker an agreement in which Macedonia was recognized under the cumbersome name "Former Yugoslav Republic of Macedonia" (FYROM; Shea 1997: 304). President Gligorov faced significant nationalist backlash at home for approving this deal, but it allowed Macedonia to be admitted to the OSCE, Council of Europe, and NATO's PFP. In the long run, economic relations with Greece grew, and it became the largest foreign investor in Macedonia. But the Greek embargo also helped stimulate the extensive smuggling that became a staple of Macedonia's underground economy.

UNPREDEP

The most concrete manifestation of Western involvement in Macedonia was the United Nations Preventive Deployment Force (UNPREDEP) that played a major role in maintaining stability in Macedonia from 1993 to 1999. On 11 November 1992, during a meeting in New York with UN Secretary General Boutros Boutros-Ghali, President Gligorov requested that the UN deploy "observers" in Macedonia "in view of his concern about the possible impact on it of fighting elsewhere in the former Yugoslavia" (Williams 2000: 43). The following day, Gligorov also discussed the deployment of UN troops with Cyrus Vance and Lord David Owen, co-chairmen of the Steering Committee of the International Conference on the Former Yugoslavia. They later wrote to the secretary-general supporting such a deployment. For the first time in history, the UN's peacekeepers would be deployed before potential outbreak of conflict, rather than after hostilities had erupted.[29] At the time, Gligorov claimed that the need for the deployment was due only to external, not internal, threats. The UN, for its part, clearly perceived an internal threat, a disagreement that would persist throughout the UNPREDEP's mandate in Macedonia. The United States would play a significant role in this force, and in fact Macedonia became the first place in the former Yugoslavia where the United States deployed ground troops. The presence of U.S. troops greatly enhanced the deterrence capability of the UNPREDEP forces. As Williams writes, the message was simple: "hands off Macedonia." Williams also notes that Gligorov's request was "a tribute to his foresight and a reflection of his keen understanding of the volatile Balkan region" (2000: 36).

The UNPREDEP forces were deployed in 1993 with the following mandate: (1) to monitor the border areas and report to the secretary-general, through the force commander, any developments that could pose a threat to Macedonia; and (2) to deter threats from any source, as well as to prevent clashes which could occur between external elements and Macedonian forces, thus helping to strengthen security and confidence in Macedonia (Williams 2000: 45). Over the course of its presence in Macedonia, however, the mandate of UNPREDEP was expanded to include three "pillars" of responsibility: political, military, and socioeconomic. The political pillar included reconciliation and mediation between the Slav Macedonian and Albanian communities, the military pillar rested on the deployment of international troops at the northern and western borders, and the socioeconomic pillar was intended to assist local communities with financial aid (Vayrynen 2003: 51). This expanded mandate included the creation of "good offices" designed to deal with civilian affairs and a special police monitoring force, CIVPOL. The UN insisted on CIVPOL's presence, "a signal that there was a link between the country's interethnic relations and its stability and that this matter was of legitimate concern to the world body" (Williams 2000: 49). This new civilian intervention eventually came to cooperate quite closely with the OSCE in brokering deals among political parties and mediating in interethnic disputes. One former Macedonian cabinet member described to me how he received numerous phone calls from the UNPREDEP political officer during the dispute, informing him that "it would not be in his interest" to back harsh measures against the renegade institution.[30] Henryk Sokalski, who led the UNPREDEP mission for much of the 1990s, writes:

> Dialogue, discretion, and quiet diplomacy were the basic tools of action. The mission developed and maintained active contacts with political forces and ethnic groups in the country as a means of promoting domestic stability. Constant efforts were made to reduce the level of mistrust among the country's political and ethnic actors and set in place a dialogue on questions regarding the rights of ethnic communities and national minorities. UNPREDEP was recognized as a significant instrument for facilitating dialogue, restraint, and practical compromise between the different segments of Macedonian society. (2003: 108)

By 1996, the UN secretary-general was openly suggesting that the most likely source of instability in Macedonia was an internal threat, which gave the UN license to expand its "advising" capabilities in political and other civilian affairs:

> The original purpose of deploying a preventive United Nations mission in FYROM was to prevent conflicts from spilling over or threatening that country. Recent developments in the region, and the enhanced international standing of the former Yugoslav Republic of Macedonia, have made such a scenario more remote. Moreover . . . it has become increasingly evident that the primary threat to the country's stability may come from internal political tensions. UNPREDEP has accordingly devoted considerable attention to strengthening dialogue between the political forces and has assisted in monitoring human rights and interethnic relations. (quoted in Williams 2000: 134)

As for the troops themselves, they were a small (at most fifteen hundred peacekeepers) but very effective entity. Besides keeping any potential external threats at bay, they succeeded in demarcating Macedonia's border with Serbia and prevented numerous incidents from erupting into large-scale conflicts.[31] The importance of the security guarantee they provided, internal or external, cannot be underestimated for a small and weak state like Macedonia, which had no army to speak of. The internal political ramifications were multifold.[32] It kept radicalism at bay and provided much-needed international legitimacy to the government.

The Macedonian political elite was deeply divided over the UNPREDEP presence, while public opinion remained quite ambivalent. The mission received the strongest support from the ruling SDSM, while VMRO opposed it, and especially its "good offices" function, which it saw as a way to undermine Macedonian sovereignty and impose foreign values on the Macedonian citizenry.[33] Ethnic Albanians were initially also ambivalent, even turning hostile when it became obvious that UNPREDEP was unwilling to raise the uncomfortable ethnic question for fear of disrupting stability.

UNPREDEP was not without its critics, however. In the late 1990s Human Rights Watch accused the UN and the OSCE of supporting the Gligorov regime unconditionally and of tolerating human rights violations in Macedonia to maintain stability: "In the name of stability, however, both the UN and OSCE tend to defend the status quo in Macedonia and downplay human rights violations within the country. Only gentle criticism is directed against a friendly government that is seen as a stabilizing force" (quoted in Williams 2000: 133). The U.S. role was also criticized in this regard since it extended uncritical support to Gligorov and Crvenkovski and largely neglected ties with VMRO. To some, this sent the message that the lack of democracy and corruption would be tolerated in the name of short-term stability. The United States was also criticized for not doing enough to address the ethnic problem:

> In fact, the Americans are in Macedonia for the wrong reasons, and are destined to accomplish nothing whatsoever. The main threat to Macedonia is internal disintegration, not invasion from outside. Despite efforts to integrate its substantial Albanian minority, the Macedonian government is facing a steadily rising Albanian opposition and, when it comes to keeping them down, Macedonia remains Serbia's potential ally.... The chances are that once the Albanian question erupts Washington will conclude that it should have stationed its troops in the near-by Greek island of Corfu; at least the weather is more welcoming there. (Eyal 1995)

The United States was clearly uncomfortable with VMRO's victory in the 1998 election, a fact captured by one Macedonian newspaper when it published a top-ten list of election "losers" that included then American Ambassador to Macedonia Christopher R. Hill (Szajkowski 2000: 266).

The UNPREDEP mission was renewed by the Security Council several times but finally ended in 1999 due to the misled foreign policy of the VMRO government, which decided to recognize Taiwan in exchange for $2 billion in Taiwanese aid and investment. China promptly vetoed an extension of UNPREDEP's mandate, which in a skewed way actually served VMRO's nationalist goals. The move, according to Vayrynen, was a "politically short-sighted exchange of Macedonia's security and stability" which "helped to line the pockets of a few individuals in Skopje" (2003: 62). The end of the UNPREDEP mission combined with the outbreak of war in neighboring Kosovo was the beginning of the end for Macedonia's tenuous stability. The accumulated dissatisfaction with illegitimate "democratic" government was bound to take its toll.

The Economics of Extreme Scarcity

Macedonia analyst Sam Vaknin has written that in the 1990s Macedonia had become a bit like a drug addict, entirely dependent on external handouts, which in turn allowed donors to demand anything of the government.[34] Indeed, "without substantial and continual serious international financial aid through the World Bank and the IMF, and specific programs to stabilize the value of the currency against a German Mark benchmark, the economy would have collapsed" (Pettifer 2001: xxxvii). At first external aid was negligible, but by 1992 it was on the increase. Although aggregate aid levels never reached those received by Bosnia, Macedonia was nonetheless a top recipient of aid, as shown in table 6.1. In exchange for aid, international financial institutions were directly involved in economic policy-making.[35]

This outside assistance notwithstanding, the Macedonian economy could not withstand the shocks of independence, and the macroeconomic effects were disastrous. The economy shrunk every year from 1990 to 1995. Industrial production declined by 43 percent in the first five years of transition, the rate of inflation soared to high of 1,691 percent in 1992, and unemployment reached 36 percent in 1993. Foreign exchange reserves were negligible. Between 1990 and 1995, GDP per capita fell from $2,200 to $700. There were no industries that could be relied on to reverse the economic decline. Though industrialization had taken place under the SFRJ, most of this industry was outmoded and had been operating in the red since at least the 1980s, if not

Table 6.1   External Assistance to Macedonia in Comparative Perspective, 1990–1998

Country	Total inflows (millions of U.S. dollars)	% GDP, annual average[a]	% GDP, annual average[b]	Per capita annual average	Per capita total 1990–1998[c]
Macedonia	1,602	4.8	3.0	89	791
Albania	1,956	11.1	4.3	62	575
Bosnia and Herzegovina	7,927	23.4	9.2	217	2,202
Bulgaria	1,482	1.5	0.4	19	181
Croatia	1,515	1.0	0.7	37	336
Romania	2,200	0.8	0.3	11	98
FRY	800	0.5	0.3	8	75

Source: Veremis and Daianu (2001: 27).
[a]Exchange rate converted.
[b]Purchasing power parity converted.
[c]Per capita of 1998 population.

earlier. Remittances from abroad, a burgeoning shadow economy, and the availability of cheap food were the only factors that kept many from falling into dire poverty.

Under the direction of international financial institutions, a number of macroeconomic stabilization measures introduced in 1993 did begin to reduce inflation. Tight monetary policy was maintained in cooperation with the IMF, and the large budget deficit began to decline. The denar was stabilized and strengthened. These macroeconomic successes, however, contributed to a rise in unemployment and a decline in production, and the downward trends continued long after they had been reversed in other transition economies. The poverty rate, meanwhile, rose steadily. According to the World Bank, poverty increased from 4 percent of the population in 1991 to over 20 percent in 1996 (Jeffries 2002: 301). To help counter the enormous social costs of marketization, the World Bank in 1998 provided Macedonia with additional credits worth $200 million (Lampe 2000: 388).

International financial institutions put considerable pressure on the Crvenkovski government to pursue privatization, and the government complied in spite of its leftist credentials. However, Macedonian privatization policy turned out to be a fiasco, with most firms "sold" to SDSM insiders at "preferential" rates. The politically connected managers who acquired the larger firms and banks could also rely on their insider status to secure bad loans from the unprivatized and government-controlled banks. This kind of privatization, besides doing little for state revenue and firm restructuring, also led to a public outcry that helped to bring the SDSM government down in 1998. Nor did ethnic Albanians, largely outsiders to state-owned enterprises, benefit at all from privatization. On the positive side, a small but observable private retail sector was appearing with European Bank for Reconstruction and Development (EBRD) assistance.[36]

In 1996 things began to look more positive as the first positive growth rates were recorded, sanctions against FRY were lifted, and Greece removed its trade embargo against Macedonia. The macroeconomic situation was now stabilized, the state budget was under control, and liberalization was proceeding. Agreements were reached to settle the foreign debt, which at $844 million was almost 28 percent of total GDP. Foreign investment began to trickle in from Greece, though at $100 million in the late 1990s it was still negligible compared to the FDI levels of other transition economies, such as the Czech Republic, where total FDI stood at $4.5 billion in the same period. It was difficult to lure investors to a country that the World Bank ranked 107th in terms of risk, behind the likes of Pakistan and Romania. Complicated rules, low visibility, a weak banking sector, and political instability continued to keep investors away (Jeffries 2002: 301).

However, any improvements recorded in aggregate indicators were hardly felt by the bulk of ordinary people. Unemployment remained high (see figure 6.1). Many of the unemployed were newcomers to the labor market and were relatively educated, making the problem even more explosive. A strict visa regime all but eliminated a safety valve for unemployment.

It is difficult to ascertain precisely how much the various negative externalities hurt the Macedonian economy. Yet, the effects were not as bad as one might have expected.[37] Sanctions- and embargo-busting fueled a thriving secondary economy that made some people rich and provided vital goods and services to others. Illicit economic activities arguably kept the rural Albanian population from erupting into revolt. There is no doubt, however, that the negative effects of the thriving underground economy were the criminality and corruption that they produced, seriously hurting the rule of law. The negative effects of the 1999 Kosovo War, which disrupted trade with FRY again and produced a mass influx of refugees, were somewhat offset by the investments provided by UNMIK and KFOR. As a prominent economist poignantly told me, post-communist Macedonia changed to a democratic politi-

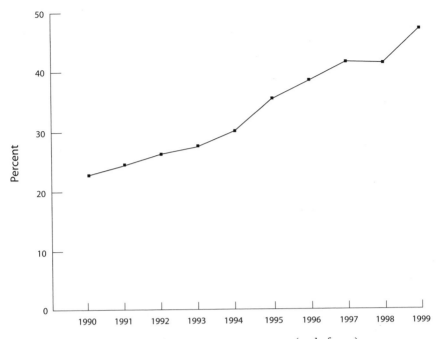

Figure 6.1. Macedonia, Unemployment Rate, 1990–1999 (end of year)
Source: Jeffries 2002: 357.

cal regime and changed to market rules, but it could not change its economic structure.[38]

The purpose of this chapter was to illustrate the nexus of economic scarcity, inequality, ethnic conflict, and state and regime illegitimacy in 1990s post-communist Macedonia. To this we must also add external sponsorship, which helped to sustain all of the above. The departure of UNPREDEP and the outbreak of war in Kosovo were the two contingent factors that brought internal contradictions to a head, and two years later the fragile balance tipped toward violent conflict and, nearly, a collapse of the state.

One of the main contradictions of 1990s Macedonia was the unwillingness of ethnic Macedonian elites to extend more rights to the ethnic Albanian community. They failed to realize that preserving the state would mean recognizing its multinational character, instead seeing multiculturalism (or *multikulti*, as my Macedonian friends say, with gentle irony) as a foreign, imposed concept. The ambiguity over Albanian rights could not continue forever: as long as the ethnic conception of the state prevailed, wrote the International Commission on the Balkans in 1998, "the state is unlikely to be accepted as legitimate by the minority (even without explicit encouragement from their 'mother nation')" (quoted in Williams 2000: 32). Ordinary Macedonians continued to believe that ethnic Albanians had too many rights. But by the end of the 1990s, tensions were so high that it would have been political suicide for any Macedonian politician to propose such an extension of rights. Indeed, it would take the West to force this on the Macedonian government in the Ohrid Agreement two years down the road. But at the time the West was too busy in neighboring Kosovo, and UNPREDEP was gone, leaving a few foreign NGOs and Western ambassadors in Skopje to keep the transition on course. It remained unclear how firm the West's security, political, and economic commitments to Macedonia were, and the harsh criticisms of Macedonia's refugee policy without a parallel effort to provide assistance during the Kosovo crisis provoked bitterness among Macedonians.[39] Sašo Ordanoski, a political commentator, remarked that Macedonia was forced to pay the bill for Serbia's injustice against Kosovo's Albanians (quoted in Liotta 2001: 305).

In contrast to FRY, concessions to the West worked in Macedonia because the state was too weak and too poor to offer resistance. Compliance with Western demands out of a sense of vulnerability was problematic because it did not reflect broad pro-Western sentiment in Macedonian society, and what was perceived as blind cooperation with the West delegitimized both Macedonian elites and their Western sponsors in the eyes of much of the public. The submission of elites to the West was not only a function of weakness and aversion to risk, for they had a real interest in maintaining power and lining their pockets with foreign largesse. This was true for both ethnic Albanian and ethnic Macedonian politicians. Both saw an incentive structure in which democratic simulation would be sufficient to reap the benefits of power.

Yet, we cannot be too cynical about the motivations behind the interethnic coalitions of the 1990s. Slavs and Albanians, after all, depended on each other for Macedonia's internal stability. And there was no question that the participation of Albanians in democratic institutions made conflict prevention more likely. The problem, again, lay in the legitimacy of these coalitions, whose members became adept at speaking the language of democracy and human rights with an eye toward the Western audience. Their behavior, however, departed from this ideal and over time it seemed that the public was more conscious of this than the West itself. The presence of ethnic Albanians in government also had the effect of raising expectations among their constituents. When ethnic Albanians saw that their leaders were not delivering, they stopped trusting them. This and the pressures of a failing economy contributed to facade democracy and regime illegitimacy.

Thus, a decade-long "oasis of peace" veiled an "oasis of corruption and crime" in 1990s Macedonia (Hislope 2002: 33). Some Western analysts, practitioners, scholars, and observers, however, failed to realize this in time, instead publishing glowing reports of Macedonian stability and incipient democracy. The lessons to them, and to the study of democratization more generally, are that Western sponsorship has limits in the face of poor economic conditions and deep societal divisions and that the illegitimate, facade democracy that the combination of the three can at best produce is unsustainable.

CHAPTER SEVEN

Populist Authoritarianism

The Federal Republic of Yugoslavia's Transition in the 1990s

> Time has shown that the policies of Milošević's socialists were consistently authoritarian, and only hypocritically national, and by their essence and results anational or anti-national.
>
> VOJISLAV KOŠTUNICA IN FEBRUARY 1996.

Authoritarianism, Milošević-style

Post-communist FRY was ruled in the 1990s by an authoritarian regime that combined Serbian nationalism, warmed-over Marxist-Titoist ideology, and a confrontational anti-Western foreign policy as forms of legitimization. At the helm of this regime were Slobodan Milošević, a former communist apparatchik turned defender of Serbian interests, and his communist successor Serbian Socialist Party (Srpska Partija Socijalistička, SPS). Milošević and the SPS took control of the most important institutions of the state, created a repressive military-bureaucratic police machine, and either marginalized or coopted opposition groups. There were frequent oscillations in ideology and policies during the 1990s, but the authoritarian leadership of Milošević and the SPS was consistent. The military, the security forces, and various paramilitary and organized crime groups were closely tied to the regime and were used to wage war in Bosnia, Croatia, and Kosovo. Milošević, like Tuđman in Croatia, used war to justify his curtailing of democracy and to create a siege mentality among the population. Moreover, the powerful military and security structures that emerged from these wars were a source of employment and regime support.

Like Tuđman's Croatia, the Milošević regime at times displayed a commitment to democratic procedures. By the end of the 1990s, in terms of the sheer reach of Milošević and the SPS in political institutions and the economy, it was more authoritarian than the Croatian case, and yet in certain areas such as media freedom the Tuđman regime was more repressive. Though some popular accounts have portrayed Milošević as a dictator akin to Iraq's Saddam Hussein, Milošević did not rule by terror or total control of information. Urbanites could watch CNN, Sky News, and the BBC on their satellite dishes. Opposition figures, like the Kosovo dissident Ibrahim Rugova, were able to travel throughout the world. Foreign-sponsored NGOs were allowed to operate, though they were often attacked as tools of foreign intelligence agencies. The regime even allowed for criticism, although it stopped short of permitting direct attacks on Milošević or his wife. There was no concerted effort to construct a cult of personality. This was in sharp contrast to the megalomaniacal tendencies of President Franjo Tuđman in Croatia.

The initial conditions of FRY's transition were characterized by an unfavorably structured economy, and a catastrophic economic situation in the formerly autonomous Kosovo province and parts of southern Serbia. Many areas of the FRY underwent only limited industrialization under communism, or at best heavy industrialization that produced inefficient industries and "political factories." Other weaknesses in the FRY economy included "low rates of capital formation, a relatively low level of technological development, a burdensome system of social administration, high tax rates and a lack of either a rational system of resource allocation or a labor market" (Thomas 1999: 163). FRY's economic structure thus could not withstand the pressures of the deepening recession, independence, and adaptation to Western markets, much less international sanctions and the economic policies of "destruction," as a famous Serbian economist called them (Dinkić 2000).

Everywhere in FRY, there was a looming social crisis related to demographic trends and the inability of the existing political system to respond effectively. Ironically, this social crisis was related in part to the spread of educational opportunities and the corresponding influx into the labor market of large numbers of young people with advanced degrees. The FRY economy of the 1980s could not absorb all of these new workers, especially in the many provincial cities and towns, and millions were left unemployed. Moreover, there was significant migration by "peasant workers" from the countryside to the cities and towns in the 1970s and 1980s, putting further pressure on a very tight labor market. The movement of such large groups of people over a relatively short span of time meant that "many remained only partially assimilated in urban life" (Thomas 1999: 26). Some estimates found that 50 to 60 percent of those involved in non-agrarian occupations in urban areas had rural origins (Thomas 1999: 26). FRY, moreover, retained the character of a largely peasant country, with overpopulation in the rural sector. These demographic realities and trends have been described by some as the "simultaneous urbanization of the village and the peasantization of the town," which had the net effect of "re-traditionalizing" FRY society (quoted in Thomas 1999: 27). Residents of small towns and the countryside would constitute a solid base of support for radical populist parties, and urban cosmopolitan culture was the target of attacks by these parties. In Kosovo, the effects of the economic crisis and the demographic trends described above were magnified due to the province's underdevelopment and helped worsen already troubled ethnic relations there. So the conditions were ripe for the rise of radical populism, especially given existing proclivities in Serbian political culture that the emerging political elite seized on. One such proclivity was toward authoritarian politics and the related development of a police and rentier state. Serbia did experiment with parliamentary democracy in the nineteenth and twentieth centuries, but these efforts largely failed and the country retreated to authoritarianism. The second proclivity was toward a sense of national victimhood that historically had been easily mobilized by politicians and expressed in the form of populist collectivist nationalism.[1] This characteristic of Serbian political culture came to the fore in the oft-cited 1986 Memorandum of the Serbian Academy of Arts and Sciences (Srpska Akademija Nauka i Umetnosti, SANU), which argued that Serbs were the victims of discrimination in the SFRJ.[2] It signaled that at least part of Serbia's intelligentsia was not in the liberal camp. The third proclivity was related to the existence of a deep cleavage between urban and rural areas and corresponding cosmopolitan versus conservative, nationalist orientations. All three of these tendencies—authoritarian political traditions, feelings of victimization, and a deep urban-rural social cleavage—came to the fore as material conditions declined and competition for resources became scarce. They were used and manipulated by elites bidding for power and exploited by Milošević and the SPS to great political advantage.

Just as it is a mistake to reduce the post-communist transition of FRY to the role of Milošević himself, it is also a distortion to see it as being driven exclusively by regime-sponsored nationalism. While Milošević and the SPS did indeed fan the flames of nationalist passion, there were groups that were far more nationalistic than the SPS. In fact, some of them were coopted by Milošević at various points in the 1990s as "ideological surrogates." Milošević himself rarely preached ultranationalism; rather, he claimed to be protecting Serbian national interests and convinced large numbers of Serbians that he would advance their cause (Cohen 2001: xiv). Yet, that he was willing, at a whim, to withdraw support for ethnic Serbs in Croatia and Bosnia and that in the end he lost Kosovo—these facts show that there was a highly instrumental dimension to his regime's nationalism.[3]

Ideological flexibility allowed Milošević and the SPS to attract a broad cross-section of the Serbian electorate and to lead the opposition into disarray. However, that the regime's strategies and levels of support remained relatively consistent even as it shifted among different ideological orientations indicated that the electorate was made up of people who simply supported the current regime in power (Gordy 1999: 9).[4]

The legitimizing principles of the regime were decidedly illiberal and infused with populist appeals. Western-style democracy was portrayed as alien to Serbian culture and history, and the regime claimed that Western states and organizations were trying to undermine Serbian state sovereignty. Since protection of Serb national interests became the regime's main rallying cry, support for separatist Serb movements in neighboring republics and war were a logical consequence. Deep divisions over fundamental questions about the state and its borders further lowered the liberal content of the Milošević regime, as did deep ethnic divisions, particularly those in Kosovo between the majority Albanian and minority Serb population. The ongoing crisis in Kosovo meant that the regime faced a neverending crisis of legitimization. When Milošević moved to rescind the province's autonomy, the Kosovar Albanians responded by boycotting rump Yugoslav federal institutions and declaring Kosovo a constituent republic. They proceeded to create their own parallel institutions, which Belgrade declared illegal.

The question for the Milošević regime in the late 1990s was one that arose for the Tuđman regime in Croatia: how long could the manipulation of fear as a basis of popular support be sustained? The answer proved to be the same: until the costs of a failing economy outweighed the "benefits" of the prevailing form of radical populism. However, the FRY case differed from the Croatian case in ways that suggested worse prospects for democratization. First, that which emerged as a response to Milošević's dictatorship as it faltered in the second half of 1990s was not a nascent liberal democratic opposition, as in Croatia, but rather an extreme rightist alternative that was to play a prominent role in Serbian politics even after Milošević was removed from power. Second, compared to Croatia, Western conditionality found a smaller receptive audience among elites in FRY. Consequently, the external impetus for liberalism was weaker.

Formal Democracy: The Record

Elections in FRY were held regularly. There were frequent reports of irregularities from the domestic opposition and external observers, and yet it was clear that Milošević and the SPS enjoyed substantial popularity. Although the elections did not formally exclude any political group, they were nonetheless perceived as illegitimate by many of FRY's minority groups, comprising over one-third of the population, who boycotted them repeatedly. Kosovar Albanians refused to recognize Belgrade's sovereignty over the province and created parallel government structures. Moreover, some Montenegrin parties repeatedly boycotted federal elections. The most notorious case of voter fraud occurred after the Belgrade municipal election of November 1996, which opposition parties won. Milošević refused to recognize the results but was forced to back down after protests at home and pressure from the international community.

Western observers gave FRY consistently poor ratings in the areas of political, civil, and human rights, placing it in the same category as Belarus, Uzbekistan, and other post-communist authoritarian regimes. The U.S. State Department declared in 1997 that the human rights situation in FRY was "very poor" (U.S. Department of State 1997). Minority rights were rarely respected, although the constitution, which declared FRY to be a "state of all its citizens," was actually more democratic than that of Croatia or Macedonia. In Vojvodina, minority groups such as the Hungarians and Croats lost much of their Yugoslav-era cultural autonomy and language rights. Ethnic Croats, many of whom came from ethnically mixed families, were subject to open harassment, and many left for Croatia. In general, a climate of intolerance marginalized non-Serbs (Miller 1997: 147).

The constitution was either amended or interpreted to promulgate the power of Slobodan Milošević. When he was president of FRY, Milošević made sure that he had wide-ranging powers, leaving the federal president as a figurehead.[5] However, when he was no longer eligible to be Serbian president, he was elected federal president and amended the constitution to assure his continued influence while installing a figurehead in the Serbian presidency.

The federal parliament largely rubber-stamped policies created by the SPS and Milošević. The Serbian parliament had greater influence, and when the SPS did not win an adequate number of seats, it was forced to cooperate with other parties. When this happened, Milošević made use of his self-created power to issue executive decrees to make policy, thereby bypassing legislative debate. The constitution gave the president wide powers to take measures that did not require the ratification of parliament and could not be challenged by the constitutional court, including the power to institute a state of emergency. By the end of the decade, the parliament was among the least-trusted institutions in Serbia, and indeed, had among the lowest levels of trust among parliaments in all of Eastern Europe (Slavujević and Mihailović 1999: 45).

The judicial system remained largely unreformed, and judges were holdovers from communist times. Though they ruled fairly on routine matters, on any cases that affected the standing of the ruling party, decisions were politicized. Criminal investigations were pursued against opposition figures, who were often imprisoned without due process. The Constitutional Court was stacked with loyalists.

Freedom of the press was guaranteed under the FRY Constitution, though all media outlets had to register with the government. Unlike Croatia, there were few libel suits against independent media outlets, but they were subject to other forms of harassment. There was at least one case of a prominent opposition journalist, Slavko Ćuruvija, killed by assassins, probably henchmen of the regime. Yet, there was also an incredible array of media sources in FRY during the 1990s. In 1997, there were more than a hundred privately owned television stations and twelve daily newspapers in Belgrade alone.[6] Moreover, international publications were widely available in Belgrade. Independent outlets such as Studio B and Radio B92 were quite popular, though the regime later attempted to shut them down. Likewise, important publications such as *NIN* and *Vreme* were openly critical of the regime. However, this seeming variety of information sources was limited strictly to a few large cities. The regime made sure that the signal of independent stations like B92 and Studio B was limited to Belgrade. The only real source of information for the millions of people living in FRY's provincial areas was the state-run Radio Television Serbia (Radio-Televizija Srbije, RTS), whose editors and producers received their orders directly from the SPS. The popular newspaper *Politika* was also firmly in the hands of the SPS. Control over state-run television gave the regime great leverage, since research showed that over 60 percent of population watched the principal news program on state television as their main source of information, while only 2 percent read newspapers (Gordy 1999: 33).[7]

Corruption and criminality reigned in the 1990s, rendering the rule of law a sham. J. F. Brown notes that while there were several post-communist states where the mafia exercised control over the government, only in FRY did the government control the mafia (Brown 2001: 72). Many top SPS officials and politicians were also directors of the most important state companies. For instance, the Serbian prime minister was director of the state company with exclusive rights to the fuel trade with Russia. The vice president of the SPS was owner and director of the Komuna publishing conglomerate. The speaker of the Serbian parliament was also the director of the largest state oil company, Jugopetrol. This kind of clientelism was at the foundation of the regime's entrenchment in power.

The First Elections

Milošević's initial rise to power had little to do with popular participation and everything to do with an intra-party coup in the Serbian League of Communists (Srpski Savez Komunista, SKS) in December 1987 in which Milošević moved to oust his longtime political mentor, Ivan Stambolić.[8] Other accounts place great emphasis on the way in which Milošević was able to seize on nationalist sentiment among Kosovo Serbs with his famous 1987 speech. Gordy (1999: 26–27), however, notes that the situation was much more complex. Milošević cleverly offered support to both the nationalist Serbian resistance movement in Kosovo and the old guard of the Communist Party, which feared the consequences of economic and political reform and was wary of any overt expressions of nationalism. Most of all, however, Milošević represented a fresh alternative to a largely discredited SKS that had failed to extract Serbia from economic crisis and was entrenched in corruption and privilege. Recognizing that Yugoslav causes had lost their potential for mass mobilization, Milošević's answer to the ideological vacuum was a brand of radical populism called the "anti-bureaucratic" revolution and filled with disparate ideological messages, among them protection of Serbian national interests and a distinctly Serbian approach to economic reform and democratization.

Milošević contended that Tito had deliberately weakened Serbia by undermining its sovereignty over the two autonomous provinces, Vojvodina and Kosovo (Bugajski 2002: 384). Moreover, he alleged that Serbs in neighboring Bosnia and Croatia were threatened by insufficient constitutional protections. Thus, he focused his efforts after becoming Serbian president in 1989 on restoring a centralized Serbian administration in Belgrade. He organized mass demonstrations in support of Serbian unification in Belgrade, Montenegro, Vojvodina, and Kosovo (Bugajski 2002: 384). Exploiting economic and ethnic grievances, he later orchestrated the ouster of the entire state and party leaderships in Novi Sad, Priština, and Podgorica, replacing them with pro-Belgrade loyalists (Bugajski 2002: 384).[9] To complete the move toward centralization, he changed the constitution so that Vojvodina and Kosovo formally lost any semblance of autonomy. The ethnic Serb populations of these regions, regardless of socioeconomic status, supported such policies because they saw the existing party leadership as corrupt and unresponsive and hoped that such changes would improve their economic situation.[10] Milošević also undermined the position of Federal Prime Minister Ante Marković and the collapsing federal institutions more generally (Gordy 1999: 29).

In July 1990, the SKS and the Socialist Alliance, a communist front organization, united to form the SPS under Milošević's leadership (Bugajski 2002: 385). The party adopted an openly nationalist platform, and yet did not part with many tenets of socialism. Under pressure from events in the rest of the communist world, the SPS reluctantly legalized opposition parties in August 1990 and called for the first multiparty elections in December 1990. But the SPS had a host of advantages, including extensive influence over the media and an electoral law that inflated its representation in the National Assembly. Moreover, it inherited an extensive organizational network from its communist predecessor, while the fledgling opposition parties were organizationally weak. Milošević and the SPS also presented a clear populist agenda with ostensibly easy solutions to FRY's socioeconomic crisis.

Milošević's well-documented use of nationalist mobilization prior to the first election worked not only because of the dissatisfaction generated by the poor economic situation in FRY but was also given strength by the rise of nationalist rhetoric in other republics, especially Croatia. The media was used to revive fears of atrocities committed against ethnic Serbs during World War II. A propaganda campaign sought to exploit public dissatisfaction with the economic situation by appealing to a sense of victimhood. The enemies in this campaign included nationalist governments in the other republics, cosmopolitanism, the Marković reformist federal government, and increasingly, Western governments. At the same time, the SPS sought to portray itself as experienced, moderate, and in tune with the public mood, using the slogan "With us, there is no uncertainty" (*S nama nema neizvesnosti*) (quoted in Gordy 1999: 32). Opposition parties, by contrast, were presented as "disorganized, corrupt, fighting among themselves, and opposed to the national interest" (Gordy 1999: 33).

The opposition, it should be said, was hardly made up only of liberal-minded parties. In fact, it is quite telling about the prevailing mood in FRY that the largest party to emerge as opposition in the first elections was Vuk Drašković's Serbian Renewal Movement (Srpski Pokret Obnove, SPO), a group that advocated openly nationalist positions such as the unity of all Serbian lands. Drašković, with his long flowing beard and three-fingered salute reminiscent of World War II–era Chetnik fighters, would only later become an ostensible liberal and opponent of the wars.[11] "Milošević's party," writes Gordy, "benefited tremendously from the SPO's extremism in 1990 and gained the ability to dismiss pro-European liberal parties as subject to 'foreign elements,' appeal to nationalist sentiment, and appear to be moderate at the same time" (1999: 34).

The election to the Serbian parliament took place in an atmosphere of uncertainty, instability, and deepening economic troubles. An electoral law had been drafted without the participation of the opposition, and a month before the elections, it was still unclear if the opposition parties would boycott or participate (Gordy 1999: 35). In the end the SPS won the most votes but did not manage to win an absolute majority despite the boost it received from the highly majoritarian electoral system. Under this electoral system, however, it was able to gain an overwhelming majority of seats (194, or nearly 78 percent of all seats), albeit amid charges of voting irregularities (Bugajski 2002: 385). No non-nationalist party did well at the polls, which shows that any politician who wished to succeed had to "offer a vision for the defense of Serbs from a variety of threats, real and unreal" (Miller 1997: 146). Serbia's minorities, together representing one-third of the total population, were offered minimal representation and were largely excluded from the political process.

Having transformed its electoral plurality into an overwhelming parliamentary majority, the SPS was able to cut short debate and "pass any and all laws and resolutions without any consideration of the position of opposition parties" (Gordy 1999: 35). The SPS was able to maintain its monopoly over all ministries and all executive positions and was actively extending its control over the two institutions that would be crucial to its rule, the police and the media (Gordy 1999: 37). However, none of this solved the problem of the SPS's legitimacy among the parts of the public that had opposed it and among Serbia's minorities, especially the Kosovar Albanians, who had entirely boycotted participation in the rump Yugoslav state.

On 9 March 1991, over a hundred thousand protestors, led by Drašković, gathered on Republic Square to protest the opposition's exclusion from state-run television. The regime responded with busloads of police officers and violence, including beatings and shootings that resulted in the death of one eighteen-year-old student. Subsequently, the military was also brought in. Two days later, the students submitted a list of demands to the regime, such as the resignation of the interior minister.

The SPS organized a counter-demonstration in New Belgrade (Novi Beograd) on the opposite side of River Sava, where many migrants from the countryside had settled to work in communist industries.[12] Indeed, the impact of the protests was tempered by their largely urban, educated, and young composition, a demographic viewed with great suspicion by provincial areas and recent migrants to the city. The SPS was able to exploit this rift effectively, but not without making concessions to some of the students' demands.[13] The decision to use the military to quell a political protest showed the politicization of state institutions (especially the military) as well as the distance to which the regime was willing to go to preserve its power. In many ways, these protests were the "last cry" before the wars rendered the regime "invincible" and allowed the opposition to be equated with treason (Gordy 1999: 42–43).

Kosovo and the Ethnic Albanians

The situation in Kosovo was also deteriorating rapidly.[14] Milošević had rescinded the province's autonomy and replaced ethnic Albanian party officials with Serbs. When the Kosovar Albanians boycotted state institutions in Belgrade, the regime sent in the army and paramilitary groups, ensuring apartheid and military rule in the province for the next ten years. Meanwhile, an outlawed shadow government of ethnic Albanians claimed to rule in Priština, and a resistance movement was being organized.

The history of Kosovo and its two main ethnic groups, the Orthodox Serbs and the mostly Muslim Albanians, has been characterized by periods of conflict and accommodation. While Serbs may have outnumbered the Albanians at one time, in recent times the Albanians have far outnumbered the Serbs; by the late 1980s they constituted over 90 percent of the population. This was due both to out-migration by the Serbs and high fertility rates among the ethnic Albanians. Owing to low rates of ethnic Albanian participation in the Partisan movement, until the 1960s Kosovar Albanians were treated with suspicion by Tito's regime, and the province was virtually a police state in which Albanians had little say. They lived as an inferior class, and the minority Serbs filled all public offices in the province. After a series of riots in Priština and the controversial removal of Aleksandar Ranković from the party's apparatus in the 1960s, Tito gradually devolved power to the Kosovar Albanians, and Kosovar Albanians controlled provincial institutions by the 1980s. An influential but corrupt ethnic Albanian party apparatus developed in Priština, and ethnic Albanians were given access to higher educational opportunities at the Albanian-language University of Priština. Serbs and Montenegrins, however, continued to dominate the police and security services. Although many ethnic Serbs did harbor legitimate feelings of victimization, in the 1980s exaggerated reports of discrimination against Kosovo's Serbs were circulated widely in the media, including accounts of rapes and killings.

As a result, ethnic tensions were high in 1980s Kosovo. Unlike Bosnia, intermarriage was almost nonexistent, and the two societies lived separately, divided by both language and religion. Any kind of compromise was made very difficult by the catastrophic economic situation. Rapid population growth had long since outstripped the Kosovar economy's capacity to provide jobs, "thereby leading to an increase in unemployment, especially among younger Albanians eager to enter the workforce" (Cohen 2001: 20). Ethnic Serbs were also afflicted by skyrocketing unemployment in the province. There was thus intense competition in the province for very limited resources in the 1980s, and one way for Belgrade politicians to bid for power was to exploit the nascent social frustration in Kosovo. This is precisely what Milošević did in 1987, with his now-infamous promise to Kosovo Serbs that "nobody will dare beat you again." Likewise, the unemployed and frustrated masses of ethnic Albanian young people were an ideal target for separatist Albanian national-ist groups. Problems in Kosovo, then, were a result of the ongoing structural problem of economic backwardness and ethnic divisions, as well as more re-cent political contingencies.

Subsequent Elections and Party Politics

The 1992 Election

Milošević called for Serbian parliamentary elections in 1992 as a way to legitimize his hold on power. In 1992, a referendum was also held in Monte-negro. Well over 90 percent of the population voted to stay with Serbia in a new entity to be called the Federal Republic of Yugoslavia, which declared itself to be the only legitimate legal successor to the SFRJ. With war raging in Bosnia and Croatia, every major political group, including the democratic opposition, was attempting to curry nationalist favor. Liberal political op-tions were virtually eliminated from the Serbian and Montenegrin political scene. Although the SPS was only able to win 30 percent of the vote, the sec-ond-largest vote getter was the neo-fascist Serbian Radical Party (Srpska Radi-kalna Stranka, SRS), which went on to form an informal "red-brown" coali-tion with the SPS. The Democratic Movement of Serbia (Demokratski Pokret Srbije, DEPOS), a coalition of fourteen parties and Serbian intellectuals of various ideological persuasions, came in third. The coalition was weakened, however, by the refusal of the Democratic Party (Demokratska Stranka, DS), which came in fourth, to join. Significantly, the 1992 elections were boycotted by some opposition parties, most ethnic Albanians, and the Slavic Muslims of Sandžak, which lowered the legitimacy of the elections and of the regime.

Earlier in 1992, after the declaration of the Federal Republic of Yugoslavia, Milošević had invited two prominent individuals, the writer Dobrica Ćosić and the Serbian-American millionaire businessman Milan Panić to be presi-dent of the FRY and Serbian prime minister, respectively. This was a clever move designed to broaden the regime's base, and with the appointment of Panić, to reach out to the West. However, both individuals subsequently be-came disillusioned with Milošević and began to criticize him openly. Panić even went so far as to ask Milošević to resign, which he declined. In retaliation for their disloyalty, Milošević began plotting to have both individuals removed. His fiercest attacks were directed at Panić, whom he accused of working at the behest of foreign powers (Cohen 2001: 166). Subsequently, Panić ran an unsuccessful campaign against Milošević in the 1992 Serbian presidential election. After being ousted, Panić returned to the United States and worked to strengthen the Serbian opposition. Ćosić was removed in favor of a Milošević henchman, Zoran Lilić.

To help remove the two and further discredit the opposition, he enlisted the help of his erstwhile informal coalition partner, the SRS. This began a pattern in which Milošević would use the charismatic and unpredictable SRS leader Vojislav Šešelj as an ideological surrogate when it was politically expedient and then openly attack and even jail him when circumstances changed. During the 1992 election, Milošević praised Šešelj, saying that he trusted him the most among opposition politicians because his party was not "dependent on foreign financial interests" and because Šešelj was not afraid to express his true political thoughts (Pribićević 1997: 58). Thus, many voters who would otherwise have voted for the SPS chose the SRS, with the understanding that they were voting for a pseudo-coalition.

However, this "red-brown coalition" ended when Milošević, increasingly worried about the negative effects of Western-imposed sanctions, decided that he would take on the role of peacemaker by supporting the ultimately unsuccessful Vance-Owen peace plan for Croatia and Bosnia. Milošević was also fearful that Šešelj was starting to threaten the SPS's communist base with all the SRS's talk of equalizing incomes (Pribićević 1997: 59). Šešelj's promise to fight corruption and organized crime also threatened the SPS, as did his overtures to certain parts of the army and police, one foundation of Milošević's rule. Thus, the coalition broke up at the end of 1992, and the SPS unleashed its media attack machine on Šešelj, calling him a war profiteer and criminal (Pribićević 1997: 60–61). Milošević dissolved the parliament and called new elections.

The 1993 Election

Dragoslav Grujić writes that in the 1993 elections "the south defeated the north, the undeveloped defeated the developed, the province defeated the metropolis, and the village defeated the city" (quoted in Gordy 1999: 52). The SPS had consolidated its rule and its propaganda campaign against the SRS worked quite well: Šešelj's party did much worse in the 1993 elections. His nationalist fire "stolen" by the SPS, Šešelj began to focus on economic problems and the fight against criminality and corruption.

The 1993 elections "played the nationalist tune and played on the collective paranoia of the whole world seeming to be against Serbia" (Jeffries 2002: 80). Vuk Drašković's SPO, the largest party in the ostensibly liberal DEPOS coalition, espoused openly nationalist positions. After the election, six deputies from the DEPOS coalition defected to the SPS. The SPS also managed to coopt another ultranationalist political grouping led by the criminal boss and paramilitary leader Željko "Arkan" Ražnjatović, the Party of Serbian Unity (Stranka Srpskog Jedinstva, SSJ).

The 1996 Federal Elections and 1996–1997 Protests

In the 1993–1995 period, little was accomplished in FRY in the way of political and economic reform. Milošević and the SPS became more deeply entrenched in positions of power, while the country was isolated internationally and paralyzed by economic sanctions. Though inflation had been stabilized somewhat, many of FRY's inhabitants lived in poverty. The vast majority of FRY's minorities and, most significantly, the Kosovar Albanians did not recognize the legitimacy of the Milošević regime. Stability in Kosovo was being maintained by special police forces with low morale.

In 1995, Milošević was afforded a political opportunity with the Dayton Agreement. He decided again to play the role of peacemaker, cooperating with the U.S.-sponsored talks to achieve an end to the war in Bosnia and Herzegovina. There was a domestic political cost, since he was seen by many nationalists to have sold out the Bosnian Serbs. However, the political capital he derived from his role in Ohio, both domestically and internationally, was significant as well.

The public was assured that the end of the war in Bosnia would lead to the end of international sanctions against FRY. Rhetoric about national issues was abandoned in favor of a focus on the economy, devastated after the years of war and sanctions. The preconditions for an economic revival were met, it was said. The slogan used by the SPS in the 1996 elections to the federal parliament was "Serbia 2000: A Step into the New Century." The DPS, the SPS's close ally in Montenegro, used similar appeals in the campaign to win seats in the National Assembly.[15] In terms of concrete solutions, the SPS's campaign proposed developmental programs for many industrial and social sectors but hardly attempted to address real problems (Slavujević and Mihailović 1999: 105). As a result, the SPS, in coalition with the Yugoslav United Left (Jugoslovenska Udružena Levica, JUL) and its Montenegrin ally, won a narrow majority of seats in the federal parliament, though an opposition coalition managed to garner nearly 24 percent of the vote and 22 seats.

However, the outcome of the federal elections masked the extent of popular dissatisfaction within the country. A dangerous rift had developed between the regime and public in urban areas. A number of opposition parties had managed to unite in local elections under the "Together" (*Zajedno*) label and win majorities in several municipalities in November 1996 runoff elections. Milošević clearly felt threatened by these results, especially since the opposition had won control of the Belgrade city council. So he arranged to have local courts annul the elections. This turned out to be a major miscalculation, as the blatant effort to steal the election led to massive protests in the winter of 1996–1997 that lasted several months. Day after day, hundreds of thousands of protestors braved the cold in Belgrade and other cities to demand that the election results be honored. The protests were expanded to other causes, among them a demand by students for certain political appointees at the university to resign. The regime attacked the protestors relentlessly with rhetoric and sometimes with physical force (Cohen 2001: 332). Given the size, strength, and duration of the protests, Milošević was obliged to recognize many of the local elections, and he also acceded to several of the students' demands.

The significance of these protests also lay in their social composition.[16] While a majority of protestors were still educated, young, and urban, among the protestors were significant groups of older people who were not so highly educated (Lazić 1999). This was a sign that the opposition to the regime was widening, though the working classes and farmers were still not well represented in the protests. In the end, the regime survived yet another election, but Milošević and the SPS were fundamentally wounded by the crisis, both domestically and internationally. The opposition, meanwhile, was emboldened.

Yet, the regime was able to survive in part due to the intense battles that occurred inside the *Zajedno* coalition after the protests were called off in February 1997. The most bitter struggle was between the DS leader Zoran Đinđić and SPO leader Drašković. The split between the two leaders had much to do with personality, but it was also related to national orientation, with Đinđić increasingly taking a pro-Western approach and Drašković continuing to espouse a nationalist and monarchist program. There were also strategic differences between the leaders, with Drašković advocating a boycott of all elections, which he saw as unfair. The split in *Zajedno* was a boon to the SPS and the SRS in the 1997 elections. The opposition leaders seemingly spent more time attacking each other than the regime. Đinđić later said that all the united opposition had fought for in the 1996–1997 protests was thrown away (Cohen 2001: 215). The greatest harm caused by the incessant bickering of the opposition parties was their own delegitimization in the eyes of the public, which helped to lead to an increasing withdrawal of the public from politics, a trend that only benefited the ruling party.

His term limit as Serbian president approaching, in 1997 Milošević engineered a formal shift of his base of power from the republican to the federal level. In July 1997 he was elected president of the FRY by the federal parliament, and subsequently transferred substantial powers and loyal personnel to the federal level.

The 1997 Elections

In the second half of 1997 popular dissatisfaction with both the regime and established opposition parties was quite high. Milošević and the SPS were blamed for having betrayed Serbian national interests and having allowed the FRY to fall into poverty. Yet, the opposition parties were also discredited because of their endless squabbling and failure to maintain a united organizational structure in the 1996–1997 protests (Cohen 2001: 220). Above all, the economic situation continued to generate intense resentment.

"The main political beneficiary of such citizen anger and despair," writes Cohen "was Vojislav Šešelj, the controversial and charismatic leader of the Serbian Radical Party" (2001: 220). Though many voters had simply withdrawn from politics, many others decided to vote for the SRS as an alternative to both the regime and opposition. The SRS, after all, was addressing the poor economic situation, albeit with simplistic populist solutions. The SRS "mobilized despair" in an increasingly delegitimized regime (Cohen 2001: 225). Šešelj, moreover, could point to his successes as mayor of the city of Zemun, where the streets were cleaner, garbage was collected regularly, and the city administration ran efficiently. The SRS had a strong showing in the 1997 Serbian parliamentary elections, winning 32 percent of the vote and 82 seats. The SPS, without enough seats to form a government, again adopted the SRS as a coalition partner. In exchange for its participation in the government, the SRS was given 16 of 36 ministries, which it proceeded to actively use in propagating its extremist goals.

Emboldened by the popularity of his party, Šešelj also ran for the office of Serbian president and, to the surprise of many, defeated Milošević ally Zoran Lilić in the second round. However, the elections were invalidated due to low turnout, and new elections were held in December 1997. This time, Milošević was ready and used every electoral manipulation he could to ensure the victory of a new henchman, Milan Milutinović. Still, the radicalism of Šešelj and the SRS enjoyed wide popularity in Serbia as a response to the deepening socioeconomic crisis. Šešelj had received close to 2 million votes, and the membership of the SRS doubled. Research showed that the SRS had taken over a significant portion of the SPS's electorate (Cohen 2001: 228). However, the low voter turnout, barely above 50 percent in the repeat presidential elections, also showed that the population was exhausted, demobilized, and distrustful of all politicians.

Meanwhile, Kosovo was on the brink. The ethnic Albanian population was increasingly losing hope of any political solution to the crisis and becoming radicalized. A separatist guerilla movement, the Kosovo Liberation Army (Ushtria Çlirimtare e Kosovës, UÇK) was organized and armed with weapons obtained by looters and sold on the black market after the 1997 breakdown of authority in Albania. In 1998 armed UÇK militias began to launch attacks on Serbian special police forces. Milošević responded with a heavy hand. Subsequent events, including the massacres of Albanian civilians by Serbian paramilitary forces, have been well documented elsewhere, as has the resulting NATO bombing of FRY from March to June 1999. The short-term effect of the NATO bombing was to compel the Serbian population to rally around the leadership temporarily. However, as the compounded effects of ten years of economic mismanagement and the destruction caused by the bombing set in and as it became clear that Milošević had lost Kosovo to international supervision, opposition rose and spread to all parts of society. Aided by the international community, the divided opposition was beginning to unite.

The Milošević regime was now in grave danger. The economy was in shambles, and the country was totally isolated. Milošević had promised in 1996 that economic sanctions would end and that Serb refugees would be allowed to return to their homes in Bosnia and Croatia, but neither promise had been fulfilled. Much of the population was living in poverty. Kosovo, for practical purposes, no longer belonged to Serbia, and the Montenegrin leadership was in open rebellion against Belgrade. The Serbian Orthodox Church and SANU were calling for Milošević to step down.[17] Though he could still rely on the support of his wife's JUL and to some extent on that of Šešelj, his power was clearly waning. In response, authoritarianism deepened: if the regime had been a "soft" dictatorship before, it moved decisively in the "hard" direction in 1999. Milošević cracked down fiercely on the opposition, using his extensive military and police apparatus. Laws were enacted to prevent criticism of the regime and to curtail the independent media. Protestors were beaten, and some opponents of the regime disappeared. Constitutional changes were enacted so that Montenegro was basically left out of political processes at the federal level.

In the spring of 2000, the SPS held an extraordinary convention at which Milošević was reelected party president by 99 percent of the delegates. Many delegates were probably under no illusions about the harm Milošević had caused the country, but given the corrupt system of privileges and the threats of trials and lustration, as well as Milošević's own indictment in 1999 by the ICTY, they had a lot to lose if the regime fell. Then the regime made a fateful move: it called for *direct* elections to the Yugoslav presidency and parliament in fall 2000. Milošević had clearly calculated that, using all of the electoral tricks and media control available to him, he would be able to secure a victory and thus legitimize his rule for another term.

The challenge was now left to the opposition, who would have to present a common front in order to defeat the regime. Milošević, after all, still had a reliable electorate ready to vote him back into power. With tactical help from the international community, they went through the painful process of unification in subsequent months. To win, the opposition would have to enlist the support of parts of society who had been suspicious of the urban democratic parties. Given the sheer depth of economic devastation, this was, for the first time, entirely possible.

The Main Parties and Their Orientations

In the 1990s, voting for parties in Serbia was generally governed by the "rule of fourths."[18] Excluding the Kosovar Albanians and Hungarians in Vojvodina, who either boycotted elections or voted for their own minority parties, we can observe that at least half the electorate voted for the two largest illiberal parties, the SPS/JUL and SRS (one fourth each). Another fourth voted for one of the opposition parties, whose liberal credentials were ambivalent.

Finally, the last fourth abstained from voting altogether. These parties, their programs, and their social bases of support speak to the illiberal character of the FRY polity in the 1990s.

The SPS and Its Bases of Support

The SPS emerged from the SKS, and beyond changing its name and adding nationalist ideology to its rhetoric, little else changed. The party inherited the funds, infrastructure, and organizational resources of its predecessor. Most members, used to party discipline and loyalty to a leader, followed Milošević as conformists. Whereas the communists regarded peasant culture and its manifestations as backward, the SPS embraced and exploited them:

> Whereas Tito's Yugoslavia relied on the acquiescence, if not necessarily the support, of urban and intellectual elites, Milošević early understood that he could not depend on their support and turned instead to rural Serbia and the areas around the "southern railway" (*južna pruga*). In turning to the peasantry and the "small towns," the regime adopted in part many of the attitudes of these groups, particularly opposition to urban life, urban culture, and the supposed contamination and artificiality of cities. These attitudes form a vital part of the nationalist side of the regime's rhetoric. (Gordy 1999: 12)

And as Gordy (1999: 11) has also observed, it was only one small step from communism's false collective of the working class to nationalism's false collective of the people. Moreover, where the Communist Party sought class enemies, the SPS found national enemies in other ethnic groups. It also found enemies in the outside world—and a global conspiracy against Serbia.

In its day-to-day functioning, the SPS oscillated among communism, socialism, nationalism, and reform, hardly unfamiliar to people who recall Tito's swings among Stalinism, "non-party" pluralism, centralism, federalism, and nonalignment (Gordy 1999: 16). Gordy notes, however, that "a single structural current runs through all of these rhetorical variants: authoritarianism" (1999: 16). He continues: "These ideological and practical inconsistencies allow the [Milošević regime], however briefly, to rely on a shifting coalition of conformists, nominally left-wing supporters of the Communist regimes of the past, right-wing nationalists who were formerly opponents of those regimes, and even some liberals who may trust in promises of eventual reform or believe that the regime can be compromised from within. In this regard, they simultaneously represent a continuation of the old regime and a limited departure from it" (1999: 17). A *Vreme* journalist put it more candidly: Milošević "succeeded in tricking both the communists and nationalists; the communists believed he was only pretending to be a nationalist, and the nationalists that he was only pretending to be a communist" (quoted in Cohen 2001: 88).

In terms of its bases of social support, the SPS was disproportionately backed by voters in poorer areas. It also had stronger support among older people. Furthermore, large numbers of SPS supporters came from rural areas and small towns, and it found stronger levels of support among less-educated voters (Gordy 1999: 52–53).[19]

The Ideological Surrogates of the SPS

Despite its clear hold on power, the SPS heavily relied on the use of ideological surrogate parties. They served a number of purposes. "By rotating its cast of ideological surrogates through the musical chairs of power," writes Gordy, "the regime protects itself from its own positions and actions" (1999: 14). Moreover, all the crucial ideological, political, and military work of the regime was performed by surrogates, and they could also be used to give the impression of pluralism. Finally, in the context of a parliamentary system, surrogates allowed the SPS to overcome its failure to win majorities in the Serbian parliament.

One important surrogate was the JUL, founded and led by the wife of Slobodan Milošević, the unpredictable Mirjana Marković. Marković espoused a hodgepodge of neo-communist views, and the JUL became an "auxiliary framework through which Milošević could attract assorted elite-level forces (mostly industrial managers, military officers, former communist apparatchiks, and some intellectuals)" (Cohen 2001: 121). Marković and the JUL became more prominent in the second half of the 1990s, helping the SPS to fight dissent with divisive rhetoric. The parties ran as a coalition in 1996 and 1997.

However, a far more important ideological surrogate in terms of its support, membership, and influence was Šešelj's SRS. The popularity of the Radicals skyrocketed in the latter half of the 1990s due to economic collapse, war, and UN sanctions. They did the "dirty work" on behalf of the SPS: organizing paramilitary units and volunteers to go fight in Croatia and Bosnia. The second most important function of the SRS was to destroy the democratically oriented opposition parties by offering an appealing alternative to the SPS.

Šešelj performed both tasks very well. According to the Serbian political scientist Ognjen Pribićević (1997: 54), the SRS was "indispensable" to Milošević and the SPS.

The SRS offered simple, populist solutions rooted in xenophobia and nationalism to complicated political, social, and economic questions. For instance, Šešelj declared that the solution to the Serbian national question was quite simple: since Serbs have the most military power in the former Yugoslavia, they should simply use it to take what is theirs (*"da upotrebe vojne snage i uzmu ono što je njihovo"*). His solution to the Kosovo problem was just as simple: Kosovar Albanians should be made to go to Albania. He also proposed a population exchange with Croatia: "We will try to quickly reach an inter-state agreement with Croatia so that, in a civilized way, we can exchange populations. If they refuse, in the civilized world there exist other, also civilized, ways that this can be accomplished" (Pribićević 1997: 55). To FRY's economic problems, he offered a variety of populist state-led solutions to redistribute income, finance public works, and yet also restrict budgetary expenditures and privatize the state sector. "Economically we are liberals," Šešelj told an interviewer in 1996, "we support liberal capitalism and the complete privatization of everything that can be privatized and not endanger the functioning of the state. Almost Thatcherism. We differ from others because we insist on a method of privatization which excludes stealing" (quoted in Cohen 2001: 223). Šešelj took advantage of the fact that a politically and socially disoriented electorate did not have the will or patience to get involved in the nuances of policy (Pribićević 1997: 55).

Šešelj proposed a Greater Serbia (*Velika Srbija*) that would include Serbia, Montenegro, Macedonia, and large parts of Croatia and Bosnia. He gave fiery speeches and boasted about atrocities committed against Croat civilians in the Krajina. He was vehemently anti-Western, frequently referring to conspiracies orchestrated against Serbia by the Vatican, Germany, CIA, Italy, and Turkey. He was also a charismatic leader who was a fearless and consistent advocate of society's deepest concerns. As such, his message resonated with the parts of population most seriously affected by Serbia's slide into poverty. These included the former middle and lower middle classes, private craftsmen, lower-ranking technicians, professionals and management personnel, small-scale entrepreneurs, skilled and semi-skilled workers and retirees, disgruntled students, and segments of the rural sector (Cohen 2001: 222). Šešelj skillfully tapped into their economic despair and sense of national humiliation. An example of his fiery, outrageous rhetoric was his threat to burn down Rome in retaliation for Italy allowing NATO planes to use its bases to bomb Bosnian Serb positions around Sarajevo in 1995. However, he toned down his most extreme rhetoric when he ran for Serbian president in 1997.

The Democratic, Somewhat Liberal, Opposition

Four major parties made up the democratic opposition: Drašković's SPO, Đinđić's DS, Vesna Pesić's Civic Alliance of Serbia (Građanski Savez Srbije, GSS) and Koštunica's Democratic Party of Serbia (Demokratska Stranka Srbije, DSS). The inability of these four parties to unite helped to keep the Milošević regime in power. Nominally, they were all liberal parties, declaring their support for democracy, human rights, the free market, and European integration.

In practice, they all dabbled in nationalism, albeit to different degrees. The GSS was the most consistently liberal, followed by the DS, the DSS, and the SPO. Drašković was unpredictable: an avowed nationalist at first, he even organized his own militia to fight in Croatia. Then he became an opponent of war, only to join the Milošević government late in the 1990s. Yet, as a traditionalist, anti-communist, and monarchist, he was able to attract a unique base of support. The DSS and DS emerged from the same party when the nationalist-inclined Koštunica split from Đinđić and founded the DSS. Yet, even Đinđić played the nationalist card, at one point supporting Bosnian Serb leader and indicted war criminal Radovan Karadžić after his split with Milošević. Nevertheless, the DS appealed mostly to educated urbanites of Belgrade.

Finally, it is worth mentioning the two Hungarian minority parties from Vojvodina: the Democratic Community of Vojvodina Hungarians (Demokratska Zajednica Mađara Vojvodine, DZMV; Hungarian: Vajdasági Magyarok Demokratikus Közössége, VMDK) and the Alliance of Vojvodina Hungarians (Savez Vojvođanskih Mađjara, SVM; Hungarian: Vajdasági Magyar Szövetség, VMSZ). Both called for the autonomy of Vojvodina, with the latter favoring a more pragmatic, conciliatory approach. With representatives in the National Assembly, the two parties were among the only minorities to have a voice at all in 1990s FRY.

Loci of Political Conflict

Patterns of party support allow us to reach some conclusions about the nature and extent of public divisions in 1990s FRY. On one level, FRY society was split between a collective, neotraditional, anti-Western, illiberal culture associated with rural areas and a cosmopolitan, civic, modernizing, liberal orientation associated with urban areas. The conditions of the 1980s and 1990s helped the former to win over the latter, but the division continued to shape public discourse and divisions within the opposition parties, for instance. The split over the appropriateness of Western liberalism proved to be the most divisive of all, especially for the opposition. FRY's democratic development was also hindered by a lack of national integration, that is, the complete withdrawal of Kosovar Albanians from the political process and the efforts of Montenegro after 1997 to withdraw from the federation.

Thomas writes about other profound divisions rooted in competing views of history:

> In Serbia ideological divisions are not necessarily connected with the pursuit of different policies; rather it is a matter of their adherence to or connection with different political traditions or cultures. These cultures may not only have a differing political content but also a radically different understanding of history and vision of the nation underpinned by familial and collective memory. In Serbia this cultural schism particularly relates to the Partisan/Chetnik and Socialist/anti-communist divide. This cultural and political chasm in the body politic is manifest in the use by contending parties of different national symbols and anthems and insignia. In practical terms this existence of alternative national political visions, which draw on the unresolved memories of civil war, means that there is no readily accepted "legitimacy" for the dominance of either side. In these circumstances the terms of the "democratic bargain" are prone to be called into doubt, the restraints on the bounds of political action are fragile, and political rhetoric tends to stray into the language of revolution. (1999: 5–6)

Table 7.1 shows how certain value divisions were manifest in the party system. A number of deep divisions emerge from this data over values such as authoritarianism, liberalism, nationalism, and modernism, with some parties attracting mostly authoritarians and others mostly liberals. For example, 63 percent of DS voters declared that belonging to Europe was important for them, while only 38 percent of SPS voters responded in this manner. Similarly deep divisions emerge over values such as nationalism, modernism, and tolerance. The kinds of cross-cutting cleavages that foster political compromise are absent, indicating low levels of liberal content.

Table 7.1   Distribution of Selected Values within the Main Political Parties
(percent of voters who agree with value)

Value	SPS[a]	SRS[b]	SPO[c]	DS[d]	DSS[e]
	Survey period October 1992				
Belonging to SCG[f] important	89	78	40	41	40
Belonging to Europe important	38	24	61	63	75
Nostalgia for the old system	72	29	9	21	15
Liberalism	17	32	70	78	71
Modernism	13	9	53	67	73
	Survey period 1993[g]				
Tolerance	3	7	35	30	58
Radicalism	74	93	24	25	19
Nationalism	53	52	20	10	10
Authoritarianism	64	47	22	12	10
Xenophobia	87	84	49	64	57
Religiosity	41	49	48	37	42
	Survey period October 1996				
Favoring private property	30	46	55	60	65
Trust in people	29	33	41	31	29
Egalitarianism	53	48	48	48	35
Conservatism	59	41	37	50	29
Post-materialist values	12	17	26	26	28

Source: Derived from Pantić (1998: 136).

[a]Serbian Socialist Party (Srpska Partija Socijalisticka).
[b]Serbian Radical Party (Srpska Radikalna Stranka).
[c]Serbian Renewal Movement (Srpski Pokret Obnove).
[d]Democratic Party (Demokratska Stranka).
[e]Democratic Party of Serbia (Demokratska Stranka Srbije).
[f]Serbia and Montenegro (Srbija i Crna Gora).
[g]Questions on tolerance and radicalism included in survey conducted May 1993. Questions on nationalism and authoritarianism included in survey conducted October 1993. Questions on xenophobia and religiosity included in survey conducted November 1993.

The Milošević Regime and the West
The Politics of Anti-Westernism

As a careful, calculating political actor, Milošević perceived that the benefits of appealing to Serbian nationalism and fomenting paranoia about the intentions of the outside world outweighed the costs of isolation and exclusion from the process of European integration. With regard to his pursuit of war in Bosnia and Croatia, some analysts have suggested that Milošević had believed internal intelligence reports, which argued that with the winding down of the Cold War, Yugoslavia was no longer of vital strategic importance to the West and thus that it would not intervene in its internal affairs. However, these factors only explain Milošević's decision to go to war and not his consistent rejection of Western liberalism and his use of populist anti-Western rhetoric throughout the 1990s.

Certainly part of the explanation is path-dependent: once he began to base his legitimacy on standing up to the West and rejecting its demands, it was harder to turn back. Even the otherwise liberal opposition parties felt that they had to toe the anti-Western line to some degree in order to be politically viable in the charged atmosphere of 1990s FRY. Being seen as a Western "lackey" was a significant political liability. Thus, that the West openly supported the ascent of Milan Panić and Dobrica Ćosić to leadership positions in the regime actually backfired, as the two leaders were later denounced as serving foreign interests by both the regime and large parts of the public. That Milošević created an atmosphere in which the Western incentives of membership in the European Union, NATO, and other international organizations had little in the way of a receptive audience among the domestic public, and thus little leverage in terms of encouraging democratization, goes far in explaining the authoritarian character of the Milošević regime. Absent a domestic impetus for liberalism and any credible promise of membership in Western institutions, the external factor could not act as a force "neutralizing" radical populism, as it did in Slovenia and Croatia.

Anti-Western sentiment deepened in the 1990s as a result of Milošević's policies and the negative effects of Western sanctions, which were exploited by the regime to demonstrate a vast conspiracy against FRY in the international community. Indeed, Belgrade bookstores were full of volumes purporting to expose Vatican, German, American, and other conspiracies to destroy Yugoslavia and annihilate the Serbs. Polls taken in the mid-1990s showed that 69 percent of respondents believed that it was necessary to keep up the fight without regard to the outside world. According to research done by the Institute of Political Studies in Belgrade, 79 percent of respondents from Serbia believed that there was a vast conspiracy against Serbia led by Germany and the Vatican (Malešević 2002: 252). Even intellectual groups had assimilated a deep mistrust of the West, as the following statement from one writers' association attests: "Western civilization is a mixture of poverty, drugs, and criminals and the fall of all moral values, and we cannot find a model for us in this" (quoted in Malešević 2002: 245).

This led to a cycle in which the West was forced to rely on negative inducements to achieve compliance, while this sort of pressure only galvanized anti-Western sentiment in FRY. Sanctions were the main instrument used by the West: they were imposed in 1991 over the war in Croatia, reinforced in 1992 over the war in Bosnia, lifted in 1995 after Dayton, reimposed in 1998 over Kosovo, and tightened in 1999 after the NATO bombing. An "outer wall" of sanctions excluded FRY from membership in any international organizations and remained intact throughout the 1990s as punishment for the undemocratic regime. Milošević, of course, understood that there was a limit to how much he could ignore Western demands, particularly since complete economic isolation would lead to conditions that could threaten his power. Thus, he made grudging concessions, mostly to have the sanctions eased.

In 1994, following hyperinflation, economic conditions were particularly bad, and Milošević knew that he would have to extricate FRY from the sanctions if he wanted to stay in power. For a tired public, it also played well to appear to have had defeated, as opposed to "given in to," sanctions.[20] It is then that he decided to play the role of peacemaker at Dayton. The sanctions were lifted, and Milošević received a significant boost at home and abroad. However, any international political capital he may have achieved internationally was wasted with his invalidation of the November 1996 local elections, for which he was sharply criticized and isolated by both the United States and the EU (Pribićević 1997: 118).

Milošević, nonetheless, was intent on cultivating a respectable image in the international community. Thus, he created a democratic façade at home and tried hard not to appear as a dictator. This was one other reason that it was strategically valuable to support extremist ideological surrogates like Šešelj's SRS: they made Milošević appear moderate and allowed him to point out to Western officials that the alternative to his rule was an extremist party. Milošević, then, was not ideologically driven in his anti-Western appeals. Rather, he saw them as politically expedient. He seemed to be always calculating about how far he could go without totally alienating the West, and how many concessions he could extract from Western officials.

Moving to Promote Regime Change

Already in 1991, Milošević came under sharp criticism from Western nations. Later, the policies of the West were driven by the imperative of ending the wars in the former Yugoslavia, and as such Milošević was embraced in

1995 when he expressed a desire to participate in the peace process. By the end of the 1990s, Western nations used the stick of isolation to punish Milošević for his democratic transgressions and in an attempt to compel democratic reform.

However, at a certain point it became clear that the policy of isolation alone was only playing into the regime's efforts to demonize the West and present Serbia as a victim. Thus, in 1998 the United States in particular decided that it would be useful to begin a campaign of support for the democratic opposition. There were strong feelings that the United States had missed an opportunity in failing to seize on the massive 1996–1997 protests by supporting the Milošević opposition.[21] This failure also made some members of the democratic opposition in FRY cynical of U.S. motives.[22]

Washington began a policy of offering support to opposition groups in the form of aid and logistical assistance, much like what was done in Croatia around the same time. By some estimates, the opposition received $25 million in financial assistance in the last two years of the 1990s (Krickovic 2001: 18). There were conditions attached to this aid.[23] One condition was that the opposition parties overcome their divisions, as this was the only way they could assure their victory over the regime. Much of the logistical support offered to the opposition was geared toward helping the opposition parties unite behind a common leader and program. The second condition was that the nationally oriented opposition parties such as the SPO and DSS cease their anti-Western rhetoric and support FRY's entry into Euro-Atlantic structures based on a fulfillment of the necessary political and economic reforms.[24] During the NATO bombing of 1999, the U.S. Mission to Belgrade evacuated, set up shop in Budapest, and received members of the Serbian opposition on a regular basis.[25] The strategy worked: the SPO, GSS, DS, and, somewhat more reluctantly, the DSS united and ran on a pro-European, liberal platform under the DEPOS coalition. Later, the nonviolent resistance movement Otpor became a major beneficiary of aid. Support for Otpor turned out to be an ideal strategy: as a nonpolitical party, it had much more legitimacy in the eyes of the public. The EU also wooed the opposition. Romano Prodi said that "Belgrade and its policies which are continuing to deny [FRY] its place in Europe, a place to which it will be wholeheartedly welcomed once a democratic government is in place" (quoted in Field 2000: 132). This also reflected a shift from exclusive reliance on the stick to the carrot on the part of the EU. Moreover, the Western-promoted democratic turnover in Croatia in January 2000 and the positive international reaction in the months that followed served as a positive demonstration effect for the opposition.

Part of the Western strategy involved funding the work of a number of U.S.-based prodemocracy NGOs, such as the International Republican Institute (IRI) and National Democratic Institute (NDI), which were instrumental in training party activists and helping to organize campaigns to encourage citizens to vote.[26] Support was also provided to alternative media outlets to help them reach rural areas. Moreover, Western-funded NGOs conducted polls that helped the opposition parties focus their programs. Critically, these polls showed that the electorate was most concerned with issues of economic survival far more than issues such as nationality.

The catch was that the United States and other Western countries had to take a very cautious approach so as not to discredit the opposition as a tool of foreign countries. The choice of DSS leader Vojislav Koštunica was a compromise in this regard: he was uncorrupted and democratic but also had strong nationalist credentials. He had been an open critic of the American effort to "export democracy," saying, "For people who have not experienced democracy it is important that democracy grow in this country. If it was somehow imported, it would not give people the right idea" (quoted in Cohen 2001: 409). Ironically, he was even more blunt about the American "Budapest strategy" that helped bring him to power: "You need to have a huge dose of arrogance to claim that a long-term U.S. goal is the improvement of democracy in Serbia. Democracy in Serbia is exclusively a Serbian goal and nobody else can claim it" (quoted in Cohen 2001: 409).

The NATO Bombing of 1999

The U.S.-led decision by NATO to pursue an air war against the Milošević regime and the events of this war have been well documented elsewhere. Despite all the debate over its utility and strategic goals, one fact is clear: the decision to punish Milošević reflected a new willingness on the part of the Western world to enforce liberal norms through military force, if necessary. Milošević's campaign in Kosovo did not represent a serious threat to European or American security, but his failure to adopt the provisions of the Rambouillet framework meant that he was not willing to play by Western liberal rules, especially with regard to minority rights. Why was he willing to risk a bombing campaign over Kosovo when he had so readily abandoned nationalist projects in Croatia and Bosnia? There is no definitive answer, but analysts have speculated that he thought he could divide the NATO alliance or that he would again be able to emerge as peacemaker after entering negotiations, thereby strengthening his position. If so, he greatly miscalculated on both counts. More than likely, he knew that losing Kosovo would be the final nail in his regime's coffin, proof that he was not capable of defending Serbian interests as he had promised in Kosovo more than a decade earlier. From the perspective of NATO, it was necessary to defend the alliance's credibility, find a new mission in the post–Cold War world, and eliminate the chief impediment to democratization and stability in the Balkans.

NATO bombed FRY for seventy-eight days before Milošević, realizing that it was his last chance to walk away and still hold power, finally capitulated[27] and signed an agreement promising to withdraw his troops from the territory of Kosovo and accept that it would become an international protectorate.[28] During the bombing itself, massacres were committed by Serbian paramilitary groups, and much of the Albanian population fled to neighboring countries. Estimates are that at least 500 civilians were killed by NATO bombs, while Serbian forces killed 10,000–12,000 Albanian civilians (Ramet 2006: 517).

During the bombing, the population initially rallied around the regime. Then support began to wane, falling sharply among nationalists as they realized that Kosovo was lost. The negative economic effects of the bombing impoverished the FRY population further. The regime was delegitimized and, as noted above, resorted to strong-arm tactics to remain in power.

Milošević delivered a speech on New Year's Eve in 1999 that again evoked the theme of Western liberal imperialism. "The West wants to conquer the whole world," he remarked, "Let us hope that the developed part of the world will come around and see the danger that they themselves are posing to the world. But we should expect that the other part of the world will find the strength to unite and stand firm" (Cohen 2001: 332). A desperate and isolated man on the eve of the new millennium, he sought alliances with the likes of Iraq, Libya, and Belarus. Meanwhile, the West had made his removal from power an explicit condition for aid and admission to any Western organizations (Field 2000: 138).

Seeking Western Largesse: Montenegro and Milo Đukanović, 1997–1999

Montenegro after 1997 is a paradigmatic example of a theoretical point made in the introduction to this study about how post-communist political elites may adopt a pro-Western stance in order to bid for political capital, even where they have no history of supporting the Western liberal project.[29] The public may or may not be behind the Western agenda, or it may be deeply divided over it; nevertheless, certain segments of society will support these elites if they see potential benefits emerging from falling in line with Western conditions. The West becomes, therefore, a source of capital in domestic political games.

Until 1996, Milošević was able to control Montenegro firmly. However, increasing dissatisfaction with FRY's isolation and the catastrophic economic situation led to a search for political alternatives in Podgorica and resistance to Milošević by the reform-minded coalition of Đukanović, who had already succeeded in placing his supporters in the federal parliament in Belgrade. The federal constitutional court, filled with Milošević loyalists, challenged this and Đukanović's subsequent election as president. In response, Montenegro's government announced that it no longer recognized the authority of the National Assembly. Milošević arranged for Momir Bulatović, a loyalist, to be elected federal prime minister (Cohen 2001: 329). In response to such battles with Belgrade, the Đukanović government in Podgorica decided to court the United States and the EU, and the West was happy to oblige, seeing in Đukanović an opportunity to promote reform in FRY.

However, a Western versus anti-Western orientation was never at the root of the Podgorica-Belgrade conflict. Đukanović had not been a pro-Western politician in the past. He had originally been one of the "golden boys" of Milošević's anti-bureaucratic revolution. He began to have reservations about the regime when Milošević removed Dobrica Ćosić and Milan Panić from office during 1993.[30] During the 1996–1997 anti-regime protests, Đukanović openly sided with the protestors. When the time was right, he used the West to raise his political standing and to gain concrete rewards. He could not have stood up to Milošević on his own: with only 600,000 people, Montenegro was dwarfed by Serbia. Embracing the West was a practical way, therefore, to pursue his political ambitions.

In the Montenegrin presidential election of October 1997, Đukanović began to criticize Milošević openly for his authoritarian practices and his failure to address the problems the country was facing. Critically, he also began to speak of Montenegro's desire to join Western structures, particularly the EU, which was a sharp departure from Belgrade's policies. Đukanović's split with the pro-Belgrade policies of Bulatović also signaled a split in the ruling DPS, with Bulatović forming the splinter Socialist People's Party (Soci-jalistička Narodna Partija, SNP) and continuing to pursue a pro-Belgrade line. The election turned into a bitter battle between Đukanović and Bulato-vić and, simultaneously, between supporters of Belgrade's policies and Mon-tenegro's continued union with Serbia and those opposing both. Two small pro-Western liberal parties, the Peoples' Party (Narodna Stranka, NS) and Liberal Alliance (Liberalni Savez, LS) agreed to support Đukanović in return for his pledge to undertake democratic reforms. The outcome of the first round of voting was extremely close, with neither candidate gaining the re-quired absolute majority. In the second round, Đukanović prevailed, with strong support from young voters and members of minority communities. Đukanović also relied on mobilizing voters along traditional Montenegrin clan lines, a strategy that was sharply attacked by the Bulatović camp as being "pre-civic" (Cohen 2001: 282).[31]

Bulatović, supported by Belgrade, mounted a fierce attack on Đukanović, claiming that he was corrupt and a stooge of the NATO countries aiming to break up the FRY (Bugajski 2002: 499). He accused his rival of election fraud and organized large demonstrations in January 1998 in an attempt to disrupt Đukanović's inauguration. Belgrade likewise tried to stir up civil strife to in-validate the election and intimidate Đukanović with Yugoslav troop move-ments. However, despite rumors that Bulatović was planning a coup and that Milošević would impose a state of emergency in Montenegro, strong interna-tional support for Đukanović probably prevented the regime from taking such drastic measures (Karatnycky et al. 1999: 658). Thus, Đukanović took office with strong international backing: fifty-six diplomats accredited to FRY attended the inauguration (Vojicic 1998).

The close results in the presidential contest reflected the deep polarization of the republic's population regarding the question of reform and relations with Serbia and, to some extent, over identity itself. Half of Montenegro's citizens identified as Serbs, and the other half as Montenegrins.[32] The Metro-politan of the Montenegrin Orthodox Church said at the time:

> At this time Montenegro is literally divided. The northern regions, workers and retirees are on the side of the Serbian option that is Momir Bulatović; the urban areas, businessmen and the youth are on the side of Milo Đukanović and independence. [Federal] army and [Montenegrin] police—each represent-ing its option—have already unsheathed the bayonets. The outcome may be bloody... very bloody... The mentality of our people is still very patriarchal,

knife, revenge, and tribal system such as exists nowhere else. The whole country is inter-connected, almost everyone knows everyone else.... Quarrels within
a family are the worst, the pain the deepest. (quoted in Cohen 2001: 334)

Đukanović, therefore, had limited legitimacy and had to tread carefully. This
only increased his need for international backing, and he began to seek it
more actively with numerous overtures to Western governments. Montenegro opened a separate trade mission in Washington, and its spokesmen distanced themselves from the FRY embassy. Representatives of the Đukanović
government were dispatched to Brussels to express their desire to cooperate
with the EU.

Increasingly operating as a quasi-independent state in terms of foreign
policy, Montenegro opened the door to foreign visitors without a visa regime.
Yet, Đukanović's regime in Montenegro also resembled the kind of "simulated" democracy described in chapter 4 for Croatia: despite the existence of
extensive democratic rules, the DPS exercised a tight hold over political and
economic life in Montenegro as well as the media. Nevertheless, Podgorica
was viewed by many Western diplomats as the back door through which to
influence developments in Milošević's Yugoslavia.[33] The simulation, however, proved to be useful in gaining concrete rewards from the West, especially since Western countries and organizations saw any counterforce to Milošević as strategically useful and hoped that democratization would spread
from Podgorica to Belgrade.[34] Hence, despite Đukanović's lack of democratic
credentials and ongoing rumors about his shady financial dealings in the contraband cigarette trade, he was embraced as the "poster boy" of the Balkans
and invited to visit Western capitals.[35]

NGOs were dispatched to Podgorica to promote reforms and educate locals in the art of Western democratic institutions. Financial assistance and
limited investment began to flow into Montenegro, including an independent bank sponsored by George Soros. The international community used
Montenegro, for instance, to set up meetings and workshops with Serbia's
political opposition, to whom Montenegro gave safe haven.[36] The ultimate
reward came in 1999, when, save for a few military installations, NATO left
Montenegrin targets off of its bombing list.

The Đukanović government used a number of traditional avenues to stim-
ulate support for its separatist agenda. For instance, it began to encourage the
Montenegrin church to assert its independence from the hierarchy of the
Serbian Orthodox Church. There was, however, a part of the population,

who, whether for personal or economic reasons, did not recognize Montenegrin identity and would never support its independence. In an atmosphere of nationalism, some had eagerly embraced the idea spread by the Belgrade regime that all Montenegrins were actually Serbs, in part because such statements were taboo under communism. The division over identity proved to be a constant threat to the legitimacy of Đukanović's agenda.[37] The West, while warning Milošević not to provoke another war with Montenegro, also opposed Montenegro's outright independence and pressured Đukanović to contain his pro-sovereignty inclinations.

Milošević did everything in his power to destabilize and discredit Đukanović's government, as did former pro-Milošević Montenegrin president and Đukanović rival Bulatović. An economic blockade was imposed on Montenegro, and troops were amassed on the border, at times provocatively straying into Montenegrin territory.[38] Đukanović was attacked for undermining social ownership and playing into the hands of "Western liberal imperialism" and excluded from the Supreme Defense Council. Podgorica retaliated by strengthening its internal security forces and with a new citizenship law that created a distinct Montenegrin citizenship.

In the end, the threat from Đukanović to Milošević was probably greater, since in acting as an independent state, Montenegro further hurt the legitimacy of the Belgrade regime. Ironically, though, one of the biggest losers after the fall of the Milošević regime in 2000 was Đukanović, who quickly lost his "poster boy" status in Western capitals. His overtures to the West would now have to depend on more than half-hearted democratic policies. A pro-Western stance as a means of bidding for power and rewards, in other words, no longer carried the same benefits under changed circumstances.

The Reproduction of Economic Decline

The economic crisis of the 1980s was especially acute in FRY, where high expectations and memories of better times fueled deep disappointment. The economic shocks associated with the breakup of the SFRJ market were severe because FRY had depended heavily on the availability of cheap inputs from the other republics and on their markets to sell its goods. Due to populist economic policies, a lack of almost any reform whatsoever, and the negative effects of war and international isolation, the economy continued its downward spiral through the 1990s. This had the dual political effect of strengthening support for radical populism (even as support for Milošević himself fell) and, in the long run, exhausting and demobilizing the population politically.

The first years of transition saw steep declines in growth. In only four years, FRY's GDP dropped by 60 percent (see figure 7.1). By 1996, 26 out of 35 branches of industry had an output that was less than 50 percent of the 1989 level. Many FRY citizens emigrated to the West, which resulted in a severe weakening of the position of the middle class (Cohen 2001: 208). The SPS-connected "new rich," meanwhile, grew richer.

The SPS's ideology called for a mixed socialist-market economy, but detailed policy proposals were few and far between. Many economic decisions were based on populist motives, which wreaked havoc on the economy. One practice employed by Milošević repeatedly from 1990 to 1993 was simply to increase the money supply to pay retirees and state-sector workers, thereby buying supporters and social peace. This proved to be disastrous. An increase in the money supply combined with strong inflationary pressures caused by a number of other factors, such as the unloading of other republics' dinar holdings in the FRY market as the SFRJ disintegrated, helped lead in 1993 to one of the largest instances of hyperinflation in world history. The monthly rate of inflation was never below 100 percent in 1993 and fell below 200 percent only in April. The end of 1993 saw genuine hyperinflation: 18,860 percent in August and 20,190 percent by November. The dinar had lost its meaning as the Serbian economy reverted to barter. In January 1994, the monthly rate of inflation averaged over 300 million percent and prices reached dizzying sums (Gordy 1999: 171).

In 1994, the economist Dragoslav Avramović was brought in as the new head of the Yugoslav National Bank and managed to curb inflation and for a time reverse declining output with a strict program of monetary restriction. However, falling inflation could not disguise continued instability in the economy. Unfortunately, Milošević had instilled Avramović with limited powers, and he could not follow through on his privatization program. Instead, he was dismissed in 1996 for advocating an end to state monopolies.

A staple of the Milošević regime's economic policy was extensive clientelism. The regime ensured that the resources available in economically devastated FRY went to regime insiders. Although clientelism marked the Tuđman regime in Croatia as well, its effects were much worse in FRY because its economic structure was weaker and because it occurred in the context of an economy that had undergone almost no liberalization. Poor initial condi-

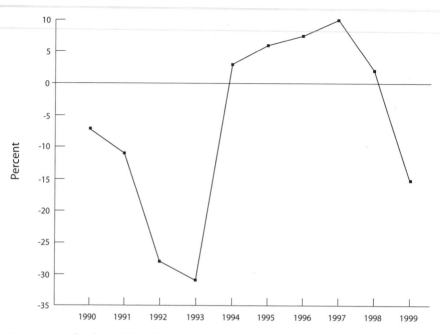

Figure 7.1. Federal Republic of Yugoslavia, Rate of GDP Growth, 1990–1999
Source: Jeffries 2002: 409.

tions, the absence of privatization, and the isolation of the FRY economy
from 1992 to 1995 due to international sanctions created an ideal milieu for
the evolution of the SPS and DPS as clientelist parties "that do not manage to
represent economic or cultural interest, but co-opt individuals from different
social strata and cultural segments by financial inducements" (Goati 1998: 25).

The SPS was the main source of patronage, doling out the state's meager
resources to loyalists and profiting from sanctions-busting and war-related
activities with the support of organized crime. Ministers and political leaders
wielded enormous influence in the economy. The economic system was dominated by 120 companies, whose heads were all political appointees and who
represented FRY's main producers, exporters, importers, and the banks. Because they operated in monopolistic conditions and received export and import privileges, the profits were large. The state and para-state economic
elites grew enormously wealthy, due not to their entrepreneurial talents but
to politically backed monopoly control over different segments of the economy. The wartime trade in arms, war materials, and stolen humanitarian aid
was very profitable. Cohen writes: "The Serbian state and para-state eco-

nomic and managerial stratum did not constitute a modernizing elite devoted to economic innovation and development, but rather a politically obedient oligarchy benefiting from the status quo" (2001: 132). The SPS adamantly opposed privatization. As one newspaper wrote in 1996, "They want things to stay as they are because they have the best of both worlds. You have companies run by general managers appointed by one political leader. These are feudal fiefs held by one man. If you privatize, you lose control—you convert your country from a tightly controlled society to an amorphous society where you do not know what to expect."[39] Limited privatization was attempted in the first years of the 1990s but was later reversed. Since there were restrictions on international capital, there was really no way for outside firms to buy FRY enterprises. By the end of the 1990s, the private sector accounted for only 40 percent of production, much of which was in the small and informal sector. The state sector, on the other hand, was inefficient and bloated and subject to soft budget constraints. The EBRD wrote: "The country's enterprises are largely unreformed and are characterized by substantial losses, soft budget constraints, widespread inter-enterprise arrears, and barter arrangements. There are no effective bankruptcy procedures. While there is a competition law in place, it has not been applied" (quoted in Jeffries 2002: 12).

The economy was characterized by a number of other negative trends in the 1990s due to poor policies and mismanagement by the Milošević regime, international sanctions, and the effects of war. FDI was limited—only $1 billion flowed in from 1990 to 1998, and most of this came from the privatization of Serbia Telecom. Macroeconomic performance was variable, but long-term trends pointed to general deterioration (Uvalić 2001: 178). There was a chronically large current accounts deficit and high gross external debt. Inflationary pressures remained. Price liberalization was only partial and was reversed on several occasions. The foreign exchange system, even after the lifting of sanctions in late 1995, remained subject to restrictions such as widespread import and export licenses, import quotas, high import duties and associated charges, the non-convertibility of the dinar, and limits on foreign exchange. Banking scandals deprived people of hard currency savings. A large part of the budget went to defense. And the unemployment rate crept upwards, surpassing 25 percent in 1995 (Jeffries 2002: 303).

Milošević was wary of reform and suspicious of free market capitalism— not so much due to his ideological convictions as his desire to stay in power at all costs. Radical reforms would strike at the heart of his power base, which rested on a vast web of political and economic patronage. Consequently, the economy continued to slide downhill. I have heard in Serbia countless stories of people who lived relatively well in the 1980s but whose lives were completely devastated in the 1990s. Many became increasingly dependent on pensions or remittances as the only source of income, lowering social autonomy and leading to general resignation. People were forced to think about basic needs rather than how to go about ousting the regime and this was a boon to Milošević (Gordy 1999).

After the Kosovo conflict, all economic indicators took a nosedive. The country's GNP in 1999 dropped to less than 40 percent of its 1989 level. Dangerously low reserves signaled that a serious international liquidity crisis was looming. The costs of the bombing and the destruction it wrought have been estimated at between $30 billion to $100 billion, of which $4 billion was the cost of physical damage, $2.3 billion was lost human capital, and $23 billion was lost potential GDP from damaged plants and disrupted trade (Uvalić 2001: 177).

Pensions and salaries were not being paid at all or paid with coupons for needed goods. The factor that kept the population at a level of basic sustenance was the fact that FRY was always able to feed itself.[40] For the first time in history, Montenegro had higher wages than Serbia. More than 40,000 people worked in 350 loss-making industries and 42,000 worked in the bloated public sector. Unemployment stood at over 40 percent. Serbia had its lowest standard of living since the end of World War II. Twenty percent of the population lived in poverty, and 50 percent lived at the subsistence level.[41]

The question of how Milošević was able to stay in power should be distinguished from the larger question of why radical populism took hold in FRY and dominated the first ten years of post-communist transition. It was clear that had the institutional and other guarantors of SPS rule been removed in the 1990s, liberal political forces would probably not have filled the vacuum. Indeed, the second-largest party in FRY throughout the 1990s was the neo-fascist SRS, and significant parts of the ostensible liberal opposition played the nationalist card.

Radical populism dominated post-communist FRY because of initial conditions of economic malaise that deepened in the 1990s. Continuing reproduction of economic scarcity was filtered through certain illiberal proclivities in FRY society to produce populist authoritarianism. Research on social attitudes in FRY indicated that "no social strata were interested or ideologically prepared to support or implement [liberal] reforms." Moreover, in the early years of post-communist transition, survey research indicated high levels of xenophobia, ethnic distance, and non-market orientation in Serbia (Sekelj 2000: 58). Bora Kuzmanović, a social psychologist, found in 1990s FRY society an uncritical attitude toward authority, a "patriots or traitors" mentality, and strong feelings of collectivism (quoted in Sekelj 2000: 58).

Certain aspects of FRY political culture that could be mobilized in conditions of economic scarcity proved especially fertile soil for Milošević's populist style. The triumph of traditional collectivist values in the Milošević years reflected in part a victory of the rural areas of FRY over the cosmopolitan, modern culture of the city. The urban-rural split in FRY society was cleverly exploited by the regime. Moreover, the regime's decision to reject Western liberalism and the corresponding lack of any credible offer of membership in the EU and other Western organizations not only fortified populist nationalism but also meant that there was no positive external inducement to curtail illiberal policies and neutralize radical groups, as there had been in Croatia, Slovenia, and Macedonia.

Milošević, despite "astutely understanding his cultural milieu, [knowing] precisely how to package and convey such nationalist appeals, and also when to adopt a new style of political discourse," had no real long-term strategy (Cohen 2001: 86). He did have an overriding interest, and that was power. He showed time and time again in his clientelist economic policies, in his manipulation of the democratic process, in his opportunistic nationalism, and in his knee-jerk foreign policy, that his chief interest was staying in power at all costs. This was not easy, as Milošević faced a permanent crisis of legitimation (Cohen 2001: xviii). Unlike his Croatian counterpart Tuđman, he could not point to a "Homeland War" or any other successful nationalist project. Instead he adopted ideological surrogates, exploited divisions in the public, blamed FRY's woes on internal and external enemies, and, when all else failed, turned to repression.

Another factor lowering liberal content in FRY was the extent and nature of public divisions as reflected in the party system. Sekelj has written that there was "no fundamental consensus in Serbia and Montenegro on either the borders and character of the state or the values on which society and the political community should be founded... the ethnic Albanian community does not recognize the state, while leading Serbian political parties... advocate a 'Greater Serbia'" (2000: 59). Liberal content in FRY was low given the complete absence from the political scene of any real liberal options for most of the 1990s.

The opposition prevailed in the tumultuous events of October 2000, Vojislav Koštunica was installed as president, and the West was elated. The DEPOS coalition took control of the federal parliament, and won Serbian parliamentary elections several months later. However, as in Croatia, Milošević was not voted out of office because of a broad condemnation of nationalism or a universal embrace of democracy. Rather, the public was expressing deep dissatisfaction with the economic situation and a deeply illegitimate regime. Nationalist sentiment remained entrenched, and there was a continuing popular distrust of the West, its institutions, and its motives.

CHAPTER EIGHT

The Yugoslav Successor States in the New Millennium

From red star to gold stars

HEADLINE IN THE SLOVENIAN DAILY *DELO* ON 1 MAY
2004, THE DAY SLOVENIA FORMALLY ENTERED THE EU,
ALLUDING TO THE OLD YUGOSLAV FLAG (WITH ONE
RED STAR) AND THE EU FLAG (WITH GOLD STARS).

The Extent and Limits of Change, 2000–2009

In the second decade of transition, external forces, and in particular the ever-increasing role of the EU, became the most important agents of democratic change in the Yugoslav successor states.[1] After 2000, Western policies toward Croatia, FRY, and Macedonia shifted from preventing conflict to an active promotion of democracy through conditionality. Especially important in this regard was the EU's process of Stabilization and Association Agreements (SAA), created in 1999 for the Balkans.[2] The SAA was designed to motivate democratic reforms while encouraging liberal elites and impatient publics with intermediate rewards on the path to full EU membership or, in the EU Commission's own words, through "an ever-closer partnership" with Europe. The power of the EU to compel reforms rested on what Pridham (2007: 446) has called its "special attraction" compared to other international organizations and the unparalleled benefits integration offered: free trade, open borders, and access to aid and investment. As part of the SAA process, an aspirant country's progress would be evaluated in periodic reports.[3] The integration process had security benefits for the EU as well. As former EU external relations commissioner Chris Patten stated, "Either we export stability to the Balkans, or the Balkans export instability to us. I know which I would prefer" (quoted in Kavalski 2006: 96).

The promise of EU membership turned out to be a powerful catalyst of democratization. However, even as the four states converged on procedural measures of democratization, they continued to diverge on measures of liberal content, demonstrating the constraints imposed by initial structural conditions. External agency, while powerful in some ways, also had limits in terms of its ability to increase liberal content in the short term.

In the first years of the new millennium, two of the states examined in this study (Croatia and FRY) underwent regime collapse triggered by electoral revolutions in which democratic political forces prevailed, another (Macedonia) was rescued from civil war by the international community, and the fourth (Slovenia) proceeded confidently on the road to the EU, formally joining in May 2004, adopting the euro in 2007, and in January 2008 assuming the presidency of the EU, the first among the post-communist member states to take on this role.

Despite the rise to power of political forces with a democratic and pro-Western agenda in Croatia and FRY in 2000 and Macedonia in 2002, initial conditions continued to shape varying levels of liberal content among them. At the same time, the increasing leverage of EU conditionality enabled all three states to make significant democratic gains in key areas such as institutional reform, elections, and the rule of law. In all three cases, EU conditionality strengthened liberal political configurations at the expense of nationalist groups and compelled formerly illiberal parties to adopt a prodemocratic stance.

Western liberalism found the most receptive audience in Croatia and helped to put it on an irreversible road to integration into the EU and NATO. However, ambivalence toward both of these organizations, and toward democracy more generally, continued to feature in public discourse and increased at the end of the decade as EU expansion appeared to stall and nationalists regrouped. Although both Macedonia and FRY made gains in their bids for membership in Euro-Atlantic organizations, substantial obstacles to building democratic legitimacy remained, illiberal groups continued to exercise influence on the political scene, deep social divisions persisted, and EU conditionality was looked at with ambivalence, lowering its ability to leverage change.

Serbia's liberal deficiencies included a sharply divided society and unresolved issues related to state borders. In May 2006, an EU-mandated referendum on independence was held in Montenegro. A sharply divided electorate voted in favor of leaving the union with Serbia, and the tiny republic has since been recognized internationally. Independence and an SAA with the EU have empowered the pro-European segment of the Montenegrin political spectrum, but factors such as corruption, a divided society, and a weak judicial sector continue to inhibit the quality of Montenegro's democracy.

In 2008, following the failure of lengthy internationally mediated talks between Priština and Belgrade, Kosovo's leaders declared independence. Most EU member states and the United States quickly recognized Kosovo's sovereignty. However, the international community still supervises its transition, 15,000 KFOR peacekeepers remain on its territory, and its economy is barely viable, with unemployment levels hovering at over 40 percent.

Nearly fourteen years after the Dayton Agreements, democratic progress in Bosnia and Herzegovina is hampered by an unwieldy federal arrangement, lingering distrust among the ethnic groups, low levels of trust in government and its institutions, and problems related to the legitimacy of the state. The international community extended the mandate of the Office of the High Representative (OHR) in 2009, and it continues to exercise substantial powers over the Bosnian polity.

Slovenia

Despite volatile party politics and coalition reshuffling, the post-2000 Slovenian political leadership remained uniformly committed to the process of democratization and European integration. As such, the dictates of the acquis communautaire continued to hold great sway over Slovenian political life, even as intense domestic political battles persisted between the communist successor LDS and the right-of-center SDP and its allies. As a result Slovenia moved more slowly than other candidate states toward completing the negotiations necessary for membership. By 2001 it was all but certain that Slovenia would be admitted to the EU along with other front-runner candidate countries. Moreover, in 2004, Slovenia was admitted to NATO, after having been excluded in the first round of expansion.

The LDS managed yet another electoral victory in the October 2000 parliamentary elections. A coalition consisting of the LDS, the United List of Social Democrats (Združena Lista Socialnih Demokratov, ZLSD), and DSUS was put together, with Drnovšek again assuming the post of prime minister.

Thus, Slovenian political life appeared to be characterized by an entrenched communist successor political class rotating among posts of power. This made the ruling party a target of fierce attacks from the right and fueled a public perception that political figures in Slovenia were simply trading seats. In 2002, Janez Drnovšek prevailed in the presidential elections to replace Milan Kučan, who stepped down after two terms. Kučan was the last of the cadre of leaders (along with Tuđman, Milošević, Gligorov, and Izetbegović) that had overseen the breakup of Yugoslavia in 1991. Anton Rop, Drnovšek's deputy and finance minister, stepped in to replace him as Premier.

Although Slovenia's economy continued to grow, its GDP per capita surpassing the poorest EU member states in the early 2000s, structural problems inherited from Yugoslav-era institutions and resistance to foreign investment limited its potential. Moreover, EU-mandated budget restrictions necessitated the laying off of state-sector workers, and unemployment increased, causing substantial discontent in a workforce that was accustomed to secure lifetime employment. The growth rate in 2003 was only 2.5 percent, the lowest since Slovenia gained its independence over twelve years before. Furthermore, the public debt had risen to over 2 billion euros since the LDS government took office.

Despite Slovenia's progress on the acquis and the government's deliberate drive toward membership, in the 2000s there was also ample evidence of public disillusionment with the EU and the reforms it mandated. Nevertheless, in 2003, Slovenians strongly endorsed membership in a referendum on EU membership, in higher numbers than their counterparts in other top-tier candidate countries. Despite their ambivalence toward Europe, Slovenians evidently did not want to risk their chances of getting in.

In Slovenia's second decade of transition, there was also evidence of a backlash from the right to both the entrenched political class and liberalism. Anti-European rhetoric became more prevalent, and xenophobia was on the rise. Playing on social frustration, groups on the right of the Slovenian political spectrum launched direct attacks on the LDS leadership. Janša's right-wing SDSS, now renamed the Slovenian Democrats (Socialni Demokrati, SD), and its ally the New Slovenia-Christian People's Party (Nova Slovenija-Krščanska Ljudska Stranka, NSi) accused the government of corruption and cronyism and attempted to oust the Rop administration. The opposition also attacked the government for supposedly giving in to Croatia in negotiations over fishing rights in the disputed Piran Bay and proposed that former communist officials be banned from public life. Threats to the LDS also came from within: disagreements in the ruling coalition led the SLS to leave in April 2004, and the Rop government was left weakened. The political battles leading up to the October 2004 election were fierce.

In late summer 2004, opinion polls showed that support for the ruling LDS was falling, while the opposition SD was gaining ground. By the time of parliamentary elections in October 2004, the SD fared extremely well, doubling its popularity compared to the previous elections. The electorate was evidently tired of the LDS's long hold on power, in spite of it being the party that had had brought Slovenia into the EU and NATO.

Overt expressions of xenophobia began to appear in public life both before and after Slovenia's accession to the EU in 2004. First, there was a fierce debate over the rights of the "erased" minorities—mostly of Bosnian or Serbian origin—who had failed to register for Slovenian citizenship in 1992 and whose status was still unresolved. Even though a court had already ruled that the erasure was unconstitutional, a referendum was organized to decide on the fate of these tens of thousands of residents of Slovenia without status. Although the referendum was invalidated due to low turnout (around 30 percent), over 90 percent of those who did take part voted to deny the "erased" rights as Slovenian citizens. As of summer 2009, only a segment of this population had been granted citizenship rights, and the NSi attempted to dismiss the interior minister who defended the Constitutional Court's upholding of the "erased" rights.[4] Second, there was a major public debate over the thirty-year-long efforts of the sizeable Muslim community to build a mosque in Ljubljana. The leader of the opposition to the project, city councilor Mihael Jarc, warned that the construction of the mosque would lead to Slovenia's "Islamization" and destroy the capital's architectural heritage. A petition drive was organized to block the mosque, and its opponents also attempted to organize a referendum, which ultimately was struck down by the courts. Although the judicial system upheld the Muslim community's rights, many thought these developments reflected a culture of intolerance and xenophobia and showed that even Slovenia, a model of democratic transition, was not immune to illiberal tendencies.[5] Another referendum was eventually held in 2008, which opponents of the mosque lost. However, the authorities failed to issue the necessary building permits. The inflammatory nationalist rhetoric surrounding the border dispute with Croatia in 2009 further illustrated this tendency.

Some observers have explained such trends as reflecting sentiments that were always beneath the surface but suppressed by the fear of Western criticism. According to one analyst, now that EU membership was assured, true public sentiments were beginning to emerge. "We are not more tolerant than any other Balkan nations," said Mišo Alkalaj, "we have just had less opportunity to show it" (quoted in Wood 2004c). However, rather than pointing to a deeply rooted culture of intolerance, such public sentiments also reflected frustration with the pace and process of European integration and all of the necessary concessions that it entailed. When Slovenia formally entered the organization on 1 May 2004, as in other new member states, the celebration was markedly subdued.

The SD coalition did not change the country's slow approach to privatization, nor did it remove barriers to FDI, which led some economic analysts to worry about the country's prospects for future growth. "The Slovenians were concerned that if they let capital come in and out at leisure, they were going to have no control over their own economy," said François Lecavalier, the top official for Slovenia at the EBRD, "The issue is whether that's going to be sufficient for continued success."[6] There were also questions about whether Slovenia's expansive welfare state was sustainable. "The transition model has expired," said Mojmir Mrak, a professor of economics at Ljubljana University. "If you want to achieve high economic growth, you need a significant change in labor policies and increased investments."[7]

The Janša government exhibited illiberal tendencies in the non-economic sphere as well: it was widely accused of manipulating the media law to stack committees with its supporters and of installing loyalists in other areas of the state administration. Polls in the fall of 2007, prior to the pending presidential elections, showed that only one-third of Slovenians approved of the government. The center-left candidate and former diplomat Danilo Türk went on to defeat veteran politician and center-right candidate Lojze Peterle with two-thirds of the vote. Türk had been a fierce critic of the Janša administration, and the campaign battles were divisive, with both sides evoking Slovenia's fight for independence in the early 1990s. A troubling indicator for liberalism was the strong showing of avowed nationalist Zmago Jelinčič in the first round, in which he won over 20 percent of the vote.

Parliamentary elections were held in September 2008. With accusations of corruption and media manipulation swirling around the Janša government, voters returned the SD to power by a slim margin. Borut Pahor, a mild-mannered young politician, became prime minister.

Zakošek notes that since joining the EU in 2004, "a change was visible in Slovenian politics from a consensus to a more confrontational and polarized model" (2007: 41). Despite the intense political battles, the democratic rules of the game were firmly rooted and legitimate in the Slovenian polity and there was public and elite consensus on the most important questions about the state and the long-term future of Slovenia in Euro-Atlantic structures. The Slovenian economy was strong, so much so that upon its entry into the EU in May 2004, with a per capita GDP of nearly $20,000, Slovenia did not qualify as a recipient of aid from Brussels. Yet, in part because of its reliance on exports, the recent worldwide recession has hurt Slovenia substantially, causing a rise in unemployment and a sharp fall in output.

Still, many see Slovenia as a model member compared to the nationalist and anti-EU antics of some other post-communist member states. Slovenia has capitalized on this success and become a bridge to the western Balkans. For several years now, Slovenian officials with expertise on the accession process have been assigned to ministries and agencies in other Balkan countries, and Ljubljana hosts a center that offers help to candidate states in how to implement the reforms necessary to join the EU.

Croatia

A coalition of reformist, pro-Western parties swept into power following the January 2000 parliamentary elections in Croatia. The program of these parties read like an EU wish list: democratizing the political system, launching economic reforms, promoting Croatia's integration into NATO and the EU, allowing for the return of displaced ethnic Serb refugees, and cooperating with the international war crimes tribunal in The Hague. A ruling coalition of six parties (*šestorka*) came together under the leadership of Ivica Račan's left-of-center SDP and Budiša's moderately nationalist HSLS. Western leaders were elated, and in the period following the election, many visited Zagreb. Likewise, Račan and his new foreign minister Tonino Picula made triumphant visits to Western capitals. The EU was now actively dangling the carrot of membership in Zagreb, but the list of conditions was daunting. The OSCE and other monitoring agencies were present in Croatia to make sure that the reforms proceeded.

The task before the new government was monumental, and it could not count on the same euphoria that had engulfed publics in other post-communist states in 1989. The economy was in bad shape, with unemployment at over 20 percent. Foreign investment was minimal. The ruling coalition moved quickly on the international front, where the rewards were greatest. In the first six months of the new government's term in office, Croatia joined the WTO and NATO's PFP program, the first step to full membership. Račan's government accomplished in a few months what Tuđman had but dreamt of for ten years, in no small part because the West was intent on providing early rewards to show other countries in the region what a prodemocracy approach can achieve.[8]

Implementing difficult domestic reforms would prove to be the greatest challenge. Reform in the state-owned media and judiciary threatened vested interests and was met with resistance. On this front the Račan government moved much more slowly. Reform was also slowed down by incessant disputes within the ruling coalition. Yet, as shown by Croatia's improving democracy evaluations, liberal change was underway.[9] However, an irreconcilable conflict developed between Račan and Budiša, the leader of the second-largest party in the coalition. This conflict to some extent revolved around personality and the pace of domestic reforms, but it was also related to Račan's willingness to make concessions to the West versus Budiša's more nationalist approach. In the end, the HSLS left the ruling coalition and split internally.

The fragility of this coalition represented a political opportunity for the formerly ruling HDZ, which, despite its defeat in 2000, held a respectable 46 seats in the parliament and used them to launch attacks on the ruling coalition, portraying it as selling out Croatia's national interests to the West. Although the HDZ and its affiliated organizations were no longer in power, they still enjoyed broad legitimacy when it came to national issues. They were able to successfully exploit the coalition's weaknesses by evoking the Homeland War, sovereignty, and national pride. The HDZ, for instance, nearly blocked the ratification of an SAA with the EU in October 2001. As economic reforms led to higher unemployment and a fall in real wages, the popularity of the ruling coalition declined and the HDZ's level of support increased.[10] The HDZ and affiliated nationalist groups also helped to make cooperation with the ICTY the most volatile issue of all in Croatian politics in the early post-authoritarian period:

> Nationalist groups in Croatia have raised the political costs of cooperation with the ICTY by effectively designing a rhetorical strategy which equates the tribu-

nal's indictments against Croatia's war heroes with attacks on the dignity and legitimacy of the so-called Homeland War (*domovinski rat*) fought on Croatia's territory against breakaway Serbs between 1991 and 1995. By extension, the nationalists argue that the indictments also attack the legitimacy of the country's newly won independence ... the *raison d'être* of the ad hoc international criminal tribunals is to obtain justice by prosecuting individuals, not nations. The nationalists' rallying cry, however, aims to turn the tribunal's mission on its head by charging that its indictments cast blame on all Croatians (Peskin and Boduszyński 2003: 1117–18).

Every indictment issued by the ICTY chief prosecutor represented a boon to the HDZ and a major setback for the ruling coalition, which, afraid of the HDZ's increasing popularity and a popular backlash, over time adopted a nationalist critique of the tribunal.[11] Although the Račan government did provide documents and witnesses to The Hague, it balked on handing over major indictees such as Ante Gotovina and Janko Bobetko, which led the EU and the United States to threaten that Croatia would be left out of Euro-Atlantic integration if it did not cooperate more fully with the ICTY. Despite all of this turmoil, Račan singlemindedly pursued EU membership with the stated goal of joining by 2007. The ruling coalition had effectively made the EU its main source of legitimacy, and the public mostly approved. In 2003, Croatia filed an application with Brussels for full membership. At the time, EU Enlargement Commissioner Günter Verheugen declared that Croatian membership could send a powerful signal to Serbia and the other western Balkan countries that the EU does reward reform (quoted in Vachudová 2005: 253). The HDZ could no longer afford to go against this momentum, and change was brewing inside the party. In May 2002, Ivo Sanader, a moderate, was elected president of the HDZ and went on to oust extremist and corrupt Tuđman-era operatives from the party. He then embarked on a campaign to modernize the party and bestow it with a pro-Western image. He actively courted Western diplomats, and in 2003 attempted to woo the United States by supporting the Iraq War and the so-called Article 98 non-extradition treaty with Washington, both of which the ruling coalition had opposed.[12] In order to accomplish this transformation, Sanader had to effectively shut out the base of the party, and speak in two languages: the nationalist one in rallies and speeches in various provincial locations and a pro-Western liberal one during receptions at Zagreb's foreign embassies.[13] The base of the party, meanwhile, seemed to accept such politics at the national level as the price of being in power while supporting more radical HDZ politicians and platforms at the local level.[14]

Parliamentary elections were called early, in November 2003, and the HDZ returned to power with 34 percent of the vote, with Sanader promising EU membership by 2007. A coalition was formed in January 2004 with HDZ, HSLS, the Democratic Center (Demokratski centar, DC, an HDZ splinter party led by Mate Granić, the former foreign minister), and the Croatian Party of Pensioners (Hrvatska stranka umirovljenika, HSU), and Sanader became prime minister. The new HDZ government was well received by the West, and in April 2004 Brussels issued an *avis*, allowing Croatia to begin formal membership negotiations. Remarkably, Sanader was also able to win the confidence of ethnic Serb parties.

Meanwhile, the economy was improving, slowly but surely. Foreign investment was on the upswing, unemployment dropped, tourists were returning to coastal resorts, and the EU Commissioner for External Affairs declared Croatia's economy to be the best prepared for admission among the second wave of candidate states. The HDZ government in some ways proved to be even more determined than its predecessor to meet the political conditions set by Brussels, and the public appeared to be growing accustomed to EU tutelage. In June 2004, Croatia was formally deemed a candidate country and also received positive messages about its bid to join NATO at the Istanbul summit.[15]

However, in 2005 Croatia reached a roadblock on its path to Euro-Atlantic integration: citing its failure to arrest ICTY fugitive Ante Gotovina and under pressure from ICTY Chief Prosecutor Carla Del Ponte, the European Commission (EC) suspended the start of membership negotiations with Zagreb. This initially provoked an array of doomsday commentary about Croatia slipping back toward nationalism, but in the end the integration process was rescued when Austria came to Zagreb's aid, insisting that it would support Turkey's advancement to EU candidacy only if its ally Croatia were included on the list as well. And so Croatia began accession negotiations in October 2005 even though Gotovina was still at large.

But authorities in The Hague and Brussels were monitoring the fugitive general's movements all along, as he was finally captured and arrested in the Canary Islands by the Spanish police in December 2005. The reaction in Croatia was remarkable for its silence: although there were spontaneous protests, there was nothing like the angry reaction precipitated by indictments in the early 2000s. I was in Dubrovnik, Croatia in the days following the announcement of Gotovina's capture, and though the media carried sensationalist play-by-play accounts of the events leading to his arrest, the streets were calm, and I found just one inflammatory piece of graffiti on a wall in old-town Dubrovnik imploring Croatians to choose Gotovina over Europe.

That Sanader was able to survive the handover of Gotovina to The Hague tribunal (although he did avoid the politically damaging spectacle of Croatian police officers arresting the fugitive) and still maintain strong levels of support indicated his strength, the continuing desire of the West to use Croatia as a motivating force for other countries in the region by showing the rewards that compliance with conditionality brings, and also the legitimacy that the pro-EU agenda acquired among the Croatian public. The promise of membership was now sufficiently credible that reforms could stay on track, showing that the intermediary rewards of the SAA process were crucial in compelling elites and the public to support reform.

The November 2007 parliamentary elections represented a culmination of these trends. The two main parties were now running on virtually identical platforms, wholeheartedly supporting both EU and NATO integration. Both parties advocated a cautious approach to market reforms. The main disagreements were over policy toward Bosnia and Herzegovina, with the HDZ continuing to support the position of Bosnian Croats. The final result was close, with a repeat HDZ triumph. The HDZ entered into a coalition with smaller, largely Euroskeptical parties, including the HSS. Sanader stayed on as prime minister and, after a lull of several months, continued to steer Croatia toward Euro-Atlantic institutions, making significant progress in negotiations with the EU by January 2009.[16] Yet, reform was still lacking in the judiciary and other key institutions, Slovenia was actively blocking negotiations in certain areas because of the border dispute, and polls suggested that the public was growing disillusioned with the EU. In June 2009, after months of failed mediation by the EU between Slovenia and Croatia, further accession negotiations were cancelled. Sweden, which took over the EU presidency in summer 2009, stated that it would no longer attempt to resolve the quarrel. Yet, EU enlargement officials (and Germany and France, which noted Croatia as an exception in calling for a halt to further EU enlargement) were careful to voice continued support for Croatia's membership, although they and analysts alike now said that this was unlikely to happen before 2012.

The Croatian economy has grown since 2000, though it has hardly been dynamic and weaknesses in its economic structure came to a head, particularly as a recession began in 2009. As in Slovenia, there is a social consensus on keeping certain vestiges of communist-era social security in place at the cost of foreign investment and dynamism. Anti-market voices have been heard along with new nationalist ones as support for the EU fell in the spring of 2009 in the face of the dispute with Slovenia, stalled EU accession, and a deepening recession. Infrastructure improved dramatically in the 2000s, however, with a new Zagreb-Split highway facilitating increasing numbers of tourists. The unemployment rate remained high at around 15 percent, and the budget deficit and ratio of foreign debt to GDP were also unfavorable. In 2009 GDP growth was expected to fall steeply.

Impediments to the consolidation of a substantive democratic order have included the continued presence of extreme nationalism in public discourse and other indicators of intolerance. Furthermore, there are unresolved issues relating to the 1990s war: although the prosecution of Croatian war crimes suspects has taken place at the domestic level, as well as at the ICTY, other crimes, such as cases related to the murders of ethnic Serbs in the 1990s, are unsolved. Many Serb refugees have not returned.

In July 2009 Prime Minister Sanader delivered a shock by abruptly stepping down from his post and ceding power to his deputy, Jadranka Kosor. He declared that he was leaving politics altogether and admitted that the border dispute with Slovenia, which had effectively blocked Croatia's EU bid, played a role in his resignation. In the meantime, members of the HDZ's right-wing old guard appeared to be reasserting their authority in the party. Several hardliners known to oppose EU conditionality, anti-corruption investigations, and ICTY cooperation were elected to top party leadership positions following Sanader's resignation. "Sanader has indeed modernized Croatia," wrote analyst Davor Butković, "but never managed to change his own party" (quoted in Loza 2009). Meanwhile, the radical nationalist HSP also reasserted its influence and inflammatory anti-Western, anti-Serb rhetoric.

These setbacks and deficiencies notwithstanding, Croatia was admitted to NATO in April 2009, its EU future was fairly certain, and its progress on building a procedurally and substantively democratic order since 2000 was immense. A border deal with Slovenia seemed imminent at the end of 2009, removing one of the last obstacles to Croatia's EU membership.

FRY (Serbia and Montenegro)

Milošević was ousted from power in October 2000 in a mass protest after he attempted to steal an election that he had clearly lost. Vojislav Koštunica, a "nationalist democrat," was installed as president of the rump Yugoslav federation, to the elation of Western governments. Finally, it appeared that an intransigent Belgrade would sign on to the liberal agenda. The DEPOS coalition, led by Koštunica's DSS and Zoran Đinđić's DS, won a plurality in the National Assembly. In December 2000, DEPOS also won the most seats in the same body, which was dominated by Serbs, and Đinđić was installed as prime minister.

The situation paralleled the one in Croatia: a liberal opposition coalition backed by the West had driven the authoritarian nationalists from power, buoyed by popular support, and there were high expectations that the economic situation would improve as well as a belief that EU membership was now a distinct possibility. However, the economic situation in FRY was much worse, the final status of Kosovo was uncertain, the Montenegrin leadership was still intent on secession, and the FRY public was much more divided over Western influence than the Croatian. The West, nevertheless, held out the carrot of future EU and NATO membership and launched an intense campaign to induce reform.

The DEPOS coalition, however, proved to be even more unwieldy than the SDP coalition in Croatia. The difference between Koštunica and Đinđić in many ways reflected the difference between Budiša and Račan, with the pragmatist Đinđić ready to meet Western demands at all costs and Koštunica very cautious about doing so. Koštunica fiercely opposed the handover of Milošević to the ICTY, and so Đinđić arranged to hand him over in secret, on the night before a U.S.-imposed deadline to do so with the threat of lost aid, infuriating Koštunica. Disagreements between the DS and DSS paralyzed the legislative work of the parliament, and the public became increasingly disillusioned with politics. Despite the removal of international sanctions, the economy continued to languish, with many FRY citizens living in poverty.[17] Corruption was rampant, organized crime groups operated with impunity, and holdouts of the former regime were present throughout state institutions. It was Đinđić's efforts to combat organized crime that led to his tragic assassination in March 2003, dealing a serious blow to reform.[18] Interior

Minister Zoran Živković took his place and declared a state of emergency and took up a determined fight against organized crime.

The lack of progress on many issues further disappointed and alienated the FRY public from politics, so much so that three elections for the post of Serbian president in 2003 and 2004 were declared invalid because turnout did not meet the required 50 percent. Political institutions were unwieldy, with many overlapping federal-republican structures. This was partially solved in spring 2002 with a EU-brokered agreement between Serbia and Montenegro that loosened the federation but also required Đukanović to move slowly on outright independence. New elections were held for the weakened post of federal president, which went to Svetozar Marović, a reformer. The agreement went into effect in 2003, and among other things formally changed the name of the state to Serbia and Montenegro (Srbija i Crna Gora, SCG), meaning that the name "Yugoslavia" was once and for all consigned to the dustbin of failed states.

By late 2003, when early elections were called because of the inability of the DEPOS coalition to govern effectively (the DSS had quit a year earlier), the part of the public that had weak liberal inclinations but had nevertheless thrown their support behind DEPOS in the hopes that the economic situation would improve had once again turned to radical populist solutions. In the December 2003 elections to the Serbian parliament, the biggest winners were Šešelj's Radicals, now led by Tomislav Nikolić. Milošević's SPS also managed to garner nearly 300,000 votes, while the democratic parties captured nearly half the vote.

These results immediately raised alarm in Western capitals. The EU repeatedly warned Belgrade that an SRS government would negatively impact SCG's bid for EU membership.[19] The SRS, fearful of plunging Serbia into renewed isolation and probably more comfortable in opposition anyway, did not seek to form a government and instead yielded to the DSS, which put together a coalition of the DSS, DS, G17 Plus (a new pro-business party led by Miroljub Labus), and Drašković's SPO. Liberalism was rescued. However, in order to control a majority of votes in the parliament, the coalition was forced to rely on nominal support from the SPS, to the chagrin of Western diplomats.

After three annulled elections due to low turnout, the post of Serbian president was still vacant. The June 2004 election turned into a contest between DS candidate Boris Tadić and Radical leader Nikolić. Brussels engaged in an all-out campaign to warn Serbian voters of the danger of a Nikolić victory.[20] Just as it appeared that Nikolić was going to win, Tadić pulled ahead and won with 53 percent of the vote, helping to ensure that Serbia would not completely stray from its troubled path toward EU membership for the moment. "Serbia has chosen the European path and European values. As the elected president of Serbia I want to fight for these values, European values, in Serbia," Tadić said shortly after the results were announced. "No doubt Serbia is closer to the European Union tonight than it was this morning. It is a great victory for the democratic Serbia," he added.[21] The EC representative in Belgrade also expressed his relief: "The EU is very, very happy with this result. This is very good for Serbia and democracy in Serbia."[22] However, that nearly half of the electorate had voted for an extremist candidate showed that both European and democratic impulses were open to challenge in Serbia and that the society was deeply divided over whether democracy and Europe represented the appropriate framework for the country. In 2004, ethnic divisions also took a turn for the worse in Vojvodina, where minorities were subject to several instances of well-publicized violent attacks. In the context of a poor economy and weak institutions, such public divisions lowered the overall liberal content of the regime.

The strength of illiberal appeals would depend on economic improvements, but before these could come, difficult restructuring would have to take place. In August 2004, Serbian workers, miners, and farmers took to the streets across the country to demand that the government raise wages and subsidies for their products. Tensions reached a climax in late July when several hundred miners from the Bor mining complex in eastern Serbia blocked the main north-south highway, creating traffic nightmares and trapping tourists on their way to Greece and Turkey. After intense negotiations, the government agreed to provide 30 million euros in financial help to the mine. *Transitions Online* reported:

> In fact . . . Koštunica inherited the same social and economic problems that the previous two post-Slobodan Milošević governments struggled with: restructuring Serbia's impoverished and decaying industrial sector while maintaining decent living conditions for the "losers of the transition." It is exactly those "losers of the transition" who are considered the main backers of the ultrapopulist opposition Serbian Radical Party (SRS)—the strongest single party in the parliament—and the Strength of Serbia party, aligned with telecommuni-

cations mogul Bogoljub Karić, whose populist agenda and rhetoric brought him an unexpected 19 percent of the vote in June's presidential elections.[23]

Liberalism, then, was under threat so long as the democratic political configurations tenuously holding on to power could not deliver a better life and convince the Serbian public that a Euro-Atlantic future was the only viable option. Serbia's pro-Western leaders also had to contend with the remnants of the Milošević regime, particularly in the security services, that were actively working to prevent reform (International Crisis Group 2004). As in Croatia, the issue of cooperation with the ICTY was extremely volatile. Belgrade cooperated with Hague prosecutors only when threatened with sanctions, and even then only at the last minute. Most Serbians distrusted the ICTY and viewed it as a biased political body. The failure of Belgrade to cooperate with the ICTY also continually left SCG behind in the race toward Euro-Atlantic integration.

In 2005, the economic situation improved, and there seemed to be progress on EU integration in addition to the announcement that SAA talks would be opened even though ICTY fugitives Karadžić and Ratko Mladić were still at large. Belgrade did take some important steps on ICTY cooperation, effectively shutting down the remaining logistical and financial support structures of both men. Koštunica would not budge from his stance on Kosovo, however, and on this and other issues he often used the threat of a SRS resurgence as a way to justify some of his uncompromising nationalist positions. Nevertheless, the popularity of the pro-Western governing coalition briefly rose.

But the failure to arrest Mladić led Brussels to suspend further SAA talks with Belgrade in mid-2006. This provoked a political crisis in Serbia, leading the chief government negotiator and Deputy Prime Minister Miroljub Labus to resign from his post. "Our government betrayed the most important interest of the country and citizens of Serbia," his resignation letter said (Mitić 2006). Liberals found themselves on the defensive yet again, while nationalists were on the rise.

Although the EU later signaled that it would back off its hard-line conditionality vis-à-vis ICTY cooperation to some degree, the runup to the pivotal January 2007 parliamentary elections was characterized by intense fights between liberal reformers and nationalists. The former framed their appeal in terms of a choice between a bright EU future and a return to the dark nationalist past. The latter, by contrast, framed the election as a choice between "patriots" who would stand up for the Serbian nation and those traitors who would be ready to sell Serbia out to foreigners. Serbian analyst Igor Jovanović wrote of this appeal: "It is a familiar xenophobic refrain that targets the usual suspects: the ICTY, UN Special Envoy Martii Ahtisaari, the U.S. and the EU" (2006). While the liberal parties used the image of a murdered Zoran Đinđić to warn against the forces of reaction, the nationalists used Milošević and Šešelj to demonstrate their commitment to defending Serbian interests. Moreover, the Radicals continued to portray themselves as clean compared to the corruption of the governing parties, which had resonated with voters in the 2003 elections.

Jovanović notes that the voters' preference for one of these two grand narratives would depend "on how well they have fared in the six years since the old regime fell. Those who have prospered in post-Milošević Serbia tend to lean toward Tadić while those who have not favor the Radicals" (2006).[24] Slobodan Antonić, a political analyst, said: "It is not a division between the future and the past, but between the winners and losers of transition, as well as between the character and look of the future state and national strategy" (Jovanović 2006).

In the end, over 40 percent of Serbian voters opted for the two main democratic parties, President Boris Tadić's DS and Prime Minister Koštunica's DSS. Both of these parties were pro-Western, though Koštunica took a more nationalist line, was less willing to make concessions to Brussels, and opposed NATO membership. The good news in terms of liberal support was that the DS (now renamed DS-Tadić to capitalize on the president's popularity) did significantly better than in 2003, gaining 27 parliamentary seats. At the same time, the level of support for the two main anti-systemic parties, the SRS and SPS remained stable, at about a third of the total vote. These results reflected the continuing split in Serbian society between Western-minded, liberal voters, who lived mostly in cities and in the north of the country, and those with a more inward-looking, nationalist orientation, concentrated in rural areas and the center and south of Serbia.

For about five months following the elections, Serbian politicians were unable to put together a governing coalition. The West pushed for another DS-DSS coalition, signaling that any coalition that included the Radicals would be seen unfavorably in the international arena. During the deadlock, the DSS teamed up with the nationalists to elect SRS leader Tomislav Nikolić as speaker, provoking alarmist commentaries in the international press and worried statements from Brussels, which quickly cancelled the signing of a visa agreement with Belgrade.

Using the nationalist threat was a way for Koštunica to extract the maximum concessions from Tadić before entering into another coalition with the DS. It worked to some extent, as the DS, despite having won more votes, agreed to allow Koštunica to continue in his role as prime minister. At the same time, Koštunica also staked a part of his legitimacy on progress with regard to EU accession, and he knew that a coalition with the Radicals would severely harm Belgrade's relations with Brussels. In this sense, he depended on the DS as much as the DS depended on the DSS. And of course Koštunica was under immense Western pressure to form a coalition with a liberal party as soon as possible.

Ultimately, a DS-DSS–G17 Plus coalition was put together, with the DS getting an absolute majority of the ministerial portfolios. For the first time, the Defense Ministry went to a DS member, raising the chances that the military intelligence services would finally be reformed. Nikolić resigned his post as speaker, and liberalism, as in 2003, was salvaged once again.

The question, remained, however, why so many people voted for the Radicals—was it primarily due to socioeconomic frustration, or is over 30 percent of the Serbian electorate simply ultranationalist? Zoran Stojiljković of the Belgrade Faculty of Political Sciences cites polls showing that only about 15 percent of the SRS electorate is truly ultranationalist.[25] The rest may be nationally oriented or suffered losses in Serbia's post-Milošević economic transition (800,000 live at subsistence levels, he notes). Moreover, the SRS's campaign ads appealed to such voters through populism: one ad showed a ruddy-faced young man saying that all he wants is a permanent job.[26] "Permanent" jobs were a feature not only of communist Yugoslavia but also of Milošević's economic populism, so in this way the SRS picked up many former SPS voters as well. What, then, explains the strong showing of the Radicals in Belgrade, where standards of living are high? Stojiljković notes that SRS voters in Belgrade were mostly refugees from Bosnia and Croatia who believed that the Radicals would somehow make their former lands a part of Serbia.

Only six months later the West was again confronted with the threat of a nationalist victory, this time in the presidential elections held in January 2008. As in 2004, the contest came down to the pro-Western liberal Tadić and the nationalist Nikolić. Once again, the EU delivered an unambiguous message about the consequences of a Nikolić victory for Serbia's EU prospects. In a bid to bolster Tadić—and his promise to bring Serbia closer to Europe and reap the economic and political benefits of closer ties—momentum grew in Brussels to grant the major concession of concluding the SAA agreement. Such a move required unanimity among the EU's twenty-seven countries. In a sign of the growing anxiety of losing Serbia, even formerly staunch tribunal backers such as Britain favored an early signing of the SAA agreement. Only the Netherlands held firm in opposition.

As pressure mounted on the Netherlands to agree to conclude the SAA agreement and the Serbian government collapsed in the wake of Kosovo's declaration of independence in mid-February 2008, the prospects of a compromise emerged. The compromise sought to balance the EU's avowed commitment to international justice with its interest in keeping Serbia on a European trajectory and staving off the election of nationalists. Days before parliamentary elections in May and with the moderates behind in the polls, the EU signed an SAA agreement with Serbia as well as agreements on trade and visa liberalization, which could be then be given positive media play in Brussels and Belgrade. However, in deference to the Netherlands and Belgium, it stipulated that the agreement would not be *implemented* without evidence of full cooperation.

This, and the resulting high turnout, helped Tadić prevail, but only by 130,000 votes. It was a remarkable victory in that nationalist fervor in Serbia was at its apogee in the runup to Kosovo's declaration of independence the following month, and it showed that a critical mass of voters did not want to abandon the EU altogether. Yet nearly half of those who cast a ballot voted for a party that was tied to war crimes and that openly advocated ethnic intolerance.

The DS-DSS coalition government weakened under the immense pressure of Kosovo's declaration of independence in February 2008. The parties and their leaders could not agree on how to deal with the EU in the aftermath of the declaration. Koštunica's DSS insisted that Serbia would not pursue further integration in the form of signing an SAA in the absence of guarantees of sovereignty over Kosovo, while Tadić's DS, backed by the G17 Plus, argued that it was not in Serbia's interest to be isolated from the integration process.[27] Brussels made its position in this dispute clear: "The EU clearly wants Serbia to decide in favor of the European perspective," said Slovenian Foreign Minister Dimitrij Rupel, representing the EU presidency (quoted in Jovanovic 2008). Although the EU member states were internally split on how much pressure to put on Serbia to cooperate with the ICTY, there was consensus on the premise that a Radical victory would threaten Serbian democracy, even more so in the wake of Kosovo's independence declaration.

The government collapsed in March 2008, and parliamentary elections were called for May. In the meantime, in the face of SRS and DSS opposition, the EU and Belgrade signed the SAA agreement, which had been initialed in the fall of 2007. This turned out to be a major psychological boost for Serbia's pro-European forces: despite the fallout over Kosovo's independence and Koštunica's populist anti-EU appeals, the big winner turned out to be Tadić's DS, who won nearly 40 percent of the vote and increased its seats by 15. The Radicals came in second, with 30 percent of the vote, while Koštunica's DSS mustered only 11 percent of the vote. The pro-European parties were clever in appealing to the economic sensibilities of voters who might have otherwise voted for the Radicals but realized that they could reap some of the benefits of progress on the road to EU membership. After much wrangling, a most surprising coalition emerged after the SPS signed on to the EU agenda and abandoned the Radicals in favor of the DS, a move that would allow the DS to pursue integration without the burden of the mercurial and increasingly nationalist Koštunica. Buoyed by the SAA prize, the pro-European perspective triumphed, but the strength of illiberal parties in the National Assembly remained formidable. Moreover, the Socialists were hardly reformed in terms of personnel changes and renouncing their authoritarian and nationalist past. Rather, their nominal acceptance of the EU was a cynical way to share in the spoils of power.

The formation of a liberal, pro-Western government and the EU's positive signals created conditions that made the sensational arrest of Radovan Karadžić in July 2008 possible. The nationalist response was greatly subdued, and Serbia's EU prospects were further strengthened. That the economy had grown robustly for several years with low inflation also helped to shape a more positive outlook on Serbia's prospects.

The rising EU tide eventually reached the recalcitrant Radicals in the fall of 2008 as the Serbian Parliament debated ratification of the SAA. Nikolić opted to support the pact despite the fierce opposition of many of his party colleagues, creating a schism in the SRS. The adoption of the EU agenda by part of the Radicals was extremely significant, a signal that Serbia was turning in the EU direction, though certainly not nearly as much as Croatia or Macedonia. The 2008 EU Progress Report on Serbia praised the country's economic growth and administrative capacity, but noted that much work remained to be done in terms of both political and economic reforms and meeting European standards. The structural problems of the Serbian economy, moreover, were hardly solved: in 2007, only half of Serbia's 3,100 former socially owned enterprises had been sold, and 15 percent were in bankruptcy. Overemployment in governmental institutions and public enterprises had not been addressed (European Stability Initiative 2007).

Positive economic growth began to undergo a sharp reversal in 2009 as the worldwide recession reached Serbia. The effects of the economic crisis and the blocking of SAA ratification by the Netherlands and Belgium over Belgrade's inability (or unwillingness) to deliver Ratko Mladić and Goran Hadžić to the ICTY continued to make Serbia's EU future uncertain. The July 2009 announcement that the EC was recommending the lifting of visa requirements for Serbians traveling to Schengen zone countries was undoubtedly designed to improve morale.

Montenegro: The Sixth Successor State

Before he was murdered in 2003, Đinđić had mostly negotiated a "velvet divorce" with Montenegro. According to Serbian-American businessman Obrad Kesić, Đinđić wished to repay Đukanović for sheltering him during the Kosovo War and also saw Montenegro as an economic burden for Belgrade (quoted in Pond 2006: 232). However, following the death of the reformist Serbian premier, the EU became worried that Montenegrin independence would destabilize Kosovo and compelled the Podgorica authorities to hold off for another three years and then hold a referendum on independence.[28] Montenegro was kept economically sustainable by outside aid and had a population of about 650,000, hardly the building blocks of a viable state. Nevertheless, the ruling party pressed ahead with its pro-independence agenda, arguing that separation from Belgrade was the only way to speed up Euro-Atlantic integration.[29]

In May 2006 Montenegrin voters endorsed independence but barely met the EU-mandated 55 percent threshold, betraying the deep splits in Montenegrin society. The Albanian and Bosniak minorities helped tip the balance in favor of independence (Pond 2006: 233). In Belgrade, the response was muted: leaders had undoubtedly been warned not to overreact by Western officials, and with Euro-Atlantic integration frozen because of the failure to apprehend Mladić and Karadžić, nobody wanted to provoke worse relations.

As for the Serbian public, many had come to see Montenegro as a drain on Belgrade's resources.[30]

Independence, better integration prospects, and strong economic growth in recent years did not necessarily advance substantive democratization, however. Nor has Podgorica's extraordinarily high level of foreign aid per capita. Weak institutions, criminality, and corruption have continued to thwart democratic reform. The opponents of independence, in fact, focused on the allegations of criminality and corruption that have swirled around Prime Minister Đukanović for years. Another challenge of the fledgling Montenegrin state has been attracting the loyalty of those 45 percent of its citizens who voted against independence in 2006, although this may be easier to overcome than in Bosnia since what it means to be "Montenegrin" is a fluid concept (Biber 2006).

Although Montenegro's pro-Western approach was rewarded by NATO and the EU with PFP status and an SAA, respectively, many procedural and substantive indicators suggest that democratization continues to be impeded by negative structural legacies. The 2006 Freedom House *Nations in Transit* report for Montenegro was sobering.[31] It found that democratic development in Montenegro declined in 2005, and its democracy score slipped closer to that of a transitional government or "hybrid regime." It received one of the lowest scores in the region, ahead only of Bosnia and Kosovo. The main democratic deficiencies noted in the report include political influence in the judiciary, security, and police services, and there was insufficient prosecution of criminality and corruption charges. The EU's 2008 progress report on Montenegro highlighted similar issues. In the beginning of 2009, with the threat of recession looming, Prime Minister Đukanović called snap elections to seek a stronger mandate for his pro-EU agenda. His coalition won easily with 66 percent of the vote, earning Đukanović a sixth term as prime minister. However, in this same period Germany vetoed giving Montenegro an immediate response to its December 2008 application for candidacy, while international monitoring organizations reported government abuses against media freedom.

Kosovo: The Seventh Successor State

It was clear after the 1999 war and UN Security Council (UNSC) Resolution 1244 that Kosovar Albanians would accept nothing less than full independence, while Belgrade politicians, backed by Russia, would not budge. Serbia's sovereignty over Kosovo was only on paper, whereas Northern Mitrovica and the various Serb enclaves in central and southern Kosovo functioned as a full part of Serbia. The seemingly stalemated conflict came to a head in the spring of 2004 when violence broke out between ethnic Serbs and Albanians in northern Kosovo, reminding the world that the situation in the province was far from stable. In the process, thousands more Serbs left the province. In October 2004 and November 2007, parliamentary elections were held for Kosovo's Provisional Institutions of Self-Government (PISG), but the territory's shrinking Serb minority boycotted them.

Negotiations that began in late 2005 were finally abandoned in December 2007, and the United States and most EU members began to support conditional independence openly, as put forward in a plan by UN Special Envoy for Kosovo and former Finnish president Martii Ahtisaari.[32] In February 2008 Kosovo declared independence amid political crisis and violence in Serbia. As of 2009 Kosovo has been recognized by sixty-three countries (including twenty-two EU member states—all except Spain, Greece, Cyprus, Romania, and Slovakia) and is undergoing a messy transition from UN to EU supervision. Unemployment is between 40 and 50 percent, and Serb-majority areas continue to function as enclaves subsidized by Belgrade. The 2008 EU progress report on Kosovo states that the country has made limited progress toward establishing a market economy, physical infrastructure is poor, and the energy supply is unreliable.[33] Although Kosovo has been promised an EU future by officials in Brussels, among western Balkans states it is the furthest from that future, and its membership in many international organizations is blocked. However, in 2009, Kosovo succeeded in joining the IMF and the World Bank.

Macedonia

Ethnic relations in VMRO-governed Macedonia continued to deteriorate after 1999, and in the spring of 2001 an ethnic Albanian rebel group calling itself the National Liberation Army (NLA; Albanian: Ushtria Çlirimtare Kombëtare, UÇK; Macedonian: Oslobodetelna Narodna Armija, ONA) launched an open rebellion against Skopje. At first the West was sympathetic to Skopje, but when Prime Minister Georgievski responded with force, both Washington and Brussels shifted their support to the Albanians.[34] The international community was determined not see a repeat of the Bosnian war in Macedonia and became involved quickly. The EU, eager to test the viability of its new

Common Foreign and Security Policy (CFSP), took the lead in pressuring Skopje to negotiate with the rebels. EU Commissioner Javier Solana was instrumental in organizing a peace conference at the lakeside town of Ohrid in August 2001. An agreement was reached in which rebels were required to hand over their arms in exchange for amnesty, while the Macedonian government promised to implement an extensive list of policies designed to give the ethnic Albanian community political and cultural rights. Included in the agreement were affirmative action–style preferences for ethnic Albanians in public institutions. Georgievski signed the agreement only under intense pressure from the West and from President Boris Trajkovski, a pro-Western moderate and former Methodist minister elected in 1999. Trajkovski enjoyed broad popularity among all ethnic groups but was tragically killed in a February 2004 plane crash. The chief ethnic Albanian negotiator at Ohrid was rebel leader Ali Ahmeti, who subsequently went on to found a new ethnic Albanian political party, the Democratic Union for Integration (Demokratska unija za integracija, DUI; Albanian: Bashkimi Demokratik për Integrimin, BDI). One carrot used by the EU to get cooperation was aid, which was needed to avoid economic collapse after the war. Polls showed, however, that the Ohrid Agreement did not benefit from the support of many Slav Macedonians, and many Albanians thought it did not go far enough and were wary of the EU, preferring to instill their trust in the United States.[35]

Ahmeti was embraced by European and American interventionists as a peacemaker and continued to enjoy direct access to many Western officials. Georgievski, by contrast, had fallen out of favor with the West for his intransigence before and during Ohrid and for widespread allegations of corruption, and he continued to lose Western support because of his anti-Western rhetoric. Following the signing of the Ohrid Agreement, a NATO peacekeeping force arrived in the country and both the EU and the United States began to supervise Macedonian politics more closely, such that the country increasingly began to resemble a protectorate in the style of Kosovo and Bosnia. "All important decisions were cleared with the American Ambassador or EU Special Representative," one government official explained to me.[36] The popularity of the VMRO government quickly declined due to the perception that it had sold out Macedonian national interests at Ohrid and also because it was perceived to be deeply corrupt. Reports by Western monitoring organizations about corruption in VMRO were strategically released to coincide with the

September 2002 parliamentary elections.[37] Analysts were now interpreting the 2001 conflict as having been intricately tied to corruption, criminality, economic scarcity, and the failure of the state to provide public goods and an acceptable standard of living.[38]

The 2002 elections were quite chaotic, and observers noted a number of irregularities.[39] In the end, the SDSM, running under the Together for Macedonia (Zaedno na Makedonija Zveza, ZMZ) coalition, prevailed and formed a coalition with Ahmeti's DUI, the largest vote-getter among the Albanian parties. Branko Crvenkovski, the SDSM leader, again became prime minister, and some ethnic Albanians were given ministerial portfolios. When Crvenkovski was elected president after Trajkovski's death in early 2004, Interior Minister Hari Kostov became prime minister.

Just as in the 1990s, Macedonia remained stable in the post-2000 period thanks to foreign supervision. Unlike the 1990s, however, the West was not content simply to assure stability: indeed, the Ohrid peace agreement was accompanied by a long list of laws relating to minority rights that the Macedonian government was obliged to implement. They would be monitored by the OSCE, the EU, and other organizations. Nevertheless, much of the day-to-day "democracy" continued to be simulated to assure Western support. While disillusionment with the state and its institutions runs deep among the public, so does ambivalence toward the West. The carrot of EU membership, for its part, has been vague and at times contradictory, although an SAA was signed in 2001, and Macedonia submitted its application for membership in March 2004.

The former ruling VMRO party was in turmoil after 2002, split between a nationalist and more moderate wing and in shock at the revelation that seven South Asian immigrants were killed by state security services under the control of former hardline interior minister Ljube Boškoski. Boškoski fled the country, as did Georgievski for a time. The latter returned and wrote an inflammatory opinion piece in a major daily newspaper calling for partition of Albanian-inhabited areas. Likewise, while out of power, DPA leader Arben Xhaferi engaged in nationalist agitation. Overall, the situation in the country was fragile, and the International Crisis Group (2003) suggested that Western countries and organizations take a more realistic look at the state of affairs: "The West must revise substantially the conventional assessment that Macedonia is the foremost political 'success story' in the Balkans. It is instead an underperforming post-conflict country still very much at risk, unable to tackle—operationally or politically—its security challenges without upsetting an uncertain ethnic balance."

Although the Western-sponsored Ohrid Framework prevented further violence in Macedonia and extended rights to ethnic Albanians, implementation was slow. Many ethnic Macedonians saw the framework as negotiated in a nontransparent manner and imposed by foreigners, and therefore viewed its provisions as illegitimate.[40] The 2004 effort to implement provisions of the Ohrid Agreement granting more power to local councils was met with rioting and violence by ethnic Macedonians opposed to the plan (Wood 2004b). Nevertheless, a November 2004 referendum organized by nationalist opposition and diaspora groups in order to question proposed changes in administrative boundaries, an Ohrid-mandated reform that would have created more Albanian-majority localities with increased autonomy, was invalidated due to low turnout. There is little doubt that the minds of some potential supporters were changed by the U.S. decision to recognize Macedonia under its constitutional name despite fervent Greek opposition, triggering street celebrations in Skopje. As *Transitions Online* reported, the EU played an important role in this outcome as well:

> Along with the United States' power to change the political mood, the failure of the referendum also demonstrated the magnetic power of the European Union in the Balkans. From the moment in August when the SMK [diaspora nationalists] managed to gather enough signatures to call a referendum, Brussels and the other EU capitals bombarded ethnic Macedonians with messages bluntly telling them that they would gravely harm their prospects of EU integration if the referendum were successful. While the EU offered no positive message in this campaign—and, because of the Greeks' veto power, obviously could not last week join the United States in recognizing Macedonia's name— the EU's warnings played an important part in the debate in Macedonia.[41]

Moreover, the government did not try to convince voters of the merits of decentralization: it simply argued that Macedonia's EU prospects would be grim if the referendum passed. Elizabeth Pond writes that: "Low turnout showed that a majority of Macedonians were becoming resigned to the Ohrid compromises as the price they must pay to get into the EU and NATO. The public had been socialized into becoming pro-EU—however fuzzy its understanding of what the EU was—and making political trade-offs on the basis of its preference" (2006: 183).

International pressure notwithstanding, that administrative reform would go ahead was quite significant as the last great hurdle to implementing the Ohrid agreement and therefore an important yardstick of progress for the EU and NATO. However, the referendum debacle hurt Kostov politically, and he soon resigned and was replaced by Vlado Bučkovski.

Under close international supervision, reforms continued, at a varying pace, after 2004. Both 2004 and 2005 were banner years for Macedonia's Euro-Atlantic aspirations. Besides becoming a member, along with Croatia and Albania, of the U.S.-sponsored "Adriatic Charter" of front-running NATO candidate states, it received several positive signals from the EU. The government's efforts at reform were rewarded at the end of 2005: first, with a relatively positive report on progress from the EU Commission (especially on ethnic relations), and then, in December 2005, with advancement to EU candidacy and lessened EU oversight in the country, although a date for the start of negotiations was not set pending progress on tackling corruption and strengthening institutions. Meanwhile, popular support for the EU stood at 90 percent (Pond 2006: 185–86).

By 2006, Macedonian leaders had "amended the Constitution of the country, changed key laws, went through a process of amnesty and disarmament, and decentralized government" (Balalovska 2006: 9). Furthermore, they had implemented most provisions of the Ohrid Agreement. However, the SDSM's inability to improve the economic situation significantly, especially the crippling levels of unemployment, helped VMRO to return to power in parliamentary elections held in June 2006.

The election campaign was monitored closely by Western organizations, with the EU and U.S. ambassadors personally observing polling stations. The West reminded Macedonians continually that an election that met international standards was a condition for further progress on the road to Euro-Atlantic integration. In the end, despite outbursts of violence and other irregularities, the election was declared to be largely free and fair (Stavrova 2006).

Upon winning the election, VMRO, led by the Sanader-like reformer Nikola Gruevski, immediately began negotiations with its former Albanian coalition partner (1998–2002), the DPA. This upset Ahmeti and the DUI, who had won more of the Albanian vote, and Ahmeti threatened violence. Skirmishes broke out in Albanian towns. The DPA regards the DUI as successor to a terrorist organization, while the DUI portrayed the DPA as corrupt and unable to defend Albanian interests. Indeed, the rhetoric and violence revealed issues of legitimacy and divisions, but it also showed how far politicians were willing to go to fight for access to government patronage. In the end, a VMRO-DPA coalition was formed with several smaller parties.

The first years in power of the new, moderate VMRO were not easy, however, in part owing to agitation from the DUI, which boycotted parliament for four months in the spring of 2007 claiming that the government was ignoring Albanians' rights. Gruevski, pandering to right-wing elements in his party, had in fact been doing little to ensure that the process of expanding minority rights moved forward. Sporadic fighting broke out between DUI and DPA supporters in ethnic Albanian areas, which gave nationalist Slav Macedonians ammunition against the Albanians more generally. The DUI ended its boycott when the government announced that a majority of Albanian deputies would be indeed needed to pass legislation.

The Slav Macedonian parties have remained deeply divided as well. In June 2007, the SDSM called for a no-confidence vote in the Gruevski government, arguing that it was hurting the country's EU prospects. It failed, with 65 deputies voting for the government and 43 against. Moreover, President Crvenkovski and Gruevski also quarreled on many issues. Pressures on the entire government increased dramatically following the disappointment of NATO's Bucharest Summit in spring 2008, at which Greece blocked Macedonia's invitation to join the alliance over the name dispute; Macedonia was scheduled to join with Albania and Croatia. The government collapsed, and early elections were called in June 2008. These tense elections were tainted by violence, mostly involving the ethnic Albanian parties, but also between the Macedonian police and Albanian civilians. One death was recorded, and voting was suspended in several ethnic Albanian districts. The OSCE recorded numerous instances of intimidation and ballot stuffing. The cause was intense rivalry between the two main Albanian parties and their supporters, no doubt in a fight for the material rewards and jobs that result from gaining a place in government. Gruevski exploited the divisions among the Albanian parties, leading the DUI to splinter into an anti-and pro-government group.[42] The flawed elections were cited later that year by the EU in its annual progress report for Macedonia, thereby hurting the country's image and membership prospects.[43]

The economic situation remained quite dire throughout the decade, with high unemployment, poverty,[44] and a dependence on a large informal sector and international aid.[45] In 2004, 78 percent of Macedonians responded that losing their jobs was their greatest fear (Ramet 2006: 567), while participants of a 2008 poll expressed the greatest dissatisfaction with their standard of living among all the peoples of the region. There was some FDI, mostly from Greece, but not enough to turn the economy around. Criminality and corruption still pervaded Macedonian institutions. In light of its assessment that Macedonia was still very far from having a mature democracy, the International Crisis Group (2003) opined that the international community must make "a more sober, less self-congratulatory" assessment of conditions in the country.[46] Parties remained the "mechanisms for distribution of patronage and running election campaigns [more] than real engines of democratic inclusion" (Pond 2006: 186). As long as economic circumstances remained poor, democratic institutions could not be legitimized. Moreover, a 2008 poll by the Gallup Balkan Monitor suggested that only a third of Macedonians thought that the Ohrid Framework was a good long-term solution to the country's ethnic problems. As of 2009, Albanian-majority municipalities, almost exclusively controlled by the DUI, were refusing to cooperate with the central government, showing that ethnic tensions were still high.

In the context of such fragile democratic institutions, democratic progress will continue to depend on the leverage of the EU and other Western states and organizations. The 2007 and 2008 EU Commission progress reports on Macedonia gave the country at best a "yellow light," stating that Skopje lacks "adequate human and financial resources" to implement in full the obligations of the SAA it has signed with Brussels (Loza 2007). The 2008 report criticized the violence surrounding the summer elections, while the 2007 report also criticized "large-scale replacement of qualified staff" in the state administration following the change of government in 2006 as well as what it described as the "political deadlock" among main political actors. In March 2009, elections were held for the mostly ceremonial post of president, resulting in the victory of VMRO candidate Gjorgje Ivanov. They, along with local elections held in 2009, were deemed free and fair by the OSCE and EU, an important boost to Macedonia following the chaotic 2008 poll.

In the fall of 2009, the EU announced a recommendation to open accession negotiations with Macedonia. However, NATO membership is still blocked by Greece owing to the name issue. It remains to be seen whether continuing delays will lead to frustration, which in turn could empower nationalists and lessen the EU's leverage to compel further reforms.

Differences in liberal content in the 1990s, and the structural factors that underpinned them, matter a great deal in explaining the post-2000 trajectories of the four successor states. This was perhaps most evident in Serbia and Croatia, where electoral revolutions in 2000 swept in a new cadre of leaders ostensibly committed to liberalism.[47] It was hard to overlook the irony in the elated Western response: throughout the 1990s the prevailing attitude in the West was that the Balkan states were predisposed to instability, ethnic conflict, and authoritarian politics. The new attitude, by contrast, seemed to indicate a newfound belief in the power of political agency: Koštunica and Račan were embraced by Brussels and Washington despite their lack of real democratic credentials.

However, the challenges the two leaders faced differed, and implementing reform and accepting Western conditions proved to be much more difficult in Serbia than Croatia. By extension, the structural challenges the West had to overcome in the former were significantly more difficult than in the latter, so the external impetus to democratize held greater sway over Zagreb than Belgrade. One would not have necessarily predicted this, however, by looking at various measures of procedural democracy for each state in the 1990s. The differences between Croatia and Serbia became even sharper in parliamentary elections held at the end of 2003 in both countries. In Croatia, roughly 40 percent of the electorate voted for parties with clear liberal credentials (SDP, HNS, HSS, LS, and the Libra party); 40 percent of the electorate voted for parties whose liberal credentials were still ambiguous (HDZ, HSLS); and 6 percent of electorate voted for decidedly illiberal parties (HSP). By contrast, in Serbia roughly 25 percent of the electorate voted for parties with clear liberal credentials (DS, G17 Plus); 25 percent voted for parties whose liberal credentials are ambiguous (DSS, SPO); and a troubling 36 percent of the electorate voted for decidedly illiberal and anti-systemic parties.[48] By 2007, the difference was even more striking, with all the Croatian parties firmly committed to democratic reform and EU accession, while a third of Serbians voted for the Radicals. The absence of the Radicals from the ruling coalitions that were ultimately cobbled together in Serbia in 2003, 2007, and 2008 was largely thanks to Western pressure and an acute sense of concern among Serbian elites over being completely left out of the integration process.

It is also telling to compare the post-2000 trajectories of the two nationalist parties that won the most votes in each election, the HDZ and SRS. Both parties came back to power in 2003 in part because they promised solutions to economic problems in response to public opinion polls showing that standard of living concerns loomed large for most voters. Thus, in both Croatia and Serbia the strong showing of nationalists did not necessarily signify a vote for a return to the past. But this is where the similarity ends. While the HDZ embraced its predecessor's goal of EU membership, cooperated with ICTY, purged radical elements from party leadership, won the backing of ethnic Serb parties, and invited ethnic Serb refugees to return to Croatia, the SRS was unreformed, was nominally led by indicted and imprisoned war criminal Vojislav Šešelj, espoused illiberal nationalism and anti-Westernism, was openly hostile toward the ICTY, and advocated a Greater Serbia that would include parts of Bosnia, Croatia, and Macedonia.

These differences reflected the different degree to which Serbia and Croatia were "co-opted" into the process of EU integration by 2008. In Serbia, nationalism was still very much a part of political discourse, distrust of the EU and NATO was pervasive, and an anti-Western stance was worn as a badge of honor. Even ostensibly liberal parties put war criminals on their party lists to prove their national credentials. Moreover, Lazić's (2007: 81) research on value orientations among Serbian political and economic elites suggests that liberalism had hardly taken root: "Political and economic elites in Serbia have not internalized liberal values… even fifteen years after pluralist democracy, and the market economy… have been introduced as the key institutional and legitimate principles of systemic regulation… during the past fifteen years only a mild shift toward liberal values occurred, and even this move was ambiguous."

By contrast, in Croatia the EU has become the least common denominator of political competition. That which began as an instrumental acceptance of EU norms on the part of elites became a process in which the beliefs of elites and the loci of political conflict were significantly altered. The 2004 EU *avis* was critical in this regard. As Croatian commentator Davor Butković argued at the time, "Failure to issue the avis would have serious consequences for political stability in Croatia. Prime Minister Sanader would lose his main foothold—foreign policy and the expected foreign political success—and the space would be open for the old, Tuđman-like, nationalist-oriented HDZ members to win greater power in the party, and, as the Parliament discussions as well as the acts of Sanader's ministers, the party still consists of a great many of those."[49] Though some segments at the base of Sanader's party were still quite nationalist, the trend was against them. This sea change from the nature of Croatian politics in the 1990s reflects three factors: (1) the acceptance of the EU agenda by the previous Račan government and its ceaseless efforts toward membership and the continuation of these efforts by the HDZ from 2003 to the present; (2) the West's efforts in Croatia and its ability to hold out a credible "carrot" of membership; and (3) domestic structural factors that made it easier for the West to coopt a sufficiently large part of the public behind the project of Western liberalism.

That parties in Serbia were still deeply divided over the West and that suspicion of Western organizations runs rampant in Serbian society—these are certainly a product of the 1999 NATO bombing and the West's support of Kosovo's independence. Serbian anti-Western sentiment was also a function of Serbia's distance from these organizations, meaning that the leverage of the EU and NATO is simply not strong enough to turn a critical mass of elites and society toward the socialization process that has taken place in Croatia.

In the context of weaker and poorer states than Serbia, Macedonian and Montenegrin elites—and to some extent the public—have embraced EU conditionality out of a perceived need for external support. Though the extent to which elites and the public in both places have been socialized to the EU's requirements was reflected in their "silence" over Kosovo's independence, in both countries EU conditionality has not been strong enough to prevent continuing cronyism and corruption.

Table 8.1 shows the varying progress of the successor states in the Euro-Atlantic accession process, which is simultaneously a strong predictor of the relative strength of the external impetus for liberalism. Table 8.2 compares Freedom House scores on procedural democracy with qualitative evaluations of liberal content in each state. It shows that even as the states have converged on procedural measures of democratization, the indicators of liberal content employed throughout this study continue to vary among them considerably.

A discernible pattern in Macedonia, Croatia, and Serbia after 2000 was a cycle in which radical populist and nationalist forces were thrown out by vot-

Table 8.1 Progress on Accession to the EU and NATO as of December 2009

Country	EU Stabilization and Accession Agreement (signed)	EU candidate status	Begin EU accession negotiations	EU membership	NATO Partnership for Peace	NATO membership
Slovenia	June 1996	July 1997	March 1998	May 2004	March 1994	March 2004
Croatia	October 2001	June 2004	October 2005	—	May 2000	April 2009
Macedonia	April 2001	December 2005	—	—	November 1995	—
Serbia	April 2008	—	—	—	December 2006	—
Montenegro	October 2007	—	—	—	December 2006	—
Bosnia and Herzegovina	June 2008	—	—	—	December 2006	—
Kosovo	—	—	—	—	—	—

Source: European Commission, http://ec.europa.eu/enlargement/press_corner/key-documents/reports_nov_2008_en.htm, North Atlantic Treaty Organization, www.nato.int/docu/basics.htm.

Note: Serbia's Stabilization and Accession Agreement has not been ratified.

Table 8.2 Democratic Progress and Liberal Content after 2000

Country	Democratic legitimacy	Nature of divisions	Strength of illiberal forces	Democracy score[a]	
				2004	2008
Slovenia	High	Normal for a democratic state	Weak	1.75	1.86
Croatia	Moderate. Certain elites and parts of the public still regard West and democracy with ambivalence	Moderate. Elites and public still divided, but this is rapidly diminishing and elites are united on EU integration	Relatively weak after transformation of HDZ	3.83	3.64
Serbia and Montenegro	Low. Evidenced by extremely low turnout at elections, Kosovo's separatism, etc. Distrust of West is widespread	Deep and divisive. Party system is deeply split between liberal, pro-Western reformers and anti-systemic nationalists. Montenegrins divided over independence	Very strong. The Serbian Radical Party received the most votes in 2003, 2007, and 2008 elections	3.83	3.79[b]
Macedonia	Low. Democracy is mandated by West. Ohrid framework is looked at with ambivalence, boycotts by Albanian parties continue	Deep and divisive. Ethnic cleavage is deep, public divided over appropriateness of Western liberalism, Albanian parties are deeply divided	Moderate. VMRO's nationalist wing enjoys broad support, although real influence is weak because of Western supervision and the EU incentive for ruling elites	4.00	3.86

Source: Democracy Scores from the Freedom House Nations in Transit series, www.freedomhouse.org/.
Note: Kosovo's democracy score for 2008 was 5.21, Montenegro's was 3.79, and Bosnia and Herzegovina's was 4.11.
[a]Democracy Scores are based on a scale from 1 to 7, with 1 representing the highest level of democratic progress and 7 the lowest.
[b]Without Montenegro.

ers, after which pro-Western parties, supported by Brussels and Washington, were brought to the fore as nationalist rhetoric lost its resonance and the public expressed its frustration with corruption in ruling parties. Domestically, the pro-European orientation of these parties was used to bid for political capital and raise hopes of better times ahead. However, as the realization set in that sovereignty must be sacrificed and that tough reforms that lead to lower living standards must be pursued, the nationalists regrouped. In Croatia, this cycle was broken when the nationalist HDZ successfully coopted, and was simultaneously coopted by, the West, and Ivo Sanader marginalized or dismissed the party's hard-line elements. In Macedonia, VMRO's nationalist outlook has also been moderated by the EU incentive, but to a lesser extent than in Croatia, as the events of 2006 and 2008 demonstrate. The key to democratization in Serbia, where pro-Euro-Atlantic parties are in a weaker position, lies in the ability of the West to sign nationalist parties onto the reform agenda by promising real rewards. The late 2008 split in the Radicals may indicate that precisely this is happening. But, as noted above, divisions in Serbian society run deep, and the EU is divided over whether to "soften" conditionality (especially on ICTY cooperation) to compensate Serbia for Kosovo's independence and to keep reforms on track. Some Serbian analysts privately worry that the sense of humiliation felt by many Serbians at the hands of the West will be successfully exploited by nationalist parties regardless of progress on EU accession.[50] Though Slovenia was never governed by radical populism, one can observe the second part of this cycle there after 2000 with the rise of nationalism in response to economic difficulties and disillusionment with the EU. Even in Slovenia, Western liberalism does not have total reach.

In 2003, following a EU-Balkan summit held in Thessaloniki that produced much rhetoric and excitement about the European future of the western Balkans, there was much hope that integration would be a reality sooner than later, and it contributed greatly to democratic gains throughout the region. Perhaps these gains were not always fully democratic when measured by the indicators of liberal content used in this study, but they were nonetheless significant as triggers of a process of socialization toward EU conditionality. However, the lack of progress in reform noted in the lukewarm reports given to the Balkan candidate states in recent years[51] with the exception of Croatia (and Macedonia in 2009) shows that the constraints to full democratization exist *in spite of* the powerful incentive of EU membership and the positive "demonstration effect" of the Croatian case.[52] This is certainly due to the continuing influence of structural constraints, but it is also a result of reduced leverage on the part of the EU, and it is driven by a perception in the candidate states that membership is still a long way off. Of course, given the failure to pass an EU constitution when it was rejected by French and Dutch voters in a 2005 referendum, the 2008 rejection of the Lisbon Treaty by Irish voters, and all the talk in Brussels of "enlargement fatigue" and "absorption capacity," this may not be much of a surprise.

That the 2007 EU Commission progress reports on accession praised the policy of conditionality while noting the lack of progress in most of the candidate countries raises an interesting conundrum, as analyst Tihomir Loza notes: "The commission's praise for the EU's conditionality principle is, however, contradicted by its own verdict on the region's progress. If the countries have largely failed to live up to expectations, it may well make sense to examine the limits of conditionality" (Loza 2007).[53]

One thing is for sure: the people of the Yugoslav successor states, Slovenia included, have become more realistic about the EU and the West more generally. Ironically, those furthest from EU membership—the Kosovars—seemed to have most favorable view of the EU in 2008, while the Croatians, who are the closest, display the most ambivalent attitudes toward Europe. Observing the EU's internal disagreements and its bias toward Turkey, they have come to see that Brussels is not just a club of rich nations, that it is not infallible, and that "EU membership is not a panacea," in the words of Loza (2006). If such realism has the effect of helping to manage expectations among the restive publics of the region, then it is not entirely a bad thing.

CHAPTER NINE

Conclusions

> In Europe there are the large countries on one side and the small on the other; there are the nations seated in the negotiating chambers and those who wait all night in the antechambers.
>
> MILAN KUNDERA, FRANCO-CZECH NOVELIST

> Myth and perception aside, enlargement is a success story. It reflects the EU as a civilian power; by extending the zone of peace and democracy, we have achieved far more through our gravitational pull than ever with a stick or sword.
>
> OLLI REHN, EU COMMISSIONER FOR ENLARGEMENT

The Determinants of Diversity

The challenge for political science is to provide an explanation for the divergent trajectories of political change that we have witnessed in Eastern and Central Europe over the past two decades. The goal of this book is to address this challenge and contribute to the study of comparative democratization by accounting for variance in regime types in the Yugoslav successor states. Furthermore, this book has aimed to contribute to the scholarship on conceptualizing democracy by specifying the kinds of regimes that emerged in each successor state in the 1990s in ways that go beyond procedural measures of democracy. Thus, substantive democracy (Slovenia) refers to procedural correctness combined with a high degree of liberal content; simulated democracy (Croatia) signifies some procedural correctness combined with some liberal content and rule by elites who don't like democracy but "fake" it to satisfy internal and external calls for liberalism; populist authoritarianism (FRY) has low liberal content, shuns many aspects of procedural correctness, and exploits feelings of victimization and social frustration to gain legitimacy;

while illegitimate democracy (Macedonia) is somewhat procedurally correct, but has low liberal content because of a population that is deeply divided and ambivalent toward the democratic project.

Two primary factors shaped each type of regime in the 1990s and beyond: (1) the initial conditions of transition in each successor state, defined by the level of economic viability on the eve of independence; and (2) the resilience or pliability of domestic structures to Western liberalism, a powerful external agent shaping democratic change in post-communist countries. According to this framework, regime outcomes should be seen as reflecting the point at which external intent (Western-promoted liberalism) and domestic interest (rooted in economic structure) meet. Put differently, there are two facets of change in the post-communist world: the external force of liberalism and the degree of internal accommodation or resistance to this force.

The starting point of the explanatory framework was structure, defined by varying levels of economic viability. These were the initial conditions of transition, but they were not rooted in any particular time, policy, or previous regime. Rather, we saw that disparities in levels of economic development have been reproduced in the area of the former Yugoslavia over time and through regimes of varying characters. The demise of communist rule did not eliminate the influence of these long-term structural legacies, and we observed how varying levels of economic viability conditioned the emergence of unique regimes in each successor state during the first ten years after communism and beyond. We have seen that structural conditions display a great deal of rigidity, so norms transferred from the outside inevitably confront them. All post-communist states also had to adapt to the new international regime of liberalism: hence, the incentives to maintain a threshold of procedural democracy were large, and as such the external factor goes far in explaining democratic simulation in Croatia, FRY, and Macedonia in the 1990s and convergence on measures of procedural correctness after 2000. But the external agent alone cannot guarantee liberal content: in chapter 8 we saw that the degree and durability of substantive democracy in the long term depends on whether the structural conditions are hospitable to the development of democracy and the penetration of external liberal norms.

Nonetheless, even if structure is not fully hospitable to the penetration of these norms, when an inability to deliver better living standards threatens the legitimacy of radical populist regimes (FRY and Croatia in 1999) or when economic collapse and a lack of internal security threaten the very existence of the state (Macedonia in 1991 and 2001), a part of the elite may nominally embrace the West in a search for support and legitimacy. In these cases similar levels of procedural correctness can exist alongside varying levels of liberal content. The ability of Western liberalism to succeed in the long term depends on the degree to which domestic structures can accommodate the external norms, but it also depends on how conditionality policies are crafted; that is, on whether rewards from the West are forthcoming. Vachudová (2005: 5) shows that when states become credible EU candidates and are exposed to all the effects of its leverage, liberal groups are strengthened and, in time, electoral games force illiberal political forces to sign on to the EU agenda and reform internally.

Rather than offering a grand new theory of post-communist transitions, this book has attempted to strike a reasonable balance between the various factors used to explain post-communist regime change: between its domestic and international determinants and between its distant and proximate precursors. It has not ignored the role of culture, institutions, or leaders, but it has shown how they emerged in particular conditions and operated within unique parameters. These parameters are defined by the two explanatory variables noted above, whose effects were charted from independence in 1991 to the present day in four ex-Yugoslav states that, in terms of historical antecedents and post-communist outcomes, represent a microcosm of Eastern Europe as a whole. Rather than being temporally rooted "legacies" in any strict sense, these explanatory factors constitute important historical *continuities* in the region: (1) a north-south historically regressive gradient of socio-economic development, and (2) the tendency of domestic politics in the small states of the region to reflect, over time, an adaptation to external regimes as well as internal realities. Despite their importance for understanding the determinants of varying paths of post-communist transition, these factors have not been sufficiently addressed by the existing literature. Encouraged by the speed and scope of what was taking place in the region, many scholars turned to voluntarist and institutionalist paradigms of politics to explain political change in Eastern and Central Europe. The constraining nature of initial structural conditions was overlooked, in part because of the way in which some scholars conceptualized democracy, which left it devoid of its liberal qualities.[1]

Furthermore, the literature on comparative post-communism has usually excluded the Yugoslav successor states as objects of analysis. Many existing works on the former Yugoslavia have focused exclusively on ethnic conflict and war without seeing them as part of the larger process of post-communist change. This book has shown that the challenges the Yugoslav successor states have faced since their independence were an integral part of their post-communist transitions. Weak state capacity in Macedonia is a consequence, not a cause, of a distinct path of post-communist regime change. Similarly, war in Bosnia and Herzegovina was the consequence of a failed democratic transition, one in which ethno-nationalist groups and projects won out over liberal alternatives. We have seen that nationalism itself, the most recognized feature of recent Balkan history, was used by elites to bid for political power and resources in conditions of scarcity and weak democratic traditions.

That three of the cases examined in this study didn't meet the criteria for liberal democracies in the 1990s was not for any lack of multiparty elections, functioning parliaments, or democratic constitutions. Still, there were key differences in their adherence to procedural correctness that neither cultural (that is, pre-communist legacies) nor institutional (post-communist construction) hypotheses can explain. Institutional design may help to explain the smooth functioning of democracy in Slovenia, but it does not explain why a parliamentary (as opposed to a presidential) system failed to create a more robust democracy in Macedonia. Macedonia, Croatia, and FRY at one time had similar electoral systems but different levels of adherence to procedural correctness. Cultural hypotheses would predict a higher level of democratization in Croatia (with a legal impersonal culture rooted in Western Christianity and a Roman-Habsburg past) than Macedonia (with a communal paternal culture rooted in Eastern Orthodoxy and a Byzantine-Ottoman past), and yet on some procedural measures, the opposite was true in the 1990s. The communist or "Leninist" legacy highlighted by some scholars of post-communism can to a large degree be held constant since the four cases share a common institutional past in Yugoslavia. And, to the extent that Yugoslav communism was "liberal" and "reformist," it cannot explain nondemocratic outcomes in the post-communist Yugoslav successor states. Eliminating culture, communism, and post-communist institutional choice as plausible hypotheses conspicuously left disparities in levels of economic development as a primary explanatory variable of post-communist regime diversity in the four cases. However, economic differences cannot fully account for variation in scores on procedural correctness either. Returning to the Macedonia-Croatia comparison, how is it that Macedonia achieved higher Freedom House scores than Croatia in the 1990s despite its much poorer economic prospects?

This question begs several related ones: does the fact that Macedonia had freer elections in the 1990s than Croatia tell us enough about differences in the character of the two regimes? Does Serbia's higher score than Croatia on media freedom allow us to predict greater chances for further democratization in the former? More generally, do procedural measures of democracy help us to understand the nature of democracy and future prospects for democratization?

We saw that as predictors of long-term democratic development, differences in the levels of procedural correctness among the four cases are less important than their levels of *liberal content,* which this study measured using a number of indicators: legitimacy (the degree to which the loci of political conflict reflect divisions over basic issues about the state); legitimizing principles (whether the legitimizing principles of the regime in power reflect liberal or illiberal appeals); and liberal representation in the party system (the number of pro- versus anti-systemic parties on the political scene). Procedural correctness, while being a normatively desirable step over repression of political and civil rights, often reflects a temporary accommodation of external conditions rather than a long-term commitment to substantive liberalism or a shift toward greater democratic consolidation. Democratic institutions and procedures are often good imitations of their Western counterparts but function quite differently in the absence of the right structural underpinnings.

The Primacy of Initial Structural Conditions

This book began by noting the "puzzle" of post-communist diversity; yet, the very term *puzzle* implies that there was little one could identify before the fact that would suggest diversity. It does not take a political scientist, much less an East European expert, to realize that states in the region embarked on very different post-communist paths because they started from very different places.

Initial conditions mattered a great deal in explaining the course of the first decade of transition and beyond. Structure is "sticky": it tends to persist and shape outcomes even as leaders and governments change. Moreover, as a set of confining conditions, it is rigid: elites find it hard to overcome the constraining influence of structure even with the best democratic intentions. Structure does not give us perfect explanatory leverage. Structural conditions, however, do allow us to understand longer-term patterns of political development. They explain why liberal political configurations have had a harder time establishing themselves on the Serbian rather than the Croatian political scene, even after the fall of authoritarian regimes in 2000. They explain why Macedonia's transition continues to be plagued by deep divisions over ethnicity and the nature of the state. They explain the weakness of populist appeals in Slovenian politics. Moreover, they explain the varying degrees of resistance the project to transfer Western liberal norms to the Balkans has encountered in the past two decades.

The embedded nature and endurance of structural conditions in the post-communist Yugoslav successor states can be demonstrated by extending the task of chapter 3: that is, tracing the relative disparities in the former Yugoslav space into the 2000s. Many indicators serve to illustrate the reproduction of economic disparities among the successor states: table 9.1 illustrates the varying dependence on trade with the EU (an important indicator of economic structure), while table 9.2 shows that in terms of per capita GDP, unemployment, and human development, the economic disparities among the successor states are significant as ever, despite impressive growth rates in the mid-2000s.

Survey results indicate that issues of economic survival topped the list of public concerns throughout the region early in the second decade of transition, surpassing issues of nationality and ethnicity, which dominated in the first. Despite just having emerged from a violent conflict between separatist Albanian fighters and the Macedonian government, in 2002 over 40 percent of Macedonian respondents cited poverty as their main concern, while less than 20 percent pointed to ethnic relations.[2] Daily life in the various Yugoslav successor states clearly reflects ongoing economic disparities. The prospects for a university student from Ljubljana these days are radically different than the very limited choices available to a student in Priština, who in most cases has limited employment prospects and even more limited international mobility due to visa restrictions.

The premise of this study was that the reproduction of economic disparities over time has fundamentally shaped political outcomes. Indeed, despite nearly two decades of post-communist change under regimes employing new ideologies and strategies, leaders in the four states are confronted in 2009 by many of the same structural opportunities and challenges faced by their pre-

Table 9.1   EU Share of Total Trade, 2007

Country	Exports	Imports
Slovenia	70.7	78.9
Croatia	60.3	64.8
Serbia[a]	55.9	55.0
Macedonia	65.1	49.5

Source: World Trade Organization, http://stat.wto.org/
[a]Without Montenegro.

decessors in the pre-communist, communist, and immediate post-communist periods. Whereas path-dependent or "critical junctures" approaches emphasize a priori unpredictable decisions made in uncertain times that shape a subsequent path of political development, this one focuses on the reproduction of a certain set of identifiable structural features over time and on how various elites and regimes have responded to these structural circumstances.[3] The issue that must now be addressed is how structural conditions are translated into distinct political outcomes.

Since the Yugoslav successor states exhibit a range of structural legacies that parallel variations in the region at large, the analysis presented in this book allows us to formulate some general propositions about the relationship between initial conditions and post-communist paths of political change. Most of Eastern and Central Europe did not suffer from a lack of industrialization but rather from the *type* of industrialization that took place under communism, which affected its chances to survive in a global economy following the collapse of Council for Mutual Economic Assistance (CMEA) markets. The type and extent of industrialization that took place under communism, in turn, depended on the relative backwardness of the state in the pre-communist period.[4]

The Political Consequences of Weak Viability

In states that had low levels of development in the pre-communist period, most industrialization took place under communism and tended to focus on heavy, capital-intensive, subsidized sectors that did not utilize comparative labor advantages, relied heavily on trade with Eastern markets, and thus had greater difficulties with the economic shock of transition, adapting to international competition, attracting foreign investment, and penetrating West-

Table 9.2   Economic Indicators, Yugoslav Successor States, 2006

Country	GDP per capita (in euros)	Unemployment rate (%)	GDP growth rate (%)	Human Development Index ranking[a] (out of 179 countries)
Slovenia	14,000	6	4.0	26
Croatia	6,000	14	4.3	45
Montenegro	3,100	15	6.5	64
Serbia	2,500	21	6.3	65
Macedonia	2,100	37	3.0	68
Bosnia and Herzegovina	2,000	40	6.2	75
Kosovo	1,100	40	3.8	n.d.

Source: European Commission, http://ec.europa.eu/. Human Development Indicators from United Nations Development Program, http://hdr.undp.org/en/statistics/.

[a]The Human Development Index is a summary composite index that measures a country's average achievements in three basic aspects of human development: health, knowledge, and standard of living. Data is from 2008.

ern markets after communism. Output collapse in these countries, as well as its negative consequences, such as unemployment, were highest in such states. Here radical populism found a willing constituency because it offered simple solutions to economic decline, played on insecurities and interethnic distrust, and appealed to traditional attitudes. Barely reconstituted communist parties, now espousing new ideologies, won the first elections. Economic scarcity intensified competition between ethnic groups. Liberal elites, by contrast, did not find a receptive constituency and only became viable political alternatives when the former communists failed to provide acceptable living standards—but even then had trouble constructing broad reformist coalitions. Without an industrial sector ready to adapt to Western markets, there were few business leaders lobbying for pro-Western policies. Vested sectoral interests in heavy industry slowed down reform, as did communist-era institutions such as the security services, because they were vital sources of employment and loci of vested interests. Radical populists depended on coalitions of rural and semirural unskilled workers and farmers *and* a political and economic elite of party insiders. Nationalist appeals resonated with both groups for different reasons: with the former because of economic hard times and cultural reasons, the latter because they could benefit by keeping resources for themselves and out of the hands of ethnic minorities.

Low levels of economic viability were also related to the development of a rentier state, which directly reinforced authoritarian politics by becoming embedded in personalized networks. Economic elites took control of the very same failing enterprises that could not be adapted to Western markets and stripped them of their assets in shady privatization deals: communist successor parties were in an especially good position to do so. In the long run, the parts of society receptive to populist appeals became disillusioned with the regime, but the entrenched elites had a vested interest in maintaining either authoritarianism and minimal reform or partial reform and a facade of democracy. To maintain power, they strengthened their hold over the most important levers of influence: the police, the security apparatus, and the media outlets. It would be a mistake, then, as Hellman (1998) has argued, to see workers, farmers, and other "losers" of transition as the primary supporters of illiberal politics in the long run.

Although these states professed support for joining Euro-Atlantic organizations, it was clear that the elite was not ready to accept the conditions needed to do so, meaning that the external impetus for liberalism was also absent. Low levels of economic viability explain the existing indicators of low liberal content: the weakness of liberal political alternatives and the illiberal legitimizing principles of ruling political configurations. Among our cases, Serbia, Montenegro, and Macedonia fall into this group (as do Kosovo and Bosnia and Herzegovina among the Yugoslav successor states), while in the larger region, Bulgaria, Romania, and Albania more or less followed this pattern of change during their initial years of transition. In Romania the former communist National Salvation Front (*Frontul Salvării Naţionale*, FSN) adopted nationalist themes and made superficial concessions to procedural democracy while keeping a firm hold on the levers of power. In Albania the former communists did not survive long but were replaced by a populist regime that took firm control of the state apparatus and was thoroughly corrupt, leading to a state of anarchy in 1997. In Bulgaria procedural correctness suffered the least despite the power of former communists, but entrenched interests continued to hinder liberal reform until the economy nearly collapsed in the late 1990s and was bailed out by international financial institutions.

The Political Consequences of Partial Viability

In states that had undergone some development in the pre-communist period or enjoyed greater geographic proximity to the West, the effect of communist industrialization was moderate, and though post-communist output collapse was serious, it did not necessarily encompass all sectors of the economy. During the transition, the political scene was witness to competition between liberal, pro-Western configurations on one hand and radical populist groups on the other. The radical populist groups appealed to segments of society disillusioned with the rapid changes that were taking place: where ethnic cleavages existed, they could also use nationalism effectively as part of their populist appeal. The liberal groups, by contrast, made appeals to those parts of the population in the best position to adapt to the market economy and global competition: in particular, educated, urban groups and those employed in industries not rooted in the communist era. These groups were also most receptive to the idea of quickly meeting the conditions for EU membership. Which configurations ultimately prevailed depended on a number of contingencies. However, in either case the political regime displayed divisions that reflected the mixed initial economic conditions. Where populist groups rose to power, they were held in check by liberal configurations. Where liberal groups prevailed, they were repeatedly threatened by extreme left- and right-wing political alternatives. Thus, partial economic viability helped shape regimes that had a mixed record of liberal content. In this study, Croatia exemplifies this path of change, while elsewhere in the region the radical populist regime of Vladimir Mečiar in Slovakia is also paradigmatic, as was the post-communist transition of Lithuania in which nationalism played a prominent role in the immediate post-independence period (Clark 2006).

The Political Consequences of Viability

In states with high levels of pre-communist development, communist-style industrialization was limited, and as a result post-communist output collapse was smaller, leaving fewer people impoverished. Liberal and pro-Western groups, whether genuinely reformed communist parties or configurations with roots in the democratic opposition, found broad support in society and prevailed in the first elections. Managers of industry, eager to attract investment and export to Western markets, saw promise in liberal economic reforms. Common incentives to stay on the liberal course meant that there was a consensus among key social groups on fundamental questions about the polity, and ethnic divisions were less likely to become divisive. Though illiberal appeals were not absent from the political scene, they were marginalized in the larger thrust toward liberalism and membership in Euro-Atlantic organizations. Thus, economic viability explains the high level of liberal content in these regimes. In the present study, Slovenia is paradigmatic, while in the larger region Hungary, the Czech Republic, Estonia, and Poland fit this pattern. In all these countries, parties with different political histories but a shared commitment to democracy, the market, Europe, and civil and political rights have alternated peacefully in power.

Discussion

The varying economic effects of different initial conditions among East European post-communist states are shown in table 9.3. Notice Janos's (2003) "distress index," which is created by adding the percentages of unemployment and output collapse, since the conditions that this index reflects directly influenced political outcomes. The magnitude of the distress index is correlated with the initial conditions. More anecdotally, as Janos writes, "This is the story of Czech beer and textiles, or Hungarian electronics and pharmaceuticals versus Romanian heavy chemicals and iron foundries, Slovakian armament factories, or Bulgarian light industries built with an eye on consumer demand in the Soviet shortage economy" (2003: 21).

We observe that countries with the highest distress indices experienced the most political turmoil after the fall of communism and were characterized by the greatest infractions against procedural correctness and the lowest levels of liberal content. Slovakia and Croatia, as noted above, are the intermediate cases here. Even after procedural correctness was instituted and economies were stabilized, the indicators of liberal content remain higher in the countries that started with more favorable structural conditions than those with poor initial conditions. Thus, illiberal and anti-Western parties played a much bigger role in Romania than Poland, and Slovaks expressed much less enthusiasm about democratic institutions compared to their Czech counterparts. For the cases that are the subject of this study, chapter 8 illustrated how differences in liberal content characterized regimes in the 2000s. The longer-term influence of structural conditions is also best observed in the varying degree to which economies have been able to recover from post-communist collapse. The lands of the former German Democratic Republic, for example, continued to be plagued by high unemployment long after reunification despite years of massive financial transfers from the former West Germany. Not surprisingly, the communist successor party there fared well in elections.

Do cross-sectional regression analyses of post-communist countries con-

Table 9.3   Extent of Communist Industrialization and Per Capita Output Collapse
(in percentages)

| Country | Communist industrialization | | | Post-communist economies | | |
	Pre-communist (1938)	Communist (1980s)	Difference	Output collapse (1994)	Unemployment (1993)	Distress[a] index
Czech Republic	59.6	66.9	7.3	19.0	3.2	22.2
Poland	37.1[b]	52.0	14.9	8.9	15.4	24.3
Hungary	35.7	47.0	11.3	16.6	13.0	29.6
Bulgaria	18.3	50.9	32.6	27.7	16.0	43.7
Romania	28.4	57.1	28.7	27.0	9.0	36.0
Slovakia	35.9	61.8	25.9	22.1	13.5	35.6
Slovenia	35.9	46.9	11.0	5.6	14.4	20.0
Croatia	22.5	38.5	16.0	16.0	17.2	33.2
Serbia	16.1	43.8	27.7	50.0	25.0	75.0
Macedonia	14.3	51.5	37.2	47.0	28.6	75.6

Source: Janos (2003: 23).
[a]The Distress index is created by adding the percentages of unemployment and output collapse.
[b]Data from 1950.

firm the finding that the initial structural economic conditions of transition are a powerful predictor of post-communist liberalism? Grigore Pop-Eleches (2007b) has employed a number of sophisticated statistical models to test the effect of various commonly hypothesized determinants of post-communist democratization.[5] Pop-Eleches finds that "the region's overlapping cultural, socioeconomic, and institutional legacies significantly shaped the preferences of political actors and the constraints of their choices."[6] Furthermore, he notes that the incorporation of structural legacies "undermines some of the earlier claims about the importance of more contingent factors, such as initial elections outcomes, institutional choices, and geographic diffusion" (2007a: 909–10).[7] While he finds that the joint predictive power of structural legacies increases over time and is significant, robust, and a formidable predictor of institutional choice, Pop-Eleches also admits that it is difficult, if not impossible, to specify "exactly which particular structural conditions matter most for the establishment of democracy and capitalism in the region" (2007b: 910). This is because of the high degree of overlap among social, cultural, economic, historical, and geographic legacies, which makes the regime outcomes somewhat overdetermined.

Since the most striking feature of the Soviet developmental model was the proliferation of energy-intensive, wasteful, and pollution-heavy industry and chemical plants meant to promote rapid industrialization and to cover the needs of defense sector, Pop-Eleches (2007b: 914) captures this feature by including the "energy intensiveness" of the communist economies at the start of transition in this model so as to test its effect on post-communist democratization. In a multivariate regression that encompasses this and a number of other structural legacies, he finds that by far the strongest predictor of post-communist democracy scores is indeed energy intensiveness and that the influence of this variable manifests itself more clearly over time (Pop-Eleches 2007b: 917). However, in another version of the same paper, he notes that energy intensiveness may simply be a proxy for a broader set of maladies from the communist period that had a negative effect on both democracy and economic reforms.[8] This brings one back to the high degree of overlap between the various legacies and other potential explanatory factors of post-communist democratization.

One solution to this problem, mentioned by Pop-Eleches in the conclusion to his study, is methodological pluralism: that is, large-N analyses need to be complemented by small-N comparative case studies to specify the precise causal mechanisms at work. But even in the context of the small-N method, it is difficult to find cases that exhibit significant variation along the independent variable of interest but are similar enough along all the other relevant dimensions to allow the researcher to attribute the variation in reform outcome to a specific legacy or mechanism. Thus, case studies can help strengthen our confidence that a particular kind of structural legacy matters more.

This study has presented a number of arguments that point away from cultural and ethnic plurality hypotheses as determinants of post-communist regime diversity in the Yugoslav successor states. This does not mean that culture and ethnicity are of no significance. Indeed, differences in political culture are evident. Although we cannot find such differences when, in survey research, we ask questions such as "Is democracy a good way of governing the country?" or "Is a strong leader better than a parliamentary system?" more nuanced indicators of political culture suggest important variations. Ronald Inglehart's index of "survival versus self-expression," a combined measure of tolerance, satisfaction, trust, and post-materialist values, not only reflects striking differences among countries but is also a powerful predictor of democratization (Inglehart 2003). Inglehart's scores for the four countries that are the subject of this book do vary, with those for Croatia and Slovenia pointing to a more democratic political culture than the scores for Serbia and Macedonia.

Yet, Inglehart (2003: 56) also notes that the strongest predictor of high self-expression values is economic development and presents evidence to show that the latter precedes the former. Culture matters, but the goal of this study was to explain how and under what conditions certain cultural predilections—and, for that matter, ethnic divisions—play a role in politics. It is in conditions of economic scarcity and insecurity that people turn to traditional values and ethnic networks. The argument, thus, is not entirely utilitarian, since feelings of security may not always reflect the most economically rational choice. Still, an investigation into economics is needed to understand the timing and salience of mobilized culture or ethnicity. Political beliefs, attitudes, and values are important intervening variables in the relationship between economic development and democracy.

Culture and ethnicity do have independent explanatory power in other ways. Ethnicity could only be mobilized in Croatia because there were real memories and grievances that underpinned the divisions between Serbs and Croats in the Krajina. Once ethnicity was mobilized, a path-dependent "spiral of ethnic politics" and nationalism ensued (Vachudová and Snyder 1997) in which national issues became the baseline of political competition. In this sense, Slovenia was lucky: despite the existence of ethnic minorities, the history and content of ethnic relations was much different. Feelings of victimization could be exploited in Serbia because feelings of victimization ran deep. Furthermore, had competition over scarce resources been at the same level in countries with a more democratic history, liberalism might have had a better chance. Still, these are necessary, but not sufficient, conditions of particular political outcomes, and socioeconomic development (particularly economic downturns and crises) is needed to understand the timing and forms of political change and mobilization. The Baltic nation of Estonia may be our best example: despite the existence of potentially troubling ethnic divisions, the country's comparatively low level of heavy industry and links to Western markets helped it to turn the economy around (Panagiotou 2001) and effectively coopt the country's Russian minority into the state- and democracy-building project.

However, disparities in economic development cannot explain higher levels of procedural correctness in Macedonia than Croatia or the election of liberal parties in Serbia in 2000 despite the persistence and deepening of poor structural conditions. Here we must turn to the second independent variable, the effect of external agency. Under what conditions will the West work as positive force for democratization? Why do different states respond differently to the project of Western liberalism?

The External Dimension of Post-communist Democratization

Absent the role of the democracy-promoting West, all of what has been said thus far leads to a rather pessimistic outlook on the prospects for full democratization in those post-communist states that did not benefit from favorable starting conditions. We do not have to look north of the Balkans to find instances in which difficult initial conditions have been overcome. Bulgaria teetered on the brink of financial collapse in 1996 and yet has emerged as a fairly stable democracy, joining the EU in 2007. It has a serious corruption problem, but this has not precluded the gradual emergence of liberal institutions and norms.

We could always be more optimistic about the prospects for democratization in Eastern and Central Europe given the existence of a strong *external* impetus toward liberalism. Unlike countries in Latin America, Asia, Africa, and the successor states of the former Soviet Union, the countries of Eastern and Central Europe not only are geographically proximate to one of the greatest centers of prosperity and innovation in the world but have also been candidates for admission to the "club" that integrates its nation states.[9] This club is "arguably the most highly and densely institutionalized region of the international system" (Schimmelfennig 2002: 1). Moreover, unlike Asians or Africans, most East European citizens see themselves as firmly belonging to the West. The external incentives to pursue liberalism, thus, are enormous. This has been particularly true given the EU's willingness to expand to include the former communist states. Unlike the "heaven" of communism that no East European ever got to see, one had only to look as near as Vienna or Rome to see the benefits of being part of the richest club of nations in the world. The promise of EU enlargement, in fact, has been the "single most important policy instrument" available to ensure a stable, prosperous, and democratic continent, simply because the benefits of joining are tremendous (Moravscik and Vachudová 2003). The international environment of the 1990s, furthermore, was the most favorable it had ever been in terms of the prospects for liberalism in East and Central Europe: Russia was weak and its influence was shrinking, and Germany was powerful but democratic and integrated into both the EU and NATO (Rupnik 1999: 3). Fukuyama's thesis about the inevitable triumph of liberalism in the post–Cold War world truly had merit in the post-communist states of Eastern and Central Europe.

While all Eastern and Central European states wanted the benefits of membership in Euro-Atlantic structures, there were significant differences in what these states were willing and able to do in its pursuit. This raises questions of domestic politics: why did the perceived benefits of EU membership outweigh the perceived costs of fulfilling admission criteria for some governments, while for others the costs of fulfilling the criteria were higher? The answer is that for some the EU represented an opportunity, while for others it did not. Joining the EU necessitated fulfilling a number of conditions that infringed not only on the sovereignty of the post-communist states but also clashed with local practices, cultures, and structures and directly endangered certain economic industries and sectors. At times the incentives for elites to meet the external conditions ran counter to any potential benefits offered to the public. At other times the horizons of membership were too long. This means that the West and domestic constituencies often pulled post-communist elites in opposite directions. The relative strength of each force at a given time helped determine political outcomes. It is no surprise that one locus of political conflict throughout the region has divided parties based on their willingness to accept the Western liberal agenda. More often than not, questions of whether and how much to comply with Western conditions have vexed and divided leaders, parties, and the voting public.

Although even early on, many analysts spoke to the importance of international factors in post-communist transitions, the relationship between processes such as EU accession and regime behavior remained under-theorized, assumed rather than proven, and bereft of causal mechanisms. In recent years more rigorous research on the effects of EU conditionality on post-communist regime change has appeared.[10]

The story of the external dimension of democratization in post-communist states is ultimately about asymmetrical power—about clients and hegemons in a new hierarchical international order. This points us to some traditional theories of international relations. There may be security benefits to EU enlargement, but the focus on building democracy and promoting human rights cannot be easily reconciled with realist and neorealist assumptions about state goals and interests. The neoliberal interpretation of events provided by international political economy (IPE) can only provide a limited explanation of democracy promotion on the part of the West given its lack of economic rationality: after all, the project to expand the EU is costly and unpopular in many of the current member states. Moreover, these theories do not account sufficiently for the way in which anticipated reactions, progress reports, and promises of rewards have allowed the West to exercise great influence over the post-communist states. Joseph Nye's elucidation of "soft power" (2004) and its focus on "cooption" and "attraction" is instructive in this regard.

In terms of accounting for the unique role of international factors in post-communist regime change, the most promising theories seem to come from the broad category of IR theory known as constructivism, particularly the literature on international socialization and the spread of norms. The literature on norms has devised frameworks that "aim to assess the conditions under which norms travel, whether across national boundaries or from the international organizations or community into states, and when they make a difference in policy" (Linden 2002: 376). For instance, Finnemore and Sikkink (1999) argue that "norm entrepreneurs" use international organizations to create a "norms cascade" in which norms held by powerful, successful states are adopted by other states that are eager to share in the group's success, reputation, and esteem. Risse and Ropp (1999: 238–39) describe a "spiral model" of norm transfer in which states at first act out of instrumental rationality and concessions in hopes of receiving rewards. Eventually, the norms become embedded in the state's institutions and modes of behavior. Earlier, Ikenberry and Kupchan (1990) hypothesized that what begins as an instrumental acceptance of a hegemon's agenda can evolve into a process in which the substantive beliefs of both elites and masses are altered. Thus, theories of norm transfer and international socialization teach us not that the West accepts only liberal democracies as members but that the condition of being a credible candidate for membership creates incentives that compel elites to make decisions that stimulate democratization (Vachudová 2005: 1; Schimmelfennig 2007: 129).[11] EU officials are well aware of this and repeat it frequently when seeking support for further expansion. Furthermore, the EU promotes the SAA process by publicly declaring that "the main motivator for reform—including the establishment of a dependable rule of law, democratic and stable institutions and a free economy—in these countries is a relationship with the EU that is based on a credible prospect of membership once the relevant conditions have been met."[12]

Constructivist theories can also help us to understand how Western norms are diffused from elites down to the public, particularly in societies where there is a weak impetus for liberalism. They help us to understand how conditionality and rewards can be used to "lock in" a path of reform in a EU candidate state. They need not espouse the rigid structuralism of dependency theory or more modern theories of neoliberal convergence in the context of globalization for two reasons. First, East European elites do have a choice, at least in theory: joining the EU or other Western organizations is not mandatory. Second, rather than representing strictly confining conditions, the liberal universalism espoused by the West and the conditionality policies associated with it represent an opportunity and source of political capital for elites. In Đukanović's Montenegro and late-1990s Croatia, we saw how a pro-Western stance can be used to bid for domestic political capital when ruling political configurations are delegitimized because of their inability to raise living standards. Elites may also adopt a pro-Western stance because they have no choice given the depth of economic malaise and security concerns: Macedonia and post-2000 Serbia are examples. In either case, the pro-Western elites need to convince their constituents that there will be real rewards in conforming to Western conditions. By embracing externally conditioned liberalism and setting their country on the path of integration into Western organizations, elites can effectively "break through" confining initial conditions. One concrete way in which this happens is through the gradual neutralization of radical populist political configurations as Western conditions and norms be-come embedded in domestic politics such that the costs of backsliding become too great. This happened in Slovenia in the 1990s, Croatia after 2000, and, more recently, Serbia and Macedonia. It also took place in Poland (where even the populist Andrzej Lepper accepted Europe, albeit reluctantly), in Romania (where after 1996 the influence of the fascist-oriented Vadim Tudor diminished), Bulgaria (where the formerly Euroskeptic socialists were partially converted and marginalized), and Slovakia (where the formerly anti-Western populist Vladimír Mečiar embraced the inevitability of the EU).[13] And most recently, the rebirth of populism, nationalism, and anti-EU rhetoric across the region, from Poland and Hungary to the Czech Republic and Estonia, are a powerful demonstration of how illiberal predilections and identity issues come to the fore as the constraining power of conditionality disappears after accession.[14]

But how can we explain *when* certain elites decide to embrace a pro-Western agenda, at least nominally? Here the answer seems to lie partially in the dynamics of political competition. When an illiberal and anti-Western regime falters because of a failing economy, it provides a political opening for opposition groups to take over, especially in the context of electoral games. A pro-Western stance becomes a beneficial source of political capital for these groups and often a source of material and organizational aid. To explain such elite dynamics, in fact, it may be useful to turn to elite competition frameworks developed in the transitology literature, such as the model developed by O'Donnell and Schmitter (1986). With regard to the strategic behavior of these elites, it also can be reconciled with rational choice approaches.[15] Such elite dynamics were very much in evidence in Croatia and Serbia in 1999, Montenegro in 1997, and Serbia in 2008. Similar dynamics could be observed in Bulgaria after 1996, and Slovakia in 1998.

However, the different situation in which Croatia and Serbia find themselves in 2009 also shows that to understand the long-term success of elite acceptance of the Western project in terms of fostering a substantively liberal regime, we must return to the structural conditions enumerated above. Simulated or partial reforms that do not benefit from public support, as we have seen in the breakdown of stability in post-2000 Macedonia, have their limits. Again, structural differences help determine the size of the part of the elite and public that is receptive to the Western liberal agenda; if this segment of society is not large enough, democracy will be constantly threatened even where procedural correctness is observed. The legitimacy of Western-dictated reforms is crucial, but there is ample evidence that these reforms are seen as illegitimate in countries without the supporting structural features. The perception of illegitimacy has been present in outbreaks of violence in Kosovo and Macedonia, inflammatory nationalist rhetoric in Bosnia, and the resistance to cooperation with The Hague tribunal on the part of governments in Zagreb, Belgrade, and Banja Luka. Two books have illustrated how Western-administered democracy in Bosnia and Herzegovina not only led to an unhealthy dependency on external actors but also decreased the legitimacy of democracy altogether.[16] And that illiberal, anti-Western parties in Bulgaria, Romania, and Serbia have waited in the wings of parliament even as democrats ruled shows that the reach of the West is never complete in the absence of strong structural underpinnings. Yet, unfavorable structural conditions can be overcome to some extent by a credible promise of membership and intermediate rewards such as aid and access to markets, rewards that are difficult for a government to refuse or give up later on. This is the tipping point at which the Western agenda takes over and becomes embedded in domestic policies and institutions.[17] In the Bulgarian case, the strong and consistent EU support for the Union of Democratic Forces (Sayuz na Demokratichnite Sili, SDS) in the late 1990s, is a good example of this dynamic.

Thus, that Western liberalism was embraced earlier in Slovenia than Croatia had to do with a greater domestic acceptance of the West in the former than the latter. That elites and part of the public finally did embrace the agenda in Croatia after 2000 reflected first and foremost an elite acceptance of Western conditions due to the delegitimization of the former regime and deep economic problems. That liberal reforms can be sustained in Croatia over time reflects favorable structural factors, the decisiveness with which the post-Tuđman governments pursued EU membership, and the credible offer of membership from the West. By contrast, that Western conditions continue to generate divisions in post-Milošević Serbia even as they have been accepted by part of the ruling elite shows the influence of less favorable structural conditions. Given that Serbia did not even sign an SAA with the EU until 2008, the West has so far held out little in the way of a credible promise of membership and thus has had less leverage over Serbian democratization.

Table 9.4 summarizes these propositions and processes and the way they played out in the four cases analyzed in this study. It employs concepts from the study of international relations, such as convergence (passive transfer through demonstration effects and "learning"), conditionality (the setting up of criteria for membership), and control (enforcing the liberal agenda through direct involvement in the domestic political process, sanctions, and intervention) to help us understand how liberal norms are transferred to the post-communist states.

Thus, political outcomes in the post-communist world depended not only on domestic structures but also on the response of these societies to the "most massive international socialization process currently underway in the international system" (Schimmelfennig 2002: 1), that is, the efforts of the West to coopt the post-communist states "into the existing institutional framework of

Table 9.4 External Impetus for Liberalism and Regime Outcomes

	Slovenia	Croatia	Federal Republic of Yugoslavia	Macedonia
Compatibility of Western liberalism with local structures	Strong	Medium	Poor	Very poor
Form of norm transfer	Contagion and convergence: passive leverage	Conditionality: positive and negative inducements	Control and conditionality: mostly negative inducements	Mixture of positive and negative inducements
Acceptance of norms by elites in 1990s	Consensus on Western liberalism	Nominal acceptance	Outright rejection	Nominal acceptance by part of the elite
Domestic political effects in the 1990s	Illiberal groups quickly marginalized; process of integration becomes main locus of political competition	Elites and public divided; external impetus for democracy moderate	Strong anti-Western sentiment; little external impetus for democracy	Public divided; anti-Western presence in politics
Resulting regime type	Substantive democracy	Simulated democracy	Populist authoritarianism	Illegitimate democracy
Effects of external influence after 2000	Some disenchantment with the EU; general consensus on appropriateness of West and liberalism	Economy falters and pro-West coalition wins; elite and public still divided. By mid-2000s, increasing consensus on integration, elites and public are coopted	Economy fails and democratic coalition wins; elites and public still deeply divided over liberalism; external impetus weak but growing by 2006	Illegitimacy comes to a head in 2001; conflict breaks out and West becomes intensely involved in domestic politics; public still deeply divided but external engagement continues to assure reform and stability

the larger liberal commonwealth" by tying membership to an extensive list of conditions (Janos 2003: 19). The processes by which this occurs are not anti-thetical to existing theories of transition and democratization. We have seen, rather, that the *sources* of these constraints, opportunities, political openings, loci of elite conflict, and public divisions often lie in the external, rather than the domestic, realm. In this sense, this study aims toward a synthesis of exist-ing theories of democratization and post-communist change with the reality of external agency, rather than a wholesale revision or rejection of any one such theory.

The Big Picture

The influence of Western conditionality notwithstanding, that the four re-gimes analyzed in this study, even those with low levels of liberal content in the 1990s, placed a premium on procedural correctness should not be a sur-prise given that in today's world the practice and rhetoric of democracy are ubiquitous. Even the most undemocratic regimes cannot afford at the very least to *pretend* to adhere to some democratic procedures, with some notable exceptions. Democracy has become an international norm, and the world's despots have learned to speak its language. President Robert Mugabe of Zim-babwe intimidated, beat, and jailed the opposition, but he did not eliminate it outright. President Hugo Chávez of Venezuela has clear authoritarian ten-dencies, but he holds elections and referenda to legitimize his rule and even accepts their results when things do not turn out in his favor, emerging as a better democrat, and thus a more legitimate leader, as a consequence. In a world where human rights and democracy are used as criteria for aid and membership in international organizations, it would be folly for any regime to disregard such norms entirely. And perhaps more important, many people are no longer willing to accept unbridled authoritarianism. Hence, in many countries, facade parliaments legislate, opposition groups hold symbolic pro-tests, minority groups have their token representatives in government bodies, foreign NGOs maintain a presence, and constitutional courts pass down rul-ings. However, the substance of democracy is missing.

Today, the majority of countries fit somewhere between democracy and dictatorship, mixing pluralism with authoritarianism in a variety of ways.[18] In this sense, both totalitarian North Korea and the democratic Netherlands are anomalies. The norm, indeed, seems to be better exemplified by the kinds of regimes that ruled in Croatia, Serbia, and Macedonia in the 1990s. All three regimes allowed for regular elections and criticism. All allowed their citizens to travel and read foreign newspapers. And yet, all three, to different degrees, were lacking in liberal content because of problems relating to legitimacy, public divisions over fundamental questions about the state, and a lack of liberal alternatives, not to mention manipulations of otherwise fair democratic rules and serious infractions against civil and human rights by those in power. The challenge for Western policymakers and donors is whether and how to encourage substantive democracy in these countries. In a July 2009 speech in Ghana, U.S. President Barack Obama noted that what happens between elections is just as important to democracy as the elections themselves.

The challenge for comparative politics is to understand the development and character of these kinds of hybrid regimes. This study has argued that in characterizing hybrid regimes, it is critical to look at various measures of liberal content. That in 1990s Serbia-Montenegro and Macedonia there were few truly liberal groups on the political scene, while in Croatia by the end of the 1990s there was a liberal opposition-in–waiting, ultimately tells us more about the challenges to democratization in each state than differences in their adherence to procedural norms. That the loci of political conflict in Slovenia were not related to questions about the borders of the state and who belongs within them is also quite telling in terms of the prospects for liberalism there. So was the refusal of many Macedonians to accept the legitimacy of the multiethnic coalitions that governed throughout the 1990s and today, or the refusal of ethnic Albanians to accept the legitimacy of a sovereign Macedonian state. For large-N studies on the determinants of democratization, the lesson is that simple operational definitions of the dependent variable will not yield reliable results. With hybrid democracy ubiquitous, political scientists will have a harder time quantifying regime type. In the Yugoslav successor states, differences in liberal content, rather than differences in procedural correctness, came to matter a great deal in the second decade of transition, even where the regimes that dominated the first ten years of transition were defeated. Put differently, if we take the level of liberal content in the 1990s to be the independent variable, it emerged as a powerful predictor of democratic success in post-authoritarian regimes that emerged with Western support after 2000.

The research agendas of political science and other disciplines that deal with human affairs are often driven by developments in the social world.

Trajectories in the study of democratization and regime change are a case in point.[19] The proliferation of democratization studies, not by accident, coincided with an unforeseen flood of change in world events rather than rapid advances in theoretical knowledge: namely, the "third wave" of democratization that began in southern Europe and then "spread" to Latin America, communist Eastern Europe, and some parts of Africa and Asia.[20] That among the countries undergoing democratization were a host of states without the "correct" cultures, social structures, or levels of development was very much at the root of highly voluntarist accounts of regime change. It also fostered the belief that, given the right institutions and political acumen, democracy could be "crafted" where there was none before.[21] Democracy, as Rustow (1970) wrote, could now be seen as the product of the "possible" rather than the "probable." In terms of foreign policy, the shift to voluntarism also coincided with Western efforts to "export" democracy to non-Western parts of the world.

More recently, there are those in Washington, London, and elsewhere that hoped for a "fourth wave" of democracy in the Greater Middle East. Wars have been waged, ostensibly with the goal of promoting precisely that. Billions of dollars have been invested in installing the right institutions, building civil society, and instructing locals in the ways of democracy. President George W. Bush's second inaugural, in January 2005, expressed great optimism about the spread of democracy in the world. Yet, daily developments in Iraq and Afghanistan and other countries have, at best, tempered any idealism about the global march of democracy. Although it is much too early to draw major conclusions, those who study regime change had to notice that "possibilism" and the feasibility of "exported" democracy were challenged in the most direct way. Germany and Japan, of course, are a testament to the potential success of externally crafted democracy and have been cited as such by proponents of the Iraq War. However, there are many differences between these two instances and the Iraqi and Afghan cases: Japan and Germany were already integrated nation-states, they had some experience with parliamentary democracy, they had a sophisticated industrial base before World War II, and they received massive amounts of aid in the wake of defeat. Divided populations, weak states, and a lack of a democratic tradition, by contrast, hinder the development of democracy in Iraq and Afghanistan.

It is equally sobering to survey negative democratic developments in states not ravaged by war. The former Soviet Central Asian states are firmly in the grip of repressive rulers, democratic institutions in Russia are under assault, coups and political violence have threatened or turned back democratization in some Latin American countries, and much of the African continent is under the control of authoritarian and corrupt regimes. Deeply divided publics have undermined recent democratic "revolutions" in states such as Lebanon, Ukraine, and Georgia. The problem in some of these cases has to do with democratic legitimacy: the inability of ostensibly democratic governments to improve the lives of ordinary people, which would instill trust in democratic governance. Shapiro has written: "If democracy does not function to improve the circumstances of those who appeal to it, its legitimacy as a political system will atrophy" (1996: 108).

In others, deep public divisions hinder democratization. Witness the popularity of the radical populist Hezbollah among Shias in Lebanon and their incredibly strong showing in rallies held just days after the massive crowds that poured into the streets in support of the "Cedar Revolution," or the weak support for Yushchenko's "Orange Revolution" among the Russian-speaking population of Eastern Ukraine. Pakistan, in which party support continues to be based on feudal loyalties, has been in a constant state of instability since the assassination of Benazir Bhutto in December 2007. The West Bank is ruled by leaders from the Fatah party who do not control and are not recognized as legitimate by a parallel leadership in Gaza, which is supposed to become part of their future state. In 2009, public divisions (and a violent crackdown by the regime) thwarted a possible democratic turnover in Iran, and the people of Honduras were divided over whether a coup d'état overthrowing a populist president was carried out in the direction of democracy or against it. In countries such as Venezuela, Russia, China, Vietnam, and Belarus, by contrast, authoritarianism itself is legitimate to the extent that it promotes higher living standards and public order.[22]

In still other cases, weak democratic institutions have turned political conflict into paralyzing protests and violence. In Thailand, tens of thousands of protesters managed to drive a government accused of corruption into internal exile and stop all international travel to and from the country in the fall of 2008. Earlier that year, months before hostilities broke out with Russia over South Ossetia, Georgia was in the midst of a political crisis in which opposition forces refused to acknowledge the results of a snap election called by champion of democracy and darling of the West President Mikhail Saakashvili following violent protests against his administration. That international observers declared that the elections were valid (albeit imperfect) did not stop the protestors. In Kenya, meanwhile, one of the few and, until now, most stable democracies in Africa, an election that did not meet international standards in early 2008 was contested by the opposition on the streets, leading to days of demonstrations and interethnic violence in which thousands may have died. Even in Greece, a member of the EU since 1981, youth protests against the government and a general strike paralyzed Athens for days in December 2008.

There is, of course, the normative question of whether liberal democracy is even desirable everywhere and at all times: scholars of Latin America have noted that democracy is not necessarily more economically or administratively efficient, or more orderly and governable, than autocratic regimes (Schmitter and Karl 1991: 85–87); Amy Chua (2003) echoed such sentiments by arguing that Western-style democracy can actually breed instability and ethnic conflict. Fareed Zakaria (2003) has argued that liberal autocracy is a better, safer, and more stable form of government for many transitional societies.[23]

One of the contributions of this study may be new ideas about the paradigm with which to regard the Balkans. Or perhaps it will cause people to assess whether it is even analytically useful to consider all of the Central and East European post-communist states under the same rubric given the very different kinds of problems faced by countries such as Macedonia and Albania compared to those faced by Slovenia, Hungary, or the Czech Republic. Such differences may override the analytical utility of the ostensibly shared communist past. In this view, variations in communist regime types themselves can be traced to certain domestic structures that predate the installation of communist rule after World War II. Furthermore, such conclusions further demonstrate that the distinction between area studies and political science is a false dichotomy: post-communist transitions are unique, but they produce dilemmas and are based on legacies that are by no means unique to the post-communist world. The difference between the post-communist states and countries in other parts of the world lies, rather, in the external sphere: namely, countries like Venezuela and Zimbabwe do not benefit from the powerful democratic incentives of Euro-Atlantic integration.

Therefore, the literature on democratic transitions of the 1980s and 1990s may have been greatly optimistic in its outlook. The notion of various stages of democratic consolidation also seems to have been refuted by developments of the past decade: in the absence of legitimacy, what appeared to be the institutionalization of democratic norms was not irreversible. More generally, however, the challenge for political scientists is to understand why the promise of the third wave of democratization and "the end of history" has not been fulfilled.

There is now a large body of evidence suggesting that the constraining influence of structural conditions is important to consider anew in the comparative study of democratization. I do not mean to suggest that we revive modernization theory or adopt crude models that generate assessments of countries' chances to become liberal democracies from aggregate income or surveys of democratic attitudes or culture. I do, however, propose that we look carefully at how different socioeconomic conditions, when filtered through distinct national political cultures and confronted with the realities of adapting to an increasingly interconnected global economy, create different parameters for democracy. Democracy does not arise out of thin air: Fukuyama (1992), whose earlier work espoused great optimism about democratic convergence, later argued that democratization in the non-Western world has taken place on the levels of ideology and institutions, while democracy remains unstable due to insufficient modernization on the levels of civil society and culture. Pop-Eleches's (2007b) statistical treatment of the post-communist world, furthermore, shows that the initial conditions of transition matter more in explaining long-term patterns of democratization, suggesting that structure is indeed a deeply entrenched force.

Finally, increasingly sophisticated large-N statistical studies continue to produce the same conclusion: that higher levels of income, usually operationalized by per capita income, are associated with higher levels of democracy, and nearly all the states that are stable democracies today are in the upper-income category.[24] Przeworski et al. (1998: 108) observe that one can correctly predict 77.5 percent of the 4,126 annual observations of regimes just by looking at per capita income. Among the sixty-four low-income countries (as so designated by the World Bank), India is the only one in which democratic institutions have survived continuously for more than a decade (Inglehart 2003: 56). However, there are a number of problems with such large-N studies and their conclusions. In the end, it is very difficult to quantify or "code" the complex variables that are potential determinants of democracy.

Thus, large-N studies must be complemented with detailed case studies that test the hypotheses derived from regression analysis, that employ more nuanced measures of development and economic structure than aggregate indicators such as per capita income, and that carefully describe the causal processes and intervening variables that lie between economic development and regime outcomes.

Prospects for the Yugoslav Successor States

Everything that has been presented here calls for some predictions on the immediate and long-term prospects of the Yugoslav successor states. The first is that economic conditions will continue to have a strong influence on political outcomes. As the appeal of nationalism has weakened and a global economic downturn has set in, issues of economic survival are at the forefront of public debate in the Balkans. The task before fragile Western-supported liberal governments is a formidable one. Elites in the region cannot count on the euphoria that characterized the initial democratic transitions of Poland or the Czech Republic, and unfulfilled material expectations can have an adverse effect on the liberal democratic project. The legitimacy of Western conditionality, and by extension the legitimacy of the organizations and states that issue the conditions, depends on real rewards: increases in living standards and a perception of progress toward membership. Rewards can also come in the form of faster disbursement of development funds, eased visa restrictions for travel to EU countries, or trade and labor mobility privileges.

Meeting Western conditions is often a painful process for candidate countries, and as such it is no wonder that pro-EU attitudes are strongest in the countries that are furthest from membership. Research shows that it is only once citizens are exposed to the economic consequences of closer EU integration that support levels can be explained by economic circumstance (Elgun and Tillman 2007). This is supported by recent survey data from the region, shown in table 9.5. The results show that Croatians, who are closest to joining the EU, evaluate their country's economic prospects and their government quite negatively and are also most skeptical about EU membership.

The public's threshold of tolerance of conditionality is lowered when negative statements are made about membership or when the economic cost of meeting them outweighs their benefit for an extended period of time. Since public expectations usually exceed both the economy's ability to turn around and the West's ability to deliver rewards, the potential for frustration is high. As noted earlier in the study, legitimacy by expectation as opposed to legitimacy by tradeoffs has its pitfalls. Bulgaria signed what was then called an Association Agreement with the EU in 1993 and formally applied for mem-

Table 9.5   Public Opinion on Key Issues, Fall 2008
(percent of respondents who agree with statement)

Country	Economic conditions are getting worse	Membership in the EU would be a good thing	Government is doing an excellent or good job
Croatia	61	29	16
Bosnia and Herzegovina	58	48	9
Macedonia	47	57	46
Serbia	42	58	25
Montenegro	28	66	55
Kosovo	25	83	53

Source: Gallup Balkan Monitor, www.balkan-monitor.eu/.
Note: Survey was conducted in September and October 2008.

bership in 1995; it joined twelve years later, in 2007, and the list of conditions that candidate countries must fulfill has only grown since then, while the appetite among current EU citizens and governments for further expansion has decreased markedly. This is why many EU leaders argued for an accelerated SAA with Serbia in 2008.[25] It remains an open question whether the patience of publics in Serbia, Montenegro, Bosnia and Herzegovina, and Macedonia, not to mention Albania and Kosovo, will hold out for so long and whether radical populism will rise if their patience does not last.

Economic problems are acute in many parts of the region and growing worse given the global recession, while political stability and ethnic reconciliation will depend on alleviating high unemployment and poverty rates. More than a quarter of Serbia's workforce—and half of its young people—are unemployed.[26] In the spring of 2007, I was with a senior U.S. official on a tour promoting interethnic cooperation in several mixed villages in central Kosovo, where half the working-age population is unemployed. In one town an elderly ethnic Serb man stepped forward and told the official in plain language that so long as people have somewhere to work and a way to feed their families, ethnic relations would be fine. Lack of trust in government and its institutions continues to hinder reform and hurt state capacity in all the successor states, so corruption will also remain at the forefront of public concern and debate for the foreseeable future. The challenge is to build state institutions that are "not too strong to interfere excessively with citizens' lives and their political and economic freedoms but strong enough to enforce positively the rule of law and avoid being captured by powerful interest groups" (Ekiert et al. 2007: 15).

Foreign aid and investment are indispensable for economic growth—and it was economic growth that underpinned the democratic development of states such as Germany, Japan, and Italy in the postwar era. At the euphoric 2003 EU–western Balkans Summit in Thessaloniki there was talk of a "Marshall Plan for the Balkans."[27] The Balkans have received a fair amount of aid from Brussels, but it is only a small portion of the total foreign aid dispensed by EU member states, and much of that is channeled toward "democracy building" rather than more tangible projects such as infrastructure (Youngs 2008: 163). As the worldwide recession reached the Balkans in 2009, the EU announced that it would not be able to provide much help. In general, the amount of aid the small states of the Balkans can expect to receive will never approach the scale of the Marshall Plan or the net transfers received by Spain, Portugal, and Greece when they joined the EU. Moreover, they must face the challenges of a highly integrated and competitive global market—and now a global recession. In 2009, growth rates and industrial production were falling, credit growth and exports declining, and perceptions of risk growing, leading EU officials to suggest that the economic woes would negatively impact enlargement.[28] Moreover the foreign investment and remittances on which the region depends have fallen sharply as well.

The countries of the region have skilled pools of labor and a potential manufacturing base, but competition from Chinese and Indian labor is fierce. The best economic hope for the Yugoslav successor states may be to cooperate so as to reestablish former markets. Slovenian manufacturers realized early in the 1990s that despite their advantages on Western markets, their goods could not compete on an equal footing with West European and American products, so they made a concerted effort to return to Serbia and other parts of the former Yugoslavia, where Slovenia's firms are active and its supermarkets ubiquitous. Croatian businesses have taken a step in this direction as well.[29]

Slovenia is a member of the EU and NATO. It is prosperous, and it is a stable and substantive, if not always fully liberal, democracy. Party politics will be volatile, and disappointment with Europe may generate some nationalist responses in Slovenia, but in the long run the country will find the right balance between its national narrative, on the one hand, and the realities of belonging to the EU, on the other.

The most likely short-term scenario for both Macedonia and Serbia is political instability exacerbated by widespread poverty. Radical populists may tone down their rhetoric, but they will continue to slow down reforms and garner support among disaffected parts of the population. Liberal parties will have to respond but can also benefit from Western pressure. In Serbia, deep divisions over the role of the West in the country's future are likely to continue. Not until Albanians in Macedonia feel that they are a full part of the political community will democracy be strengthened there. Polls taken at the end of the decade show that one in three Macedonians fear an outbreak of inter-ethnic violence.[30] Even the democratic minimalist Rustow (1970) assumed national unity as a necessary precondition for democracy. On the positive side, the EU Special Representative model of intervention has worked quite well, and the 2009 presidential and local elections were peaceful (though few ethnic Albanians voted). Significant delays in progress on both EU and NATO accession could threaten Macedonia's internal security.

Though much work remains to be done, Croatia has solidified its future as a European democratic state. Economic difficulties, Euroskepticism and nationalist tendencies in the ruling party may complicate the process, but Croatia's progress on accession negotiations and widespread support among current member states mean that the larger momentum toward Europe and reform will not be reversed. Moreover, the government can credibly use the need to fulfill dictates of the acquis communautaire as an "excuse" for unpopular reforms. The 2007 reelection of the reformed and "Christian-Democratized" HDZ, and the indistinguishable pro-Euro-Atlantic platforms of HDZ and its rival, the SDP, can be interpreted as the result of widespread support for EU membership, to whose conditionality the public has now been socialized, in spite of, or perhaps rather because of, their ambivalence toward the EU as an organization.[31] However, if Croatia's membership were to be delayed significantly by the border dispute with Slovenia or other external factors, it would not only empower the nationalists who currently seem to be making a comeback but also serve as a conspicuous negative model for the country's southern neighbors.

In 2009, Montenegro's leaders ("oligarchs," as one Montenegrin analyst called them) are still benefiting from a post-independence "honeymoon" in terms of general public satisfaction and levels of EU support.[32] The country's constitution is inclusive, which has helped diffuse ethnic tensions. However, the pro-EU honeymoon is unlikely to last forever. Poverty is a serious issue, corruption is endemic, unemployment is high, and the country's economic structure is weak.[33] Elites will have to work hard to maintain the momentum for change, but disappointment will certainly set in. There are formidable obstacles to overcome, and continued public support for EU conditionality is not guaranteed. But the longstanding pro-Western rhetoric of Montenegro's politicians and the enthusiasm of its population toward the EU provide for a more optimistic outlook than that of Serbia, even as the country's institutions and economy are weaker.

Bosnia and Herzegovina and Kosovo have the most uncertain futures of all, and they also face the most dire economic circumstances with, unemployment rates exceeding 40 percent. In Bosnia, although progress has been made on reform and institution building, and an SAA has been signed, crucial reform bills, as well as a new constitution, have not passed due to obstructionism from all sides. That which has been accomplished, however, is to a large degree thanks to the heavy-handedness of the international community's High Representatives (HRs), who continued to exercise sweeping powers through 2009. The leaders of Republika Srpska have consistently obstructed measures that would strengthen the Bosnian state, only relenting when threatened with EU accession slowdown or when overruled by the OHR. It is clear that in order for Western-sponsored "democracy" to be legitimized in Bosnia, locals must be given a greater stake in their future and problems of state legitimacy need to be overcome. In a 2008 survey, Bosnians expressed the lowest levels of trust in their institutions of all the peoples in the region.[34] This is undoubtedly in part because local leaders are more accountable to their international supervisors than Bosnians themselves. A former HR, Paddy Ashdown, admitted as much when he noted upon taking office that the international community had focused so much on elections after Dayton that it had forgotten the importance of building stable, legitimate institutions. But the de facto ethnic division of the country, and its accompanying problems of legitimacy, may not be overcome in the coming years. And it is quite troubling that support for the EU has fallen from 80 percent to 50 percent in just one year and that interethnic relations appear to be at a low point.[35] Some EU diplomats have resigned themselves to Bosnia's entry into the EU not as a unitary state but in its current, problematic, highly decentralized form.[36] Kosovo's leaders, like those of Montenegro, are buoyed by public euphoria over independence, but the economy is very weak, Kosovo's Serbs refuse to sign on to the new state, the transition from UN to EU oversight has been fraught with difficulties, and the country lacks adequate international recognition.

Those post-communist states that became EU members in May 2004 joined the Schengen system on 21 December 2007, meaning that their citizens could now travel passport-free in the twenty-four-nation Schengen zone. On that very day I boarded a train from Vienna to Katowice, Poland, a route that I had taken numerous times, and as we crossed the Czech and Polish borders I marveled that for the first time a succession of border police did not enter the compartment to check my passport. This is a remarkable thing, both symbolically and practically, but it also underscored the fact that citizens of that other part of Eastern and Central Europe—the Balkans—need visas to travel virtually anywhere and reminded me of how far behind these countries are in the EU integration process. In 2009 former Macedonian vice premier Ivica Bocevski noted that 70 percent of Macedonians between the ages of 16 and 30 had never been to an EU member state, including Bulgaria.[37] The July 2009 EC recommendation to lift Schengen visa requirements for citizens of Serbia, Macedonia, and Montenegro was a welcome announcement demonstrating the success of conditionality, but in order to go into force it still needs the approval of the EU Council, the EU Parliament, and the member states; for the time being, it leaves Albanians, Kosovars, and Bosnians in the "Balkan ghetto." Nevertheless, the announcement was designed as an intermediate reward, an interim solution to the problem of stalled enlargement.

In the end, democracy can succeed given the continued and active engagement of the West and the enduring "soft power" of the incentive of membership in Euro-Atlantic structures. The countries of the "western Balkans," as "the former Yugoslavia minus Slovenia plus Albania" are now known to policymakers in Brussels and around the world, owe their existing democratic orders to Western involvement. Continued engagement on the part of the West depends in large part on developments beyond the control of the governments and people of the region. Though it remains an influential force in the region, the United States, preoccupied with two wars, has gradually ceded responsibility for the region to the Europeans. U.S. president Barack Obama barely mentioned the Balkans during his campaign (Tcherneva 2008), though there have been signs of renewed engagement since then on the part of the United States, including a visit by Vice President Joe Biden to the region in mid-2009. The momentum for further EU expansion will depend on the readiness of current EU members to accept new members: after the admission of Bulgaria and Romania in 2007, "expansion fatigue" and "absorption capacity" were commonly heard phrases in Brussels and other West European capitals. However, after its initial rejection by Irish voters in 2008, in 2009 the Lisbon Treaty was approved in Ireland in a repeat referendum and its implementation was underway at the end of 2009. French President Nicolas Sarkozy openly stated that the act of Irish rejectionism in the first referendum directly threatened further EU expansion, while forty European intellectuals, activists, and commentators wrote an open letter imploring the EU not to make the latest impasse an impediment to further enlargement (Safarikova 2008). Eurobarometer polls have revealed that less than 50 percent of Europeans support the admission of Croatia, Macedonia, and Serbia and Montenegro, while Albania, along with Turkey, came in dead last in terms of support for its membership among citizens of current EU members.[38] The Netherlands and Belgium are staunch opponents of advancing Serbia in the SAA process so long as the two fugitive war crimes suspects are at large.[39] With the exception of Croatia, and in 2009, Macedonia, the lukewarm reports that the EU gave to the western Balkan states suggest that membership is still a rather distant prospect for Bosnia and Herzegovina, Serbia, Montenegro, Albania, and Kosovo.

Sustained feelings of distance from the EU can only weaken the impetus for further reform and empower radical populist forces in the domestic politics of the candidate states. The EU is well aware of this: following the rejection of the EU Constitution by French and Dutch voters in 2005, Commissioner for Enlargement Olli Rehn told the European Parliament Foreign Affairs Committee: "If the EU went wobbly about the Western Balkans' long-term prospect of membership, our positive influence would be seriously eroded."[40] Having declared 2009 "the Year of the Western Balkans," it appears that the EC has taken Rehn's words to heart. Yet, in this very same year, both French and German leaders declared that EU expansion needs to be slowed down. Commentators have noted widespread exhaustion in the EU regarding the Balkans. Again, Enlargement Commissioner Olli Rehn has been forced to undertake damage control, assuring the candidate states that enlargement is on track and imploring France and Germany to support its continuation, saying that the EU cannot take a "sabbatical" from its works "for stability and progress in the Western Balkans, which is provided by the European perspective."[41] These sentiments were echoed by U.S. Deputy Assistant Secretary of State Stuart Jones in May 2009.

Nevertheless, in 2009, all of the Yugoslav successor states are either part of Europe or committed to joining it, a fact that offers great hope for democracy, stability, and security in the region. Until now, Western conditionality has helped to shape convergence in procedural, if not always liberal, democracies. The rise of lasting and liberal democracies in the Balkans will depend on whether the western and southeastern parts of the continent converge in terms of prosperity as well, and on whether all the Yugoslav successor states are offered a future as equal partners in a Europe "whole and free."[42]

Notes

Introduction

1. In 2003 the rump Yugoslav Federal Parliament ratified a EU-sponsored agreement to change the name of the Federal Republic of Yugoslavia to "Serbia and Montenegro." In 2006, Montenegrins voted in favor of independence, and a sovereign Montenegro was recognized internationally. In writing about the pre-2003 period, I will refer to "FRY," except when discussing differences between the governments in Belgrade and Podgorica. When writing about the post-2003 period, I will refer to "Serbia and Montenegro," and after 2006 each of the two as independent states. In February 2008, the former Serbian province of Kosovo, administered since 1999 by the international community, declared independence and as of late 2009 is recognized by sixty-three countries. Approximately 62 percent of UN member states recognize Macedonia by its constitutional name ("Republic of Macedonia"); others, in deference to Greek objections, recognize it as the "Former Yugoslav Republic of Macedonia," or FYROM.

2. Žarkovic-Bookman (1991: 249) defines economic viability as the ability to sustain economic growth and acceptable living standards in the aftermath of secession at levels that prevailed prior to independence.

3. Stokes (1999), for instance, argues that the post-communist Balkan states are undergoing a delayed process of national consolidation, one that started in the nineteenth century on the Western half of the continent.

4. Nationalism comes in many forms (Greenfeld 1992) and is not necessarily detrimental to liberalism. Here I have in mind aggressive, exclusionary, and ethnic nationalism.

5. See, for instance, Šarinić (1999), Dizdarević (1999), Mamula (2000), and Mesić (2004). In an excellent volume, Sabrina Ramet (2006) reviews and critically analyzes these memoirs and other works on the Yugoslav wars. Also see Ingrao and Emmert (2009), whose recently published volume addresses many of the most sensitive controversies surrounding the breakup of Yugoslavia using the tools of historiography.

6. Pleština (1996) makes this point for the case of Croatia. The first free elections in all republics were held in 1990, while violent conflict did not break out until 1991 and 1992. A poignant example of the willingness of influential elements within the Croatian HDZ to pursue war is portrayed in the BBC documentary *Death of a Nation*. On camera, a widow tells the story of her husband, an ethnic Croatian police com-

mander in Slavonia who was killed by HDZ functionaries for attempting to promote peace between local Serbs and Croats.

7. Interview with Mirjana Kasapović, Zagreb, January 2002. Other writings about the former Yugoslavia have been preoccupied with the role of a few infamous leaders. Though the leading role of these individuals cannot be denied, it is also important to remember that they rose to positions of authority under certain conditions, and in many cases they were elected and supported by large numbers of people, often in multiple elections.

8. Following Jowitt's (1992) famous explication of the "Leninist Legacy," a number of scholars suggested that post-communist states with the legacy of a liberal communist regime would find democratic transition easier (Millar and Wolchik 1994; Hanson 1995; Baranyi and Volgyes 1995).

9. The comparative case study approach is described in George (1979), Collier (1991), and Lijphart (1971).

10. This section is based in part on Grzymała-Busse's (2002) own methodological justification for her path-breaking study on the regeneration of former communist parties, which also examines four cases.

CHAPTER ONE: Post-communist Diversity

1. While Latin America "restrains the universe of causes," it is less successful at "expanding the range of results" (Bunce 2003: 169). The post-communist region, by contrast, is useful on both counts. Charles King (2000) has termed these diverse outcomes the "mercurial dependent variables" of post-communism.

2. Transitologists focus mainly on elite dynamics and choices, especially splits within the elite during the political opening created by a crisis. It is the high uncertainty of transition periods that leaves room for contingency and agency.

3. For example, Wandycz (1992), Suny (1993), Janos (2000), Horowitz (2004), Darden and Grzymala-Busse (2005), and Wittenberg (2006).

4. The cultural differences between Eastern and Western Christianity are discussed in Janos (2000: 38–41), Kharkhordin (1999), and Stan and Turcescu (2000).

5. A powerful early elaboration of the importance of the communist legacy was Jowitt (1992), speaking to scholars and policymakers who saw the post-communist states as a tabula rasa onto which instructions for democracy and the market could be written. Stark (1992) made a similar argument in the context of path dependence. Works that emphasize the varying legacies of different kinds of communist regimes include Millar and Wolchik (1994), Hanson (1995), Ekiert (1996), Poznanski (1996), Baranyi and Volgyes (1995), Greskovits (1998), Grzymala-Busse (2002), Kopstein (2003), and Ekiert and Hanson (2003).

6. For instance, Poznański (1996).

7. Roeder (2001) makes this argument for the Soviet successor states.

8. Recent examples include Ishiyama and Velten (1998), Fish (1998a, 1998b), Fish (1999), Kopecky and Mudde (2000), Fish (2001), and McFaul (2002). Rationalist approaches may also be included here as a subset of the larger approach; however,

they have rarely been applied in explaining post-communist democratization, since rational choice usually assumes a much more stable institutional environment than that which characterized the breakdown of communist regimes and emergence of democracy in formerly communist states. One interesting use of rationalism to explain post-communist politics is Roeder (1994).

9. Staniszkis (1992) has written about the great leverage elites had immediately following the collapse of communism. During such periods, the constraints of the social environment are significantly attenuated, the weight of the past becomes less decisive, and social reality tends to be more malleable, allowing us to think of transitions in terms of "crafting" (Diamandouros and Larrabee 2000: 27).

10. Stark (1992) was the first to formulate a theory of path dependence for post-communist "transformations." Beyer et al. (2001) provide a critical evaluation of Stark's hypothesis based on empirical data.

11. An example of the application of transitology to post-communism is the volume by Linz and Stepan (1996).

12. The comparability of post-communist transitions to other "third wave" cases has been the subject of intense scholarly debate. Such a debate between Valerie Bunce (skeptical of the utility of such comparison) and Terry Lynn Karl and Philippe Schmitter (proponents of comparison) appeared in *Slavic Review* in 1995.

13. On the "why of the why," see Kopstein and Reilly (1999), who expand on Fish's (1998b) finding that the outcome of the first free elections is the best predictor of the extent of post-communist economic reform.

14. M. Steven Fish, who previously employed multivariate regression to explain post-communist democratization and economic reform (1998a, 1998b), later noted the pitfalls of this method (Fish 2001). First, the number of hypotheses is large relative to the number of cases. Second, reliable data are often missing. Third, since post-communist "outcomes" are not really outcomes at all but instead a dynamic process, standard regression cannot really capture the process and its causes.

15. See Dryzek and Holmes (2002).

16. Interview with Ivan Šiber, Zagreb, November 2001.

17. According to the New Democracies barometer, which posed this question to representative samples of the population in various post-communist countries. See Fink-Hafner and Haček (2001a), table 3.

18. Popularized in works such as Anzulović (1999) and Drašković (1982).

19. Or, alternatively, the incentive structure may lead elites to pursue policies that encourage ethnic inclusion. Timothy Snyder (2003) observes that, encouraged by Brussels, Polish elites in the 1990s crafted successful policies to peacefully integrate the country's Ukrainian, Belarussian, and other minorities into the post-communist Polish state, thereby maintaining harmony where there was a historical basis for conflict.

20. Interview with Ivo Banac, Dubrovnik, Croatia, July 2002. Ramet (2006: 599) reminds us not to confuse Tito's mythical status as a great leader with democratic legitimacy.

21. Meier (1999) mentions the repression of these returning guest workers. I have spoken with several former Fulbright scholars from various parts of the former Yugoslavia who received surprise visits and interrogations from the secret police after returning home from study and research in the United States.

22. Former U.S. Ambassador to Yugoslavia Warren Zimmerman's (1996) account of the dissolution was one such reaction.

23. One well-known volume based on the experience of Latin American and Asian states is Haggard and Kaufman (1995).

24. See the data in Ekiert et al. (2007: 9). This makes the post-communist experience significantly different than that of Latin America, although Slovenia democratized successfully despite comparatively slow economic reforms.

25. Interview with Davor Gjenero, Zagreb, December 2001.

26. Moore (1996) argues that these findings are usually based on poor methodology: on insufficient measures of democracy, for instance.

27. For instance, Rueschemeyer et al. (1992) and Huber et al. (1993).

28. For instance, Almond and Verba (1963); Apter (1965); and Putnam (1993).

29. On "intellectuals as bad guys," see Drakulić (1999).

30. Susan Woodward (1995a) provides an especially illuminating explanation of how the oil crisis and other structural changes in the economy starting in the 1970s had especially grave consequences for Yugoslavia.

31. Žarko Puhovski mentioned this in an interview in Zagreb, January 2002.

32. In a June 2002 presentation to the Seminar on Security and Cooperation in Southeast Europe in Dubrovnik Croatia, the economist Ljubiša Adamović put this even more bluntly: some of the Yugoslav successor states were simply too poor to be independent.

33. Interview with Phillipe Schmitter, Ljubljana, July 2002.

34. Conditionality is a strategy of reinforcement used by the EU, NATO, and other organizations to compel and reinforce democratization in post-communist states, with the ultimate goal of membership in these organizations. In exchange for progress on adopting liberal democratic norms, post-communist states have been given intermediate rewards such as praise, positive progress reports, financial assistance, military protection, and visa liberalization. By contrast, a noncompliant post-communist state is publicly criticized, and these rewards are withheld (Schimmelfennig 2007: 127).

35. For example, Pridham et al. (1997), Linden (2002), Kubicek (2003), Jacoby (2004), Kelley (2004), Pridham (2005), Vachudová (2005), Schimmelfennig et al. (2006), Grabbe (2006), and Epstein (2008).

36. See the 1995 BBC documentary film *Death of a Nation*.

CHAPTER TWO: Characterizing Regime Type

Epigraph: Przeworski (1999:16).

1. Schumpeter understood democracy in terms of free elections. He defined the "democratic method" as "that institutional arrangement for arriving at political deci-

sions in which individuals acquire the power to decide by means of a competitive struggle for the people's vote" (1950: 269).

2. On democratic quality, see, for example, Diamond and Morlino (2005).

3. Elkins (2000) has shown that gradations of democracy yield better results in quantitative tests.

4. As Munck (2009: 1) observes, the question of how to measure progress on democracy is hardly limited to the academic sphere: with the explosion of democracy promotion programs since the end of the Cold War, it is a central question for policymakers as well.

5. For instance, Bollen (1990), Inkeles (1991), Collier and Levitsky (1997), Elkins (2000), and Coppedge (2004). Bollen (1990) and Inkeles (1991) have examined quantitative democracy scores constructed in alternate ways to see how consistent they are with one another. Moore points out that although the findings are somewhat comforting, quantitative measures of democracy are still not sufficiently authoritative to "make possible fine-grained analysis of its causes and correlates" (1996: 41). Collier and Levitsky (1997) criticize the constant adjustment of definitions of democracy to fit new cases.

6. For a survey of popular understandings of democracy in post-communist countries, see Dryzek and Holmes (2002). The World Values Survey also contains an interesting cross-national analysis of democratic attitudes that includes post-communist states.

7. The distinction is discussed in Linz and Stepan (1996), among others.

8. Robert Dahl's (1982: 11) defining conditions of democracy are as follows: (1) control over government decisions about policy is constitutionally vested in elected officials; (2) elected officials are chosen in frequently and fairly conducted elections in which coercion is comparatively uncommon; (3) practically all adults have the right to vote in the election of officials; (4) practically all adults have the right to run for elective offices in the government; (5) citizens have the right to express themselves without the danger of severe punishment on political matters broadly defined; (6) citizens have the right to seek out alternative sources of information, and alternative sources of information exist and are protected by law; and (7) citizens . . . have the right to form relatively independent associations or organizations, including independent political parties and interest groups.

9. These are a combination of criteria outlined in Moore (1996), Diamond (1999), and Bugajski (2002).

10. However, despite their many advantages, Freedom House (FH) scores are far from perfect measurement instruments. Munck (2009) notes the following shortcomings: (1) the indicators used to construct the FH index of political rights have changed over the years; (2) the relationship among the various attributes on the FH "checklist" used to construct the Political Rights and Civil Liberties indices are not considered; (3) FH does little to subject the process of measurement to public scrutiny; (4) the various attributes of democracy used by FH and the weight assigned

to them are not sufficiently rooted in democratic theory; and (5) the aggregation procedure is not adequate.

CHAPTER THREE: The Development of Disparity

1. There is a literature on intra-state regional economic differences and their consequences in places other than Yugoslavia. See, for instance, Hechter (1975), Nairn (1977), Gourevitch (1978), and Žarkovic-Bookman (1991).

2. This division roughly corresponds to an older division between the Eastern (later Byzantine) and Western Roman Empires, which at the time of their existence were already associated with different levels of development.

3. These industries were great beneficiaries of the Austro-Hungarian market prior to the formation of the first Yugoslavia and thus were substantially hurt when the market for the goods they produced was reduced from 59 million to 12 million when the Hapsburg Empire was dissolved. Serbia's market, by contrast, was increased from 1.9 million to 12 million. As Singleton (1986: 152) and Pleština (1992: 11) note, this difference was at the root of subsequent battles over development policy, with Croatia and Slovenia consistently arguing for an outwardly oriented economy and Serbia content with a self-contained national market.

4. The preceding paragraph is based on several sources, including Tomasevich (1955), Pleština (1992), Lampe (2000), and Mazower (2000). Singleton (1986: 151) notes that the legacy of Habsburg rule for Slovenia was that its roads and railways were well linked to Austria. The backbone of this system was the *Südbahn* and connected Vienna with Trieste via Maribor and Ljubljana. Croatia was also linked with Budapest. In Slovenia, commercial agriculture, public education, roads, and light manufacturing began to develop as early as the mid-eighteenth century with Theresian reforms in the Habsburg Empire (Woodward 1995b: 38). By contrast, in many parts of the south, Woodward notes that people were "still mired in pre-capitalist relations with respect to religion, colonial oppression, and the nation embodied in the feudal power of a landholding class" (1995b: 39).

5. Pleština (1992: 144), note 7.

6. On this crisis and on conditions in the countryside more generally, see Tomasevich (1955).

7. This bureaucratic apparatus was overwhelmingly made up of Serbs, leaving Croats and Slovenes disgruntled, with no parallel avenues to achieve professional and material satisfaction (Janos 1997: 27–31).

8. For more on the human and economic costs of World War II, see Hoffman and Neal (1962), Horvat (1976), Rusinow (1977), and Žerjavić (1989). On the different conditions faced by Partisan committees after the war in the north and south, see Woodward (1995b: 60–61).

9. On the eve of World War II, over 75 percent of the Yugoslav population engaged in agriculture as a primary source of income. According to some estimates, there was a 44.4 percent surplus in the agricultural labor force. In areas such as Dalmatia this figure was over 68 percent, while in Vojvodina it was only 2.4 percent

(Singleton 1986: 154). The per capita national income of the first Yugoslavia has been estimated at between $60 and $70 (Rusinow 1977: xviii).

10. This and subsequent references to aggregate development indicators are based on "social product," which is roughly GNP minus unproductive services.

11. Analyzing the first years of the communist Yugoslav state, Pleština writes: "The fundamental prerequisite for a socialist society as well as for national and political equality, of prime importance in multi-national Yugoslavia, was economic equality which was to be achieved by the equalization of living and working conditions throughout Yugoslavia. This logically entailed... equalizing conditions between republics and regions to circumvent the possible development of a quasi-colonial relationship between a developed center and a less-developed periphery" (1992: 16).

12. I rely heavily in this section on Dijana Pleština's (1992) groundbreaking work on regional development in communist Yugoslavia. I am indebted to Dr. Pleština for her helpful advice in Zagreb in the winter and spring of 2002. Articles by Bombelles (1991) and Ocić (1998) were also very useful in preparing this section.

13. Bosnia and Herzegovina was not considered an LDR during the time of the second Five-Year Plan owing to the intense military industry buildup that had occurred there, a decision that represented a substantial economic setback for the republic (Pleština 1992, 49).

14. Despite favoritism toward the DRs, Croatia was often left behind politically because of its role in World War II, low membership in the Communist Party, and the Slovene identity of the top architects of Yugoslavia's economic policy, Edvard Kardelj and Sergej Krajger.

15. Even in the best of times, only 7 percent of residents of the SFRJ self-identified as Yugoslav. See Lampe (2000); on Yugoslavism, see Djokić (2003).

16. Several authors have provided analyses of the Croatian Spring, among them Ramet (1984).

17. In the south, the people used a term of political slang standing for the ties between party members and protected industry: *Čaršija*, a word of Turkish origin meaning "market" (Woodward 1995b: 36, note 19).

18. From the early 1950s to the early 1970s, Yugoslavia's GDP was growing at an average of 6 percent per year, the output of the industrial sector at 10.1 percent, exports at 11.1 percent, imports at 9.8 percent, and investments at 8.2 percent. Overall, GDP per capita increased 250 percent. Infant mortality was cut by more than half, literacy increased (in Bosnia and Herzegovina and Kosovo, illiteracy rates fell from over 80 percent in the prewar period to below 20 percent in the 1980s), as did ownership of consumer durables, showing that some of the benefits of overall growth did trickle down to the masses. The distribution of wealth also became much more equitable. And between 1950 and 1970, the Yugoslav economy managed to keep pace with the growth rates of advanced capitalist countries (Janos 2000: 276–77).

19. On the problem of the centralization needed for reform, especially with reference to the pressure exerted by international financial institutions in the 1980s for Yugoslavia to centralize, see Woodward (1995b).

20. On this crisis, see Horvat (1985), Lydall (1989), Woodward (1995a, 1995b), and Lampe (2000).

21. For an analysis of the problem of unemployment in Yugoslavia, see Woodward (1995b).

22. This subsection has benefited from conversations with Tvrtko Jakovina of the History Department at Zagreb University, Croatia; see also Jakovina (2003).

23. On U.S. aid during the early years of communist Yugoslavia, see Lampe (2000), especially ch. 9.

24. During the initial years of Yugoslav development, fully one third of Yugoslavia's investments in production came from foreign aid and loans, while the growing balance of trade deficit was covered by "soft" Western assistance.

25. This definition of economic viability is also used in Žarkovic-Bookman (1991: 249).

CHAPTER FOUR: Simulated Democracy

Epigraph: Interview with Mirjana Kasapović, Zagreb, January 2002.

1. The name of the party has also been translated as "Croatian Democratic Community." The problem lies in the word *zajednica*, which can be translated as either "community" or "union."

2. Interview with Jože Mencinger, Ljubljana, June 2002.

3. Woodward has described the economic policies that adversely affected the Croatian hinterland and Bosnia. According to Woodward, these included "an economic policy aimed at promoting exports to Western markets and declining domestic investment in transport, construction and industries such as mining, timber, and heavy industry," which led to deindustrialization and economic decline (1995b: 161).

4. Research shows that two-thirds of the HDZ constituency resided in rural areas or small towns (Grdešić 1991).

5. Interview with Davor Glavaš, Zagreb, November 2001.

6. Interview with former HDZ official, Zagreb, December 2001.

7. The OSCE reported that irregularities in elections included arbitrary and non-transparent changes in constituency boundaries, restrictions of criticism of the government in the state-run media, and flawed election administration such as outdated and inaccurate voter lists. OSCE report quoted in Karatnycky et al. (1999: 178).

8. For an excellent quantitative/content analysis study of the HDZ's advantages, such as unequal access to and bias in the media at election time, see Vrčan et al. (1999).

9. One famous case is that of Miroslav Kutle, an HDZ tycoon who controlled *Slobodna Dalmacija*, an influential newspaper on the Croatian coast. After the fall of the HDZ regime in January 2000, he was prosecuted on charges of corruption.

10. Between 1994 and 1997, independent newspapers and journalists faced about seven hundred libel suits (Ottaway 2003: 116).

11. Interview with Ivna Bajšić, Zagreb, April 2002.

12. In its first six months in office, the HDZ replaced 280 judges with HDZ loyalists. In 1992 and 1996 the president of the Supreme Court was fired for failing to bow to Tuđman's decisions. The constitutional court was able to hold out the longest, but it, too, was eventually replaced with HDZ loyalists in 1999 (Ottaway 2003: 114).

13. A 1994 U.S. State Department report maintained that "Serbs continued to suffer from ever-present, subtle, and sometimes even open discrimination in such areas as the administration of justice, employment, housing, and the free exercise of their cultural rights" (quoted in Cohen 1997:120, note 54).

14. Interview with Ljubomir Čučić, Zagreb, July 2000.

15. The rebellion was the so-called Croatian Spring, also known as *Maspok*, which brought together reformist communists, nationalist cultural organizations, and a number of extremist Croatian nationalists wanting to take advantage of the situation to promote their goals.

16. Interview with Davor Gjenero, Zagreb, November 2001.

17. It is estimated that immediately prior to the first elections, 27,000 party members left the SKH and migrated to the HDZ (Cohen 1997: 78).

18. The events surrounding this rebellion are well documented in Glenny (1993).

19. See the BBC documentary *Death of a Nation*.

20. Interview with Goran Čular, Zagreb, December 2001.

21. Interview with Mate Granić, Zagreb, December 2001.

22. See, for instance, Mesić (2004).

23. Interview with Mate Granić, Zagreb, December 2001.

24. Many war crimes committed by the Croatian Army against Muslim and Serb civilians have been documented. The worst example was the massacre at Ahmići in April 1993. Over ten thousand Croats died in this "war within a war" as well as a great many Muslims.

25. Recently, the Bosnian Serb leadership finally admitted to the planning and execution of this war crime.

26. For some, this is also evidence of the secret cooperation between the Croatian and Serbian armies. According to former UNPROFOR commander Michael Rose, a secret deal had almost certainly been struck between Milošević and Tuđman to allow Croats to retake the Krajina in exchange for preventing the Muslims from achieving victory over the Serbs in Bosnia and not asking for too much at Dayton. According to Rose, the prospect of a Muslim state among them was the worst possible scenario for both Serbs and Croats (Rose 1998).

27. See the excellent report by the Helsinki Committee (2001).

28. Several years later, as Croatian military leaders were accused of war crimes against Serb civilians in the International Criminal Tribunal for the former Yugoslavia (ICTY), this became a liability for the United States.

29. On Dayton and Tuđman's role in it, see Holbrooke (1998).

30. Kasapović (2001: 5) notes that there was no other post-communist democracy with such frequent and radical changes in its electoral system.

31. Interview with former HDZ official, Zagreb, May 2002.

32. Many of my Croatian associates who were students in the 1990s complained of the various privileges that students from Herzegovina received.

33. Bartlett (2003: 57) reports that different security services had come under the control of different factions of the HDZ, and these services were used to attack and discredit individuals who had fallen out of favor with the regime, such as former prime minister Hrvoje Šarinić.

34. Interview with Mate Granić, Zagreb, December 2001.

35. The independent media often published stories describing the lavish lifestyles of HDZ-affiliated tycoons.

36. For a biographical sketch of Tuđman, see Rogel (2004: 141–146). Zimmerman's (1996) observations on Tuđman are also insightful.

37. Apparently, his authoritarian tendencies were quite evident even then. He was unwilling to compromise, liked to give many speeches, and fired any staff who did not display complete loyalty to him. He also did a poor job of managing the organization's finances. Interview with Andrea Feldman, Zagreb, January 2002.

38. Interview with Žarko Puhovski, Zagreb, February 2002.

39. I have discussed the misappropriation of funds with a former staff member of the Croatian Diplomatic Corps familiar with the situation at the time.

40. Interview with former HDZ official, Zagreb, March 2002.

41. Based on personal correspondence and interviews in 2000.

42. The HSP was formed in February 1990 by the young dissident Dobroslav Paraga, who also led paramilitary units in Slavonia. It declared itself to be a continuation of Starčević's nineteenth-century right-wing movement. However, it was unable to gain many votes in the first elections. In 1993, after a fierce internal struggle, Ante Ðapić replaced Paraga as leader of the HSP. Paraga accused the HDZ of orchestrating his removal, and there is evidence that the HDZ wanted someone they could control more easily (Irvine 1997: 2). Meanwhile, Paraga formed his own party, the HSP-1861, and began to champion human rights. Interview with Dobroslav Paraga, Zagreb, November 2001.

43. The emphasis on the NDH as a political reference point for the HDZ regime was shown in its extensive rehabilitation of NDH symbols and personalities, after whom many squares and streets were renamed. There was also an all-out effort to purify the Croatian language by purging it of Serbian elements.

44. The degree to which the Roman Catholic Church was complicit in the HDZ's nationalist project has been a matter of some controversy. Though certain clerics, especially in rural areas, did openly support the HDZ, Bellamy (2002) argues that urban Roman Catholic leaders (as well as the Pope himself) were critical of the Tuđman regime.

45. Research shows that HDZ voters were more inclined toward authoritarianism than others (Grdešić 1991).

46. Interview with former member of HDZ, Zagreb, March 2002.

47. For more on the SDP's public avowal of social democracy, see the its website, at www.sdp.hr/.

48. For a history of the HSS, see Biondich (2000). At first there were actually several parties that claimed to continue the prewar Radić tradition.

49. Interview with Davorka Matić, Zagreb, June 2002.

50. This refers to the execution of thousands of Ustaša sympathizers and non-communists by Tito's Partisans at the conclusion of World War II.

51. Šiber (2001) has shown that an individual's family history (which camp they belonged to in World War II) helped determine voting patterns in the founding elections.

52. See, for instance, Šarinić (1999). For the testimony of current President Stjepan Mesić at the International Criminal Tribunal for the former Yugoslavia, see www.un.org/icty/.

53. There was also fighting in 1993, when Croatian forces launched as assault in the northern Dalmatia region and regained control over an airport and a key bridge linking central Croatia with the coast. This prompted the Krajina Serbs to fire shells into central Zagreb, one of the only times that the territory of the capital witnessed warfare.

54. For an analysis of how Croatian military strategy could be linked to the domestic political situation, see Kearns (1996).

55. Interview with Ivna Bajšić, Zagreb, February 2002.

56. Interview with U.S. diplomat, Zagreb, May 2002.

57. Interviews with Karen Gainer of the National Democratic Institute, Zagreb, November 2001; the staff of the International Republican Institute, Zagreb, March 2002; and Iva Bajšić of GONG, Zagreb, March 2002.

58. See the discussion in Bićanić (2001: 168–69).

59. However, Bićanić (2001: 169) argues that the decision not to introduce a war economy had a negative impact. For instance, high interest rates pushed many businesses into bankruptcy.

60. The kuna had been the currency in the wartime NDH and thus was a symbolic statement about the nature of the new regime, a very negative one for the regime's detractors.

61. Though not high enough for an economy undergoing postwar reconstruction, argues Bićanić (2001).

62. Projects included railway and hospital modernization (Bartlett 2003: 101–2).

63. Interview with Vojmir Franičević, Zagreb, February 2002.

64. On the winners of transition and semi-reform, see Hellman (1998). For an account of various tycoon scandals, see Bartlett (2003: 113).

65. There were some negative externalities, however: the war in Kosovo and the 1999 NATO bombing of Yugoslavia disrupted tourism.

66. *The Economist*, 10 January 1998, pp. 37–38.

67. Interview with Ivo Banac, Dubrovnik, June 2002.

68. Interview with Žarko Puhovski, Zagreb, March 2002.

69. See the interview with Škrabalo in Markovich (1997).

CHAPTER FIVE: Substantive Democracy

Epigraph: Quoted in Magaš (1993: 134).

1. In fact, Harris notes that in 1986, 61.1 percent of respondents in Slovenia agreed that "a strong arm that knows what it wants would be of more use to our society than all the slogans about self-management" (2002: 141).

2. Harris (2002: 134). Harris also notes that the immigrant population voted for Slovenian independence.

3. Interview with Rudi Rizman, Ljubljana, June 2002.

4. Ibid.

5. On the institutions of Slovenian democracy, see Lukšič (2001).

6. Strictly speaking, the Slovenian system was neither unicameral nor bicameral. The National Council has limited powers, and it acts as a consultative body. See Mrak et al. (2004: 56).

7. There is some contention over Slovenia's record on human rights in the early 1990s especially with regard to the judiciary (Ramet 1997a: 208).

8. Fink-Hafner (1994: 387), however, also emphasizes the role of political mobilization from below in pushing for these first free elections.

9. Interview with Alenka Krašovec, Ljubljana, June 2002.

10. In practice, over time the prime minister and government have acquired even more power than the constitution might suggest (Gow and Carmichael 2000: 142).

11. A key element in the SNS's program was its fight against citizenship and social welfare rights for refugees, guest workers, and other migrants from the southern republics of the former Yugoslavia. Jelinčić argued that citizenship should be an "honor" that is "hard to earn" (Kuzmanić 1999: 125). As such, the SNS called for the cancellation of the existing citizenship law, the revocation of the citizenship of all non-Slovenes who had gained citizen's rights after 25 December 1990, and the reduction of the number of non-Slovenians in Slovenia by 90 percent (Kuzmanić 1999: 125). Its economic program was short and called for the closure of all socialist-era "political" factories, which would achieve several nationalist (and, surprisingly, environmental) objectives: workers from other republics would go home, freeing housing and jobs for young Slovenians, and energy would be freed up (as the political factories consumed 40 percent of Slovenia's potential energy). Thus, there was a "synergy" among the SNS's biggest enemies: "heavy, dirty industry; socialism; and workers from the other Yugoslav republics" (Kuzmanić 1999: 125). There was one more critical element of the SNS's platform: throughout the 1990s, it opposed EU membership for Slovenia, calling it the "totalitarian dictate of Europe" (Kuzmanić 1999: 125). Paradoxically, SNS was also pro-choice and anticlerical.

12. Interview with Alenka Krašovec, Ljubljana, June 2002.

13. These included: responsibility over the nuclear power plant at Krško; demarcations of the land and sea border; fishing rights in Piran Bay; and the rights of the Croat minority in Slovenia.

14. See polls noted by Fink-Hafner (1994: 397).

15. Interview with former Slovenian legislator, Ljubjlana, April 2002.

16. Ibid.

17. Ibid.

18. Ibid.

19. However, Ferfila and Phillips note that "the extent of the Slovenian depression can be exaggerated.... After the major North American recession in the early 1990s, average incomes only returned to pre-recession levels in the late 1990s, at about approximately the same time as Slovenian incomes recovered to 1989 levels. Indeed, this comparison underscores an important point—the economic success of Slovenia not only in comparison to other transitional economies, but also to major Western economies" (2000: 177–78).

20. Interview with Jože Mencinger, Ljubljana, June 2002.

21. Studies show that FDI has been an important factor propelling improvements in technology and quality in advanced transition economies such as Hungary (Bojnec 2000: 1334).

22. That Slovenia's model of privatization has inhibited firm performance, however, is a matter of debate. Though international financial institutions have been sharply critical of Slovenian policies as hurting efficiency, Ferfila and Phillips (2000) present enterprise-level evidence to argue that the effect of manager-buyout privatization was not negative at all.

23. Bojnec (2000: 1335). Bojnec notes that typically 40 percent of a company's shares were transferred free of charge to state funds; 20 percent was allocated to employees free of charge; and the remaining 40 percent was privatized using a variety of methods, though priority was given to labor and management buyouts at a substantial discount.

24. Interview with Bogomil Ferfila, Dubrovnik, June 2002.

25. On corporatism in Slovenia and its relation to communist-era institutions, see Ferfila and Phillips (2000: ch. 2).

26. In an analysis of Slovenian enterprises carried out in 1996 and 1997, Bojnec (2000) found that capital for investment was lacking in enterprises subjected to "insider" or delayed privatization. By contrast, enterprises set up during the transition period received much higher levels of investment.

27. *Progress Towards Accession*, quoted in Jeffries (2002: 369–70).

CHAPTER SIX: Illegitimate Democracy

Epigraph: Quoted in Georgievski (2001).

1. On the history of the development of a Macedonian national identity, see Poulton (1995) and Brown (2003). Allcock observes "there can be little doubt about the success of the project to create a Macedonian *nation*, but the conditions of that success have confirmed the problematic nature of Macedonia's position as a state" (1999: 162).

2. Hislope (2002, 2003) in particular has written extensively about the connection linking corruption, organized crime, nationalism, and armed rebellion in Macedonia. The 2001 war is covered in chapter 8 of this volume.

3. Interview with Mirjana Maleska, Skopje, June 2003.

4. For example, see Szajkowski (2000).

5. Much of the data presented here is based on Karatnycky (1999).

6. See the interview with Gligorov in Liotta (2001). The JNA also took with it critical infrastructure, such as the radar equipment at Skopje International Airport.

7. Interview with Vasko Naumovski, Skopje, June 2003.

8. Interview with Dane Taleski, Skopje, June 2003.

9. Interview with Vasko Naumovski, Skopje, June 2003.

10. Interview with Denko Maleski, Skopje, June 2003.

11. Interview with Ilo Trajkovski, Skopje, June 2003.

12. This subsection is based in part on my conversations with a number of Macedonian scholars, analysts, and members of political parties in June 2003.

13. Interview with Kristina Balalovska, Washington, D.C., July 2003.

14. VMRO-DPMNE was actually one of a number of political parties to have appropriated the VMRO designation for its identity. All claimed to be a continuation of the original VMRO, founded in 1893 and based in Thessaloniki, Greece. VMRO-Fatherland, VMRO-United, and the VMRO-Goce Delchev-Radical Democratic Party were others, though their influence was minimal compared to the dominant VMRO-DPMNE; for this reason the VMRO label, rather than the cumbersome VMRO-DPMNE, is used throughout.

15. Interview with Dane Taleski, Skopje, June 2003.

16. Interview with Kristina Balalovska, Washington, D.C., July 2003.

17. Interview with ethnic Albanian politician, Skopje, June 2003.

18. Interview with Vasko Naumovski, Skopje, June 2003.

19. Interview with Lidija Naum, Skopje, June 2003.

20. Interview with Ilo Trajkovski, Skopje, June 2003.

21. On ethnicity, identity, and the history of ethnic relations in Macedonia, see Poulton (1995), Cowan (2000), Barker (2001), Drezov (2001), and Brown (2003). On the ethnic Albanian minority in particular, see Najčevska et al. (1996) and Pettifer (2001). This section draws heavily on Hislope (2003).

22. Interview with a Macedonian political analyst, June 2003.

23. The birthrate among ethnic Albanians was 25 births annually per 1000 people in the 1990s. Over half of Macedonia's Albanians are under the age of 27. The average family size of Albanian families was six members. By comparison, the Macedonian birthrate was 1.7 children per family (Balalovska 2003).

24. Personal communication with Ivan Krastev, Toronto, February 2003.

25. Interview with Habib Massoud, Skopje, June 2003.

26. Ibid.

27. The information about elections comes from an interview with Chris Deliso, Kumanovo, June 2003.

28. Interview with VMRO official, Skopje, June 2003.

29. At least until the conflict of 2001, the UNPREDEP mission had been hailed as a successful international preventive peace mission. Its success has been attributed

to its comprehensive, yet clear and flexible mandate (Vayrynen 2003: 51). The total costs of conflict prevention were determined to be $255 million, compared to the costs of a potential conflict, estimated to cost $15 billion to $143 billion, depending on its length (Vayrynen 2003: 52). The UNPREDEP mission produced a remarkable number of analyses by participants and observers, including Leatherman (1999), Williams (2000), Ackermann (2000), Vayrynen (2003), and Sokalski (2003).

30. Interview with former Macedonian cabinet minister, Skopje, June 2003.

31. For examples, see Williams (2000) and Sokalski (2003).

32. Interview with Denko Maleski, Skopje, June 2003.

33. Interview with Vasko Naumovski, Skopje, June 2003.

34. See his interview with Chris Deliso at www.antiwar.com.

35. Interview with Macedonian official, Skopje, June 2003.

36. Interview with Lidija Naum, Skopje, June 2003.

37. Interview with Kristina Balalovska, Washington, D.C., July 2003.

38. Interview with Ljubiša Adamović, Portland, Oregon, March 2003.

39. Interview with Kristina Balalovska, Washington, D.C., July 2003.

CHAPTER SEVEN: Populist Authoritarianism

1. Popov (1996) notes that there is a "tradition" of populist nationalism in Serbia. Lenard Cohen traces a political culture of victimization to the early twentieth century. Interview with Lenard Cohen, Sarajevo, July 2002.

2. Nationalist rhetoric was also voiced at this time by the Serbian Writers' Union (Udruženje književnika Srbije, UKS). These pronouncements were meant to reflect the frustrations of the peasantry and not necessarily urban dwellers.

3. He also did little to help the flood of ethnic Serb refugees that migrated to Serbia proper in the 1990s.

4. This aspect of Serbian political culture is also captured in a popular anecdote. In 2000, when Vojislav Koštunica was a candidate for President of FRY, a farmer told him that he would vote for Koštunica if he (meaning Koštunica) happened to be in power one day.

5. According to Slavoljub Đukić, when Milan Panić asked Milošević why he had allowed Dobrica Ćosić to occupy the post of federal president while he was "only" president of Serbia, Milošević answered: "Milan, it isn't important where I'm at. For Serbia I'm a kind of Khomeini." Quoted in Cohen (2001: 164).

6. Interview with Damian Murphy, Belgrade, April 2002.

7. This is why large numbers of Serbians were left completely in the dark about the war in neighboring Bosnia and did not know about the massacre at Srebrenica, for instance. In the long run, even independent media outlets turned to strictly entertainment programming as disenchantment with politics grew.

8. I deal in this section mainly with the Serbian parliamentary elections, since it was the Serbian legislature that mattered most in shaping the development of postcommunist FRY. There were, however, also elections to the federal parliament and

elections to Montenegro's legislature, which mattered more in the second half of the 1990s.

9. Montenegro also held elections in 1990 that produced a victory for the Democratic Party of Socialists, led by Momir Bulatović, who initially distanced himself from Belgrade but then became a Milošević ally.

10. Interview with Marko Romčević, Novi Sad, July 2001.

11. For more on Drašković and his writings, see Vujačić (1995).

12. Interview with Goran Lapčević, Toronto, February 2001.

13. Many of these students subsequently emigrated to the West (Gordy 1999: 44).

14. On the history of Kosovo, see Malcolm (1998) and Cohen (2001: ch. 1). This subsection is largely drawn from the accounts of these two authors. Kosovo is called "Kosova" in Albanian.

15. Interview with Serbian political analyst, Belgrade, March 2002.

16. For a comprehensive account of the protests, see Lazić (1999).

17. The Church was devastated by the loss of Kosovo and supported Milošević's efforts to retain it. "We blame Milošević not for trying to defend the nation but for failing," said one bishop (Cohen 2001: 320).

18. Interview with Zoran Slavujević, Belgrade, April 2002.

19. The 1992 data actually probably undercounts the real level of SPS support, since many strong SPS supporters voted for the SRS that year.

20. Interview with Živorad Kovačević, Belgrade, April 2002.

21. Interview with U.S. diplomat, Belgrade, March 2002.

22. Interview with Marko Romčević, Novi Sad, July 2001.

23. Interview with U.S. diplomat, Zagreb, May 2002.

24. Interview with European diplomat, Belgrade, March 2002.

25. Anonymous interview with U.S. diplomat, Zagreb, June 2002.

26. Interview with Damian Murphy, Belgrade, April 2002. On Koštunica, see Cigar (2002).

27. Cohen (2001: 202) provides several reasons why Milošević capitulated when he did: he could not count on national unity forever; morale in the army was low; he could extract his military forces intact; his power would have been threatened by a ground invasion; NATO was cohesive; and he could not expect any help from external actors, such as Russia.

28. Šešelj and the Radicals fiercely opposed the agreement, saying it was a sell-out.

29. This subsection benefits from Cohen (2001).

30. Interview with Tatjana Radulović, Dubrovnik, June 2002. For more, see the biographical portrait of Đukanović at www.esiweb.org.

31. Montenegrin society was traditionally divided by clans, and the ties binding them persist to this very day and influence politics and economics. See Banac (1984: 45) and Anzulović (1999: 46).

32. Even in the late nineteenth century, there were divisions in Montenegro over whether to continue independence or pursue a union with Serbia.

33. Interview with European diplomat, Belgrade, June 2002.

34. Interview with EU official, Zagreb, June 2003.

35. Interview with Montenegrin political analyst, Dubrovnik, June 2002.

36. At various points, both Vuk Drašković and Zoran Đinđić were in exile in Podgorica.

37. However, on a positive note, public opinion research indicated that Montenegrins had more confidence in their institutions than Serbians (Cohen 2001: 331).

38. Milošević was warned, however, that NATO would take action if he provoked a military conflict with Montenegro.

39. *International Herald Tribune*, 21 August 1996, p. 2.

40. Interview with Radovan Vukadinović, Zagreb, June 2002.

41. See Economist Intelligence Unit, *Serbia Country Report* (2000).

CHAPTER EIGHT: The Yugoslav Successor States in the New Millennium

Epigraph: Delo, 1 May 2004, www.delo.si.

1. Updates on post-2000 political developments in this chapter, unless otherwise noted, are drawn from *Transitions Online* (www.tol.cz), Radio Free Europe–Radio Liberty (www.rferl.org), the *Southeast European Times* (www.setimes.com), *Vjesnik* (www.vjesnik.com), and B92 (www.b92.net). All poll results, unless otherwise noted, are from www.balkan-monitor.eu. References to EU progress reports are from http://europa.eu/rapid/.

2. At the 2003 Thessaloniki Summit, the EU reaffirmed its commitment to integrating the Balkan states into European structures.

3. See http://ec.europa.eu/enlargement/.

4. On the treatment of "outsiders" in Slovenia, see Pajnik et al. (2001).

5. As of January 2009, the mosque has still not been built.

6. *International Herald Tribune*, 29 March 2007. Slovenia has very low levels of FDI compared to other top-tier transition countries. From 1989 through 2005, foreign direct investment in Slovenia totaled $1,536 per person, compared with $5,061 in the Czech Republic and $4,229 in Hungary, according to the 2006 Transition Report by the European Bank for Reconstruction and Development. www.ebrd.com.

7. Ibid.

8. Interview with EU official, Zagreb, June 2003.

9. See www.freedomhouse.org.

10. See *Nacional*, 28 May 2001.

11. See Peskin and Boduszyński (2003).

12. On the U.S.-EU quarrel over Article 98 and its effect on Balkan politics, see Boduszyński and Balalovska (2004).

13. See *Globus*, 5 July 2004.

14. Interview with Chris Lamont, Zagreb, June 2003.

15. Nevertheless, in November 2004 another "cold shower" came when the Financial Times estimated that Croatia was unlikely to enter the EU before 2011. "Such predictions in the media have a very negative effect on the general public mood, especially since so much has been invested in this project but the results are still mea-

ger," says political analyst Vlatko Cvrtila. Quoted in *Transitions Online*, 8 November 2004.

16. See interview with Foreign Minister Gordan Jandraković in Rijeka Novi List, 2 February 2008.

17. The poverty rate was over 40 percent in 2002. See Economist Intelligence Unit (2003).

18. Personal correspondence with a Serbian political analyst. This was also widely reported in the Serbian and Western press.

19. *Transitions Online*, 4 January 2004. www.tol.cz.

20. See, for instance, the interview with EU High Representative for Common Foreign and Security Policy Javier Solana in *Koha Ditore*, 16 February 2004.

21. Quoted in *Transitions Online*, 30 June 2004. www.tol.cz.

22. Ibid.

23. Ibid.

24. Seventy-five percent of Serbians say they spend all of their salary on food and clothing.

25. Quoted in *Transitions Online*, 31 January 2007.

26. Ibid.

27. Koštunica was appealing to genuine public sentiment: polls at the time showed that 74 percent of Serbians were not willing to accept the acceleration of EU integration if losing Kosovo was a condition (Jovanovic 2008).

28. The U.S. apparently disagreed but deferred to Brussels. See Pond (2006: 233).

29. See, for instance, the interview with Đukanović in *Utrinski Vesnik*, 29 April 2006.

30. Personal communication, Serbian analyst, December 2006.

31. See www.freedomhouse.org.

32. The unveiling of the proposal in February 2007 stimulated violent protests by Kosovar groups who wanted nothing less than full independence. I was in Kosovo then and could hear the gunshots as international police forces fired on the demonstrators with rubber bullets, ostensibly to prevent them from damaging property. Two young protestors were accidentally killed. Lingering tear gas made one's eyes sting for many hours afterwards.

33. See http://europa.eu/rapid/.

34. Apparently this was also due to lobbying in Washington by émigré Albanian groups. Anonymous interview with U.S. diplomat, Skopje, June 2003.

35. Interview with Kristina Balalovska, Washington D.C., July 2003.

36. Interview with Macedonian government official, Skopje, June 2003.

37. Interview with Chris Deliso, Kumanovo, June 2003.

38. For example, see Vaknin (2002). Vaknin describes a society in which criminal gangs are tied to politicians, and regard Macedonia as a vital route for trafficking. He writes: "Crime and war provide employment, status, regular income, perks, and livelihood to many denizens of Macedonia, Albania, and Bulgaria. They constitute an outlet for entrepreneurship, however perverted. Fighting for the cause and smuggling often means travel abroad (for instance, on fundraising missions), five-star ac-

commodation, and a lavish lifestyle. It also translates into powers of patronage and excesses of self-enrichment. Moreover, in ossified, socially stratified, ethnically polarized, and economically impoverished societies, war and crime engender social mobility. The likes of Hashim Thaçi and Ali Ahmeti often start as rebels and end as part of the cosseted establishment. Many a criminal dabble in politics and business. Hence the tenacity of both phenomena. Hence the bleak and pessimistic outlook for this region. The 'formal' economies simply cannot compete."

39. See the report of the Macedonian Helsinki Committee at www.nhc.no/php/files/documents/Publikasjoner/Rapporter/Valgobservasjon/2002macedonia.pdf.

40. Public opinion polls indicated that only 30 percent of Macedonians support the provisions of Ohrid (Balalovska 2003).

41. *Transitions Online*, 10 November 2004.

42. In fact, Gruevski wanted both Albanian parties in his government, but fighting among them and resistance from hardline factions in VMRO prevented this from happening. Author's personal communication with Macedonian political analyst, May 2009.

43. See http://europa.eu/rapid/.

44. In 2003, one-fourth of the country's 2 million citizens lived in poverty and in 2004, unemployment stood at 37 percent. RFE/RL Report, 12 December 2003; Ramet (2006: 567).

45. International aid was well over $100 million in 2002 and was entirely used to overcome budgetary problems. A plethora of Macedonian NGOs is also addicted to foreign grants but does little in terms of fulfilling the stated mission. Starting an NGO is also the easiest way to make money, as it provides the safest flow of money and source of employment (Dimitrov 2003).

46. See the report "Macedonia: No Time for Complacency" at www.crisisweb.org.

47. On electoral revolutions, see Bunce and Wolchik (2007).

48. For an analysis of these elections, see Boduszyński (2004).

49. See *Jutarnji List*, 16 February 2004.

50. Personal communication with Serbian political analyst, December 2007. This analyst noted that in terms of institutional strength, Serbia easily matches Croatia and wins over the other candidate states, and the EU knows this.

51. See http://ec.europa.eu/enlargement/key_documents/reports_nov_2007_en.htm.

52. The 2007 progress reports note that the EU hopes that Croatia will send "a strong signal to other Western Balkans countries on their own membership prospects, once they fulfill the necessary conditions." See http://ec.europa.eu/enlargement/key_documents/reports_nov_2007_en.htm.

53. Grabbe (2006) argues that the potential of conditionality has not been realized because of inconsistency and lack of precision in the EU's membership criteria.

CHAPTER NINE: Conclusions

Epigraphs: Kundera (2006: 33); http:europa.eu.int/rapid/start/welcome.html/.

1. Anderson (2001: 59) observes that much of the literature adopted a minimalist

definition of democracy. Munck (2009: 13) notes that many quantitative researchers pay sparse attention to the quality of the democracy measures that they employ.

2. See the results of the 2002 IDEA survey at www.idea.int.

3. On path dependence, see Pierson (1996); on post-communism and path dependence, see Stark and Bruszt (1998); on "critical junctures," see Collier and Collier (1991).

4. As Gerschenkron (1962) reminds us, late development necessitates extensive state involvement in an effort to "catch up," and this involvement can become a liability to democracy later on.

5. Horowitz (2003) also presents results that point to the importance of certain initial conditions in explaining post-communist outcomes.

6. Pop-Eleches also shows that "some of the statistical discrepancies in the legacy-democracy link are due to the fact that different regime indicators capture distinct aspects of democracy" (2007b: 908). For instance, ethnic plurality explains the gap between political institutions and actual rights, while imperial legacy may better explain institutional configurations.

7. Ekiert et al. (2007: 13) also note the growing evidence that structural constraints and historical legacies greatly influence political outcomes in the region.

8. From Pop-Eleches's presentation at the 2003 Annual Meeting of the American Political Science Association, Philadelphia, Pennsylvania.

9. Levitsky and Way (2005).

10. Pridham et al. (1997), Whitehead (2001), Kurtz and Barnes (2002), Kubicek (2003), Levistky and Way (2005), Pridham (2005), Vachodová (2005), and Grabbe (2006).

11. Schimmelfennig notes that after the European Council offered Turkey candidate status in 1999 and judged it by the same criteria as other countries, "it triggered more serious and thorough democratic reforms than ever before in more than thirty years of Turkish association with the European Union" (2007: 130).

12. See http://europa.eu.int/comm/external_relations/see/actions/sap.htm/.

13. It is interesting to note that in the northwest "tier" of Eastern Europe it is the former right-wing opposition that has become increasingly Euroskeptic (witness the phenomenon of Václav Klaus in the Czech Republic), while in the Southeast "tier" former communists and some right-wing populists have been converted to the EU (like Serbia's Tomislav Nikolić).

14. Rupnik (2007) and Butora (2007) cover the (re)emergence of nationalism and populism in many post-communist countries after entering the EU. The 2009 edition of *Nations in Transit* found that illiberal proclivities were on the rise throughout the region. It registered declines in seven countries and stagnation in two. See www.freedomhouse.org.

15. For instance, see Roeder (1994).

16. See Chandler (2000) and Bose (2002). Western-imposed norms also have not succeeded in fostering loyalty toward the Bosnian state among many ethnic Croats and Serbs (Wood 2004a).

17. Grabbe writes: "Priority setting at domestic level involves some strategic choice, but processes of Europeanization tend to develop a logic and momentum of their own which do not depend wholly on top-down direction from government. Instead, EU tasks are written into the work-programmes of national ministries and a layer of local officials becomes 'Europeanised' through contact with the EU and through training courses and participation in EU programmes. The routinisation of EU practices has a long-term effect" (2006: 203).

18. See Carothers (2002), Levitsky and Way (2002), and Ottaway (2003).

19. A similar point is made in Whitehead (1993).

20. On the third wave, see Huntington (1991).

21. On political crafting, see Di Palma (1990).

22. Larry Diamond (2009) argues that economic development based on a single natural resource, such as that which has taken place in Venezuela and Russia and helped prop up authoritarianism, is distorted and unsustainable (oil revenue also makes these states less receptive to outside pressure for democratization).

23. Diamond (1999: 30) has noted that save for two tiny island states, there are no autocracies in the world that could possibly qualify as liberal. In other words, it is difficult to envision civil and human rights in the absence of political liberties.

24. See Lipset (1960), Cutright (1963), Dahl (1971), Jackman (1973), Huntington (1984), Bollen (1990), Rueschemeyer et al. (1992), Lipset, Seong, and Torres (1993), Burkhart and Lewis-Beck (1994), Londegran and Poole (1996), Przeworski and Limongi (1993, 1997), and Przeworski et al. (1998). Mainwaring and Perez-Linan (2003) find that Latin America is an exception in this regard. My thanks to Scott Mainwaring for providing the data and for his advice.

25. Personal communication with Victor Peskin, December 2008.

26. *Transitions Online*, "After the Rupture." 7 January 2008. www.tol.cz/.

27. See the declaration of this summit at http://ec.europa.eu/enlargement/enlargement_process/accession_process/.

28. See the analysis at www.iiea.com.

29. Personal communication with Vlatka Blagus, December 2008.

30. See www.balkan-monitor.eu.

31. Fish and Krickovic (2003) have written about the Christian Democratic transformation of the HDZ.

32. See the 15 June 2009 commentary by Milan Popović in *Vijesti*, www.vijesti.cg.yu.

33. A Gallup poll analyst suggested in 2009 that the threshold of tolerance with respect to corruption is too high in Montenegro. See www.balkan-monitor.eu.

34. See www.balkan-monitor.eu/.

35. Ibid.

36. Personal communication with EU diplomat, October 2008.

37. Quoted in MIA news agency, 5 June 2009. www.mia.com.mk.

38. See http://ec.europa.eu/public_opinion/.

39. However, some in Brussels privately admit that the ICTY cooperation issue

has become a convenient excuse to use in slowing down enlargement, given the current lack of public support for further expansion in EU member states. Personal communication with Victor Peskin, December 2008.

40. From http://europe.eu.int/rapid/start/welcome.htm/.

41. Agence France Presse, 17 March 2009.

42. A formulation first used by U.S. president George H. W. Bush during a speech in Mainz, Germany, in May 1989.

References

Ackermann, Alice. 2000. *Making Peace Prevail: Preventing Violent Conflict in Macedonia*. Syracuse, NY: Syracuse University Press.

Allcock, John B. 1999. "Macedonia." In *The States of Eastern Europe. Volume II: South-Eastern Europe*, ed. David Turnock and Francis W. Carter. Aldershot, U.K.: Ashgate.

Almond, Gabriel A., and Sidney Verba. 1963. *The Civic Culture: Political Attitudes and Democracy in Five Nations*. Princeton, NJ: Princeton University Press.

Anderson, Richard D., M. Steven Fish, Stephen E. Hanson, and Philip G. Roeder, eds. 2001. *Postcommunism and the Theory of Democracy*. Princeton, NJ: Princeton University Press.

Anzulović, Branimir. 1999. *Heavenly Serbia: From Myth to Genocide*. London: C. Hurst.

Apter, David E. 1965. *The Politics of Modernization*. Chicago: University of Chicago Press.

Balalovska, Kristina. 2003. "Between 'The Balkans' and 'Europe': A Study of the Contemporary Transformation of Macedonian Identity, 1991–2002," *New Balkan Politics* 6/7.

———. 2006. *Macedonia 2006: Towards Stability?* Rome: Ethnobarometer Working Paper 11.

Banac, Ivo. 1984. *The National Question in Yugoslavia: Origins, History, Politics*. Ithaca, NY: Cornell University Press.

Baranyi, Zoltan, and Ivan Volgyes. 1995. *The Legacy of Communism in Eastern Europe*. Baltimore: Johns Hopkins University Press.

Barker, Elisabeth. 2001. "The Origin of the Macedonian Dispute." In *The New Macedonian Question*, ed. James Pettifer. London: Palgrave.

Barker, Rodney S. 1990. *Political Legitimacy and the State*. Oxford: Oxford University Press.

Bartlett, William. 2000. "Economic Transformation and Democratization in the Balkans." In *Experimenting with Democracy: Regime Change in the Balkans,* ed. Geoffrey Pridham and Tom Gallagher. London: Routledge.

———. 2003. *Croatia: Between Europe and the Balkans*. London: Routledge.

Bellamy, Alex J. 2001. "Croatia after Tudjman: The 2000 Parliamentary and Presidential Elections." *Problems of Post-Communism* 48, no. 5.

———. 2002. "The Catholic Church and Croatia's Two Transitions." *Religion, State, and Society* 30, no. 1.

Benderly, Jill, and Evan Kraft. 1994. *Independent Slovenia: Origins, Movements, Prospects*. New York: St. Martin's.

Bernik, Ivan. 1997. *Dvojno odčaranje politike: Sedem socioloških razprav o nastajanju postsocialističnih družb*. Ljubljana: Fakulteta za družbene vede.

Beyer, Jürgen, J. Wielgohs, and H. Wiesenthal. 2001. *Successful Transitions: Political Factors of Socio-Economic Progress in Postsocialist Countries*. Baden-Baden: Nomos.

Bieber, Florian. 2006. "Looking Each Other in the Eye." *Transitions Online*, 23 May. Available at www.tol.cz.

Bićanić, Ivo. 2001. "Croatia." In *Balkan Reconstruction*, ed. Daniel Daianu and Thanos Veremis. London: Frank Cass.

Biondich, Mark. 2000. *Stjepan Radić, The Croat Peasant Party and the Politics of Mass Mobilization, 1904–1928*. Toronto: University of Toronto Press.

Boduszyński, Mieczysław P. 2004. "The Return of Nationalists in Serbia and Croatia: Is Democracy Threatened?" *WWICS EES Newsletter*, September/October.

Boduszyński, Mieczysław P., and Kristina Balalovska. 2004. "Between a Rock and a Hard Place: Croatia, Macedonia, and the Battle over Article 98." *Problems of Post-Communism* 51, no. 1: 18–30.

Bojnec, Stefan. 2000. "Restructuring and Marketing Strategies at Macro and Micro Levels: The Case of Slovenia." *Europe Asia Studies* 52, no. 7: 1331–48.

Bollen, Kenneth A. 1990. "Political Democracy: Conceptual and Measurement Traps." *Studies in Comparative International Development* 25, no. 7: 7–24.

Bombelles, Joseph T. 1991. "Federal Aid to the Less Developed Areas of Yugoslavia." *East European Politics and Societies* 5, no. 3 (Fall): 439–65.

Bose, Sumantra. 2002. *Bosnia after Dayton: Nationalist Partition and International Intervention*. Oxford: Oxford University Press.

Brady, Henry E., and David Collier. 2004. *Rethinking Social Inquiry: Diverse Tools, Shared Standards*. Lanham, MD: Rowman and Littlefield.

Brinar, Irena. 1999. "Slovenia: From Yugoslavia to the European Union." In *Back to Europe: Central and Eastern Europe and the European Union*, ed. Karen Henderson. Philadelphia: UCL Press.

Brown, James F. 2001. *The Grooves of Change: Eastern Europe at the Turn of the Millennium*. Durham, NC: Duke University Press.

Brown, Keith. 2003. *The Past in Question: Modern Macedonia and the Uncertainties of Nation*. Princeton, NJ: Princeton University Press.

Bugajski, Janusz. 2002. *Political Parties of Eastern Europe: A Guide to Politics in the Post-Communist Era*. Armonk, NY: M. E. Sharpe.

Bukowski, Charles. 1999. "Slovenia's Transition to Democracy: Theory and Practice." *East European Quarterly* 33, no. 1 (March): 69–96.

Bunce, Valerie. 1999. "The Political Economy of Postsocialism," *Slavic Review* 58, no. 4.

———. 2000. "Comparative Democratization: Big and Bounded Generalizations." *Comparative Political Studies* 33, no. 6/7.

———. 2003. "Rethinking Recent Democratization: Lessons from the Postcommunist Experience." *World Politics* 55.

Bunce, Valerie J., and Sharon L. Wolchik. 2007. "Favorable Conditions and Electoral Revolutions." *Journal of Democracy* 18, no. 4 (October).

Burkhart, Ross E., and Michael S. Lewis-Beck. 1994. "Comparative Democracy, The Economic Development Thesis." *American Political Science Review* 88, no. 4, 903–10.

Butora, Martin. 2007. "Nightmares of the Past, Dreams of the Future." *Journal of Democracy* 18, no. 4 (October).

Cabada, Ladislav. 2001. "Konsolidacija Demokracije v Postjugoslovanskem Prostoru v Primerjavi s Postsovjetsko Evropo." In *Demokraticni Prehodi II*, ed. Danica Fink-Hafner and Miro Haček. Ljubljana: Fakulteta za Družbene Vede.

Cardais, S. Adam. 2008. "Europe: Jekyll and Hyde." *Transitions Online*, 30 June.

Carothers, Thomas. 2002. "The End of the Transition Paradigm." *Journal of Democracy* 13, no. 1.

Chandler, David. 2000. *Bosnia: Faking Democracy after Dayton*. Sterling, VA: Pluto Press.

Chua, Amy. 2003. *World on Fire: How Exporting Free Market Democracy Breeds Ethnic Hatred and Global Instability*. New York: Doubleday.

Cigar, Norman. 2002. *Vojislav Koštunica and Serbia's Future*. London: Palgrave.

Clark, Terry D. 2006. "Nationalism in Post-Soviet Lithuania: New Approaches for the Nation of Innocent Sufferers." In *After Independence*, ed. Lowell W. Barrengton. Ann Arbor: University of Michigan Press.

Cohen, Lenard J. 1993. *Broken Bonds: The Disintegration of Yugoslavia*. Boulder, CO: Westview Press.

———. 1997. "Embattled Democracy: Post Communist Croatia in Transition." In *Politics, Power, and the Struggle for Democracy in South-East Europe*, ed. Karen Dawisha and Bruce Parrott. Cambridge, U.K.: Cambridge University Press.

———. 2001. *Serpent in the Bosom: The Rise and Fall of Slobodan Milošević*. Boulder, CO: Westview Press.

Collier, David. 1991. "New Perspectives on the Comparative Method." Working paper, Institute of Governmental Studies, University of California, Berkeley.

Collier, David, and Steven Levitsky. 1997. *Democracy "with Adjectives": Conceptual Innovation in Comparative Research*. Notre Dame, Indiana: Helen Kellogg Institute for International Studies.

Collier, Ruth Berins, and David Collier. 1991. *Shaping the Political Arena*. Princeton, NJ: Princeton University Press.

Coppedge, Michael. 2004. "Quality of Democracy and Its Measurement." In *The Quality of Democracy: Theory and Applications*, ed. Guillermo O'Donnell, Jorge Vargas Cullell, and Osvaldo M. Iazzetta. Notre Dame: University of Notre Dame Press.

Cowan, Jane, ed. 2000. *Macedonia: The Politics of Identity and Difference*. London: Pluto Press.

Croatian Helsinki Committee for Human Rights. 2001. *Military Operation Storm and Its Aftermath*. Zagreb: Croatian Helsinki Committee for Human Rights.

Čular, Goran. 2000. "Institucionalizacija Strankarskega Sistema v Nekonsolidirani Demokraciji: Primer Hrvaške." In *Demokraticni Prehodi I*, ed. Danica Fink-Hafner and Miro Haček. Ljubljana: Fakulteta za Družbene Vede.

Cutright, Phillips. 1963. "National Political Development: Measurement and Analysis." *American Sociological Review* 28 (April).

Dahl, Robert. 1956. *A Preface to Democratic Theory.* Chicago: University of Chicago Press.

———. 1971. *Polyarchy, Participation, and Opposition.* New Haven: Yale University Press.

———. 1982. *Dilemmas of Pluralist Democracy: Autonomy vs. Control.* New Haven: Yale University Press.

Darden, Keith, and Anna Grzymala-Busse. 2005. "The Great Divide: Pre-Communist Schooling and Post-Communist Trajectories." Presented at the annual meeting of the American Political Science Association.

Di Palma, Giuseppe. 1990. *To Craft Democracies: An Essay on Democratic Transitions.* Berkeley: University of California Press.

Diamandouros, P. Nikiforos, and F. Stephen Larrabee. 2000. "Democratization in South-Eastern Europe: Theoretical Considerations and Evolving Trends." In *Experimenting with Democracy: Regime Change in the Balkans,* ed. Geoffrey Pridham and Tom Gallagher, 24–64. London: Routledge.

Diamond, Larry. 1999. *Developing Democracy: Toward Consolidation.* Baltimore: Johns Hopkins University Press, 1999.

———. 2009. "The Shape of Global Democracy." *Brown Journal of World Affairs* 15, no. 2.

Diamond, Larry, and Leonardo Morlino, eds. 2005. *Assessing the Quality of Democracy.* Baltimore: Johns Hopkins University Press.

Dimitrov, Petre. 2003. "Corruption Rife among Macedonia's NGOs." *TOL Wire,* 1 August. Available at www.tol.cz.

Dinkić, Mlađan. 2000. *Ekonomija Destrukcije.* Belgrade: VIN.

Dizdarević, Raif. 1999. *Od smrti Tita do smrti Jugoslavije.* Sarajevo: Svjedok.

Djokić, Dejan, ed. 2003. *Yugoslavism: Histories of a Failed Idea, 1918–1992.* London: Hurst.

Drakulić, Slavenka. 1999. "Intellectuals as Bad Guys." *East European Politics and Societies* 13, no. 2.

Drašković, Vuk. 1982. *Nož.* Belgrade: Zapis.

Drezov, Kyril. 2001. "Macedonian Identity: An Overview of the Major Claims." In *The New Macedonian Question,* ed. James Pettifer, 47–59. London: Palgrave.

Dryzek, John S., and Holmes, Leslie. 2002. *Post-Communist Democratization: Political Discourses across Thirteen Countries.* Cambridge, U.K.: Cambridge University Press.

Dyker, David A. 1990. *Yugoslavia: Socialism, Development, and Debt.* London: Routledge.

The Economist. 1998. "The Croatians are Coming." Vol. 346, no. 8050 (10 January 1998): 43–44.

Ekiert, Grzegorz. 1996. *The State against Society: Political Crises and Their Aftermath in East Central Europe.* Princeton, NJ: Princeton University Press.

Ekiert, Grzegorz, and Steven Hanson. 2003. *Capitalism and Democracy in Central and*

Eastern Europe: Assessing the Legacy of Communist Rule. Cambridge, U.K.: Cambridge University Press.

Ekiert, Grzegorz, and Jan Kubik. 1999. *Rebellious Civil Society: Popular Protest and Democratic Consolidation in Poland, 1989–1993*. Ann Arbor: University of Michigan Press.

Ekiert, Grzegorz, Jan Kubik, and Milada Anna Vachudova. 2007. "Democracy in the Post-Communist World: An Unending Quest?" *East European Politics and Societies* 21, no. 1: 7–30.

Elgun, Ozlem, and Erik R. Tillman. 2007. "Exposure to European Union Policies and Support for Membership in the Candidate Countries." *Political Research Quarterly* 60, no. 3 (September).

Elkins, Zachary. 2000. "Gradations of Democracy? Empirical Tests of Alternative Conceptualizations." *American Journal of Political Science* 44: 293–300.

Epstein, Rachel. 2008. *In Pursuit of Liberalism: International Institutions in Postcommunist Europe*. Baltimore: Johns Hopkins University Press.

European Security Initative. 2007. *The Cost of Non-Europe: Textile Towns and the Future of Serbia*. Discussion Paper. Berlin, Germany. Available at www.esiweb.org.

Eyal, Jonthan. 1995. "From Bad to Worse to Bosnia." *The Spectator*, 17 June.

Ferfila, Bogomil, and Paul Phillips. 2000. *Slovenia: On the Edge of the European Union*. Lanham, MD: University Press of America.

Field, Heather. 2000. "Awkward States: EU Enlargement and Slovakia, Croatia, and Serbia." *Perspectives on European Politics and Society* 1, no. 1: 123–46.

Fink-Hafner, Danica. 1994. "Slovenia in a Process of Transition to Political Democracy." In *Civil Society, Political Society, Democracy*, ed. Adolf Bibič and Gigi Graziano, 387–408. Ljubljana: Slovenian Political Science Association.

Fink-Hafner, Danica, and Miro Haček, eds. 2001a. *Demokraticni Prehodi I*. Ljubljana: Fakulteta za Družbene Vede.

———. 2001b. *Demokraticni Prehodi II*. Ljubljana: Fakulteta za Družbene Vede.

Finnemore, Martha, and Kathryn Sikkink. 1999. "International Norm Dynamics and Political Change." *International Organization* 52 no. 4: 887–917.

Fish, M. Steven. 1998a. "Democratization's Requisites: The Postcommunist Experience." *Post-Soviet Affairs* 14, no. 3.

———. 1998b. "The Determinants of Economic Reform in the Post-Communist World." *East European Politics and Societies* 12, no. 3: 31–78.

———. 1999. "Postcommunist Subversion: Social Science and Democratization in East Europe and Eurasia." *Slavic Review* 58, no. 4.

———. 2001. "The Dynamics of Democratic Erosion." In *Postcommunism and the Theory of Democracy*, ed. Richard D. Anderson et al., 65–95. Princeton, NJ: Princeton University Press.

Fish, M. Steven, and Andrej Krickovic. 2003. "Out of the Brown and into the Blue: The Tentative 'Christian-Democratization' of the Croatian Democratic Union." *East European Constitutional Review* 12, no. 2/3 (Spring-Summer): 104–12.

Franičević, Vojmir, and Evan Kraft. 1997. "Croatia's Economy After Stabilization." *Europe-Asia Studies* 49, no. 4 (June).

Friedman, Milton, and Rose Friedman. 1980. *Free to Choose: A Personal Statement.* New York: Harcourt.

Friedrich, Carl J. 1972. *Tradition and Authority.* New York: Praeger.

Fukuyama, Francis. 1992. *The End of History and the Last Man.* New York: Avon Books.

Gantar, Pavel. 1994. "Discussions on Civil Society in Slovenia." In *Civil Society, Political Society, Democracy,* ed. Adolf Bibič and Gigi Graziano, 355–68. Ljubljana: Slovenian Political Science Association.

George, Alexander L. 1979. "Case Studies and Theory Development: The Method of Structured, Focused Comparison." in *Diplomacy: New Approaches in History, Theory, and Policy,* ed. P. G. Lauren. New York: Free Press.

Georgievski, Zvezdan. 2001. "Macedonia: Albanians Must Have Equal Rights." *Network of Independent Journalists - NIJ,* no. 224, 29 May.

Gerschenkron, Alexander. 1962. *Economic Backwardness in Historical Perspective.* Cambridge, MA: Harvard University Press.

Glavaš, Davor. 1994. "Roots of Croatian Extremism." in *Mediterranean Quarterly* (Spring).

Glenny, Misha. 1993. *The Fall of Yugoslavia: The Third Balkan War.* New York: Penguin.

Goati, Vladimir. 1989. *Politička anatomija jugoslovenskog društva.* Zagreb: Naprijed.

———. 1998. "Introduction: Political Development in the Federal Republic of Yugoslavia (1990–1996)." In *Elections to the Federal and Republican Parliaments of Yugoslavia (Serbia and Montenegro) 1990–1996: Analysis, Documents, and Data,* ed. Vladimir Goati, 12–34. Edition Sigma.

Gordy, Eric. 1999. *The Culture of Power in Serbia: Nationalism and the Destruction of Alternatives.* University Park: Pennsylvania State University Press.

Gourevitch, Peter. 1978. "The Second Image Reversed: The International Sources of Domestic Politics." *International Organization* 32, no. 4: 881–912.

Government of the Republic of Slovenia. 2001. *Facts about Slovenia.* Ljubljana: Government Public Relations and Media Office.

Gow, James, and Cathie Carmichael. 2000. *Slovenia and the Slovenes: A Small State and the New Europe.* London: Hurst.

Grabbe, Heather. 2006. *The EU's Transformative Power: Europeanization through Conditionality in Central and Eastern Europe.* Hampshire, U.K.: Palgrave.

Grdešić, Ivan, Mirjana Kasapović, Ivan Šiber, and N. Zakošek. 1991. *Hrvatska u Izborima '90.* Zagreb: Naprijed.

Greenfeld, Liah. 1992. *Nationalism: Five Roads to Modernity.* Cambridge: Harvard University Press.

Greskovits, Bela. 1998. *The Political Economy of Protest and Patience: East European and Latin American Transformations Compared.* New York: Central European University Press.

Grzymała-Busse, Anna. 2002. *Redeeming the Communist Past: The Regeneration of Communist Parties in East Central Europe.* Cambridge, U.K.: Cambridge University Press.

Gurr, Ted. 1970. *Why Men Rebel.* Princeton, NJ: Princeton University Press.

Habermas, J. 1976. *Legitimation Crisis.* Boston: Beacon Books.

Haggard, Stephan, and Robert Kauffman. 1995. *The Political Economy of Democratic Transitions.* Princeton, NJ: Princeton University Press.

Hanson, Stephan. 1995. "The Leninist Legacy and Institutional Change." *Comparative Political Studies* 28, no. 2 (July): 306–14.

Harris, Erika. 2002. *Nationalism and Democratisation: Politics of Slovakia and Slovenia.* Burlington, VT: Ashgate.

Hechter, Michael. 1975. *Internal Colonialism: The Celtic Fringe in British National Development, 1536–1966.* London: Routledge.

Hellman, Joel. 1998. "Winners Take All: The Politics of Partial Reform in Postcommunist Transitions." *World Politics* 50, no. 2.

Hirschman, Albert O. 1970. *Exit, Voice, and Loyalty; Responses to Decline in Firms, Organizations, and States.* Cambridge, MA: Harvard University Press.

Hislope, Robert. 2002. "Organized Crime in a Disorganized State: How Corruption Contributed to Macedonia's Mini-War." *Problems of Post-Communism* 49, no. 3.

———. 2003. "Between a Bad Peace and a Good War: Insights and Lessons from the Almost-War in Macedonia." *Ethnic and Racial Studies* 26, no. 1: 129–51.

Hoffman, George W., and Fred Warner Neal. 1962. *Yugoslavia and the New Communism.* New York: Twentieth Century Fund.

Holbrooke, Richard. 1998. *To End a War.* New York: Random House.

Horowitz, Donald L. 2000. *Ethnic Groups in Conflict.* Berkeley: University of California Press.

Horowitz, Shale. 2003. "Sources of Post-Communism Democratization: Economic Structure, Political Culture, War, and Political Institutions." *Nationalities Papers* 31, no. 2.

———. 2004. "Identities Unbound: Escalating Ethnic Conflict in Post-Soviet Azerbaijan, Georgia, Moldova, and Tajikistan." In *Ethnic Conflict and International Politics: Explaining Diffusion and Escalation,* ed. Steven Lobell and Philip Mauceri. New York: Palgrave-Macmillan.

Horvat, Branko. 1976. *The Yugoslav Economic System: The First Labor-Managed Economy in the Making.* White Plains, NY: International Arts and Sciences Press.

———. 1985. *Jugoslavensko društvo u krizi: Kritički ogledi i prijedlozi reformi.* Zagreb: Globus.

Huber, Evelyne, Dietrich Rueschemeyer, and John D. Stephens. 1993. "The Impact of Economic Development on Democracy." *Journal of Economic Perspectives* 7, no. 3.

Huntington, Samuel P. 1984. "Will More Countries Become Democratic?" *Political Science Quarterly* 99, no. 2: 193–218.

———. 1991. "Democracy's Third Wave." *Journal of Democracy* 2, no. 2.

———. 1993. *The Third Wave: Democratization in the Late 20th Century.* Norman: University of Oklahoma Press.

Ikenberry, G. John, and Charles A. Kupchan. 1990. "Socialization and Hegemonic Power." *International Organization* 44, no. 3 (Summer 1990): 283–315.

Inglehart, Ronald. 2003. "How Solid Is Mass Support for Democracy, and How Can We Measure It?" *PS Online*. Available at www.apsanet.org.

Inglehart, Ronald, and Christian Welzel. 2005. *Modernization, Cultural Change, and Democracy*. Cambridge, U.K.: Cambridge University Press.

Ingrao, Charles W., and Thomas A. Emmert, eds. 2009. *Confronting the Yugoslav Controversies: A Scholars' Initiative*. West Lafayette, IN: Purdue University Press.

Inkeles, Alex, ed. 1991. *On Measuring Democracy*. New Brunswick, NJ: Transaction Publishers.

Inotai, Andras, and Peter Stanovnik. 2004. "EU Membership: Rationale, Costs, and Benefits." In *Slovenia: From Yugoslavia to the European Union*, ed. Mojmir Mrak, Matija Rojec, and Carlos Silva-Jauregui. Washington, DC: World Bank.

International Crisis Group. 2004. "Serbia's Changing Political Landscape." International Crisis Group Europe Briefing No. 32, 22 July. Available at www.crisisgroup.org.

Irvine, Jill A. 1997. "Ultranationalist Ideology and State-Building in Croatia, 1990–1996." *Problems of Post-Communism* 44, no. 4: 30.

Ishiyama, John T. and Matthew Velten. 1998. "Presidential Power and Democratic Development in Post-Communist Politics." *Communist and Post-Communist Studies* 31, no. 3: 217–33.

Jackman, Robert W. 1973. "On the Relation of Economic Development to Democratic Performance." *American Journal of Political Science* 17: 611–21.

Jacoby, Wade. 2004. *The Enlargement of the European Union and NATO: Ordering from the Menu in Central Europe*. Cambridge, U.K.: Cambridge University Press.

Jakovina, Tvrtko. 2003. *Američki komunistički saveznik: Hrvati, Titova Jugoslavija i Sjedinjene Američke Države, 1945–1955*. Zagreb: Profil.

Janos, Andrew C. 1984. *The Politics of Backwardness in Hungary*. Princeton, NJ: Princeton University Press.

———. 1986. *Politics and Paradigms: Changing Theories of Change in Social Science*. Stanford, CA: Stanford University Press.

———. 1989. "The Politics of Backwardness in Continental Europe, 1780–1945" *WorldPolitics* 41, no. 3 (April): 325–58.

———. 1997. *Czechoslovakia and Yugoslavia: Ethnic Conflict and the Dissolution of Multinational States*. University of California, Berkeley: Institute of International Studies.

———. 2000. *East Central Europe in the Modern World: The Politics of the Borderlands from Pre- to Postcommunism*. Stanford, CA: Stanford University Press.

———. 2001. "From Eastern Empire to Western Hegemony." *East European Politics and Societies* 15, no. 2: 221–49.

———. 2003. "From Eastern Empire to Western Hegemony: East Central Europe under Two International Regimes." In *Cultural Legacies in Post-Socialist Europe: The Role of the Various Pasts in the Current Transformation Process*, ed. Michael Minkenberg and Timm Beichelt.

Jeffries, Ian, ed. 2002. *The Former Yugoslavia at the Turn of the Twenty-First Century: A Guide to the Economies in Transition*. London: Routledge.

Jovanović, Igor. 2006. "Patriots, Traitors, Reformers, and Radicals." *Transitions Online,* 21 December. Available at www.tol.cz.

Jović, Dejan. 2001. "Yugoslavia and Europe: Breaking Up, Making Up." *Open Democracy,* 14 June. Available at www.opendemocracy.net/debates/article-2-42-205.jsp.

Jowitt, Ken. 1992. *New World Disorder: The Leninist Extinction.* Berkeley: University of California Press.

Judah, Tim. 1997. *The Serbs: History, Myth, and the Destruction of Yugoslavia.* New Haven: Yale University Press.

Kaldor, Mary, and Ivan Vejvoda, eds. 1998. *Democratization in Central and Eastern Europe.* London: Continuum.

Karatnycky, Adrian, Alexander J. Motyl, and Charles Graybow. 1999. *Nations in Transit 1999.* New York: Freedom House.

Kasapović, Mirjana, ed. 2001. *Hrvatska politika 1990–2000.* Zagreb: Fakultet Političkih Znanosti.

Katzenstein, Peter J. 1985. *Small States in World Markets: Industrial Policy in Europe.* Ithaca, NY: Cornell University Press.

Kavalski, Emilian. 2006. "From the Western Balkans to the Greater Balkans Area: The External Conditioning of 'Awkward' and 'Integrated' States." *Mediterranean Quarterly* 17, no. 3.

Kearns, Ian. 1996. "Croatian Politics: The New Authoritarianism." *Political Quarterly* 67, no. 1: 26–35.

———. 1998. "Croatian Politics: Authoritarianism or Democracy?" *Contemporary Politics* 4, no. 3.

Kelly, Judith G. 2004. *Ethnic Politics in Europe: The Power of Norms and Incentives.* Princeton, NJ: Princeton University Press.

Kharkhordin, Oleg. 1999. *The Collective and the Individual in Russia: A Study of Practices.* Berkeley: University of California Press.

King, Charles. 2000. "Post-Post Communism: Transition, Comparison, and the End of 'Eastern Europe.'" *World Politics* 53, no. 1 (October): 143–72.

King, Gary, Robert O. Keohane, and Sidney Verba. 1994. *Designing Social Inquiry: Scientific Inference in Qualitative Research.* Princeton, NJ: Princeton University Press.

Kitschelt, Herbert. 1992. "Political Regime Change: Structure and Process-Driven Explanations?" *American Political Science Review* 86, no. 4.

———. 1999. "According for Outcomes of Post-Communist Regime Change: Causal Depth or Shallowness in Rival Explanations." Paper presented at the annual meeting of the American Political Science Association, Atlanta, Georgia.

Kopecky, Petr, and Cas Mudde. 2000. "Explaining Different Paths of Democratization: The Czech and Slovak Republics." *Journal of Communist Studies and Transition Politics* 16, no. 3: 63–84.

Kopstein, Jeffrey. 1999. "Post-Communist Democracy: Legacies and Outcomes." *Comparative Politics* 35, no. 2: 250.

Kopstein, Jeffrey, and David A. Reilly. 2003. "Explaining the Why of the Why: A

Comment on Fish's 'Determinants of Economic Reform in the Post-Communist World.'" *East European Politics and Societies* 13, no. 3.

Krickovic, Andrej. 2001. International Intervention and Recent Regime Changes in Croatia and Serbia." *Berkeley Slavic Center Newsletter,* Fall.

Kubicek, Paul J., ed. 2003. *The European Union and Democratization.* London: Routledge.

Kundera, Milan. 2006. *The Curtain: An Essay in Seven Parts.* New York: HarperCollins.

Kurtz, Marcus J., and Andrew Barnes. 2002. "The Political Foundations of Post-Communist Regimes: Marketization, Agrarian Legacies, or International Influences." *Comparative Political Studies* 35, no. 5: 524–53.

Kuzmanić, Tonči. 1999. "Slovenia: From Yugoslavia to the Middle of Nowhere?" In *Democratization in Central and Eastern Europe,* ed. Mary Kaldor and Ivan Vejvoda. London: Pinter.

Lajh, Damjan, and Danica Fink-Hafner. 2001. "Primerjalni Vidik Konsolidacije Stranskarskih Aren v Nekdanjih Jugoslovanskih Republikah." In *Demokraticni Prehodi II,* ed. Danica Fink-Hafner and Miro Haček. Ljubljana: Fakulteta za Družbene Vede.

Lampe, John R. 2000. *Yugoslavia as History: Twice There Was a Country.* 2d ed. Cambridge, U.K.: Cambridge University Press.

Lazić, Mladen, ed. 1999. *Protest in Belgrade: Winter of Discontent.* Budapest: Central European University Press.

Lazić, Mladen. 2007. "Spread of Value Orientations among Political and Economic Elites in Serbia." *Romanian Journal of Political Science,* no. 2: 67–83.

Leatherman, Janie. 1999. *Breaking Cycles of Violence: Conflict Prevention in Intrastate Crises.* West Hartford, CT: Kumarian Press.

Levitsky, Steven, and Lucan Way. 2002. "The Rise of Competitive Authoritarianism." *Journal of Democracy* 13, no. 2.

———. 2005. "International Linkage and Democratization." *Journal of Democracy* 16, no. 3 (July): 20–34.

Lijphart, Arend. 1971. "Comparative Politics and the Comparative Method." *American Political Science Review* 65, no. 3: 682–93.

———. 1977. *Democracy in Plural Societies: a Comparative Exploration.* New Haven: Yale University Press.

Linden, Ronald H. 2002. "Conclusion: International Organizations and East Europe—Bringing Parallel Tracks Together." In *Norms and Nannies: The Impact of International Organizations on the Central and East European States,* ed. Ronald H. Linden. Lanham, MD: Rowman and Littlefield.

Lindstrom, Nicole. 2004. "European Integration and Ethnic Reconciliation in Croatia and Serbia." *WWICS EES Newsletter,* May-June.

Linz, Juan J. 1978. *The Breakdown of Democratic Regimes: Crisis, Breakdown, and Reequilibration.* Baltimore: Johns Hopkins University Press.

Linz, Juan J., and Alfred C. Stepan. 1996. *Problems of Democratic Transition and Consolidation: Southern Europe, South America, and Post-Communist Europe.* Baltimore: Johns Hopkins University Press.

Liotta, P. H. 2001. *Dismembering the State: The Death of Yugoslavia and Why It Matters.* Lanham, MD: Lexington Books.

Lipset, Seymour Martin. 1960. *Political Man: The Social Bases of Politics.* Garden City, NY: Doubleday.

Lipset, Seymour Martin, Kyoung-Ryung Seong, and John Charles Torres. 1993. "Social Requisites of Democracy." *International Social Science Journal,* no. 136 (May): 155–75.

Londegran, J. B., and K. T. Poole. 1996. "Does High Income Promote Democracy?" *World Politics* 49, no. 1: 1–30.

Loza, Tihomir. 2006. "Let's Just be Friends." *Transitions Online,* 18 December. Available at www.tol.cz.

———. 2007. "Delaying the Inevitable." *Transitions Online,* 7 November. Available at www.tol.cz.

———. 2009. "Before It Hits the Fan." *Transitions Online,* 2 July. Available at www.tol.cz.

Luebbert, Gregory. 1991. *Liberalism, Fascism, or Social Democracy.* New York: Oxford University Press.

Lukšič, Igor. 2001. *Politični Sistem Republike Slovenije: Ocrt.* Ljubljana: Znanstveno in Publistično Središče.

Lydall, Harold. 1989. *Yugoslavia in Crisis.* Oxford: Clarendon Press.

Magaš, Branka. 1993. *The Destruction of Yugoslavia: Tracing the Break-Up, 1980–92.* New York: Verso.

Mainwaring, Scott, and Aníbal Pérez-Liñán. 2003. "Levels of Development and Democracy: Latin American Exceptionalism, 1945–1996." *Comparative Political Studies* 36, no. 9: 1031–67.

Malcolm, Noel. 1998. *Kosovo: A Short History.* New York: Harper Perennial.

Malešević, Sinisa. 2002. *Ideology, Legitimacy, and the New State: Yugoslavia, Serbia, and Croatia.* London: Frank Cass.

Mamula, Branko. 2000. *Slučaj Jugoslavija.* Podgorica: CID.

Mazower, Mark. 2000. *The Balkans: A Short History.* New York: Modern Library.

McFaul, Michael. 2002. "The Fourth Wave of Democracy and Dictatorship: Noncooperative Transitions in the Postcommunist World." *World Politics* 54, no. 2 (January): 212–44.

Meier, Viktor. 1999. *Yugoslavia: A History of its Demise.* London: Routledge.

Mesić, Stipe. 2004. *The Demise of Yugoslavia: A Political Memoir.* Budapest: Central European University Press.

Millar, James L., and Sharon Wolchik, eds. 1994. *The Social Legacy of Communism.* New York: Cambridge University Press.

Miller, Nicholas. 1997. "A Failed Transition: The Case of Serbia." In *Politics, Power, and the Struggle for Democracy in South-East Europe,* ed. Karen Dawisha and Bruce Parrott. Cambridge, U.K.: Cambridge University Press.

Mitić, Aleksander. 2006. "The Silent Treatment." *Transitions Online,* 5 May. Available at www.tol.cz.

Moore, Barrington. 1996. *Social Origins of Dictatorship and Democracy.* Boston: Beacon Press.

Moore, Mick. 1996. "Is Democracy Rooted in Material Prosperity?" In *Democratization in the South. The Jagged Wave,* ed. R. Luckham and G. White, 37–68. Manchester: Manchester University Press.

Moravscik, Andrew, and Milada Anna Vachudová. 2003. "National Interests, State Power, and EU Enlargement." *East European Politics and Societies* 17, no. 1: 42–57.

Mrak, Mojmir, Matija Rojec, and Carlos Silva-Jaurequi, eds. 2004. *Slovenia: From Yugoslavia to the European Union.* Washington, DC: International Bank for Reconstruction and Development.

Munck, Gerardo L. 2009. *Measuring Democracy: A Bridge between Scholarship and Politics.* Baltimore: John Hopkins University Press.

Nairn, Tom. 1977. *The Break-up of Britain: Crisis and Neo-Nationalism.* London: NLB.

Najčevska, Mirjana, Emilija Simoska, and Natasha Gaber. 1996. "Muslims, State, and Society in the Republic of Macedonia: The View From Within." In *Muslim Communities in the New Europe,* ed. Gerd Nonneman, Tim Niblock, and Bogdan Szajkowski. Berkshire, U.K.: Ithaca Press.

Nye, Joesph S., Sr. 2004. *Soft Power: The Means to Success in World Politics.* New York: Public Affairs.

Ocić, Časlav. 1998. "The Regional Problem and the Break-up of the State: The Case of Yugoslavia." *Acta Slavica Iaponica,* no. 16.

O'Donnell, Guillermo, and Philippe C. Schmitter. 1986. *Transitions from Authoritarian Rule: Tentative Conclusions about Uncertain Democracies.* Baltimore: John Hopkins University Press.

Offe, Claus. 1984. *Societal Preconditions of Corporatism and Some Current Dilemmas of Democratic Theory.* Notre Dame, Indiana: Helen Kellogg Institute for International Studies.

Oh, Seung Eun. 2003. "The Role of the Past in the Present: Lessons from the Case of the Croatian Democratic Union." Unpublished manuscript presented at the Association for the Study of Nationalities annual meeting.

Ottaway, Marina. 2003. *Democracy Challenged: The Rise of Semi-Authoritarianism.* Washington, DC: Carnegie Endowment for International Peace.

Pajnik, Mojca, Petra Lesjak-Tušek, Marta Gregorčič, and Olga Vuković. 2001. *Immigrants, Who Are You? Research on Immigrants in Slovenia.* Ljubljana: Peace Institute.

Panagiotou, R. A. 2001. "Estonia's Success: Prescription or Legacy?" *Communist and Post-Communist Studies* 34, no. 2 (June 2001): 261–77.

Pantić, Dragomir. 1998. "Vrednosti birača u Srbiji." In *Elections to the Federal and Republican Parliaments of Yugoslavia (Serbia and Montenegro) 1990–1996: Analysis, Documents, and Data,* ed. Vladimir Goati, 111–44.

Perry, Duncan M. 1997. "The Republic of Macedonia: Finding Its Way." In *Politics, Power, and the Struggle for Democracy in South-East Europe,* ed. Karen Dawisha and Bruce Parrott. Cambridge, U.K.: Cambridge University Press.

Peskin, Victor, and Mieczysław P. Boduszyński. 2003. "International Justice and Domestic Politics: Post-Tudjman Croatia and the International Criminal Tribunal for the Former Yugoslavia." *Europe-Asia Studies* 55, no. 7: 1117–42.

Petrin, Tea. 1995. *Industrial Policy Supporting Economic Transition in Central-Eastern Europe*. Berkeley: Institute of International Studies, University of California.

Pettifer, James. 2001. "The New Macedonian Question." In *The New Macedonian Question*, ed. James Pettifer. London: Palgrave.

Pierson, Paul. 1996. "Path Dependence, Increasing Returns, and the Study of Politics." *American Political Science Review* 94, no. 2: 251–67.

Pleština, Dijana. 1992. *Regional Development in Communist Yugoslavia: Success, Failure, and Consequences*. Boulder, CO: Westview Press.

———. 1996. "Democracy and Nationalism in Croatia: The First Three Years." In *Beyond Yugoslavia, Politics, Economics and Culture in a Shattered Community*, ed. S. P. Ramet and L. Adamović. Boulder: University of Colorado Press.

Pond, Elizabeth. 2006. *Endgame in the Balkans: Regime Change, European Style*. Washington, DC: Brookings Institution Press.

Pop-Eleches, Grigore. 2007a. "Between Historical Legacies and the Promise of Western Integration: Democratic Conditionality after Communism." *East European Politics and Societies* 21, no. 1: 142–61.

———. 2007b. "Historical Legacies and Post-Communist Regime Change." *The Journal of Politics* 69, no. 4: 908–26.

Popov, Nebojša, ed. 1996. *The Road to War in Serbia: Trauma and Catharsis*. Budapest: Central European University Press.

Poulton, Hugh. 1995. *Who are the Macedonians?* London: Hurst.

Poznanski, Kazimierz. 1996. *Poland's Protracted Transition: Institutional Change and Economic Growth, 1970–1994*. Cambridge, U.K.: Cambridge University Press.

Pribićević, Ognjen. 1997. *Vlast i oprozicija u Srbiji*. Beograd: Radio B29.

Pridham, Geoffrey. 1990. "Political Actors, Linkages, and Interactions: Democratic Consolidation in Southern Europe." *West European Politics* 13, no. 4: 103–17.

———. 2005. *Designing Democracy: EU Enlargement and Regime Change in Post-Communist Europe*. Basingstoke: Palgrave Macmillan.

———. 2007. "Change and Continuity in the European Union's Political Conditionality: Aims, Approach, and Priorities." *Democratization* 14, no. 3: 446–71.

Pridham, Geoffrey, Eric Herring, and George Sanford, eds. 1997. *Building Democracy? The International Dimension of Democratisation in Eastern Europe*. London: Leicester Press.

Przeworski, Adam. 1999. "Minimalist Conception of Democracy: A Defense." In *The Democracy Sourcebook*, ed. Robert A. Dahl, Ian Shapiro, and Jose Antonio Cheibub. Cambridge, MA: MIT Press.

Przeworski, Adam, José Antônio Cheibub, and Fernando Limongi. 1998. "Culture and Democracy." *World Culture Report: Culture, Creativity, and Markets*. Paris: UNESCO Publishing.

Przeworski, Adam, and Fernando Limongi. 1993. "Political Regimes and Economic Growth." *Journal of Economic Perspectives* 7, no. 3: 51–69.

———. 1997. "Modernization: Theories and Facts." *World Politics* 49: 155–83.

Pusić, Vesna. 1994. "Dictatorships with Democratic Legitimacy: Democracy Versus Nation." *East European Politics and Societies* 8: 383–401.

Putnam, Robert D. 1993. *Making Democracy Work: Civic Traditions in Modern Italy.* With Robert Leonardi and Raffaella Y. Nanetti. Princeton, NJ: Princeton University Press.

Ramet, Pedro. 1984. *Nationalism and Federalism in Yugoslavia, 1963–1983.* Bloomington: Indiana University Press.

Ramet, Sabrina Petra. 1993. "Slovenia's Road to Democracy." *Europe-Asia Studies* 45, no. 5.

———. 1997a. "Democratization in Slovenia—the Second Stage." In *Politics, Power, and the Struggle for Democracy in South-East Europe,* ed. Karen Dawisha and Bruce Parrott. Cambridge, U.K.: Cambridge University Press.

———. 1997b. *Whose Democracy? Nationalism, Religion, and the Doctrine of Collective Rights in Post-1989 Eastern Europe.* Lanham, MD: Rowman and Littlefield.

———. 2006. *The Three Yugoslavias: State-Building and Legitimation, 1918–2005.* Washington, DC: Woodrow Wilson Center Press.

Risse, Thomas, and Stephen C. Ropp. 1999. "International Human Rights Norms and Domestic Change: Conclusions." In *The Power of Human Rights: International Norms and Domestic Change,* 234–78. Cambridge, U.K.: Cambridge University Press.

Roeder, Philip G. 1994. "Varieties of Post-Soviet Authoritarian Regimes." *Post-Soviet Affairs* 10, no. 1: 61–101.

———. 2001. "The Rejection of Authoritarianism." In *Postcommunism and the Theory of Democracy,* ed. Richard D. Anderson et al. Princeton, NJ: Princeton University Press.

Rogel, Carole. 2004. *The Breakup of Yugoslavia and its Aftermath.* Westport, CT: Greenwood Press.

Rose, Michael. 1998. *Fighting for Peace.* London: Harvill Press.

Rueschemeyer, D., E. H. Stephens, and J. D. Stephens. 1992. *Capitalist Development and Democracy.* Cambridge, MA: Polity Press.

Rupel, Dmitrij. 1994. *Slovenia's Shift from the Balkans to Central Europe.* New York: St. Martin's.

Rupnik, Jacques. 2007. "From Democracy Fatigue to Populist Backlash." *Journal of Democracy* 18, no. 4 (October).

———. 1999. "The Postcommunist Divide." *Journal of Democracy* 10, no. 1 (January).

Rusinow, Dennison I. 1977. *The Yugoslav Experiment, 1948–1974.* London: Royal Institute of International Affairs.

Rustow, Dankwart A. 1970. "Transitions to Democracy: Toward a Dynamic Model." *Comparative Politics* 2, no. 3.

Sabič, Zlatko. 2002. "Slovenia and the European Union: A Different Kind of Two-Level Game." In *Norms and Nannies: The Impact of International Organizations on the Central and East European States,* ed. Ronald H. Linden. Lanham, MD: Rowman and Littlefield.

Safarikova, Katerina. 2008a. "Balkans: No More Yawns." *Transitions Online,* 24 July.

———. 2008b. "Enlargement: Monsieur Non." *Transitions On-Line,* 26 June.

Šarinić, Hrvoje. 1999. *Svi moji tajni pregovori sa Slobodanom Miloševićem: Između rata i diplomacije, 1993–1995.* Zagreb: Globus International.

Schierup, Carl-Ulrik. 1999. "Memorandum for Modernity? Socialist Modernisers,

Retraditionalisation, and the Rise of Ethnic Nationalism." In *Scramble for the Balkans: Nationalism, Globalism, and the Political Economy of Reconstrucion*, ed. Carl-Ulrik Scheirup. Hampshire, U.K.: Macmillan Press.

Schimmelfennig, Frank. 2002. "Introduction: The Impact of International Organizations on the Central and Eastern European States—Conceptual and Theoretical Issues." In *Norms and Nannies: The Impact of International Organizations on the Central and East European States*, ed. Ronald H. Linden. Lanham, MD: Rowman and Littlefield.

———. 2005. "Strategic Calculation and International Socialization: Membership Incentive, Party Constellations, and Sustained Compliance in Central and Eastern Europe." *International Organizations* 59, no. 4: 827–60.

———. 2007. "European Regional Organizations, Political Conditionality, and Democratic Transformation in Eastern Europe." *East European Politics and Societies* 21, no. 1: 126–41.

Schimmelfennig, Frank, Stephan Engert, and Heiko Knobel. 2006. *International Socialization in Europe: European Organizations, Political Conditionality, and Democratic Change*. Basingstoke, U.K.: Palgrave Macmillan.

Schimmelfennig, Frank, and Ulrich Sedelmeier, eds. 2005. *The Europeanization of Central and Eastern Europe*. Ithaca, NY: Cornell University Press.

Schmitter, Philippe, and Terry Lynn Karl. 1991. "What Democracy Is and Is Not." *Journal of Democracy* 2, no. 3.

Schumpeter, Joseph. 1950. *Capitalism, Socialism, and Democracy*. New York: Harper and Row.

Schwartz, Mladen. 2000. *Hrvatska nakon Tuđmana: Studija o nacionalnom usudu*. Zagreb: Iuvenalis Samizdat.

Sekelj, Laslo. 2000. "Parties and Elections: The Federal Republic of Yugoslavia—Change without Transformation." *Euro-Asia Studies* 52, no. 1: 57–75.

Shapiro, Ian. 1996. *Democracy's Place*. Ithaca, NY: Cornell University Press.

Shea, John. 1997. *Macedonia and Greece: The Struggle to Define a New Balkan Nation*. Jefferson, NC: McFarland.

Šiber, Ivan. 2001. "Političko ponašanje birača u izborima 1990–2000." In *Hrvatska Politika 1990–2000*, ed. Mirjana Kasapović. Zagreb: Fakultet Političkih Znanosti.

Singleton, Frederick Bernard. 1986. *A Short History of the Yugoslav Peoples*. Cambridge, U.K.: Cambridge University Press.

Slavujević, Zoran Đ., and Srećko Mihailović. 1999. *Dva Ogleda o Legitimitetu: Javno mnenje o legitimitetu treće Jugoslavije*. Beograd: Institut Društvenih Nauka and Friedrich Ebert Stiftung.

Snyder, Timothy. 2003. *The Reconstruction of Nations: Poland, Ukraine, Lithuania, Belarus, 1569–1999*. New Haven: Yale University Press.

Sokalski, Henryk J. 2003. *An Ounce of Prevention: Macedonia and the UN Experience in Preventive Diplomacy*. Washington, DC: United States Institute of Peace Press.

Stan, Lavinia, and Lucian Turcescu. 2000. "The Romanian Orthodox Church and Post-Communist Democratization." *Europe-Asia Studies* 52, no. 8: 1467–88.

Staniszkis, Jadwiga. 1992. *The Dynamics of Breakthrough in Central Europe*. Berkeley: University of California Press.

Stanojević, Miroslav. 1994. "Changing Power Structures: Trade Unions, Privatisation, and the End of Self-Management—The Slovenian Case." *European Journal of Development Research* 6, no. 1: 164–74.

Stark, David. 1992. "Path Dependence and Privatization Strategies in East Central Europe." *East European Politics and Societies* 6: 17–54.

Stark, David, and Laszlo Bruszt. 1998. *Postsocialist Pathways: Transforming Politics and Property in East Central Europe.* Cambridge, U.K.: Cambridge University Press.

Stavrova, Biljana. 2006. "Ade Over?" *Transitions Online,* 10 July. Available at www.tol.cz.

Stoilovski, Dragan. 1999. *Makedonija vo medjunarodnite odnosi 1991–1998.* Skopje: Pecasnica 2-ru Avzust S.

Stokes, Gale. 1999. "Containing Nationalism: Solutions in the Balkans." *Problems of Post-Communism* 46, no. 4 (July/August): 3–10.

Suny, Ronald G. 1993. *The Revenge of the Past: Nationalism, Revolution, and the Collapse of the Soviet Union.* Stanford: Stanford University Press.

Szajkowski, Bogdan. 2000. "Macedonia: An Unlikely Road to Democracy." In *Experimenting with Democracy: Regime Change in the Balkans,* ed. Geoffrey Pridham and Tom Gallagher. London: Routledge.

Tcherneva, Vessela. 2008. "Balkans: On the Periphery of the New World Order." *Transitions Online,* 13 November. Available at www.tol.cz.

Thomas, Robert. 1999. *Serbia under Milošević: Politics in the 1990s.* London: Hurst.

Tomac, Zdravko. 1992. *Iza zatvorenih vrata: Tako se stvarala hrvatska država.* Zagreb: Sveučilišna Tiskara.

Tomasevich, Jozo. 1955. *Peasants, Politics, and Economic Change in Yugoslavia.* Stanford, CA: Stanford University Press.

Toš, Niko, et al. 1995. *Dozorevanje Slovenske Samozavesti.* Ljubljana: Centar za raziskovanje javnega mnenja in množičnih komunikacij.

Toš, Niko, and Vlado Miheljak, eds. 2002. *Slovenia between Continuity and Change, 1990–1997.* Berlin: Edition Sigma.

Tull, Stephen M. 2003. "The European Union and Croatia: Negotiating 'Europeanization' amid National, Regional, and International Interests." In *The European Union and Democratization,* ed. Paul J. Kubicek. London: Routledge.

United States Department of State. 1997. "1997 State Department Human Rights Report." Washington, DC: Department of State, Bureau of Democracy, Human Rights, and Labor.

Uvalić, Milica. 2001. "Regional Cooperation in Southeast Europe." In *Balkan Reconstruction,* ed. Daniel Daianu and Thanos Veremis. London: Frank Cass.

Vachudová, Milada Anna. 2005. *Europe Undivided: Democracy, Leverage, and Integration after Communism.* Oxford: Oxford University Press.

Vachudová, Milada Anna, and Tim Snyder. 1997. "Are Transitions Transitory? Two Types of Political Change in Eastern Europe since 1989." *East European Politics and Societies* 11, no. 1: 1–35.

Vaknin, Sam. 2002. *The Macedonian Lottery.* Available at http://samvak.tripod.com/nm102.html/.

Vankovska, Biljana, and Hakan Wiberg. 2003. *Between the Past and Future: Civil-Military Relations in the Post-Communist Balkans.* London: I. B. Tauris.

Vayrynen, Raimo. 2003. "Challenges to Preventive Action: The Cases of Kosovo and Macedonia." In *Conflict Prevention: Path to Peace or Grand Illusion?* ed. David Carment and Albrecht Schnabel. Tokyo: United Nations University Press.

Vejvoda, Ivan. 2000. "Democratic Despotism: Federal Republic of Yugoslavia and Croatia." In *Experimenting with Democracy: Regime Change in the Balkans,* ed. Geoffrey Pridham and Tom Gallagher. London: Routledge.

Vojicic, Branko. 1998. "Who is Milo Djukanovic?" Part 2. *Alternative Information Network Review* 56 (February 1998).

Vrčan, Srdan, et al. 1999. *Pakiranje Vlasti: Izbori u Hrvatskoj 1995. i 1997.* Zagreb: Alinea.

Vujačić, Veljko. 1995. "Communism and Nationalism in Russia and Serbia." Ph.D. dissertation, Department of Sociology, University of California, Berkeley.

Wandycz, Piotr S. 1992. *The Price of Freedom: A History of East Central Europe from the Middle Ages to the Present.* London: Routledge.

Weber, Max. 1968. *Max Weber on Charisma and Institution Building: Selected Papers.* Edited and with an introduction by S. N. Eisenstadt. Chicago: University of Chicago Press.

Whitehead, Laurence. 1996. "Democratic Regions, Ostracism, and Pariahs." In *The International Aspects of Democratization: Europe and the Americas,* ed. Laurence Whitehead. Oxford: Oxford University Press.

Whitehead, Laurence, ed. 2001. *The International Dimensions of Democratization: Europe and the Americas.* Oxford: Oxford University Press.

Williams, Abiodum. 2000. *Preventing War: The United Nations and Macedonia.* Lanham, MD: Rowman and Littlefield.

Wittenberg, Jason. 2006. *Crucibles of Political Loyalty: Church Institutions and Electoral Continuity in Hungary.* Cambridge, U.K.: Cambridge University Press.

World Bank. 1999. *Slovenia. Economic Transformation and EU Accession,* Vol. 2: Main Report. Washington, DC: World Bank.

Wood, Nicholas. 2004a. "An Effort to Unify a Bosnian City Multiplies Frictions." *New York Times,* 15 March.

———. 2004b. "Ethnic Macedonians Riot Over New Laws That Aid Albanians." *New York Times,* 24 July, p. 3.

———. 2004c. "For Slovenia, New Alliances are Raising New Issues." *New York Times,* 27 February, p. 6.

Woodward, Susan L. 1995a. *Balkan Tragedy: Chaos and Dissolution after the Cold War.* Washington, DC: Brookings Institution.

———. 1995b. *Socialist Unemployment: The Political Economy of Yugoslavia, 1945–1990.* Princeton: Princeton University Press.

Youngs, Richard. 2008. "What Has Europe Been Doing?" *Journal of Democracy* 19, no. 2 (April).

Zakaria, Fareed. 2003. *The Future of Freedom: Illiberal Democracy at Home and Abroad.* New York: W.W. Norton.

Zakošek, Nenad. 2007. "The Heavy Burden of History: The Political Uses of the Past in the Yugoslav Successor States." *Romanian Journal of Political Science,* no. 2.

Zapp, Kenneth. 1996. "Compromise in Slovenia Produces a Unique Privatization Process." *Problems of Post-Communism* 43, no. 3 (May-June): 60–71.

Zarkovic-Bookman, Milica. 1991. *The Political Economy of Discontinuous Development: Regional Disparities and Inter-Regional Conflict.* New York: Praeger.

Žerjavić, Vladimir. 1989. *Gubici stanovništva Jugoslavije u drugom svjetskom ratu.* Zagreb: Jugoslavensko viktimološko društvo.

Zimmermann, Warren. 1996. *Origins of a Catastrophe.* New York: Random House.

Index

Mieczysław P. Boduszyński received his Ph.D. in political science from the University of California, Berkeley. He has taught at the University of San Diego, European University of Tirana, and Temple University, Japan campus, and conducted research in the former Yugoslavia as a Fulbright Scholar. His articles have appeared in *Problems of Post-Communism* and *Europe-Asia Studies*. Currently, Boduszyński is a career Foreign Service Officer with the U.S. Department of State. He has served at the U.S. embassies in Tirana, Albania, Pristina, Kosovo, and Tokyo. The doctoral dissertation on which this book is based was the recipient of the American Political Science Association's Comparative Democratization Section Prize for the Best Dissertation in the Comparative Study of Democracy. The views expressed in this book are those of the author and do not necessarily reflect those of the U.S. Department of State or the U.S. government. All interviews with diplomats were conducted before the author joined the Foreign Service.